The Foundation of Japanese Power:

Continuities, Changes, Challenges

William R. Nester

Lecturer in Far East Politics
School of Oriental and African Studies
University of London

M. E. Sharpe, Inc.
Armonk, New York

First published in 1990

Published in the United States by M. E. Sharpe, Inc.
80 Business Park Drive, Armonk, New York 10504.

Published in Great Britain by The Macmillan Press Ltd.

Printed in Great Britain.

Library of Congress Cataloging-in-Publication Data
Nester, William, R., 1956–
  The foundation of Japanese power : continuities, changes,
challenges / By William Raymond Nester.
    p. cm.
  ISBN 0–87332–755–1
  1. Investments, Japanese—Asia, Southeastern 2. Joint ventures—Asia, South-
eastern. 3. Japan—Foreign economic relations—Asia, Southeastern. 4. Asia,
Southeastern—Foreign economic relations—Japan. 5. Capitalism—Japan. I. Title.
HG5740.8.A3N47 1990
332.6′7352059—dc20   90–34055
                                                                   CIP

To Yoshiko, for all we share

Contents

1 Introduction

When the Japanese buried Emperor Hirohito on 24 February 1989, they buried a man important not so much for what he did, as for what he represented. Although he reigned for 62 years as the 124th emperor in a line stretching back over 1500 years, for Japanese Hirohito represents much more than a colorful and mysterious past. The Emperor's long reign straddled Japan's schizophrenic twentieth century: the promising steps toward democratization and internationalization of the 1920s, the mad, rapid descent into the fascism and militarism of the 1930s, the horror of defeat and shame of Occupation during the 1940s, and the steady growth into an economic superpower since. With Hirohito's death and the ascension of a new, young emperor, Akihito, to the throne, Japan has become psychologically whole again, confidently reinterpreting its past as passionately as it continues to expand its global economic power.

It was Japan's tremendous, ever growing wealth and power rather than the past, however, that brought the representatives of 163 nations – 54 heads of state and 109 representatives – to Hirohito's funeral.[1] Hats literally in hand, the representatives of almost every nation on earth were paying homage to an economic superpower whose recent ascent atop the world economy will deepen into the indefinite future. Prince Phillip nicely symbolized the rest of the world's deepening economic dependence on Japan when he bowed, not to Hirohito's casket, but to Emperor Akihito. It is not just governments that recognize Japan's economic power. A 1989 poll indicated that 54 per cent of Americans thought Japan was now the world's greatest economic power while only 29 per cent felt the United States still retained the title.[2]

How real are these élite and mass perceptions of Japanese power? By most measures, Japan has replaced the United States as the world's most dynamic economic power. Although its GNP is still only 60 per cent the size of America's, Japan's economy will surpass that of the United States within a decade if current growth rates hold. Japanese are already richer than Americans – in 1988, the per capita income of Japanese was $19 500 compared to $18 400 for Americans. Of the OECD countries only Switzerland had a higher per capita income than Japan's. Japan's huge wealth resulted from economic growth rates that annually averaged 10 per cent between

1

1950 and 1973, and almost five per cent since, almost twice the average growth of other OECD countries. Japan's inflation rate averaged only 0.9 per cent between 1984 and 1987, compared to an OECD average of 3.0 per cent, and an American average of 4.2 per cent. In 1987, its unemployment rate was 2.8 per cent compared to an OECD average of 7.0 per cent and an American average of 6.1 per cent.[3]

But the most vital indicators of Japanese power are its tremendous trade and current account surpluses that will continue into the indefinite future.[4] Between 1982 and 1985 Japan's trade surplus rose from $18.6 billion to $55.9 billion, and its current account surplus from $6.8 billion to $49.1 billion. Then in 1986, Japan's trade and current account surpluses almost doubled to $92.8 billion and $85.8 billion, followed by a moderate increase to $96.3 billion and $87.0 billion, respectively, in 1987. Meanwhile, as stated, although the United States actually enjoyed a modest trade surplus of $2 billion in 1980, it has continually run trade deficits since that peaked at $171.2 billion in 1987, with Japan accounting for $59.8 billion of that year's deficit.[5] Although America's overall trade deficit declined to $137 billion in 1988, almost half of the deficit continued to be with Japan.

Japan's 1987 current account surplus was 3.7 per cent of GNP, compared to an OECD average deficit of –0.4 per cent, and an American deficit of a mind-boggling –3.5 per cent of GNP.[6] That same year, Japan's accumulated current account surplus was the world's largest at $880 billion, while America's accumulated deficit of –1.406 trillion made it the world's worst debtor nation. Japan's accumulated net foreign assets in 1987 of $241 billion were also the world's largest, bolstered by a $33.4 billion surge in direct foreign investment that year alone.[7] Of its overseas assets, $61.6 billion is invested in the United States and $25.1 billion in Europe.[8] Recent multibillion dollar purchases have included Firestone Tire and Rubber Company, CBS Records, and the Intercontinental Hotels group. Although Japan's trade surplus declined slightly to $93.0 billion in 1988 while its current account surplus dropped by $10 billion to $78.0 billion, some analysts estimate that Japan's trade surplus will rise to over $100 billion in 1989 fueled by over 5 per cent economic growth.[9]

Japanese corporations have spearheaded this tremendous economic and trade growth, and their corporate culture and strategies have become models for ambitious businessmen everywhere, analyzed in hundreds of books and articles. Of the world's top 1000 firms, 345 are now Japanese, and those Japanese firms own 47 per cent of the total assets.[10] In comparison, American firms number 353 of the top 1000 firms, but own only 32 per cent of the total assets. In terms of market value, the world's five largest corporations, 18 of the top 25 and 32 of the top 50 are now Japanese. In stark contrast, American firms number only four of the world's top 25 firms, and 11 of the largest 50. By drastically cutting costs and improving productivity, Japan's corporations adapted quickly to the yen's strengthening from 240 yen to the dollar in September 1985 to 125 yen to the dollar in 1988. Japan's corporate profits rose an average 19.3 per cent in 1987 and over 20 per cent in 1988.[11] Japan's corporate power is in part based on its technological power. A 1987 US Academy of Engineering report revealed that Japan had technologically leapfrogged the United States to dominate 25 of 34 key technologies, which included such strategic industries as semiconductors, telecommunications, superconductors, and the fifth generation computer.[12]

Japan's immense financial power has surpassed that of the United States as well – Japan is now the world's banker while the United States has deteriorated into the world's largest debtor nation, with over one-third of America's national debt now owned by Japan. The world's eight largest banks, and 16 of the top 25 banks are now Japanese, and Japanese banks hold more than twice the asset of their American counterparts. Of American banks, only Citicorps at number ten was ranked among the world's top 25; the next largest, Chase Manhattan, was a distant 36th.[13] America's deepening financial dependence on Japan became terribly clear when the October 1987 stock market crash was sparked after Japanese investors stopped buying US treasury bills. But does Japan's trade, manufacturing, corporate, technological and financial domination of the world economy necessarily mean that it is the world's most powerful nation?

While virtually all observers acknowledge that Japan is now an economic colossus, either battling for or already dominating the world's markets, technologies, and finance, some counter that the United States is still the world's greatest power because of its huge nuclear and conventional military. If measured by the traditional notion of power based largely on a country's military size, it is true that the United States is still the world's greatest power, although Japan has the world's third largest military in terms of spending.

inequalities that characterize most other industrial nations. In many ways Japan's political development has been just as successful. Japanese readily abandoned the authoritarian system that carried them into World War II and adapted to an American-imposed democracy. Today Japan is a dynamic, multiparty liberal democracy in which the people enjoy the full spectrum of human rights.

Yet, despite these remarkable developments, perceptive observers can point out as many continuities as changes. Such core values of Japanese society as patron-client and group relations, particularistic ethics, the importance for groups to maintain a harmonious façade despite inner conflicts, and the equal importance for rivals to cooperate behind the scenes as fiercely as they publicly compete remain unchanged. These values in turn shape the actual running of Japan's modern institutions in ways far different from how similar institutions operate within the United States and West Europe. For example, on the surface, relations between seemingly rival political parties or corporations may appear highly competitive and even antagonistic; in reality those same institutions may secretly cooperate to a degree unknown in the West.

It is impossible to understand Japanese power without understanding how Japan's élite has adapted to a range of both internal and external development challenges by carefully managing a dynamic interaction between continuity and change throughout Japan's modern political economy. This theme will be explored through the four parts of the book. The first part gives an overview of Japan's political economic development which, since 1945, has been guided by a 'governing triad' of the conservative political, bureaucratic and corporate élite. The section begins with a chapter analyzing the continuities and changes within the governing triad over the past four decades, and the neo-mercantilist policies they have pursued. This discussion is followed by a chapter on Japan's political economic culture, reasoning that it is impossible to understand government and corporate policies and their results without understanding the underlying cultural values, institutions, and behavior in which they are rooted. The next three chapters analyze Japan's modern political, economic, and corporate development 'miracles', respectively. Quotation marks bracket the word 'miracle' because, as will be seen, these developments were in reality not miracles at all in the sense that they involved some sort of divine intervention. Instead, each resulted from a variety of interrelated internal and external factors.

analyzed in hundreds of books and articles. Of the world's top 1000 firms, 345 are now Japanese, and those Japanese firms own 47 per cent of the total assets.[10] In comparison, American firms number 353 of the top 1000 firms, but own only 32 per cent of the total assets. In terms of market value, the world's five largest corporations, 18 of the top 25 and 32 of the top 50 are now Japanese. In stark contrast, American firms number only four of the world's top 25 firms, and 11 of the largest 50. By drastically cutting costs and improving productivity, Japan's corporations adapted quickly to the yen's strengthening from 240 yen to the dollar in September 1985 to 125 yen to the dollar in 1988. Japan's corporate profits rose an average 19.3 per cent in 1987 and over 20 per cent in 1988.[11] Japan's corporate power is in part based on its technological power. A 1987 US Academy of Engineering report revealed that Japan had technologically leapfrogged the United States to dominate 25 of 34 key technologies, which included such strategic industries as semi-conductors, telecommunications, superconductors, and the fifth generation computer.[12]

Japan's immense financial power has surpassed that of the United States as well – Japan is now the world's banker while the United States has deteriorated into the world's largest debtor nation, with over one-third of America's national debt now owned by Japan. The world's eight largest banks, and 16 of the top 25 banks are now Japanese, and Japanese banks hold more than twice the asset of their American counterparts. Of American banks, only Citicorps at number ten was ranked among the world's top 25; the next largest, Chase Manhattan, was a distant 36th.[13] America's deepening financial dependence on Japan became terribly clear when the October 1987 stock market crash was sparked after Japanese investors stopped buying US treasury bills. But does Japan's trade, manufacturing, corporate, technological and financial domination of the world economy necessarily mean that it is the world's most powerful nation?

While virtually all observers acknowledge that Japan is now an economic colossus, either battling for or already dominating the world's markets, technologies, and finance, some counter that the United States is still the world's greatest power because of its huge nuclear and conventional military. If measured by the traditional notion of power based largely on a country's military size, it is true that the United States is still the world's greatest power, although Japan has the world's third largest military in terms of spending.

But increasingly power, or the ability to get others to do things they ordinarily would not do to advance one's own interests, is based on economic rather than military prowess. The more economically interdependent the world becomes, the easier it is for states to maintain or enhance their security and other national interests through trade and diplomacy rather than warfare. Although some states continue to either threaten to go to war or actually attack their rivals to resolve differences, their numbers are decreasing, while the golden age of militarism when great powers got away with gunboat diplomacy and sabre rattling to advance their interests is largely a thing of the past.

In the 1980s the United States did invade tiny Grenada and bomb Libya, and continues to fund various anti-communist guerrilla groups in farflung regions, but the effectiveness of these actions is highly questionable. Since 1945 the costs of military action have steadily risen while the benefits have just as steadily fallen. Throughout the postwar era, the balance of nuclear terror and mutually assured destruction (MAD) have prevented the Soviet and American military blocks from going to war when they would likely have done so if equipped with only conventional forces. And with the diffusion of conventional military technology throughout the world, as the Americans found out in Vietnam and the Russians in Afghanistan, it is virtually impossible for a conventional power to defeat a popular insurgency equipped with state-of-the-art weapons. International morality expressed through such forums as the United Nations and mass media is still a slight but growing check on policy-makers considering a military option. Although wars make headlines, most are civil rather than international wars.[14] In 1987, although 23 of about 170 sovereign states were involved in war, 22 were civil wars, and only one war – the Iran-Iraq war – was between states. As the twentieth century rapidly comes to an end, peace between states rather than war has become the natural condition of humankind.

Japan was the first nation to understand this fundamental change in international relations and the nature of power. Japan's devastating defeat in World War II convinced its leadership that the national goals of achieving economic and military security, rapid modernization, great power status, and international prestige could only be accomplished through economic means. Japan's incredible success in achieving all its national goals in turn accelerated the shift in international relations from traditional military-based power to contemporary economic-based power.

Japanese power rests on several key international pillars. Japan could never have achieved its immense wealth and power without the revolutionary land, labor, corporate, and political reforms forced through by the American Occupation (1945–52) that set the stage for Japan's later rapid economic growth. Likewise, Japan has continually relied on America's nuclear umbrella to guarantee its military security while enjoying virtually unlimited access to America's huge domestic market, cheap technology, and sponsorship in a continually expanding open world economy whose maintenance costs remain largely borne by the United States. I have explored in detail elsewhere Japan's 'free ride' to global economic power.[15]

In this book I will concentrate on exploring the domestic basis of Japanese power – in particular the ability of Japan's bureaucratic, political, and economic leadership to create rational policies geared to continually expanding Japan's wealth and converting it into power, which in turn is used to create still more wealth, and so on, all to the end of achieving the national goals of economic and military security, rapid modernization, superpower status, and international recognition of all Japan's accomplishments. The ability of Japan's élite to adapt traditional Japanese institutions, behavior, and policies to contemporary challenges is the essence of Japan's domestic source of power.

Some old Greek long ago once said that you cannot step into the same stream twice. This may be an alarming thought to anyone who has ever lived beside a stream and daily taken sustenance, cleanliness, or peace of mind from its waters. Though it might swell with Spring rain, wither from Summer drought, or darken with pollution, surely the stream itself does not change; its essence remains water nourished by the same lesser streams above to be eventually dissolved into the same greater body of water below.

Obviously change and continuity are dynamically intertwined in most worldly phenomena, including nations. Few nations exemplify the paradox of continuity and change as dramatically as Japan. Within two generations Japan developed from a war-devastated, poverty-stricken nation to become a global economic superpower with the world's second largest GNP and one of its highest per capita incomes. Japan's economic growth was as egalitarian as it was high speed: about 90 per cent of Japanese consider themselves middle class, and indeed Japan has little of the obvious poverty and inequalities that characterize most other industrial nations. In many ways Japan's political development has been just as successful. Japanese readily abandoned the authoritarian system that carried them into World War II and adapted to an American-imposed democracy. Today Japan is a dynamic, multiparty liberal democracy in which the people enjoy the full spectrum of human rights.

Yet, despite these remarkable developments, perceptive observers can point out as many continuities as changes. Such core values of Japanese society as patron-client and group relations, particularistic ethics, the importance for groups to maintain a harmonious façade despite inner conflicts, and the equal importance for rivals to cooperate behind the scenes as fiercely as they publicly compete remain unchanged. These values in turn shape the actual running of Japan's modern institutions in ways far different from how similar institutions operate within the United States and West Europe. For example, on the surface, relations between seemingly rival political parties or corporations may appear highly competitive and even antagonistic; in reality those same institutions may secretly cooperate to a degree unknown in the West.

It is impossible to understand Japanese power without understanding how Japan's élite has adapted to a range of both internal and external development challenges by carefully managing a dynamic interaction between continuity and change throughout Japan's modern political economy. This theme will be explored through the four parts of the book. The first part gives an overview of Japan's political economic development which, since 1945, has been guided by a 'governing triad' of the conservative political, bureaucratic and corporate élite. The section begins with a chapter analyzing the continuities and changes within the governing triad over the past four decades, and the neo-mercantilist policies they have pursued. This discussion is followed by a chapter on Japan's political economic culture, reasoning that it is impossible to understand government and corporate policies and their results without understanding the underlying cultural values, institutions, and behavior in which they are rooted. The next three chapters analyze Japan's modern political, economic, and corporate development 'miracles', respectively. Quotation marks bracket the word 'miracle' because, as will be seen, these developments were in reality not miracles at all in the sense that they involved some sort of divine intervention. Instead, each resulted from a variety of interrelated internal and external factors.

If one or more of these key factors had been missing, Japan's development in each area would have been significantly different.

The next two parts will analyze Japanese policy-making and policies, respectively. Part II will examine in depth the roles, sources of power, and relations within the closely knit governing triad of the conservative political, bureaucratic, and corporate élite. Although this triad continues to dominate economic policy-making, policy differences both between and within each leg are increasingly evident as Japan's political economy becomes more complex and difficult to manage. One chapter will be devoted to each leg of the triad. The section will conclude with a chapter on the ruling triad's many 'insider' and 'outsider' political auxiliaries. Although the mass media can be critical of individual politicians and decisions, it is clearly an insider political auxiliary as it continues solidly to support Tokyo's neo-mercantilist policies and rally around the flag on all trade issues. Other insider political auxiliaries, such as the farm and small-business lobbies, continue to dominate policy-making, affecting their respective interests, although they have no influence on other policy areas. Traditionally outsider political auxiliaries such as consumer groups, the opposition parties, and labor are playing a greater symbolic if not substantive role in increasing numbers of policy areas. They cooperate closely with the ruling triad behind the scenes while continuing their public opposition. Part III analyzes Japan's actual postwar policies, with chapters devoted to macroeconomic, industrial, and foreign policies, respectively.

The final part analyzes Japanese power from the present into the twenty-first century. What challenges does Japan face in the coming decades as it becomes a post-industrial society and solidifies its financial and technological leadership over the world economy? What are the implications for the rest of the world? How will Tokyo respond to the growing foreign demands that Japan should use its tremendous wealth to start giving as much as it takes from the world economy? As the new hegemon over the world economy, will Japan emulate precedessors like Britain and the United States by abandoning neo-mercantilism and embracing liberalism? Or will Tokyo continue to follow policies focused solely on enriching Japan, often at the expense of others?

For Japanese, the answer to all these problems lies in the word internationalization, but there are vastly conflicting views over what this actually entails. The April 1986 Maekawa report represented the still minority view that internationalization means that Japanese must not only open their markets but their minds to the rest of the world. Most of Japan's political economic élite, however, see internationalization as merely a more subtle form of neo-mercantilism; Japanese corporations must globalize their operations to solidify their power while the government coughs up more aid and defense funds to divert foreign criticism focused on 'free rides' and 'unfair trade'. In this sense internationalism becomes indistinguishable from nationalism. Whether Japan's 'internationalization' eventually becomes genuine or remains nationalistic remains to be seen. But one thing is certain, Japan's power over the world economy will continue to deepen well into the twenty-first century.

NOTES

1. *The Times*, 26 February 1989.
2. The poll was conducted by the Washington Post-ABC News Poll in February 1989, *International Herald Tribune*, 19 February 1989.
3. 1989 *OECD Development Cooperation*, p. 45.
4. It should be pointed out that according to the Alice in Wonderland world of neo-classical economic theory, trade, current account, and budget deficits are actually considered good. Milton Friedman has been the most consistent champion of the Reagan administration policies that tripled America's national debt in eight years and converted America's trade surplus of $2 billion in 1980 to a $171 billion deficit by 1987.
5. *Far Eastern Economic Review*, 29 September 1988.
6. 1989 *OECD Development Cooperation*.
7. *Economist*, 13 August 1988.
8. *International Herald Tribune*, 13 December, 1988.
9. *Far Eastern Economic Review*, 12 January 1989, 2 February 1989, *International Herald Tribune*, 13 December 1988.
10. *Businessweek*, 17 July 1989.
11. Merril Lynch, *Japan Economic Commentary*, 25 October 1988, p. 8, FAR EASTERN ECONOMIC REVIEW, December 15, 1988.
12. Clyde Prestowitz, *Trading Places*, p. 76.
13. *Businessweek*, 26 June 1989. *Los Angeles Times*, 19 July 1988.
14. *Economist* (12 March 1989).
15. William Nester, *Japan's Growing Power Over East Asia and the World Economy: Ends and Mean*. (London: Macmillan, 1990)

Part I
Japan's Development 'Miracles'

1 The Governing Triad: Models of Development and Policy-making

How did Japan manage in just 40 years to develop from a war-devastated, poverty-stricken country into its present position as the world's financial and technological superpower? A half dozen schools of thought have attempted to answer this question, but to varying extents the explanations they offer fall short of providing a completely satisfying understanding of Japan's postwar development. The 'Japan is unique' and 'neo-classical' schools severely underestimate while the 'Japan Inc' school overestimates the role of the governing triad of bureaucracy, Liberal Democratic Party (LDP), and big business world (zaikai) in managing Japan's development into an economic superpower. The 'free ride' and 'developmental' schools are much more realistic in analyzing where power lies and how it is used in Japan's political economy, while presenting a range of factors behind Japan's economic success. Yet, they too ultimately fail to explain the considerable changes that Japan's political economy has undergone over the past 40 years.

After first examining these different interpretations of Japan's policy-making and development models, this chapter will discuss in detail the two models that provide the most realistic analysis of Japanese policy-making and economic development: corporatism and neo-mercantilism.[1] In a corporatist system, political and economic actors are limited to the major interest blocks such as big business, labor, and landowners with each major interest block organized hierarchially and holding monopoly control over its sector. Other interest groups are poorly represented and have little influence on politics or power. The state's role is to determine the participants, rules, and policies, while coordinating policy-making among the major blocks. Sometimes political parties are major interest groups themselves, other times they merely ratify decisions made by negotiations between the major interest blocks elsewhere. Neo-mercantilism is a development strategy whereby the state actively intervenes in the economy to bolster strategic sectors with a range of subsidies, import barriers, and export promotion that gives those firms an

11

advantage over their foreign rivals. Although corporatist states are not necessarily neo-mercantilist, any government that wants to follow a neo-mercantilist development strategy must organize the targeted industries along corporatist lines.[2]

FLAWED MODELS OF JAPANESE POLICY-MAKING AND DEVELOPMENT

Until recently the 'Japan Inc.' model was the most popular way of describing Japanese policy-making and policies.[3] Japan was presented as a monolithic society of conformists ruled over by a brilliant élite, and run like a corporation with the government the headquarters and each enterprise a corporate division. This model may have provided a somewhat accurate, though exaggerated description of Japan during the Occupation and 1950s, but quickly became obsolete as Japan's political economy grew in complexity throughout the 1960s. With increased economic power the corporate world became less dependent on the bureaucracy for such handouts as foreign exchange, import protection, and technology – and thus more independent in charting their own investment decisions. Growing affluence allowed concerned Japanese citizens the opportunity to clamor for government relief from such socio-economic problems as pollution or the high cost of medical care, and after a nationwide consensus had emerged in favor of change, the government responded with sweeping legislation dealing with those problems. Political and economic pluralism eroded the bureaucracy's role in governing society, while virtually all the other ministries began chipping away at the domination of MITI and the MOF over economic policy-making itself.

Equally inaccurate is the 'Japan is unique' school which argues that Japan's economic 'miracle' resulted not from Tokyo's bureaucracies or industrial policies, but from Japan's national character.[4] Most Japanese believe Japan's economic success simply results from hard work, consensus, loyalty, and 'racial purity', sentiments exemplified by Prime Minister Nakasone's 1986 remarks that the United States was declining economically because of the inferior intelligence of its blacks, hispanics, and other minorities. According to 'Japan is unique' adherents, if organizations do play a role on the economic level, it is at an enterprise rather than national level. Japanese are assumed not only to work harder than anyone else, but to organize themselves into groups based on the 'three unique national treasures' – lifetime employment, the seniority wage system, enterprise unionism – which because of 'racial purity' cannot be duplicated elsewhere.

The increased popularity of the 'Japan is unique' school among Japanese and some foreign advocates has paralleled Japan's growing economic dynamism, and is a central pillar of the very emotional nationalism building up across the country. For example, foreign criticism of Japan's unfair trade practices – however well argued – is denounced as 'Japan bashing' or scapegoating Japan for the failures of other nations to work hard enough. After all, if economic success depends solely on hard work and racial purity, then by definition any foreign allegations about such Japanese practices as 'dumping', non-tariff trade barriers, or thefts of technology are grossly untrue.

Of course, neither hard work, the 'three national treasures', nor 'racial purity' accounts for Japan's economic success. People work hard all over the world. While Japanese certainly work about 250 to 450 more hours a year than their OECD counterparts, Japan's productivity is about average among the industrial countries. Thus it can be argued that in terms of productivity, although Japanese may work much longer, people in other countries work much more intensely. Likewise the 'three national treasures' are hardly unique. For example, recent studies of the best run American corporations such as IBM, Hewlett Packard, or Black and Decker show that they also use modified variations of lifetime employment, seniority wages, and enterprise unionism.[5] It could be that any successful corporation must employ similar means to build up the loyalty and productivity of its workers. Finally, the 'racial purity' thesis is easily dismissed. Eerily similar to the arguments of German and Japanese ultranationalists during the 1930s and 1940s, it neglects the reality that three to four per cent of Japan's population represent minority groups of various kinds that suffer discrimination from other Japanese. American productivity remains about ten per cent higher than that of Japan, something 'Japan is unique' adherents cannot explain when they assert that 'racial purity' is essential for economic success.

Like the 'Japan is unique' school, the 'neo-classical economic' model completely avoids discussing the role of industrial policies in Japan's economic success and instead claims that the rapid economic growth occurred in the world's most open economy characterized by intense inter-firm competition and government-business ties no closer than in other countries. The government's role has been confined to rational macroeconomic policies that resulted in an extremely high savings/investment ratio which in turn fueled Japan's rapid economic growth. Patrick claims that Japan's economic performance is 'due primarily to the actions and efforts of private individuals and enterprises responding to the opportunities provided in quite free markets for commodities and labor. While the government has been supportive and indeed has done much to create the environment of growth, its role has often been exaggerated'.[6] Chen echoes Patrick's assertion by arguing that for Japan state 'intervention is largely absent. What the state has provided is a suitable environment for the entrepreneurs to perform their functions'.[7]

For different reasons, Japanese government and business leaders, along with many Western economists, have embraced this neo-classical model as the explanation of Japan's economic success. While knowing full well that such things as industrial policies, various kinds of cartels, import barriers, and export offensives were as important as competition in creating a dynamic economy, Japanese promote this view to help undermine foreign criticism of Tokyo's trade practices and calls for increased financial contributions to alleviate world problems. Western neo-classical economists argued this view because their ideology allows no other explanation. In reality, although Tokyo followed sound macroeconomic policies throughout the postwar era, they in themselves were not enough to account for its rapid economic growth, and, as will be seen, Japan may have some of the world's lowest tariffs but most of its markets remain protected by webs of subtle non-tariff barriers.

The 'Free Ride' school also focuses on one narrow group of factors behind Japan's economic success.[8] Its adherents claim that Japan was able to develop into an economic superpower because throughout the postwar era the United States did all it could economically to build up Japan to help contain the Soviet Union. Washington allowed Japan uninhibited access to an expanding world economy and cheap technology while maintaining high import barriers. With its military security guaranteed by America's nuclear and conventional umbrella, Tokyo could channel all its energies and capital into developing strategic industries which would in turn capture world markets and bring back enormous wealth to Japan. Tokyo's contributions to defense and foreign aid remain niggardly despite Japan's transformation into an economic superpower and the world's largest creditor nation. But again the counter to this argument is that while Japan's free ride on the world economy and defense was an important factor behind its economic success, other factors were equally important.

In contrast to the above arguments, which are generally superficial and tend to focus on one side of Japan's development and policy-making, Chalmers Johnson has advocated a much more sophisticated explanation of Japan's economic success that has systematized many of the arguments of the other schools.[9] Johnson contrasts the 'plan rational', developmental state of Japan with the 'market rational' United States. A plan rational state is usually a late industrializing country that must catch up with other more advanced industrial countries by developing its economy through elaborate, rational economic plans. Japan exemplified the plan rational state both in the Meiji era with its goals of a 'strong country/strong military' (fukoku kyohei) and 'overtake America and Europe' (obei ni oikose) of the postwar era. To achieve this, Tokyo followed pragmatic indus-trial policies designed to help Japan economically catch up to and eventually leapfrog its industrial rivals. Rational industrial policies promoted strategic industries through a wide range of subsidies, protection, and export support. In contrast, the United States exemplifies a market rational state where the consumer, not the producer, is king, and markets, not the state, determine the econ-omy's direction.

But policies alone were not enough. As important was the 'bureau-cratic-industrial complex', or web of related institutions dedicated to promoting these policies. Johnson points out that the three sacred treasures of lifetime employment, seniority wage system, and enter-prise unionism advocated by the 'Japan is unique school' were 'not the only special institutions, and they are certainly not the most sacred. Others include the personal savings system; the distribution system; the "descent from heaven" (amakudari) of retired bureau-crats from the ministries into senior management positions in private enterprises; the structure of industrial groupings (keiretsu, or the oligopolistic organization of each industry by conglomerates); the "dual economy" together with the elaborate structure of subcontract-ing it generates; the tax system; the extremely low degree of influence exercised over companies by shareholders; the hundred-odd "public corporations; and, perhaps most important of all, the government-controlled financial institutions, particularly the Japan Development Bank and the . . . Fiscal Investment and Loan Plan" '.[10]

While this web of institutions and procedures has clearly contrib-uted to Japan's economic success, like the 'Japan Inc' model, the

'Developmental State' model lays too much emphasis on governing triad collaboration and not enough on the tremendous changes that have swept Japan's political economy in the past quarter century. Competition has been as important as cooperation in giving Japanese corporations an edge over their foreign rivals. And these institutions are hardly unique – South Korea, Taiwan, and Singapore have erected many of these same institutions in their own countries, with the same results of high growth and affluence.

While Johnson's arguments are very inciteful in putting all the factors behind Japan's policy-making and rapid economic development in perspective, they fail to account for the changes that have occurred in Japan throughout the last decade. Johnson claims that 'the Japanese system remains plan rational, and the American system is still market rational'.[11] But it is a mistake to continue to call Japan a plan rational state when its bureaucracy is having increasing difficulties managing the economy, the LDP is increasingly taking the initiative in policy-making, and the corporate world daily grows more complex and financially powerful, while foreign governments are slowly prying open Japan's protected markets.

CORPORATIST POLICY-MAKING AND NEO-MERCANTILIST POLICY: MODELS AND REALITIES

The Corporatist model of policy-making and economic development provides the best framework with which to analyze Japan's political economy. Schmitter defines corporatism as 'a system of interest representation in which the constituent units are organized into a limited number of singular, compulsory, non-competitive, hierarchially ordered and functionally differentiated categories, recognized or licensed (if not created) by the state and granted a deliberate representational monopoly within their respective categories in exchange for observing certain controls on the selection of leaders and articulation of demands and supports'.[12] George builds on Schmitter's definition by writing that the 'essence of corporatism is a pattern of interest group-state bureaucracy relations of interdependence: formal inclusion of interest groups in government administration for purposes of assistance in policy implementation, in exchange for guaranteed access to government officials, legitimation of interest groups in ministerial advisory and consultation processes . . . and bureaucratic protection and patronage. The end product of corporatised relations between the state and interest groups is cooperation between the various parts of the public and private sectors in the pursuit of commonly agreed policy goals. Corporatism can also result in diminished levels of organizational autonomy . . . Interest groups become the instrument of mobilization where the state, in determining the economic and social priorities, sees a need to intervene in the operations of the free market and countenance various forms of assistance and control over sectors of the economy'.[13]

In a corporatist system the state acts not only as a referee in policy issues, but determines who the major contenders will be in any policy, and is also a dominant actor itself in most issues. In contrast, the state plays a minimal role in a pluralist system. Although written over two centuries ago, Adam Smith's words still capture the essence of the state's role in a liberal political economy: 'the sovereign (state) has only three duties . . . first, the duty of protecting the society from the violence and invasion of other independent societies; secondly, the duty of protecting as far as possible, every member of society from the injustice and oppression of every other member, or the duty of establishing an exact administration of justice; and thirdly, the duty of erecting and maintaining certain public works and certain public institutions, which it can never be for the interest of any individual, or small number of individuals'.[14]

Pempel blasts pluralist theory, arguing that 'the notion of a free market has been based on assumptions divorced from the realities of individual and group motivation and behavior . . . political assumptions undergirding liberalism and pluralism have . . . proven theoretically inadequate in dealing the challenges posed by . . . the centrality of the state in determining national economic priorities'.[15] The concept of free markets for both politics and economics evolved in the relatively prosperous, secure havens of Britain and the United States with their traditions of a limited state in the eighteenth and nineteenth centuries. Shortly after its independence, the United States embraced liberal forms of politics and economics while Britain slowly opened its markets and political system throughout the nineteenth century.

Despite the strenuous efforts of the two successive hegemons over the world system, first Britain in the late nineteenth and early twentieth century and America since 1945, to cajole other states into embracing liberalism, very few states have purely pluralist political economies. Even the United States, although generally considered to epitomize a pluralist political economy, has experienced a growing role of the state in the economy. For the most part, the United States has an unlimited number of active political and economic groups representing virtually every aspect of society. While the ability of these groups to safeguard or enhance their respective interests differs greatly, weaker groups can augment their influence through coalitions and trade offs with more powerful groups. Political parties competing in federal, state, and local governments are the most important institutions for mediating these conflicting interest groups. In America's pluralist system, the government's role is primarily regulatory, ensuring that all interest groups have the legal right to represent themselves, and to abide by the decisions made in the political and economic marketplaces. Yet this generally pluralist system has a number of corporatist elements such as the 'iron triangles' between industries, politicians, and bureaucracies pushing for government protection. America's most successful industries – aerospace and agriculture – resulted from rational industrial policies that targeted those industries for development with a range of subsidies, import protection, and technology sharing.

In contrast to the handful of states with mostly pluralist economies like the United States, Hong Kong, Australia, Canada, and Britain, the vast majority of liberal democratic states combine elements of both corporatism and pluralism. It can be difficult to categorize states which have a pluralistic political system of free, competitive elections while the economy is managed along corporatist lines. The intermediary categories of neo-pluralism and neo-corporatism may help. Neo-pluralist states differ from purely pluralist states in that through free competition a number of major interest blocks have emerged to dominate policy-making, although those interest blocks by no means hold a monopoly of power over the interests they claim to represent. In neo-pluralist systems, although all interests remain free in principle to compete for influence in the system, the major interest blocks can often use their collective clout to shape the laws to their own advantage. The state's role continues to be one of regulation and mediation, but certain agencies or institutions may be captured by powerful interest groups. Likewise political parties remain relatively free to compete but may be overly dependent on particular interest groups. West Germany provides a good example of a neo-pluralist state. Although West Germany had a generally pluralist economy managed by liberal policies up through the early 1970s, the quadrupling of oil prices in late 1973 plunged the country into the same stagflation that afflicted the entire world economy. Bonn responded by taking a much more active role in managing the economy and relations between its major interest groups. Although relations between management and labor had always been cooperative, the government reinforced the ties between them as much as possible.

Neo-corporatist states differ from corporatist states in that while the most important policy-making issues remain monopolized by the major interest blocks, other interest groups are allowed a limited but sometimes significant role in some areas, and even a token representation in major policy areas. Political parties become increasingly important in forming coalitions of interest groups and in sharing responsibility with the state for policy-making. In corporatist states the major actors are generally the bureaucracy, big business, and organized labor which negotiate over various management-labor wage/unemployment, and social welfare issues. Corporatist literature has gathered a wide variety of states under the corporatist rubric, although these states may vary widely in their degree of corporatism or neo-corporatism, the interest groups represented, and the central issues dealt with. Most Western European states are identified as being either corporate or neo-corporate states.[16] Austria, Sweden, and Norway are generally considered corporatist states while Denmark, West Germany, and Switzerland are often labeled neo-corporatist states. France is a good example of a corporatist state. Paris manages cooperation between the major economic blocks, guides the economy through five year plans, and outright owns many of the most important industries.

States in other regions of the world such as Latin America and East Asia have corporatist political as well as economic systems.[17] In most Latin American states the major groups are the bureaucracy, big business, landowners, military, church, and multinational corporations in countries like Peru, Guatemala, and Ecuador, while industrial labor forms a major interest group in countries like Brazil, Argentina, Mexico, and Chile. The state's major role is to maintain élite interests in all issue areas, with no concern for mass welfare or overall economic viability. The state's power extends indirectly throughout most aspects of the political economy. Parties are relatively unimportant; there is often little change in government, and when it occurs coups are often more important than elections. The Newly Industrializing Countries (NICs) of East Asia, including South Korea, Taiwan, and Singapore, provide yet another type of corporatism. The major actors include the bureaucracy, big business, and the military (except in Singapore) whose major role is to maximize economic development through export-led growth. Although consumer or labor groups are not represented, their interests are served by policies that promote a relatively egalitarian distribution of income and mass prosperity. Like Latin American corporatist states, the state's power extends throughout the country, generally through one party, and opposition parties remain impotent, while elections are often rigged.

Both before and after 1945 Japan passed through a number of different political economic orientations. In the pre-1945 period, while the goals of becoming an economic and military great power, and the means of mercantilism and imperialism to attain those goals remained the same, specific policies, actors, and opportunities to influence policy-making differed greatly. From 1868 to the early 1920s, Japan represented a bureaucratic-dominant corporatist model. The élite was dominated by the genro and bureaucracy while the military, zaibatsu (industrial combine), parties, aristocracy, and landlords played a secondary role in policy-making, and the masses of peasants and growing population of industrial workers and urban laborers were completely shut out from power.[18] During this period the government followed two phases of economic policies. From 1868 through the early 1880s Tokyo attempted directly to own and develop strategic industries like steel, shipbuilding, and armaments. But the failure of these state enterprises to overcome development problems led Tokyo to sell them off to private investors in the 1880s.

Yet Tokyo's economic policies and policy-making remained highly dominated by the state throughout this period despite this shift from public to private ownership. The state either formed or approved and then dominated all important interest groups involved in policy-making; those not approved were outlawed. For example, the prewar ancestor of the contemporary Agricultural Association (Nokyo), which serves as the corporatist group representing farmers, consisted of the producer cooperatives (sangyo kumiai) and agricultural associations (nokai), both established and regulated by successive laws from 1899. The Japanese Chamber of Commerce began as a government-approved organization in 1878. Legal regulation was often accompanied by an officially recognized government advisory role, the imposition of semi-administrative duties, and the receipt of government subsidies.[19]

During the 1920s, however, Japan enjoyed a brief period in which politics followed a neo-corporatist model while the economy as a whole was neo-pluralist. The government played a relatively insignificant role in the economy during this time while in 1925 it gave all men over 25 years of age the right to vote. Still, while peasants could vote, they generally voted according to the dictates of local political bosses while labor unions and leftist parties were periodically suppressed. Among the élite, however, there emerged a corporatist balance of power among the bureaucracy, military, parties, zaibatsu, aristocracy, and landlords similar to that of many Latin American countries today. Thus Japan had a corporatist political structure on top of a relatively *laissez-faire* economic structure.

This delicate balance of power among the élite shifted steadily in favor of the military after the 1931 invasion of Manchuria up through Japan's final defeat in 1945. The government assumed increasingly greater control over Japan until in 1940 all Japanese political, economic, social, and even religious groups were dissolved into the Imperial Rule Assistance Association (IRAA). While the government had absolute political control it fell short in its attempt to assert totalitarian controls over the economy, which even by 1945 remained a mixed economy. Policy-making was thoroughly corporatist with the military leading the inner circle of bureaucracy, zaibatsu, aristocracy, and landlords, and token representatives of peasants, workers and left-wing parties.

Japan's political economic orientation has passed through three distinct phases throughout the postwar era, and seems to be entering a fourth. During the Occupation and up through the mid-1960s Japan represented a bureaucratic-dominant corporatist state, in the mid-1960s up through the mid-1970s a corporatist state, and since then increasingly a neo-corporatist state. As Japan's economy continues to open up to the world and as Japanese become increasingly affluent, pressure groups will increasingly jostle with the dominant economic groups that favor continued economic growth over all to advocate policies which raise Japan's quality of life in such areas as more leisure time, lower priced goods, and better housing. Japan's policy-making may become increasingly neo-pluralist while its neo-mercantist policies slowly lose their vigor.

Although the patterns, actors, and priorities of policy-making may have shifted since 1945, the goal of becoming an economic superpower through steady export-led economic growth has remained constant as has the means to attain this via neo-mercantilist industrial, technology, and trade policies. The ruling élite remains dominated by the interdependent governing triad of LDP, bureaucracy, and big business (zaikai) tied by common interests in economic growth, wealth, and Japanese resurgence, and solidified by school ties, marriage, and retiring of bureaucrats into the industries they formerly 'regulated' (amakudari). The mass media has been a largely unwitting auxiliary through its reporters cooption in press clubs and publishers' membership in the élite. Although the press is sometimes critical of the government on domestic issues, it rallies around the flag on international issues. The governing triad has also succeeded in cooping the opposition parties, labor federations, and consumer and environmental groups through various payoffs and concessions. George writes that although the pluralists 'successfully challenged the notion of a rigid and exclusive three-sided power structure in which a hierarchy of "interests" dictated that the claims of big business groups automatically prevailed over those of other voluntary organization . . . the continuing hegemony of the LDP, however, and the central role which Japanese public officials in the national bureaucracy continued to play in setting and implementing policy goals, left the core party and bureaucratic elements in the elite alliance intact. The outcome was a new variant of the old elite model'.[20] Meanwhile the economy remains far from approximating the liberal ideal of free markets. Ronald Dore argues that Japan does not have markets in the neo-classical liberal sense of the word, but 'only a network of established customer relations'.[21]

The 'bureaucratic-dominated corporatist' or 'governing triad' model from 1945 to the mid-1960s closely approximated the Japan Inc model discussed earlier. The economic ministries of MITI and the MOF dominated policy-making and policies, while the LDP, big business, and farm interests played supporting roles, and the labor federations, and opposition parties were largely ignored. J. A. A. Stockwin succinctly describes the interdependent relations among the governing triad: 'the LDP depended on the bureaucracy for technical expertise and legislative initiative; the bureaucracy depended upon the LDP for parliamentary majorities in favour of government legislation, and for jobs on retirement; the LDP depended upon big business for electoral funding; big business depended upon the LDP for political backing, advantageous policies and political stability; big business depended upon bureaucracy for favors in the drawing up and implementing of legislation; the bureaucracy depended upon big business for jobs upon retirement'.[22]

The ruling triad threw its policy-making efforts behind Japan's rapid economic growth, which in turn depended on pushing neo-mercantilist policies. A senior MITI official explains both the strategy and justification behind neo-mercantilism:

> MITI decided to establish in Japan industries which require intensive employment of capital and technology, industries that in consideration of comparative cost of production should be the most inappropriate for Japan, industries such as steel, oil-refining, industrial machinery of all sorts, and electronics . . . From a short run, static viewpoint, encouragement of such industries would seem to conflict with economic rationalism. But, from a long-range viewpoint, these are precisely the industries where income elasticity of demand is high, technological progress is rapid, and labor productivity rises fast. It was clear that without these industries it would be difficult to employ a population of 100 million and raise their standard of living to that of Europe and America with light industries alone; whether right or wrong (in a neo-classical economic sense), Japan had to have these heavy and chemical industries . . . (the government) has been able to concentrate its scant capital in strategic industries.[23]

Japan's policy-makers completely rejected the neo-classical idea of free markets for several reasons. As the MITI official pointed out, a *laissez-faire* attitude by Tokyo would have condemned Japan to remain forever behind the more advanced industrial countries, rather than surpass them as it has by following neo-mercantilist policies. Tokyo understood that comparative advantage did not have to be inherited as neo-classical theorists argued, but instead could be created. Japanese policy-makers also rejected the neo-classical idea that all industries are of equal value. Clearly, some industries are far more important than others in creating wealth and stimulating economic development. Thus Tokyo created comparative advantage for its industries by targeting strategic sectors of the economy with a vast range of subsidies, import barriers, cartels, and export promotion. Although most of the economy remains in private hands and most transactions are determined by general market principles of supply and demand, the state takes an active role in developing strategic sectors and protecting declining ones.

Policy-making during this first phase typically followed a zig-zag course from the middle level of the relevant economic bureaucracy to acceptance by the minister, after which the bill or policy was sent for approval to the appropriate LDP policy bureau and then to the LDP Executive Council, when in turn it was sent to the appropriate

Diet policy committee and then on for ratification by the Diet. During this period about 85 per cent of all the ministry bills submitted were passed by the Diet, and they in turn composed about 95 per cent of all bills passed during this time.[24]

The 'corporatist' or 'tight governing triad' model from the mid-1960s to the mid-1970s emerged in response to related internal and external developments. Partly as a result of liberalization steps taken by Tokyo in response to foreign pressure and the entrance fee for the OECD, and partly because of the growing complexity and wealth of Japan's economy, influence over policy-making became increasingly diffused among the different segments of the triad, with the relative influence of any segment varying from one issue to the next. The zaikai's bargaining power grew as its dependence on the bureaucracy for subsidies, import protection, and export promotion lessened. The LDP's Policy Affairs Research Council (PARC) became increasingly important as its bureaus acquired policy-making expertise. The amakudari of bureaucrats into both the zaikai and LDP accelerated these trends. Policy-making turf battles and deadlocks grew as power devolved both between and within each segment. As they moderated their positions, the opposition parties, labor federations, and other interest groups were occasionally allowed to emerge from the political wilderness to play a token role on certain issues.

Japan's political economy has increasingly become characterized as a 'neo-corporatist' or 'loose governing triad' model from the mid-1970s through to the present. Although the governing triad continues to dominate policy-making, the actors vary in strength and participation according to the issues. The focus of policy-making is increasingly blurred as foreign governments and corporations begin to make an impact, and the LDP policy 'tribes' (zoku) play an increasingly important role in policy-making. Meanwhile, new ministries are challenging the role of MITI and the MOF in specific areas of economic policy-making. For example, MITI and the Ministry of Post and Telecommunications continue to battle over various high technology policies, while the Ministry of Education actually blocked MITI's attempt in the mid–1980s to reduce software protection from 50 to 15 years.

Stockwin writes that 'what is singular about the Japanese system of economic management is the intensity and frequency of consultation within the government-industry complex as a whole, and the strategic goal-orientation of Japanese government and industry . . . information flows quickly through the system, and participants on both government and industry sides are under intense pressure to obtain results'. In this dynamic policy-making and implementation system Stockwin finds no real focus of economic policy-making, arguing that the participants and their relative influence vary according to the issue: 'the balance of power among all the participants is constantly shifting, even if it is shifting within relatively predictable parameters'.[25] Pempel agrees with Stockwin, pointing out that it is 'difficult to speak meaningfully of any single policy-making process in Japan'.[26]

The bureaucrats domination of policy-making is clearly past. According to Chikara Higashi, a former MITI official, it is the special interest policy zoku rather than the bureaucracy which now dominates policy-making. Although in the past, the bureaucrats wrote 90 per cent of the laws, in the late 1980s as much as 25–50 per cent were written by LDP policy committees, while 'no policy can be formulated and no legislation passed without the approval of the relevant zoku'.[27] Most ministry officials overwhelmingly agree that policy-making power has shifted from their hands to the politicians. A 1986 survey by the *Mainichi Shimbun* revealed that although 60.3 per cent of officials polled in 18 different ministries agreed that postwar prosperity was the result of their leadership, only 20 per cent claimed that they still dominated economic policy-making.[28] Apparently, some of the traditional arrogance with which bureaucrats viewed the rest of humanity (kanson minpi) has been transferred to the politicians as well. Higashi relates an incident in 1985, in which the PARC Chairman asked MOF to make some changes in the FY1986 budget. When MOF refused, the Chairman called the MOF leaders to a meeting, sharply tongue-lashed them saying, among other things, that 'petty bureaucrats should not create petty arguments', and then kicked them out of his office while warning them not to come back.[29]

One important reason for the bureaucrat's declining power has been the proliferation of interest groups over the past decade. For example, the number of organizations lobbying MOF's Tax Bureau for favors rose steadily from 48 in 1966 to 198 in 1983, then almost doubled to 358 in 1986 when Nakasone's tax reform proposals were first aired.[30] Many of these interest groups are being represented in the Diet. In 1983, there were 144 politicians in the Lower House, or 28.2 per cent of the total of 511 members, who had either held or were holding official leadership positions in interest groups. In the Upper House there were 102 interest group officials or 40.5 per cent of the total membership of 252. Altogether, 246 or 31.1 per cent of 776 Diet members represented interest groups. Labor union officials (92) formed the largest interest group in the Diet, followed by farmers (38), business (16), health/welfare (16), sports (14), religious or ideological (13), professional (13), youth (9), and forestry or fishery groups (9).[31] Many professional associations have political arms; for example, the Japan Doctors' League operates as the political front for the Japan Medical Association and the Japan Dentists' Political League for the Japan Dentists' Association.

The power of most interest groups, however, is undermined by the factionalism endemic to Japan's political culture. Even Big Business' political arm, Keidanren, is becoming increasingly split between those who advocate a relatively open economy and those who insist on retaining subtle although no less powerful non-tariff barriers. Despite these growing divisions, the corporate world will remain united in its support of and interdependence with the LDP. The recent amalgamation of the labor federations into Rengo, however, poses potential problems for the JSP and DSP which traditionally relied on the General Council of Trade Unions (Sohyo) and the All Japan Labor Federation (Domei) for their financial and organizational support. The Private Sector Trade Union Council (Rengo) will support both parties and encourage closer collaboration between the JSP and DSP.

Today, the Clean Government Party (CGP) is the only political party which is dominated by an outside group. And even the Sokka Gakkai's power over the CGP has been cloaked by the formal split between the two in the 1970s and conscious attempts to distance themselves since. Interest groups that are simply mouthpieces for a particular political party are almost as rare: for example, the Free Lawyers' Association is simply the political arm of the JCP. Most interest groups, however, are generally autonomous. Many broad interest areas are split between two or more groups, each affiliated with a different political party. For example, Although most small- and medium-sized business groups support the LDP, some work with parties like the Japan Socialist Party (JSP), Democratic Socialist Party (DSP), or Japan Communist Party (JCP). Among professional groups the Free Lawyers' Association is aligned with the JCP, the Second Tokyo Lawyers' Association with the JSP, and the Japan Lawyers' Federation with the LDP. Almost one quarter of the agricultural association (Nokyo) Diet members between 1949–80 belonged to either the JSP or DSP.

Many interest groups, however, while independent of the parties, are dominated by the bureaucracy. Often the bureaucracy will assign different interest groups certain responsibilities for implementing policies that affect them. For example, Japan's Agricultural Federation, Nokyo, performs a wide range of administrative functions under the agriculture laws. These extra departmental groups (gaikaku dantai) represent a specialized form of administrative or institutional interest group which act like auxiliary government organs. The gaikaku dantai conform to the bureaucracy's regulations in return for being consulted and having a voice on relevant policies, as well as receiving financial grants to perform their administrative functions. These semi-official functions can include technical, planning, informational, research, inspection, promotional, funding, and public relations areas. There are now over 5000 such groups in Japan.[32]

The influence of most of these interest groups on policy-making, however, remains limited. Any interest group's impact on policy-making depends on its relationship to the policy-makers. Since 1945, Japanese policy-making has been dominated by the bureaucracy, with growing assistance from the LDP since the 1960s. Thus, any interest group desiring a voice in a particular policy must go through either the bureaucracy or LDP. Since the LDP has dominated Japanese politics and was a key participant in policy-making throughout the postwar era, its political backers have a strong voice in policies affecting them. Formally, interest group demands are channeled through the LDP PARC. The opposition parties and their respective interest groups, however, have been largely excluded from the LDP policy-making process. Until recently, they have also been largely excluded from the bureaucratic channels of policy-making, although they are allowed increasing token representatives on the largely ornamental policy advisory councils (shigikai).[33] Although George identifies Japanese corporatism as being shaped by a variety of factors including 'historical tradition, organizational factors, party alignments, and government economic priorities', he sees the basis of Japan's continued corporatism in 'the long and continuous period of one-party rule by the LDP which has elevated the political support patterns of interest groups to a critical determinance of policy access. For groups aligned with the Opposition this has meant limited direct access to authoritative decision – makers and limited direct participation in policy-making'.[34]

The continuing web of financial and policy ties between and within each leg of the governing triad was sharply highlighted by the Recruit scandal that plagued the Takeshita administration for most its tenure. The Recruit Corporation is a small keiretsu (industrial group) of 27 subsidiaries which includes Japan's largest private employment agency, several weekly advertising publications, and a financial firm whose combined sales in 1987 were $2 billion. One of Recruit's subsidiaries, the Recruit Cosmos Company, sold underpriced stocks to 159 leading members of Japan's political parties, ministries, and corporations shortly before the company went public on 30, October 1986, after which the insiders resold their stocks, pocketing over a 100 per cent profit on shares they had held only several months, with average profits ranging from $160 000 to $330 000 each. Some of the more prominent Recruit beneficiaries include all the LDP faction leaders, three Takeshita Cabinet Ministers including MOF Minister Kiichi Miyazawa, Deputy Prime Minister and head of the EPA Ken Harada, and MOF Minister Takashi Hasegawa, DSP Chairman Saburo Tsukamoto, Takashi Kato, a former vice-minister at the Labor Ministry, Jiro Ushio and Ken Moroi the vice-chairmen of the Japan Association of Corporate Executives and the Japan Federation of Employers' Association, Speaker of the House Kenzaburo Hara, Rules and Administration Committee head Toshio Yamaguchi, and three top executives of NTT including its Chairman Hisahi Shinto. In addition, Diet members of every political party except the JCP, officials in the Labor and Education ministries, and executives in dozens of corporations all received shares.

Although it is not illegal to receive unlisted shares, it is considered unethical if the sale is used to buy influence. The possibility that share recipients engaged in influence peddling caused 20 of them – all senior politicians and officials – to resign, including MOF Minister Miyazawa. All those who resigned had carelessly bought the stock in their own names. Most of the recipients, however, managed to evade any responsibility by buying the shares in the names of their relatives or aids, and then denying any knowledge of the transaction. For example, three close associates of former Prime Minister Nakasone – two aides and the executive of one of his political organizations – received over 29 000 shares for a profit of $470 000, while Prime Minister Takeshita's 12 000 shares were brought through several friends and relatives.

Recruit received a range of benefits from its generous sale of shares to Japan's élite. Recruit's Chairman, Hiramasa Ezoe, was appointed to four government advisory groups (shingikai) with the Education and Labor ministries, including the very important Tax Systems Research Council. The Labor Ministry relaxed its advertizing regulations for Recruit. In addition, 13 former members of the previously government-owned NTT parachuted down to work for Recruit, taking their connections and inside information with them. Although a newcomer to telecommunications, Recruit was allowed to jump the line of more established firms and lease high speed electrical circuits on NTT telephone lines. Even more controversial was NTT's secret sale of two supercomputers to Recruit. In 1986, Prime Minister Nakasone had agreed to a Reagan administration request that NTT buy more supercomputers to help alleviate Japan's huge trade surplus of over $60 billion. Although Cray's supercomputers are the world's most advanced, NTT had continued to buy from Japanese sources in order to promote Japan's technological development.

As the scandal unfolded it revealed a web of bribery, kick-backs, and coverups. One of the Recruit Directors, Hiroshi Matsubara, repeatedly tried to bribe Yanosuke Narazaki, a Diet member of the United Social Democrat Party and strong advocate of a complete investigation of the scandal. Matsubara's last bribery attempt was secretly videotaped and shown later that night on the television news. A Recruit company spokesman claimed that Matsubara was acting on his own. Eventually Matsubara and Recruit's Chairman, Hiramasa Ezoe, as well as NTT Chairman Hisashi Shinto, were arrested on various corruption charges.

The Recruit scandal reveals that the financial ties not just within the ruling triad, but with the opposition parties as well, remain firmly in place. Japan's political economy continues to run on money politics (kinken seiji) and is dominated by the ruling triad. Although Japan's élite repeatedly claims that its markets are the world's most open, some business success in Japan clearly depends on the amount of money a firm can pass to those in power behind the scenes rather than its product's ability to compete in free markets.

CONCLUSION

Japan's policy-making will eventually shift from neo-corporatism into neo-pluralism as the economy continues to prosper, diversify, and slowly open, while society's values increasingly shift from industrial standard of living to post-industrial quality of life issues. Consumer, housing, old-age, minority, and foreign interest groups will become increasingly vocal and visible, if not decisive, in relevant issues. Despite these changes, the governing triad will continue to dominate policy-making, even as the bureaucracy, LDP, and zaikai become increasingly divided over specific policies and issues. The Diet will remain a rubber-stamp for decisions made elsewhere since economic prosperity and the continued fragmentation of the opposition parties will keep the LDP in power.

Despite these changes, Japan will continue to follow essentially neo-mercantilist economic policies; Tokyo will continue to use largely cosmetic 'liberalization' steps and promises to mask its rational macroeconomic and industrial policies designed to continually push the economy to a higher technology base by targeting strategic industries for development with subsidies, export promotion, and a web of non-tariff import barriers. The reason for continued neo-mercantilism is simple: its beneficiaries are so deeply entrenched politically, that significant change is all but impossible. Calder shows several ways in which the political system reinforces neo-mercantilism. Japan's multimember electoral districts make 'extremely small shifts in the total vote . . . crucial to a candidate's election prospects. As a result, LDP legislators tend to be highly sensitive to a constituency pressure, especially from relatively well-organized grassroots pressure groups such as agriculture and small business . . . The LDP's complex factional structure, grassroots constituency-sensitive orientation, and strong domestic interest-group ties . . . inhibit the party from making decisive independent policy initiatives . . . ; trade policy is biased in favor of inefficient domestic agriculture and labor-intensive manufacturing . . .' which 'have virtually no international interests other than to resist foreign encroachments into Japanese domestic markets'.[35] The voting power of these groups is bolstered with 'iron triangle' clientalist relationships with the appropriate bureaucrats and politicians. Meanwhile, the 'bureaucracy and big business are still powerful in the policy process . . . especially on delicate trade policy questions, where . . . initiatives directed toward liberalization of existing barriers are often politically controversial'.[36] Thus with virtually every area of Japan's economy protected by a corporatist group, Japan's neo-mercantilist policies and governing triad will persist into the indefinite future.

NOTES

1. Stockwin advocates combining the liberal democratic and authority maintenance models, in which the ruling triad's ability to dominate both access to policy-making and the actual policies exists with a broad liberal democratic framework; *Dynamic and Immobilist Politics in Japan*, p. 12. Other corporatist explanations include Gavan McCormick and Yoshio Sugimoto (eds), *Democracy in Contemporary Japan*; Jon Woronoff, *Politics The Japanese Way*; Chalmers Johnson, *MITI and the Japanese Miracle*; T. J. Pempel, 'Corporatism with Labor', in Phillipe C. Schmitter and Gerhard Lehmbruch (eds), *Trends Toward Corporatist Intervention*; and Karl van Wolferen, 'The Japan Problem', *Foreign Affairs*, vol. 65, Winter 1986–87. For a good discussion of various international economic strategies see Robert Gilpin, *The Political Economy of International Relations*.
2. T. J. Pempel writes that 'state-societal interaction will be more "corporatist" in regard to the activities of one economic sector or one interest than in regard to another'. Pempel and Tsunekawa, op. cit., p. 234.
3. See Haruhiro Fukui's 'Studies in Policy-making: A Review of the literature', in T. J. Pempel (ed.), *Policy-making in Contemporary Japan*, for an extensive review of the pluralist-élitist discussion of the pluralistic-élitist views of Japan's policy economy.
4. Virtually any government or business spokesperson can be found echoing these views. See chapter 13 for an in-depth discussion of Japan's growing nationalism as examplified by its Nihonjinron literature.
5. See Dale Peters, *In Search of Excellence*.
6. Hugh Patrick and Henry Rosovsky, *Asia's New Giant: How the Japanese Economy Works*, p. 239.
7. Edward Chen, *Hyper-Growth in the Asian Economies*, pp. 183–4; see also Milton and Rose Friedman, *Freedom To Choose*.
8. See Chalmers Johnson, *MITI and Japan's Modern Economic Miracle*, chapter 1 for an in-depth discussion of this and other schools.
9. Ibid., pp. 18–25.
10. Ibid., p. 12.
11. Ibid., p. 20.
12. Schmitter, op. cit., p. 13.
13. Aurelia George, 'Japanese Interest Group Behavior', in Stockwin, op. cit., pp. 122–3, 131.
14. Adam Smith, *The Wealth of Nations*.
15. Pempel, op. cit., p. 231.

16. See Schmitter, op. cit.
17. Ibid. See also Linn A. Hammergren, 'Corporatism in Latin American Politics', *Comparative Politics*, vol. 9, no. 4, July 1977, or Kent Calder and Roy Hofheinz, *The Eastasian Edge* for a fuller explanation.
18. See chs. 3 and 4 for details of the genro and zaibatsu, respectively.
19. George in Stockwin, op. cit., p. 126.
20. Ibid., p. 107.
21. Ronald Dore, *Flexible Rigidities*, p. 248.
22. J. A. A. Stockwin, *Dynamic and Immobilist Aspects of Japanese Politics*, p. 10. See also Robert A. Scalapino (ed.), *The Foreign Policy of Modern Japan*, T. J. Pempel, *Policy and Politics in Japan: Creative Conservatism*, Michael Minor, 'Decision Models and Japanese Foreign Policy Decision Making', *Asian Survey*, vol. 25, no. 12, December 1985, and E. S. Krauss and Michio Muramatsu, 'The Conservative Policy Line and the Development of Patterned Pluralism in Postwar Japan', in Kozo Yamamura and Yasukichi Yasuba, (eds), *Japan's Political Economy*.
23. Quoted in *OECD Report*, 1972.
24. Hans Baerwald, *Party Politics in Japan*, p. 112.
25. Stockwin, op. cit., p. 12.
26. Pempel, op. cit., p. 398.
27. Chikara Higashi, *Japan's Economic Internationalization*, p. 71.
28. Ibid.
29. Ibid.
30. Ibid., p. 73.
31. George, op. cit., in Stockwin, pp. 109–11.
32. Ibid., p. 124.
33. Ibid., pp. 120–4.
34. Ibid., pp. 132–3.
35. Kent Calder, 'Japanese Foreign Economic Policy Formation: Explaining the Reactive State', *World Politics*, vol. 40, no. 4, July 1988, pp. 530–1.
36. Ibid., p. 530.

2 The Political Economic Culture

Shortly after Emperor Hirohito died on 7 January 1989, Crown Prince Akihito ascended the throne and performed the ritual of accepting the sacred mirror, sword, and necklace that have symbolized imperial rule for over 1500 years. The imperial transition, however, did not end there. Emperor Akihito performed a series of elaborate rituals over the next year that culminated in his formal ascension at Kyoto's imperial shrine on the anniversary of his father's death. There Akihito performed the ritual of Daijosai whereby he was ritually transformed into a woman, impregnated by the gods, and finally reborn as a god. Only then did he truly become an emperor.

These mysterious, arcane rituals contrast starkly with the impressions that strike foreign visitors when they first arrive in what is increasingly the world's economic capital – Tokyo. Most newcomers are dazzled by Tokyo's seeming modernity – the skyscrapers, fast, efficient transportation system, mass affluence and lack of noticeable poverty, and armies of blue-suited businessmen and stylishly attired women. In just 170 years after it was dragged from its self-imposed isolation into the modern world economy, Japan seems to have either equaled or surpassed its industrial rivals in mastering such Western institutions as parliamentary democracy, high technology, multinational corporations, international trade, and even the fine arts.

How can Japan seem at once so thoroughly modern and yet retain such primordial rituals as exemplified in the imperial succession? Are the values surrounding the imperial institution an anachronism or an integral part of contemporary Japan? What role, if any, does contemporary Japan's mixture of traditional and modern values and institutions play in enhancing Japanese power?

This chapter will analyze the continuities and changes in Japan's political economic culture, and how they affect Japanese power. But what is culture? In its common usage, the word 'culture' conjures up images of such things as Beethovan sonatas, Rembrandt paintings, and Russian ballets enjoyed mostly by a blue-blooded 'old money' élite; wealthy Boston families have culture, Texas oil million-

33

aires do not. Actually, culture is much more than just artistic events and possessions enjoyed by a privileged few. Michelangelo's brilliant Sistine Chapel paintings may at once personify the artistic heights of both a culture and an individual while Pope Julius II may represent the ultimate patron, but culture is not confined to any one group or individual; everyone is an active participant within a culture whether they realize it or not.

The essence of any culture is a group sharing the same organizational, technological, and psychological values and patterns of behavior which are distinct from those of other groups. But although distinct from one another, cultures do not develop in isolation; the more complex a culture the more it both borrows from and lends to other cultures, which in turn leads to its further enrichment. Through such media as trade, warfare, diplomacy, and religious missions, ideas spread from one culture to the next, and are in turn interpreted through and integrated within a culture's core values.

For social scientists, the primary group identified as a culture changes markedly depending on the period of history. Anthropologists studying the neolithic era identify cultures with broad regional or even continental characteristics such as a common style of arrowheads or pottery. As local cultures developed within stone-age America or Africa the tribe became the primary group for analysis. For much of history the boundaries of a culture reflected the frontiers of great military empires such as those of Babylon, Rome, or China, or great religious empires such as those of Medieval Christianity or Islam. At the same time social scientists identify countless sub-cultures within these overarching cultures.

Social scientists analyzing the modern world, however, identify nation-states as the primary cultural group. Nation-states are not the same thing as nations. While nation-states are identified as any state internationally recognized as holding sovereignty within its boundaries, nations are defined as 'a group of people with a common way of perceiving, organizing, modifying, and acting within a clearly defined territory, conscious of their group's distinction from other nations, and either holding or aspiring to national sovereignty'.[1] Nation-states first emerged in Europe during the 1500s with the break-up of the power of the medieval church. By the mid-twentieth century, as a result of a long process of first colonization by the European countries and eventual independence the entire world was organized into almost 170 sovereign nation-states ranging from continental size giants like the Soviet Union or United States to micro-states in the South Pacific and Caribbean Sea.

Only four countries in the world – Iceland, Portugal, Bangledesh, and Koreas – can include 100 per cent of their inhabitants within their national culture; all other nation-states have significant sub-cultures or even other national cultures within their territory. Countries like Britain, France, or the United States, while enjoying well-defined and pervasive national cultures, have large ethnic, regional, or religious sub-cultures as well. Most nation-states, however, whether they are industrialized countries like Canada or Belgium or industrializing countries like India or Nigeria, are trying desperately to forge a common culture within their borders among nations which often hold widely different values, languages, institutions, and histories.

The concept of culture becomes even more problematic when we introduce related concepts like 'political culture' and 'political economic culture'. Political culture is the sub-system of values, institutions, and behavior within a culture encompassing politics. Politics, of course, is not confined simply to such formal areas as government institutions and procedures, but includes virtually everything associated with the distribution of and struggle for power or influence within a given culture, such as the attitudes of citizens towards their government and their degree of participation within the system, the informal channels by which individuals or groups compete to influence government policy-making, or the way individuals are socialized into the system. Political economic culture is an even broader concept. It includes both political culture and such areas as how businesses compete or collude with each other, labor-management relations, or the ways political and economic institutions interact with and influence each other.

A distinctly Japanese political economic culture has been evolving for over 1500 years while its roots stretch back even further, originating from such far-flung regions as Southeast Asia, China, Northeast Asia, and Central Asia. Chapters 3, 4 and 5 will analyze the evolution of Japan's political economy up through the present day. This chapter focuses on the values, institutions, and patterns of behavior that comprise Japan's modern political economic culture. The chapter will first identify the psychological and sociological basis of Japanese culture, and then demonstrate how these cultural values, institutions, and behaviors are manifested in Japan's modern political economy.

THE PSYCHOLOGICAL AND SOCIOLOGICAL BASIS OF JAPANESE CULTURE

Japanese behavior has mystified Westerners ever since the Portuguese traders and missionaries first arrived in the mid-sixteenth century. How could a people produce both the timeless serenity of a zen temple and the unbridled savagery of the 'rape' of Nanjing, or such a single-minded drive to excel among its students and businessmen while traditional values laud the importance of resignation, serenity, and fate? Is the modern Japan of noisy, crowded, and polluted concrete urban jungles the same that extolls the virtues of nature?

What most long-term residents of Japan eventually understand is that a vast unity underlies such seeming paradoxes and contradictions. It is important to remember that the more complex and developed a culture becomes, the greater the likelihood that some of its values will at times seem to conflict. For example, how do Americans resolve the seeming contradiction between the value that people should be free to pursue and enjoy material wealth and the equally cherished value in equality and a 'level playing field'?

One of the first things a foreign resident realizes is that the West and Japan have very different concepts of the individual. From its Judeo-Christian-Greek cultural roots through the Renaissance up to the human potential movement of today, Western culture has stressed the importance of an individual striving to realize his full potential as a human being, to fulfill the Delphic challenge to 'Know Yourself'.

In contrast, Japanese consider the individual to be of little importance; the Japanese word for individualism – kojinshugi – conveys an image of selfishness and egoism. Individuals are invariably described as a 'nail which must be hammered down' (deru kugi wa utareru). Between 1953 and 1983, there was actually a large drop in those who preferred to push their own ideas from 41 per cent to 30 per cent, while those who tended to follow custom increased from 35 to 37 per cent, those who said the individual should come first remained constant at 25 per cent, and those who said Japan should come first dropped from 37 per cent to 30 per cent.[2] The group, not the individual, is the basic building block of society, and the group's character and identity is transferred to each individual within it. The peasant toiling in a rice paddy or the salaried clerk behind a desk build their individual identity around their village or company, respectively.

While wandering poets like Basho or masterless samurai (ronin) are the subject of countless romantic stories, for Japanese the tragedy of these characters lies in their rootlessness and lack of identity as human beings. Personal achievements or ideas pale beside those of the group. When asked what they do, Japanese businessmen will invariably say they work for their company rather than declare themselves an engineer or accountant. Yet, by Western standards, the group demands a high price for its extension of security and a sense of identity to the individual. Individual differences in taste, morals, or goals are suppressed by group concensus.

Another value that quickly becomes apparent to the foreign resident is the hierarchy that pervades all aspects of Japanese society whether it be within or between groups and individuals. Inequality is considered natural and good. Individuals should know and dedicate themselves to fulfilling their role within a group's hierarchy of roles, just as each group must obey its proper place in relation to other groups in society. The hierarchial structure of traditional Japan was considered fixed and just. Whether they be peasants, samurai, merchants, or artisans, each had their respective role to play and each was dependent on the others to fulfill theirs. Modern Japan, however, allows individuals and groups to change their place within their respective hierarchy depending on their relative degree of enterprise and hard work. The fierce competition between students or companies is fueled by the realization that rising to the top of the pyramid is possible through a single-minded dedication to excel.

But cooperation is just as important, both between individuals and groups, as is competition. 'Connections' (kone) are a vital means of advancing ones position within a group or that of a group within society. Relations both between individuals and groups are organized around patrons (sempai) and followers (kohai). The patron extends life-long protection and advantages to his followers in turn for undying loyalty and conformity. This patron-follower relationship is reinforced by the concept of 'amae' which is described as the psychological dependence of a child on its parent.[3] By pampering their children, Japanese mothers create in them a life-long dependence need for others to take of them. For Japanese, a group becomes a new family and the patron a parent-surrogate. The patron-follower relationship – 'oyabun/kobun' – of more traditional Japanese groups, literally means parent-role/child role. This need to be indulged within a group extends even to such areas as honeymoons where a thriving industry caters to the needs of newlyweds to be with others even on such an intimate occasion.

Thus, because of the importance of patron/follower relations, connections may well be much more important than merit in determining the relative success of individuals or groups within Japanese society. For example, although automobile companies generally compete fiercely among themselves, there is a clear hierarchy among them which may be determined more by connections than merit. By producing consistently excellent automobiles, Honda is the number one Japanese automobile-maker in the vast open American market. Yet, in Japan Honda is a distant third behind Toyota and Nissan. Why? The answer lies in connections rather than quality. Both Toyota and Nissan were founded in the prewar era with massive government promotion and have thus since enjoyed long-established connections throughout Japan's political economic élite. The postwar upstart Honda, on the other hand, is largely locked out of these connections and, despite having superior products, must look to foreign markets for most of its growth. Invariably connections are more important than merit in determining the degree of relative success between individuals or groups.

The Japanese language both reflects and reinforces this obsession with rank. With a half dozen ways each to say 'I' or 'You', and a vast intricate range of honorifics or blunt terms depending on whether one is speaking up or down to someone, it becomes very difficult to speak on equal terms in Japanese. Women's speech is much more honorific than that of men, reflecting the inferior status of women in Japanese society. Japanese businessmen meeting for the first time will bow uniformly, speak politely, and exchange business cards. Then the behavior changes markedly as the businessman from the 'superior' company assumes a somewhat haughty attitude while the representative from the 'inferior' company becomes instantly humble and self-effacing.

This concept of hierarchy is extended to international relations – just as there is no equality between individuals or groups, nations also struggle with each other for higher status within the global hierarchy of nations. Before 1945, this position in the international pecking order was determined by the size of a nation's empire and military; in the postwar era by such indicators as economic growth rates, size, and per capita income. An engrained sense of hierarchy provided an extra stimulus for the Meiji leaders to attempt to overthrow the unequal treaties imposed by the Western powers and eventually surpass them by creating a modern, powerful Japan; for Japan's postwar leaders, this obsession with becoming 'Number One' has fueled their drive to economically surpass the West and particularly the United States. To this end of becoming the 'superior' country in the world, Tokyo has single-mindedly pursued neo-mercantilist policies designed continually to upgrade Japan's economy to higher technological levels. This obsession has paid off; in 40 years Japan rose from its decrepit, war-devastated Third World economic level to become the world's banker and most dynamic economy.

A particularistic ethical system is an integral part of the Japanese values of the group and hierarchy. The Western individual attempts to develop as a human being within universal guidelines of right and wrong. For Japanese, however, right and wrong depend on the situation rather than some external standards like the Ten Commandments. Takie Sugiyama Lebra in her book, *Japanese Patterns of Behavior*, identifies three distinct Japanese ethical categories. 'Intimate' behavior occurs in informal situations with close family, friends, or co-workers. Individuals are relaxed and can behave increasingly uninhibitedly often in relation to the amount of alcohol they have consumed. 'Ritualistic' behavior occurs in formal settings both within and between groups, and is carefully prescribed according to the respective status of the participants.

Finally, and most puzzling to foreign observers, is 'Anomic' behavior which occurs in situations where there are no clear relationships or guidelines. In anomic situations when the individual is beyond the guidance of his group, or the group itself is unrestrained by other Japanese groups, anything goes. This is because for Japanese a sense of guilt is inseparable from their social relationship; guilt, responsibility, and atonement come from failing the group rather than all-knowing, all-powerful God.

During World War II, anomic behavior was revealed in several ways. Without clear boundaries of what was considered proper behavior, Japanese troops slaughtered millions of East Asians for no apparent reason. Although considered barbarous by international standards, most Japanese believe there was nothing wrong with such behavior and view the War Crimes Trials in Tokyo and elsewhere as unjust. Likewise, Japanese troops fought fanatically against their enemies, often dying to a man in massive human wave attacks that had little chance of success. Yet, after capture, having lost their group identity and moral guidelines, many Japanese POWs collaborated openly with their captors even to the extent of betraying their former units.

But Japanese are not completely without internal constraints. Without group guidance, internal constraints on the individual come from a sense of 'On', or deep obligation to ones benefactors. Like original sin for Christians, all Japanese are considered to be born with 'on', whether it be to one's parents, or their benefactors, or to society as a whole. Debts are repaid to one's benefactors through loyalty and sacrifice. The 'on' between individuals is never equal, but is instead asymmetrical and hierarchial. This web of obligations rather than rights limits the ability of an individual to act freely. Lebra describes the paradox of individual power in Japan that 'the higher up one goes along the hierarchy of authority, the higher the price one seems to pay in freedom and authority, partly because of the taboos surrounding authority but mainly because of the higher concentration of social obligations in the person of the authority figure.[4]

In a relativistic world that at times resembles a Hobbesian war of all against all, Japanese assume that everyone in a conflict is responsible to varying extents, reasoning that 'even a thief may be 30 per cent right'. There is no absolute truth that can be perceived through rationally examining the situation. Instead, what truth does exist is relative and is hidden in paradoxes and contradictions. For example, the 17 Hitachi and Mitsubishi executives arrested for attempting to buy what they were told were stolen IBM secrets, not only felt they were doing nothing wrong but instead angrily accused the FBI and IBM of wrong-doing. Most Japanese agree with this particularistic ethic that 'right' is whatever benefits the group and 'wrong' anything that hinders it. A recent survey of Japanese college graduates reported that 51 per cent felt they would follow their company 'even if it involved doing something unfair or violating social justice'.[5]

The emphasis on organizing society and the identities of individuals around groups, combined with the values of hierarchy and a particularistic ethical system inevitably breeds conflict. According to Flanagan and Richardson, Japanese 'society is a series of concentric rings emanating out from the individual at the center and representing diminished levels of intimacy with increasing distance. Respect, obligation, and trust fall off rapidly when we move beyond the spheres of intimate associates and meaningful acquaintances. As a result, outsiders and strangers are frequently viewed with a coolness and suspicion, if not outright hostility and distrust.'[6]

Japanese get around these inevitable conflicts, in part, by differen-tiating between two interrelated concepts – Tatemae (principles) and Honne (reality), in which Tatemae is often used as a smokescreen to mask Honne. For example, any important decision will be decided only after a series of long, intricate behind-the-scenes negotiations (nemawashi) followed by a ritualistic formal meeting during which the decision is announced. The 'ten market opening steps' presented by Tokyo to the world during the 1980s were tatemae obscuring the honne that in reality the more obvious trade barriers like tariffs and quotas were simply replaced by more subtle ones like administrative procedures and semi-official cartels. Export surpluses continued to mount dramatically throughout the 1980s despite repeated claims by officials that Japan now had the world's most open markets. But it is considered a breach of Japanese etiquette to point out the difference between tatemae and honne. When foreigners expose the gap between Japanese economic tatemae and honne, they are accused of 'Japan bashing'. Japanese try to avoid open conflict at all costs even if it means merely hiding it behind declarations of harmony and goodwill. Unfortunately, this distinction between tatamae and honne can result in even greater conflict between Japanese and foreigners when the latter take the former's promises at face value.

Although conflicts between groups are common, there are often considerable conflicts within groups as well among patron/follower factions struggling for power. As can be imagined, these internal conflicts are covered up even more vigorously than conflicts between groups. Yet, this cover-up also has a negative side-effect. Flanagan and Richardson write that as a consequence, 'the myth of internal unity is bought at the expense of promoting the myth of external war. The more emphasis on preserving harmony within the group, the greater the difficulty in effectively cooperating with outside groups'.[7]

Japan's view of its trade conflicts with the rest of the world epito-mizes this dilemma. Although Japan has huge and continually rising trade and current account surpluses, has replaced the United States as world banker with the world's ten largest banks, and has one of the world's largest per capita incomes, Japanese see themselves as beseiged by foreigners making unreasonable demands on Tokyo to open its markets further. Despite a $60 billion trade surplus with the United States in 1987, it is America that is 'bashing' Japan, and not the other way round.

Although Japan confronts the same conflicts and problems experienced by other industrial countries, most Japanese, when asked, will instead describe their land as characterized by harmony and oneness. In terms rather startling to foreigners who are familiar with pre–1945 history, Japanese consider themselves to be members of a 'pure, unique [implying superior] race'. In reality, of course, there are a number of both ethnic minority groups – Koreans, Chinese, Okinawans, and Ainu, and cultural minority groups – burakumin (an 'untouchable' class), hibakusha (atomic bomb victims), and konketsujin (mixed-race people) that number as much as five per cent of the population. Discrimination against these minority groups is deeply imbedded in Japanese society and will continue into the indefinite future despite the political efforts of these groups to achieve equality. But the important thing for Japanese is nonetheless to believe that they are actually members of a 'pure unique race'.

The core values and institutions of Japanese culture – its group and hierarchical basis, particularistic ethical system, emphasis on status and connections, and the importance of masking unpleasant realities with idealistic gestures – are lubricated by two seemingly contradictory values: fatalism and will-power. There is a whole inter-related range of concepts dealing with Japanese fatalism including 'akirame' (resignation), 'innen' (karma), or 'mono no aware' (the impermanence of all things). In contrast to the West where individuals generally have the freedom to shape their lives according to their desires or abilities (erabi culture), Japanese must instead adapt themselves to the demands of a tightly-knit society that gives them security in exchange for loyalty (awase culture). Some examples of 'adjustments' Japanese must make include the fact that as many as 40 per cent of all Japanese marriages are still arranged by a go-between, Toyota workers must own a Toyota, and employees are not really free to decline participation in group calisthetics. A recent survey indicated that 44 per cent of Japanese youth compared to only 9 per cent of American youth listed 'luck or fate' as the first or second most important factor in being successful.[8] Yet, at the same time most Japanese share the belief that almost anything can be achieved if one works and tries hard enough. Dismissing the decisive effects of the Occupation reforms or participation in an open, expanding world economy, most Japanese believe that the real secret behind their country's economic success is simply hard work reinforced by Japanese spirit (Yamato Damashi). This combination of fatalism and will-power enables most Japanese to bend to unavoidable demands while taking full advantage of opportunities that arise.

From childhood through old age, Japanese are repeatedly socialized into the core values and beliefs of their culture through a wide range of institutions. As in other societies, the family is the most important means of instilling Japanese culture into its citizens. Such child-rearing practices as breast-feeding for as long as two years, parent-child joint bathing and sleeping, no use of babysitters, and the 'ombu' (carrying a baby on ones back) shape individuals who are psychologically passive and dependent on others for security. Even Japanese discipline reinforces this tendency. Generally, children are spoiled and parents will try to appease a crying child rather than punish it. In contrast to the Western practice of 'grounding' children at home when they are bad, Japanese children are often shut out of the house and told not to return until they have repented. Families socialize children to be afraid of strangers and outsiders while looking to familiar groups for security. The worst punishment is ostracism (mura hachibu) by one's group.

The values of cooperation, hierarchy, obedience, hard work, and group identity are reinforced throughout a child's formal education. The Education Ministry imposes national uniform standards of class content, dress, and behavior for all students. The emphasis is on repetitive memorizing of 'correct' answers rather than creative or critical thinking. Exams at the end of high school will determine what university the student will be accepted into, and in turn, what company he will be employed at after graduation. Because of the intense competition, ambitious students must spend years attending cram-schools (juku) after school in the hope of getting the edge over their rivals. Even school clubs become mostly classes in Japanese etiquette. Unlike their Western counterparts, who are encouraged to become well-rounded individuals, Japanese students are only allowed to join one club, and most club activities seem to be built around teaching the proper relationship between superiors (sempai) and juniors (kohai).

Large Japanese companies have become famous for instilling group loyalty through long training sessions that last up to a year, joint songs, calesthenics, after-work drinking sessions, week-end golf and retreats, and end of the year parties. It is said that Japanese companies hire people rather than skills; by taking its employees from newly graduated high school or college students it can mold them into becoming loyal followers of the corporate culture. The seniority-based wage system (nenko seido) or elevator system, in which employees steadily receive annual incremental wage increases and promotions, the life-time employment guarantee, and the low job mobility between firms all serve to reinforce an employee's dependence on and loyalty to his company.

But recently, the most influential force in shaping the views of Japanese towards their own country and the outside world has been the increasing flood of mass media dedicated to promoting and exploring the 'uniqueness' of Japanese culture (Nihonjin Ron). In his book, *The Myth of Japanese Uniqueness*, Peter Dale explores this Nihonjin Ron phenomena in depth, exposing its growth as a mass media industry, its repeated claims that the Japanese are a 'pure, unique race', and the often absurd arguments made to support this central theme (one very famous Japanese scientist even claimed Japanese brains were different from those of the rest of humanity). Through such media as 'academic' literature, television, radio, movies, and even 'manga' (adult comic books which compose 28 per cent of all Japanese publications), Japanese receive daily and repeated doses of these themes of Japanese uniqueness and superiority. Without any tradition of critical thinking taught in the schools or practiced in society at large, most people simply accept the Nihonjin Ron claims at face value. For example, Prime Minister Nakasone's 1986 statement that America's economic problems stemmed from the 'inferior intelligence of blacks, Puerto Ricans, and Mexicans' while Japan's success flows from the superior intelligence of its people merely reflected the views of most Japanese. To Japanese, such statements are not racist or ethnocentric, but simply fact. A 1983 survey revealed that 53 per cent of Japanese felt 'superior' to Westerners and only 8 per cent felt 'inferior' to Westerners, a sharp contrast from survey results 30 years earlier in which only 20 per cent of Japanese felt superior, while 28 per cent felt inferior.[9] That a public survey would ask such a question of relative superiority or inferiority among nations is revealing in itself. It is difficult to imagine such a survey question asked in any other OECD country.

INSTITUTIONS OF JAPANESE POLITICAL ECONOMIC CULTURE

How are these general Japanese cultural values and institutions of hierarchy, the group, particularistic ethics, and so on, manifested within Japan's political economy? As will be seen in the next three chapters, factionalism is a constant organizing theme throughout

Japan's political economic development. Every group is composed of smaller groups, each organized around a patron and his hierarchy of followers. Mutual loyalty, protection, and promotion are based on the relationships between its members and the solidarity of the group itself, rather than on the ideals or issues on which it is based.

Almost all the postwar political parties are actually mini-party systems composed of varying numbers of factions, each competing fiercely with the others for domination of the party itself, while uniting and competing as a whole just as fiercely when faced with an external challenge from other parties. The Liberal Democratic Party (LDP), Japan Socialist Party (JSP), Democratic Socialist Party (DSP), and Clean Government Party (CGP) (and even the small New Liberal Club (NLC) during its short existence) are all plagued by factionalism. Factionalism in these parties revolves around personalities rather than ideology; even the heated policy debates within the JSP mask deeper personal ties. Only the Japan Communist Party (JCP) is generally considered faction-free.

But the basis of these relationships is power rather than sentimentality, and in Japanese politics the degree of one's access to power is in direct proportion to the amount of money at ones disposal to pay for it. Prime Minister Kishi captured this relationship succinctly when he said that 'Politics is money'. Each of the parties traditionally had a major source of funds: big business and agriculture for the LDP, the more radical trade federation Sohyo for the JSP, the mainstream labor federation Domei for the DSP, and the Sokka Gakkai religion for the CGP. The JCP's ability to finance itself solely from sales of its daily newspaper *Akahata* (Red Flag) frees it from dependence on a powerful vested interest. But the parties are able to offer their candidates only a fraction of the funds necessary to win elections; factions compete fiercely with each other for financial patrons. LDP factions will go so far as to set up an annual quota of funds for each traditional corporate backer.

For example, both the Nakasone and Takeshita factions within the LDP rely on the construction industry for large amounts of their cash flow. Yet, it is to the advantage of the construction industry as a whole, and individual groupings and firms within it, to spread their contributions among the five different factions within the LDP, thus ensuring their needs will be met by whichever faction is dominant. Big contributors will in turn receive such rewards as winning government contracts through pre-bid collusion coordinated by the involved Diet member, bureaucratic, and corporate members, kickbacks of

10–20 per cent of the government contract, and protection against foreign competition.

Power, of course, if managed properly, begets more power; the larger a faction the more funds it attracts which in turn enables it to make more payoffs during elections that thus improves its members' chances of beating their opponents. The multi-member electoral districts contribute to factionalism by giving each faction an opportunity to run its own candidates. Party factions often compete more fiercely with each other than with the other parties during elections.

But even factions often do not provide enough money for their members to win an election. As a result, politicians organize their own koenkai, or financial support group, within their districts. The koenkai's purpose is to maintain a steady flow of funds from powerful local groups, whether it be a business association or industry, agricultural cooperative, labor group, or rural hamlet, which then mobilizes its block of voters behind the candidate during elections. In office, the Diet member then pushes through pork-barrel legislation (patronage) or bureaucratic initiatives that aid his key financial backers.

As part of one's loyalty to one's group, Japanese will generally suppress their individual preference and vote for the candidate espoused by their group. Voting turn-out in Japan is high – 70 per cent – compared to barely 50 per cent in the United States. But this high voter participation masks a general disinterest and cynicism about politics. Japan can be described as a 'spectator' political culture in which a high voter mobilization based on social obligations and community solidarity is accompanied by low genuine participation. In contrast, America has a 'cheerleader' political culture with its relatively low mobilization but high genuine participation in terms of political discussions, campaign volunteers, contributions, bumper stickers, and yard signs.

Although Japanese generally vote according to their group's wishes, conflicts occur when an individual is a member of two or more groups. In this case the wishes of the dominant group will take precedence. For example, an individual is both a factory worker and member of the Sokka Gakkai religion – his union tells him to vote for a DSP candidate while his religion urges him to vote CGP. Since the Sokka Gakkai's emotional hold over him is stronger than that of his company, he will vote for the CGP candidate.

Individuals not strongly affiliated with a group will generally vote for a local personality rather than a party, even though because of strict party discipline the individual candidate's personal views will be suppressed if he is elected. In 1958, over 45 per cent of the electorate voted on the basis of personality while only 32 per cent voted on the basis of party. However, this emphasis on personality rather than party is changing. In 1980 the figures were 49 per cent in favor of a party while 38 per cent voted for a person.[10] Generally speaking, older, rural, and less educated people tend to vote more for a personality, while younger, urban, better educated people vote for a party. Again, the multi-member districts contribute to this personalism since they often pit people of the same party against each other in the same district so personality can be more important than party.[11] And the growing emphasis on party rather than personality may merely reflect the stronger involvement of local groups in politics, as they mobilize their members around local candidates who if elected have the best chance of furthering the group's interests. An LDP koenkai leader once said that his members 'would have voted for a communist if I told them'.[12]

There is a growing cynicism about politics. In 1953, 43 per cent of Japanese said they should leave political matters to politicians while 38 per cent disagreed; in 1983 only 33 per cent said politicians should be left alone while 60 per cent disagreed. Between 1958 and 1983 the percentage of those polled who said they always voted in national elections dropped from 62 per cent to 39 per cent. There is also a growing number of independent voters. In 1953 41 per cent supported the LDP, 23 per cent the JSP, and only 19 per cent claimed to be independents; by 1983 the ranks of LDP and JSP supporters had fallen to 39 per cent and 13 per cent of the electorate respectively while 32 per cent claimed to be independent.[13] And the fact that despite low claims of support the LDP and JSP received 48 per cent and 19 per cent of the vote, respectively, while voting turnout was above 70 per cent of the electorate shows how far most Japanese can still be mobilized to vote for a party despite their personal preferences.

The tendency of Japanese to vote according to the 'recommendation' (suisensei) of their patrons tends to focus their attention on local rather than national politics. The whole purpose of participating in politics is seen to be to gain the support of elected officials for one's group. Thus, two out of every three Japanese agree in surveys that local events are more important than national events. Yet this participation is very passive and ritualized – confined to voting and small financial contributions. Surveys indicate that while 80 per cent of Americans want to do something for their country, only 46 per cent of Japanese do, and these figures fall to 54 per cent and 8 per cent, respectively, if such a contribution involves sacrificing self-interest. Japanese are more cynical about politics in particular and human nature in general than Americans by a two-to-one margin by agreeing to the following statements: 'people usually look out for themselves', Japan (75 per cent), US (43 per cent); 'people usually try to help others', Japan (25 per cent), US (59 per cent); 'people take advantage of others', Japan (71 per cent), US (33 per cent); 'people try to be fair', (Japan 29 per cent), US (67 per cent). Japanese express a similar inability to affect decisions made by others or receive equal treatment from others by agreeing with such statements as show: 'freedom to complain about a family decision', Japan (30 per cent), US (52 per cent); 'freedom to complain about a job decision', Japan (38 per cent), US (81 per cent); 'people like me can't affect an unjust national law', Japan (42 per cent), US (75 per cent) or 'local law', Japan (58 per cent), US (77 per cent); 'everyone receives equal treatment from government', Japan (25 per cent), US (83 per cent), or from the 'police', Japan (34 per cent), US (85 per cent). Sixty-three per cent of Japanese said they needed a good connection to contact government as opposed to 26 per cent of Americans. Over twice as many Japanese (69 per cent) as Americans (33 per cent) said that problems were too great for individuals to influence. In response to the statement that 'Individual rights and freedom are more important than filial piety and repayment of favors' only 22 per cent of Japanese supported individual rights while 78 per cent favored group values.[14]

Political apathy and fatalism becomes self-fulfilling – the more passive Japanese are, the more easily they are manipulated and the less chance there is for the few activists to achieve positive results, which in turn makes Japanese all the more passive and fatalistic. Thus politics remains dominated by élites while any opposition remains fragmented and ineffectual. In classic tactics of divide and rule, the LDP plays off one opposition party against another. More often than not, in a political system characterized by open favoratism and the laddling out of pork-barrel gifts to loyal followers, opposition groups with similar interests usually see themselves as rivals rather than allies. Environmental, consumer, and labor groups focus their activities on solving local problems that directly affect themselves, and have generally failed to unite at an effective national level. Only the government can unite all the groups successfully into a mass movement.

Japanese apathy and cynicism affect international relations as well. For Japanese the ability of those in power to favor their supporters, enrich themselves, and undermine their foes is not only to be expected but just; for Western people such actions are perverse deviations from the ideals of impartiality and fairness. Thus, Westerners are continually frustrated by continued Japanese neo-mercantilist policies affecting industrial development, trade, and negotiations despite Tokyo's repeated claims that it now has the world's most open economy. In turn, Japanese cannot understand the repeated international calls for a 'level economic playing field' or reciprocity between Japan and its trading partners.

All this emphasis on on favoritism, voting blocks, and pork-barrel politics may sound corrupt to many Westerners. But political cultures differ as to the level and type of corruption they will allow; what is considered corrupt in one culture may be perfectly acceptable in another. And a political culture's corruption threshold can change dramatically over time. Rural elections in the United States during the nineteenth century used to be decided by the candidate who could dispense the most whiskey and money, and until recently most American cities were organized as political machines composed of a hierarchy of patron-client relationships and voting blocks very similar to those of Japanese politics today. While Congress enacted legislation in the 1970s designed to limit contributions from individuals and groups to $1000 and $5000, respectively, interest groups organized as political action committees (PACs) seem to play an even greater role in influencing elections and legislation.

Japanese have mixed feeling about the corruption or 'black mist' (kuro kasumi) that pervades politics. They greet exposures of nepotism, pork-barrel politics, vote-brokers, and huge payoffs with a mixture of cynicism and fatalism. Politics is considered to be a dirty but essential business, and structural corruption (kozo oshoku) inevitable. A combination of an ethical system based on one's loyalty to one's group rather than universal standards, plus the custom of gift-giving which makes the recipient beholder to the giver, makes much of what would be considered corruption in the West perfectly acceptable behavior in Japan. For example, a recent survey indicated that over 77 per cent of Japanese think dishonesty sometimes necessary to get ahead compared to 41 per cent of Americans. Almost 70 per cent of Japanese would follow custom or circumstances when making a decision while only 30 per cent would use universal standards, and 55 per cent agreed that it is better to make political donations as requested without complaint to save the group's face, while only 21 per cent disagreed.[15]

There is, however, a distinction between official fund-raising (omotegane) and backroom dealing (urugane). Japan has some of the strictest election laws in the world to regulate the amount of money and channels through which it changes hands. No house-to-house campaigning, signature drives, or presents of food, alcohol, or money to voters are allowed during the allotted three weeks of campaigning. Likewise, the amount of public speeches, spending, campaign materials, and media advertisements are all carefully proscribed. In reality, however, all these regulations are routinely violated, often on a massive scale. For example, as the Recruit scandal has revealed, one way of getting around contribution limits is for a company to sell a candidate or vote-broker something – like land or stock issues – at a cheap price and then either buy it back at a higher price through a dummy company or let the recipient sell it later when the price rises. It is said that parties report as little as 10 per cent of the contributions they actually spend and receive. Only the JCP actually reports accurate financial figures.[16]

The two Tanaka scandals and their aftermath reveal a great deal about how the Japanese view corruption. In October 1974 the monthly journal *Bungei Shunju* carried a long article exposing the blatant means the Prime Minister had used to collect and dispense vast sums of money that helped give him the LDP's largest faction. But the daily newspapers hesitated to report the scandal since it is commonplace and its exposure would disturb national harmony. It was only after the stories began to appear in foreign newspapers that the Japanese picked up the scandal, thus forcing Tanaka to resign in November. The Lockheed scandal, whereby Tanaka and other politicians were paid over $2 million to facilitate the government procurement of Lockheed jets, would never have come to light without the Congressional hearings on government corruption in February 1976. Tanaka was eventually arrested in July, resigned his LDP membership shortly thereafter, and was eventually given a five-year jail term for corruption in January 1983. He remains free on appeal. Yet, despite or perhaps because of all the adverse publicity, Tanaka has been re-elected five times since the scandal broke, remained leader of the largest LDP faction until a 1986 stroke and later faction coup allowed Takeshita to take his place, and was the 'King-maker' behind the selection of Ohira, Suzuki and Nakasone as Prime Minister. By the time the scandal broke, Tanaka's power was so entrenched that he was able to remain Japan's 'shadow Shogun'. Money continued to pour into Tanaka's coffers, which enabled him to keep his faction intact. During the 1983 election all LDP factions except for his lost Diet members. He continued to be re-elected in his district in part because it receives the highest per capita government spending in Japan.

There is some sign, however, that the corruption tolerance threshold may be lowering. Although the sale of stocks to 159 of Japan's highest ranking élite including politicians from all the parties except the JCP, bureaucrats, and corporate executives was not illegal, a dozen of the 30 buyers who were publicly named have been forced to resign their respective political, Cabinet, or corporate positions. In February 1989 the LDP lost a by-election in a traditionally 'safe' seat in Fukoaka, in part because of the scandal, and in April Prime Minister Takeshita's popularity reached a low of 2.8 per cent. These reverses for the LDP in particular and Japan's élite in general may be more a popular reaction to such things as the new three per cent value added tax, the failure of Japan's strong yen to translate into lower prices for consumers, and continuing high land prices, as to the Recruit scandal itself. Still it will force politicians and businessmen to become far less blatant and much more ingenious in devising new channels of political funding.

Another characteristic of Japan's political economic culture is the ritualization of conflict. Generally speaking, open conflict is avoided at all costs while the opposition is instead coopted and their protests expressed through mutually agreed channels. For example, the LDP gives the opposition parties certain periods in Diet proceedings to criticize government policy (tatemae), while in reality (honne) the opposition (except for the JCP) votes in favor of government bills 90 per cent of the time. Labor's annual 'Spring offensive' (Shunto) provides another example of ritualized conflict. Unions 'strike' for a day or two to demonstrate their 'sincerity' in fighting for better pay and conditions. In reality the management – labor settlement is usually reached before the strike takes place and the strikers go out of their way to avoid disrupting the company's business.

Anomic behavior, however, can occur when consensus between opposing groups breaks down. Confrontation rather than cooperation was the norm between the LDP and the opposition parties throughout the 1950s and reached a peak with the 1960 mass protests against the government attempts to push through revisions of the US – Japan security treaty. The opposition members clogged the aisles ('cow walking') trying to prevent the LDP from voting. Fighting broke out and finally Prime Minister Kishi had the police eject the opposition, whereupon the remaining LDP members quickly voted for the treaty revision.

Although management-labor confrontation gave way to cooperation during the 1950s, and LDP-Opposition party confrontation to cooperation during the 1960s, fringe areas of Japan's political economy remained violent through the 1970s. For example, in March 1972 the Red Army tortured to death 14 members suspected of disloyalty; in 1974 Burakumin activists took over Yoka High School, captured 52 teachers, and spent the night torturing them for alleged discrimination – 43 were hospitalized; and activists protesting the building of Narita Airport frequently resorted to violence throughout the early 1980s.[17] But these are all exceptions to the generally ritualized or suppressed handling of conflict in Japan.

The LDP cooption of the opposition parties is only one strand in a web of interlocking relations that connect all aspects of Japan's political economy, which is presided over by an interrelated élite composed of ranking members of the LDP, bureaucracy, and corporate world. By consulting endlessly with the corporate world and among themselves, the ministry and LDP committees devise policies designed to continually promote the development of Japan's economy to higher technology-based levels while continuing to protect inefficient sectors such as agriculture, heavy industry, and construction, among others. In return, big business provides bureaucrats with high-paying second careers when they retire and massive funds to the LDP and its factions. These ties among the ruling triad are further solidified by a common educational background – most are graduates of Tokyo University or other top Japanese schools – and even marriage. The fact that now over one-third of all Japanese LDP Diet members inherited the position from their fathers is a startling indication of how entrenched the triad has become. Behind the seemingly cozy relationships and the highly successful industrial policies and dramatic economic growth it produces, however, rage often bitter policy battles both between and within different legs of the triad over specific interests.

The corporate world provides an excellent example of the dynamic relationship between cooperation and completion in Japanese politics. The vast majority of large companies are affiliated with a Keiretsu, or corporate group. A keiretsu may include a central bank that gives cheap preferential loans to the other members, a trading company to handle much of its trade, and a range of related companies including raw material refiners (petrochemicals, oil), heavy (steel, shipbuilding, automobiles). and consumer (electronics, computers) industries. Keiretsu strategy over investments, product development, or technology sharing is coordinated by monthly Presidents' meetings. In classic Japanese patron-client style, each company within a keiretsu sits atop a pyramid of medium – and small-sized companies which provide components in return for guaranteed business. Generally speaking, keiretsu compete fiercely with each other during periods of economic expansion, which cooperating closely through a variety of price, export, or production cartels during recessions presided over by the relevant economic ministry.

A dual economy between the dynamic, highly profitable big corporations and the vast range of often inefficient medium – and small-sized companies remains an enduring feature of Japan's political economy. Only about 25per cent of all Japanese workers are actually members of a company that provides job security until retirement; the other companies will fire their workers during recessions just like most Western companies. Although the system is not 'life-time' employment, since the retirement age is 55 while the life expectancy is almost 76 years, most of the larger companies do guarantee long-term employment in return for the single-minded dedication of their workers. Blue-collar workers are hired after graduating from high school and white-collar workers after graduating from college, and each then enters a pay and promotion 'escalator' that will last until retirement. With their jobs guaranteed, pay increases dependent on company profits, and job mobility restricted, since even if they found a job elsewhere they would have to start at the bottom of that company's escalator, workers passively work hard while demanding little of the company union.

CONCLUSION

In less than 40 years Japan developed from an impoverished, inefficient country into one with the world's most dynamic economy and one of its largest per capita incomes. This leap from poverty to prosperity has been accompanied by enormous socio-economic change. Although over half the population was rural in 1950, today over 90 per cent of the population lives in urban areas. During the same period the percentage of junior high school students going to high school rose from 30 per cent to 95 per cent, while high school graduates going on to college rose from 9 per cent to 40 per cent. Urbanization and prosperity have meant a shift in Japan's family structure from the extended families of several generations under one roof in the early postwar years to the predominant nuclear family pattern at present. As the birth rate declines and life-expectancy lengthens, over 20 per cent of all Japanese will be over age 65 by the year 2000. Quality of life issues such as the environment, consumer rights, leisure time, and care of the aging are increasingly competing with economic development and trade issues for centre ring in the policy circus. Japan's 'internationalization' has become the new buzz-word, although no one seems to know exactly what it means. Foreign pressure on Tokyo to open its markets and people's minds to the outside world, combined with Japan's shift from an industrial into a post-industrialist society, has led to government calls for Japanese to start spending as hard as they save and playing as hard as they work.

Yet despite these rapid and profound changes since 1945, the overall values, institutions, and patterns of behavior that underly Japan's political economic culture have remained constant. Although for most Japanese the primary focus of loyalty and security may have shifted from one village to the work place, the emotional ties are no less binding; traditional values built around the group, hierarchy, patron-follower relations, and a particularistic ethical system characterize the blue suited salarymen just as strongly as they did their bare-footed peasant ancestors. A succession of institutions such as the family, school, company, and mass media continually socialize the Japanese deeper into a uniform traditional value system. Although a consensus within Japan's ruling triad on most issues becomes increasingly difficult to forge, the ties that unite the LDP, bureaucratic, and corporate élite grow ever more deeply rooted and intricate. Change will accelerate as Japan vaults into the twenty-first century, but it will merely obscure underlying cultural continuities that have endured for over 1500 years. And the persistence of these traditional values of hierarchy, groupism, self-sacrifice, and conformity in new forms and institutions will continue to be an enormous source of Japanese power.

NOTES

1. 'Nation' in the *Encyclopedia of the Social Sciences*.
2. Yasumasa Kuroda, *et al.*, 'The End of Westernization and the Beginning of New Modernization in Japan', *Arab Journal of the Social Sciences*, vol. 2, no. 1, April 1987, p. 26.
3. See Takeo Doi, *The Anatomy of Dependence*.
4. Takie Sugiyama Lebra, *Japanese Patterns of Behavior*, p. 47.
5. Bradley Richardson and Scott Flanagan, *Politics Japan*, p. 144.
6. Ibid., p. 134.
7. Ibid., p. 153.
8. Ibid., pp. 145, 157.
9. Kuroda, op. cit., pp. 25–7.
10. Flanagan and Richardson, op. cit., p. 172.
11. Ibid., p. 173.
12. Taketsugu Tsurutani, 'The LDP in Transition: Mass Membership Participation in Party Leadership Selection', *Asian Survey*, vol. 20, No. 8, August 1980.
13. Kuroda, op. cit., pp. 28–30.
14. See Flanagan and Richardson, op. cit., chs. 3–5.
15. Richardson, Flanagan, op. cit., Chapter 5.
16. Ibid., p. 192.
17. Ibid., p. 273.

3 The Political 'Miracle'

Japan's transformation from its mass poverty and war devastation of 1945 to its current position as the world's greatest economic power has been guided by an extremely powerful state. By most measures, the post–1945 Japanese state is characterized as a highly democratic political system. The 1947 Constitution guarantees the 'natural' human freedoms of speech, assembly, and religion for all Japanese citizens, and created a parliamentary system in which they could express their political will. A half dozen parties compete in national elections which occur on average every two years. Although conservative parties have ruled Japan for all but eight months since 1945, they have governed at the will of the people. The ruling Liberal Democratic Party (LDP) has presided over rapid, continuous, relatively equitable economic growth that has transformed Japan into one of the world's most developed countries. Less well-known but equally impressive has been the ability of Japan's political system to deal successfully with such pressing problems as crime, pollution, poverty, and education. Throughout the postwar era, success has bred success: political stability allowed Tokyo to concentrate on achieving economic growth which in turn contributed to continued political stability and the ability to continue its growth policies while overcoming other social problems, and so on.

Japan's postwar democratic development seems a 'miracle' when contrasted with the leadership of the 1930s and early 1940s that attempted to erect a totalitarian political system that controlled not just the behavior, but even the thoughts of the population. Considering how total the wartime government's control over politics, and how recently it occurred, how deep are Japan's democratic roots? How could a population be so politically malleable that it could enthusiastically support both totalitarian and democratic political systems? Is Japan's present political system as democratic as it seems? How closely does Japanese politics correspond to the system outlined in the Constitution?

These and related questions will be answered in two sections, addressing respectively each side of the great divide – 1945. Each section will analyze the continuities and changes, and difference between the ideals (tatemae) and reality (honne) on which each regime has based its rule, paying particular attention to the ways in which political power is seized, maintained, and lost.

PRE-1945 POLITICAL DEVELOPMENT

It is important to distinguish states from regimes. A state is a clearly defined territory in which a ruling élite exercises complete control or sovereignty over its inhabitants. A regime is the arrangement of institutions either created or inherited by the ruling élite to govern the state. For example, the state of France has existed since the Middle Ages. At first the French state was confined to the area around Paris, but over the centuries it has gradually increased the territory under its control to its contemporary boundaries. From the Middle Ages to the French Revolution one regime presided over France: a monarchy based on hereditary succession. Since the French Revolution of 1789, however, 15 distinct political regimes have presided over the state of France, including five republics, one absolute and one constitutional monarchy, and two emperors.

There is an important distinction between pre-modern and modern states. In pre-modern states, sovereignty or supreme power generally resided in the concept of the monarchy. For example, under the British monarchy the death of a king is announced with the words: 'The king is dead, long live the king!' While kings come and go the monarchy, or sovereign state, endures. The masses of inhabitants in a pre-modern state are subject to the monarchy's sovereign power. In a modern state, sovereignty theoretically lies with its mass population or citizens. Modern states have slowly extended the concept of the people's sovereignty from men of property to all men and at present all women. Modern states generally use elections to determine the citizen's will over who should rule. Of course, modern states are represented by a range of different types of regimes which vary in the degree to which they allow the mass citizenry a choice over those who govern, and the policies they follow. Both industrial democractic and communist states are considered modern, in part because the masses play an important role in the politics of each.

Because Japan did not have a written language before the seventh century, it is difficult for historians to determine exactly when the archipelago was first united into one state. A 297 AD Wei dynasty chronicle based on second-hand reports describes Japan as composed of hundreds of 'kingdoms' which warred incessantly against each other. Each kingdom or clan was organized on a strict hierarchy both within and between classes, and was presided over by a high priest or priestess whose most important role was to maintain harmony through rites of divination and purification. During this time many of the clans were loosely allied under High priestess Himiko of the Yamato clan.[1] This confederation under the nominal authority of the Yamato High Priestess corresponds to that of France during the Middle Ages. During that time, the French king was sovereign in his small territory around Paris, but held nominal authority over his vassals in what is now much of the rest of France.

The Wei chronicle captures the early decades of the Kofun era (250–650 AD) during which the Yamato clan centered in the Kansai area slowly spread its control over the rest of the archipelago. Yamato power reached a height during the fifth century when High Priest Nintoku not only received tribute from 55 clans to the East and 66 to the West, but also from 15 clans in Korea. Over the centuries the Yamato clan achieved sovereignty over the other clans as much by compromise as conquest; rival clans were coopted with titles and spoils in return for allegiance to the Yamato High Priest. Yamato rule was legitimized by the claim that its High Priest had descended from the Sun Goddess Amaterasu, who sat atop the heirarchy of the thousands of local gods (Kami) which populated Japan and in which all the clans believed. Never all-powerful, the Yamato chief ruled over his minions through a Council of State composed of all the great clan chiefs. Political, economic, and religious power were arranged on parallel heirarchial, interdependent lines.

Since the Yamato clan first began to unite the independent clans of the Japanese archipelago into a state over 1500 years ago, Japan's political history has followed two distinct, often interrelated, cyclical patterns. The first pattern involves the rise, maturity, and fall of a political regime; the second is the cyclical pattern of Japan's relations with the outside world. Before 1945, six distinct regimes ruled over the Japanese state: The Yamato regime (250–710), the Aristocratic (710–1150), the Minamoto (1150–1350), the Ashikaga (1350–1550), the Tokugawa (1600–1868), and the Meiji (1868–1945). During this same period Japan experienced four distinct phases of intensive contact with and cultural borrowing from foreign civilizations: Chinese and Korean (fifth to eleventh centuries), Chinese (thirteenth to fourteenth centuries), Iberian (sixteenth century), and Western (1854–1941).

The rise, maturity, and fall of Japanese regimes was similar to that of regimes elsewhere. Because of mismanagement, overconfidence, and decadence, a ruling élite would gradually lose both the power and legitimacy of its rule over the state. Ambitious clans or political factions would take advantage of the regime's growing weaknesses by further undermining its rule by first secretly and then openly challenging the old regime's right to rule the state. Civil war would result, during which the challengers would eventually win. The new regime would then attempt to consolidate its rule by increasing both its power and legitimacy; new institutions of control over the state would be created while old institutions, rituals, and values would be carefully followed to assure the ruled that the new ruler's power was legitimate.

Often a challenger to an old regime would augment its power and legitimacy by using foreign religious, political, economic, or military techniques. All four of Japan's pre-1945 cycles of foreign relations corresponded either to the strengthening of an old regime or its overthrow by a new regime. In the seventh century the Soga clan used the universalistic tenets of Buddhism which had only recently arrived in Japan to help undermine the legitimacy of the Yamato regime which continued to base its rule on Shintoism. The long period of aristocratic rule was based on such Chinese institutions as a bureaucracy and emperor. The Ashikaga regime reinforced the legitimacy of its rule by filling the élite's leisure time with a range of Chinese aesthetic pursuits. The Tokugawa clan used Western military techniques to defeat its rivals and take over the state, and then bolstered the legitimacy of its power by adapting Confucian ideas of loyalty and hierarchy to its regime. The Meiji élite followed the same process of first taking power and then legitimizing that power through Western military, political, and economic ideas.

These periods of foreign relations all began when a foreign power or powers attempted to establish relations with Japan. During the first two periods when Japan's foreign relations were centered on China, the relationship was based on tribute from 'the land of the rising sun' to the 'land of the setting sun'. The latter two periods, when Japan's foreign relationship was largely with the West, was based on trade. At first the influx of foreign ideas, techniques, and institutions would be greeted with suspicion by most Japanese élites. But gradually the foreign ideas and practices would acquire a large following, and eventually be embraced either by the existing regime or by a political challenger. The ruling élite's acceptance of the foreign influences would lead to its wholesale adoption by the upper class, whereupon the foreign ideas, institutions, or techniques would be 'Japanized' or integrated into Japan's traditional culture. Finally, the Japanese élites would reach a cultural saturation point where it was felt enough had been gained from the foreign influences, and any greater influx would undermine Japanese culture. A reaction against foreign culture would eventually lead the regime to completely sever Japan's relations with the outside world.

This reaction against foreign culture was most dramatic during Japan's two recent periods of foreign relations. In 1641 the Tokugawa regime inaugurated the policy of sakoku or isolationism whereby almost no foreigners were allowed in and no Japanese allowed out of Japan. Japan's only contact with the outside world was at the port of Nagasaki where Dutch and Chinese were allowed a limited trade. During the 1930s, instead of retreating from the world, Japan reacted against its intensive period of cultural borrowing from the West by attempting to carve out a vast, autonomous empire in East Asia which would exclude all Westerners.

No institution represents these two political patterns of regime change and cultural borrowing better than the Japanese imperial line. The ultimate source of legitimacy for any regime has been ritual acceptance by the imperial line. In turn, different regimes have augmented the symbolic power of the emperor either by manufacturing native traditions or borrowing foreign trappings. For example, the Yamato regime's claim that its High Priest was the direct descendant of Amaterasu was based on its possession of the three sacred treasures: a mirror representing the body of Amaterasu, the sword of Susa, Amaterasu's rival, which represents the conquest of Yamato's chief rival Izumo and its local god, and Amaterasu's necklace which was passed down to each succeeding Yamato high priest.

The High Priest Shotoku Taishi (574–622) attempted to further solify and legitimize Yamato rule by meshing Confucian and Buddhist ideas with native institutions. He introduced the Chinese institution of 12 court ranks in 603, and the following year enacted his 17 Articles of Government (604) which basically converted his position from that of high priest into an emperor. A century later the claims of the imperial line to divine origins were codified with the court's compilation of the Record of Ancient Matters (Kojiki) in 712 and the Chronicles of Japan (Nihonshoki) in 720. The Court mixed ancient myths with its own fabrications in a way that showed the Yamato clan really was the descendant of Amaterasu. The Kojiki and Nihonshoki contain no strong heros or gods who play an important role, and no interest in metaphysics; the emphasis is on the survival and eventual triumph of a lineage despite a constant struggle for power.

Japan's concept of emperor is very different from that of China's. China was ruled by a powerful emperor whose legitimacy rested on a 'mandate of Heaven', which essentially meant that revolt was justified when the emperor failed to fulfill his duties to promote peace and prosperity for the empire. The Japanese emperor, in contrast, was considered benevolent and virtuous by definition; he did not have to prove anything. But although the mandate was given to the imperial line in perpetuity, the Japanese emperor reigned but rarely ruled; real power was exercised by a behind-the-scenes élite.

The imperial sanction of a new regime was a time-consuming step-by-step legitimation process that generally paralleled the regime's consolidation of power. The Tokugawa regime was built on the military and political skills of three great generals. Oda Nobunaga captured Kyoto as early as 1568 and began centralizing his power over the newly conquered provinces, but he was assasinated in 1582, before he could achieve national unity or receive any sort of imperial support. His successor, Toyotomi Hideyoshi, finally conquered the rival clans in 1585, received the title of Imperial Regent later that year, and three years later gathered all his vassals in front of the emperor and required them to repeat their oath to him while swearing to protect the imperial line. Upon his death in 1598, Hideyoshi was succeeded by Tokugawa Ieyasu, who decisively crushed a revolt against Tokugawa rule in 1600. In 1603, Ieyasu received the title of Shogun which combined the duties of imperial prime minister and commander-in-chief. Each regime underwent a similar step-by-step process of imperial approval.

But legitimacy ultimately rested on the regime's control over any actual or potential challengers. Throughout Japanese history, factions won and maintained power by constructing elaborate structures of horizontal and vertical controls. Japan's mountainous terrain fragmented political power among hundreds of small clans; no one clan, however ambitious, could challenge the existing regime on its own. Clans could only achieve regional power, and ultimately take over the state, by forming coalitions with other clans which conferred nominal leadership in return for a division of the spoils. The leading clan's allies would be divided within three ranks based on their degree of loyalty and geographical proximity. The Tokugawa regime systemized these divisions the most clearly. The Shimpan were the 23 clans that had fought with the Tokugawa from the very beginning and whose loyalty was beyond doubt. They got the greatest share of the spoils in rice land and actually administered national affairs. The 145 clans that had joined later were called the Fudai, and were given rice lands that formed a buffer zone around the Shimpan located in the eastern and central regimes. Finally, the Tozama were composed of the 97 former enemy clans located mostly in the outlying regions.

Power also rested on a strict class basis. The Yamato regime had systematized a three-layer society composed of the aristocratic Uji, the artisan and peasant Be, and the Yatsuko slave classes. Strict class divisions were carried on 1000 years later by the Tokugawa clan which segmented society into five classes with the samurai rulers at the top, followed in descending order by the peasant, artisan, merchant, and untouchable classes.

The need to achieve both power and legitimacy was enormously complicated for the Meiji leaders who toppled the Tokugawa regime in 1868. In order to maintain power, the new Meiji regime faced two interrelated legitimacy challenges – one internal, one external. Having toppled the discredited Tokugawa with the war cry 'Honor the Emperor, Expel the Barbarians', with the Emperor's sanction, the Meiji élite were already well on their way toward legitimizing their rule in the eyes of most Japanese. Throughout Japanese history, the imperial throne's 1500 year unbroken lineage of reign rather than rule, made it the natural focus of any political faction powerful and ambitious enough to attempt a takeover; by remaining above politics the imperial institution had never lost its legitimacy despite the tyranny and corruption of the regimes over which it presided. In 1869, the Meiji leaders then moved the Emperor to the Tokugawa capital of Edo, which was renamed Tokyo (Eastern Capital) to symbolize both the legitimacy and modernization policies of the new regime. With the Emperor's support and by justifying all their actions according to 'imperial will', the Meiji government gained internal legitimacy with fewer challenges than previous regimes.

But this task was complicated by the new élite's need also to legitimize its rule in the eyes of the international community. Commodore Perry's gunboats had forced Japan open in 1854, further discrediting the Tokugawa regime, and giving the ambitious clans (Han) – Satsuma, Choshu, Tosa, and Hizen – the opportunity to challenge and overthrow the old regime. Yet, upon taking power, the Meiji leaders feared that failure to quickly modernize could result in Japan suffering a fate similar to that of China: being carved up into spheres of influence by the Western powers. To prevent this, Japan had to embark on a rapid political, economic, and military revolution; the more modern Japan became, the greater the chance of reversing the 'unequal treaties' imposed by the West. Within a generation of taking power, the Meiji leaders had succeeded in creating the institutional foundations of a modern state, and crushed or coopted any opposition to their rule.

Shortly after taking power, in April 1868, the government issued its five article Charter Oath which acted as the general guidelines for the modernization program. The Oath promised that: (1) all policies would be based on wide consultation; (2) individuals would be free to pursue their own interests; (3) national interests would come before all other interests; (4) old customs would be abolished in favor of modern practices; and (5) knowledge would be sought throughout the world. These five articles simultaneously served as the guidelines for coopting any potential rivals and modernizing the country.

The Meiji leader's first step in the long modernization process was to create a formal modern government (Seitaisho) composed of a Daijokan or council which presided over seven departments including Executive, Shinto, Finance, War, Foreign Affairs, and Civil Affairs departments as well as a bicameral Legislative Department consisting of an upper Council of the Meiji élite and rubber stamp lower representative assembly made up of other Han representatives. Initially, the government included a coalition of 106 representatives from the court and 19 Han, with most members coming from Satsuma, Choshu, Tosa, and Hizen, but these ranks were thinned to 22 representatives from seven Han in June 1868. Power was further consolidated in 1869, when the governing council's membership was limited to 26 representatives of the four original coup Han.

The government's next step was to spread its power, which was largely confined to Tokyo and the provinces of the coup leaders, nationwide. First the Tokugawa lands were confiscated and turned into prefectures with governors appointed by Tokyo. Then the government convinced the lords (Daimyo) of the four leading Han to return their titles to the Emperor, who in turn appointed them governors of their prefectures. In 1871 the approximately 200 Daimyo of the remaining Han gathered in Tokyo and collectively returned their Han to the Emperor, who then abolished the Han, and consolidated them into 75 prefectures. The Daimyo and their samurai followers were then pensioned into retirement and all their debts absorbed by Tokyo, while all Han military forces were demobilized and the castles confiscated by the state. In 1888 the number of prefectures was reduced to 43; governors continued to be appointed by the state.

That same year (1871), in addition to agreeing to take-over the samurai's huge debts, the government further softened the abolition of the Han by encouraging the creation of Consultative Assemblies (Kaigi) at the prefecture, district, and village levels. This move at once fulfilled the government's promise in the Charter Oath to widely consult influential leaders before making policies while creating safety valves for political tensions and dissent that could be closely observed by Tokyo.

Tokyo was just as successful in creating a modern military establishment, as it had a modern government. In 1871 the coup leaders' forces were converted into an Imperial Guard of 10 000 men who were trained by a French advisory group in modern tactics, weapons, and organization. With the abolition of all Han military forces and confiscation of their castles that same year, the government now held unchallenged military power. The next important step in creating a modern military was taken with the Conscription Law of January 1873 which abolished all differences between samurai and commoners and subjected all males over 21 to the draft.

The new modern army's ability was tested by the Satsuma Rebellion of 1877, when one of the original coup leaders, Saigo Takamori, led a revolt of 30 000 disgruntled ex-samurai after the government rejected his plan to invade Korea. The decisive defeat of Saigo's samurai by the 40 000-man national army composed of conscripted commoners symbolized the transition from a traditional to a modern Japan; modern firepower and tactics, not samurai spirit and sacrifice, were the key to victory in the new age – a vital lesson later forgotten by Japan's leadership of the 1930s and 1940s.

The government used its modern army and navy not just to maintain power at home but to carve out an empire abroad. Japanese imperialism started with the takeover of the Ryukyu Islands in 1872, and was followed by the punitive military expedition against Taiwan in 1874, and the forced opening of Korea to Japanese trade in 1876. These ventures were rewarded with a negotiation of a treaty with St Petersburg whereby Russia agreed to renounce its claim to the Kurile Islands in return for the abandonment of the Japanese claim to

Sakhalin. This agreement was Tokyo's first equal treaty with a 'Western' country.

Complete acceptance by the West, however, had to wait another 20 years. In 1894, impressed by Japan's modernization, London announced it would end its extraterritorial rights in Japan by 1899. The other Western powers followed suit and by 1911 Japan had received both its legal and tariff rights. Japan's stunning victory over China in 1895 led London to form an alliance with Tokyo in 1902. Japan's even more dramatic victory over Russia in 1905 gave it undisputed control over the Korean peninsula, reinforced its commercial interests in Manchuria and China, and stimulated an industrial take-off at home.

Japan's imperial and economic expansion seemed interrelated as Tokyo gobbled up German colonies in the Pacific during World War I while rapidly expanding its economy by exporting goods throughout East Asia as the Western powers were preoccupied with war in Europe. Although it was rebuffed in its 21 Demands on China in 1916 that would effectively have made the country a Japanese colony, and gained few tangible benefits from its Siberian expedition (1918–22), Tokyo's status in the world continued to rise as it was made one of the Big Five countries at the Versailles Conference in 1919 and signed a number of military disarmament treaties at the Washington Conference in 1922.

The Meiji regime's legitimacy was just as steadily solidified at home as it was abroad. During the 1870s Tokyo faced a political challenge potentially almost as distabilizing as Saigo's revolt. The same government split which had led to Saigo's revolt led other disgruntled leaders to form an opposition party. In 1874 the faction which favored war with Korea lost out, resigned from the government, began urging fulfillment of the Charter Oath promise of an elective national assembly, and in 1875 formed the Patriotic Society (Aikoku-sha) to lobby for its goals. The Patriotic Society inspired a number of other political groups to rise during this time with similar demands for representation. The pressure created by this so-called Popular Rights Movement (Minken Undo) payed off when the government issued an Imperial Rescript later that year, promising to grant a constitution by gradual stages, and formed a Senate (Genro-in) to draft it.

The popular rights movement was followed by the emergence of a nascent party movement in the early 1880s to lead the pressure for a constitution. The opposition rallied around two parties, the Jiyuto

(Liberal) and Rikken Kaishinto (Constitutional Reform Party), while the government in 1882 formed its own party, the Teiseito (Imperial Rule Party), to counteract their growing influence. The Teiseito was not effective in coopting the opposition, so the following year the police were given the power to break up political meetings and censor the press, thus forcing the opposition parties to go underground.

But in the late 1880s the government followed up this suppression by fulfilling its promise to enact a constitution. A House of Peers and new nobility class was created in 1884; a Cabinet replaced the Diajokan the next year; and a Privy Council composed of imperial appointees to approve the constitution and advise the Emperor emerged in 1888. By the time the formal constitution was granted in 1889, all its institutions were in place except the Diet, the government's major concession to the idea of popular representation.

Granted by the Emperor to his subjects, the 1889 Constitution essentially legalized the imperial institution as an absolute, sacred monarchy which embodied the spiritual essence of Japan (Kokutai). The constitution decreed that the first duty of all imperial subjects was to serve the Emperor without question. Legally, the Emperor held absolute power, but ruled through a Cabinet, who were in turn selected from the Diet. The Cabinet was in charge of all state affairs except the army and navy ministries, which were accountable only to the Emperor.

In reality the Emperor was no less a figurehead than before. For over 1500 years there had always been a difference between the formal, ceremonial power (tatemae) of the Emperor, and the informal, behind-the-scenes real power (honne) of the regimes that claimed to rule on his behalf – the new system was no different. Real power remained in the hands of a small behind-the-scenes élite (Genro), who were not even mentioned in the Constitution. The genro's power would slowly subside during the early twentieth century until, for a brief period during the 1920s, Japan actually began to experience Cabinet government. Cabinet governments in turn would be superseded in the 1930s by an increasingly autocratic, militaristic élite unaccountable to anyone but themselves.

The genro, however, did not emerge as a distinct ruling body until almost 20 years after the Meiji coup. Initially, real power was concentrated in the hands of Saigo Takamori, Okubo Toshimichi, and Kido Koin, who ruled via the 26-member Daijokan. Saigo, of course, later lost power and his life during the short-lived Satsuma rebellion. The Genro-in was created in 1875 to supplement the Daijokan and act as a senate and law-making body. But the Daijokan was abolished in 1885 and the Genro-in in 1890, without either becoming more than a rubber stamp for decisions made by Okubo, Kido, and others.

It was after the Daijokan was abolished, however, that the famous seven-member Genro (of elder statesmen) emerged to wield real power. The original Genro included Matsukata Masayoshi (1835–1924), Inoue Kaoru (1836–1915), Yamagata Aritomo (1838–1922), Kuroda Kiyotaka (1840–1900), Ito Hirobumi (1841–1909), Oyama Iwao (1842–1916), and Saigo Tsugumichi (1843–1902). Later additions to the list always include Saionji Kimmochi (1849–1940) and Katsura Taro (1848–1913). All were from either Satsuma (Matsukata, Kuroda, Oyama, Saigo) or Choshu (Inoue, Yamagata, Ito). Each was the son of a samurai family of moderate or low status born between 1835 and 1843, had been active in the Restoration movement, and had risen to membership in the Genro through achievements in either economic, military, or foreign affairs. They cemented their group with a web of financial and marriage ties.[2]

The Genro served as the government's real Cabinet, with each member taking turns as Prime Minister. When a prime minister resigned he would suggest a successor after consulting with the other Genro. The nominee would then ritually reject the offer, suggesting one 'more competent.' Meanwhile court officials would encourage one or another genro to take the post until someone finally accepted. The Prime Ministership generally alternated between Satsuma and Choshu. Although the Genro were sometimes split over serious issues, they shared the philosophy that government should be run by the leaders of the bureaucracy who had national interests at heart rather than the narrow interests of the political parties.

The Genro wielded power by a variety of means. The most common was to meet casually at each others homes to discuss issues, and allow the subsequent decision to filter out to formal government leaders who were responsible for its implementation. If an issue was particularly pressing, one or more Genro could make a Specific Request for a meeting (Genro kaigi), during which the same process of consensus-building and later government implementation would take place. A Genro-Daijin Kaigi was a formal meeting of the genro and major Cabinet Ministers, which was usually followed up by an Imperial Conference (gozon kaigi) which was convoked by the court to approve major decisions made at earlier meetings.

The Genro ruled through three phases of gradually declining influence. The first phase lasted from 1889 to 1901, and was characterized by direct rule. During the second phase (1901–12), however, their ranks were reduced to five, and they withdrew from direct rule since they had essentially accomplished the Meiji goals of creating a modern and independent Japan. Although their meetings and influence on daily matters were gradually reduced, they were still consulted on all important issues, particularly international events. The final phase lasted from 1912 to 1940, during which time the remaining four Genro played merely a symbolic role in general decision-making.

The Genro played a vital role in Japan's initial modernization drive. As a behind-the-scenes power, the Genro provided a detached, non-partisan, long-range outlook which contributed to the development and stability of a new system undergoing enormous strains and challenges. However, leadership and policy problems increased as their influence diminished, and the Genro left a legacy of an authoritarian government ruled over by a behind-the-scenes élite unaccountable to the popular will, which culminated in the totalitarianism and fascism of the 1930s.

Many historians argue that without the Genro, the relatively viable two-party Cabinet system of the 1920s would never have occurred. The Constitution created a Lower House with a limited electorate of 450 000, representing only 1 per cent of the population. Although the Diet had no powers to initiate legislation, it could refuse to approve a budget submitted by the government, in which case last year's budget would be used. Despite its largely rubber-stamp role and the continual government attempts to suppress the parties through surveillance, arrests, and bribes, the creation of a Diet did immediately lead to an active mobilization of voters by a competitive party system.

The Genro aided the two-party system by alternating their choice of a party to fill the Cabinet. Whenever the Genro felt conditions were ripe, the Prime Minister would be asked to resign and a new prime minister would be chosen to lead a Cabinet, after which an election would be held to ratify the results. Scalipino writes that, 'Had the political mechanism operated automatically and alone via the party-election system, it is likely that the party in power would have remained in power. Government patronage shading into multiple forms of corruption would have ensured this, and indeed, a party in power had never lost an election up to this point. But via the instrumentality of the Genro, Japanese leadership was changed without the use of elections, and the new Cabinet proceeded to ratify its power via the electorial process, thus making possible an alternation of power between the parties . . . Had it not been for the Genro, Japan would probably have had a dominant-party system'.[3]

The political support of these parties was based not on mass support but on ties with 'families of influence' in each particular region, support from local and prefectural office holders, and access to funds. Within each major party, moreover, 'factional rivalries were often severe. Factional leaders frequently competed with each other, seeking to expand their district or national bases through favors and funds to local leaders. The major parties were thus themselves federations, loosely knit coalitions that were capable of being dissolved and reformed with different alliances being effected'.[4]

Although factionalism has been a central characteristic of Japan's political culture since the country's beginning, post-1889 party factionalism was exacerbated by the multi-member district system which created an electoral war of all against all, stimulating as much competition within as between parties. Despite this effect, it can be argued that multi-member districts helped preserve a balance of power between the parties since single-member districts would have solidified one party in power.

Vast sums of money, not differences over issues, became the key to electoral victory both before and after an election. Although millions of yen changed hands before an election, after winning an election the party in power would attempt to 'buy' as many minor and independent politicians as possible, usually adding ten to 20 additional seats to its ranks and thus solidifying its majority.[5] In fact, until the participation of socialist parties in the 1920s, there were no significant political differences between the parties. Both the Minseito and Seiyukai shared the same pragmatic program and philosophy of supporting fiscal conservatism, agrarian and business interests, the suppression of radicals at home, and expansion abroad.

Although the Meiji constitution created a national assembly and electoral system which evolved into a two-party system and universal male suffrage by 1925, Japan was far from being a genuine democracy. According to Scalipino, a party in power never lost an election during this period. Power did alternate by means of elections, but only when 'neutral', non-party governments presided over such elections. 'True alteration in power between parties took place as a result of the Genro system, with the senior Japanese statesmen selecting prime ministers when, in their opinion, conditions necessitated a change. These prime ministers then proceeded to use elections to ratify their power.'[6] Despite these limitations, the system developed dramatically during this time. From the first election in 1890 up to the election of commoner Hara Kei in 1919, the parties gradually evolved from being considered subversive challengers to the system, to becoming essential parts of the system.

Another important related political development was the rise of interest groups. As might be expected, the first interest groups were business groups, and these were encouraged by the Meiji government as part of its economic development and political stabilization policies. In 1878 the Bureau of Commercial Development created the Tokyo Chamber of Commerce (Tokyo Shoho Kaigisho) to stimulate corporate cooperation and to serve in an advisory role to the government. The organization of business interests was furthered by the Chamber of Commerce Act of 1890. Agricultural interest were not organized on a national scale until much later – the Federation of Agricultural Cooperatives (Sangyo kumiai) was authorized in 1909, and by 1915 93 per cent of the towns and villages had local cooperatives. The following year the Imperial Agricultural Association was established by law and centralized a number of local farm organizations.[7] After their establishment, both business and agricultural interests became active in supporting sympathetic politicians and lobbying key Dietmen and bureaucrats. Because of their lack of mass dues-paying membership, both parties became closely tied to these groups for most of their funds.

The rise of labor interest groups and the first attempts of labor-based parties to participate in elections caused a severe backlash from both business and agricultural groups. The first labor union was the Society of Friendship and Love (Yuaikai), created in 1912 by Suzuki Bunji and 14 of his friends. Its ranks and that of similar labor unions gradually swelled despite constant police and business harassment. The rise of these labor unions, in part, stimulated the creation of the Industrial Club in 1918, which proved much more effective than Chamber of Commerce in influencing politics. Mitsui and Mitsubishi contributed 100 000 yen each to the Industrial Club and alternated its presidency. The Industrial Club took a particularly hard line on labor issues; for example, it protested against labor attempts to insert a labor clause in the Versailles Treaty, pushed through the 1919 Management Labor Collaboration Association (kyochokai) designed to coopt labor, and strongly opposed the labor union acts of the mid-1920s. Its influence and efforts, however, were not strong enough to prevent a 1924 act that allowed labor unions to elect their own representatives, or a 1925 act that attempted to regulate female and child labor.

Labor and tenancy unions mushroomed during this period, becoming an increasingly vocal if not powerful force in Japanese politics. By 1929, although there were over 300 000 union members represented by a variety of labor and tenant organizations, this represented only a fraction of 1.6 million in industry as a whole. The Japan Federation of Labor (Nippon Rodo Sodomei), formed in 1919, was the most effective of all the unions in mobilizing demands for improved working conditions. In response, the corporate world created the Harmonization Society (Kyochokai) to coopt moderate unionists and isolate the radicals.

While the unions were neutralized with both suppression and cooption, the government at first used mostly suppression to deal with the birth of a variety of socialist parties that accompanied the labor movement. In succession, the Socialist Party formed in 1921, the Communist Party (1922), and Labor-farm Party (Rodo Nominto, 1926) were suppressed shortly after their creation. By the end of the decade, however, the peaceful activities of most remaining socialist parties were tolerated, if closely watched, by the government.

Although urban and rural unrest had been building for some time, and have in fact been constants throughout Japanese history, they reached a height during the rice riots that spread across the country in 1918 in reaction to high inflation, food shortages, mass poverty, and political suppression. Housewives, students, laborers, and peasants clamored for relief via a variety of economic and political reforms. The government responded in 1919 by replacing the discredited Terauchi Cabinet with one led by Hara Kei, a commoner and head of the Seiyukai. As the first prime minister chosen from outside the inner-oligarchy, the Hara government marked the acceptance of the political parties as equal partners within Japan's governing élite of aristocrats, upper bureaucrats (mombatsu), agricultural interests, big business (zaibatsu), and military leadership (gumbatsu), and inaugurated a decade of party-led Cabinets. As the Genro steadily faded in influence, the party leaders played an increasingly important role in policy-making and were the logical choice to mediate mass demands on the political system. Though important symbolically, the Hara Cabinet was little more successful than its predecessors in alieviating mass poverty and demands for greater representation, and ended ominously with Hara's assassination in 1921.

Eventually, it became clear to Tokyo that the time had come to coopt the more moderate elements of these increasingly vocal and violent mass demands for greater political participation. In 1925 the government took two actions which seemed dramatically to advance Japan's political development. First, the Diet passed a bill granting universal suffrage to all males over 25 years of age, thereby increasing the electorate from three to 14 million voters. At the same time it reduced the army's strength from 21 to 17 divisions.

These democratizing trends in politics were paralleled by similar advances in political philosophy. The most significant were the teachings of Professor Minobe Tatsukichi (1873–1948) of Tokyo University, who from 1911 taught that the Emperor was an 'organ of the state' rather than the essence of the state itself, thus softening the absolutist role the Constitution had assigned the Emperor. Although he stopped short of calling for popular sovereignty, Yoshino Sakuzo (1878–1933), another Todai professor, taught that the people's livelihood should be the focus of government.

How democratic was this 'Taisho Democracy' of the 1920s? Certainly the inauguration of party governments and universal male suffrage, reduction of the army, and grudging acceptance of labor unions and socialist parties were all very important steps in Japan's democratization. Yet it must be remembered that all the parties – mainstream and socialist alike – were controlled by small élites dependent on powerful interest groups for financial and organizational support. For example, the Seiyukai was considered the spokesparty for the huge zaibatsu Mitsui, while Minseito fronted Mitsubishi. In addition, only six of the 11 premiers who led 'party governments' during this time were actually party men; the other five were career bureaucrats or military officers. The assasination in office of three of these six party premiers raises considerable doubts about the legitimacy of these governments. But perhaps the most sinister development of all was the 1925 Peace Preservation Bill, enacted the same year as the universal male suffrage law. The Peace Preservation Bill greatly enlarged government controls over any group deemed subversive by creating the Thought Police (Kempeitai), designed to root out any 'dangerous thoughts'.

Offsetting the spectrum of political parties and interest groups that mushroomed during this era, was the growing popularity of ultranationalist secret societies whose membership included some of the most influential men in society. These ultranationalist groups had begun to emerge in the late nineteenth century to advocate imperialism abroad and a purified Japanese state led by the Emperor at home. The Black Ocean Society (Genyosha, 1881) and Amur Society (Kokuryukai, later the Black Dragon Society, 1901) advocated incorporating Korea and Manchuria into the Japanese empire, while suppressing socialists and dangerous thoughts at home. The Japan Patriotic Society (Nihon Kokusuikai) was formed in 1919 by bureaucrats and businessmen who called for harmony between labor and business, suppression of leftists, and expansion throughout East Asia. The organization eventually included 100 000 members. The Anti-Red League (Sekka Boshidan, 1922) emphasized Japan's unique character and 'special mission in Asia'. Other ultranationalist organizations include the Jimmu Society (Jimmu-kai), Heavenly Sword Party (Tenkento), Blood Brotherhood (Ketsumeidan), and Cherry Society (Sakura-kai). These ultranationalist sentiments were most systematically articulated by Kita Ikki (1885–1937) who wrote 'An Outline Plan for the National Reorganization of Japan' in which he advocated a military coup to fulfill the ideals of imperial rule and remove corruption from around the throne, promotion of harmony among all classes, and fulfillment of Japan's mission to liberate Asia from the West.

By the late 1920s Japan faced a deepening economic crisis of slow growth, vast gaps between the rich and the impoverished mass urban and rural poor, corruption, unemployment, and inflation that threatened to undermine the dramatic but largely shallow-rooted political economic developments that had taken place since the Meiji coup. Rather than being the solution to Japan's problems, the emerging democratic political and economic institutions were increasingly scape-goated as its cause. Increasing numbers of the Japanese political and economic élite rejected the democratic developments and took up the cry of the ultranationalists for a return to traditional authoritarian institutions and outlooks. Just as Japanese leaders had increasingly turned to the throne in the tumultuous years leading up to the Meiji coup, during the 1920s most Japanese came to believe that a revival of emperor worship and Japanese spirit at home and expansion abroad would resolve the crisis.

The catalyst for this transformation from 'Taisho democracy' to 'Showa fascism' came with the army's takeover of Manchuria in 1931. Faced with this *fait accompli*, the government unanimously approved the action. The parties competed with each other to sound the most patriotic, although the more thoughtful politicians expressed doubts behind closed doors. Even the left began advocating militarism and fascism. A public show trial of 400 jailed communists during in 1931–32 resulted in all except a handful renouncing their faith and embracing the government position. The more moderate socialists quickly followed suit. By endorsing the army program while continuing to call for labor reforms, the Social Mass Party (Shakai Taishuto), a coalition of moderate left parties, steadily increased its popularity and received 37 seats in 1936.

Attacks by fanatical right-wing groups were another impetus for backing further Japanese imperialism. In February 1932 the Minseito campaign manager and the chairman of Mitsui were assassinated. This was followed by the assasination of Prime Minister Inukai and armed attacks on Tokyo's police department and other government leaders on 15 May 1932. As a result, the élite formed a 'national unity government' under Admiral Saito, and allowed the army and navy ministers to dominate the choice of subsequent prime ministers and Cabinets, and have a free reign to expand abroad. Even these changes failed to quell the constant right-wing campaign of pressure and intimidation. On 26 February 1936, the right made its strongest bid for power when it led the revolt of the 1st Division in Tokyo and takeover of the War Ministry, Police Headquarters, General Staff Headquarters, and Diet Building. The revolt lasted three days before the rebels surrendered.

According to Masao Maruyama, February 1936 proved the turning point in Japan's steady shift to the right.[8] In the years leading up to the 1st Division revolt, Japan's political system was dominated by 'fascism from below' in which the government embraced right-wing policies and ideas in response to fanatical outside pressure groups. But after the government crushed the revolt and coopted the remaining right-wing groups, Japan's political system became characterized by 'fascism from above' in which the élite led rather than followed a systematic transformation of the political economy into one based on a fascist state philosophy, totalitarian controls, and overseas aggression.

Although the government never achieved total control over the economy, it did create a totalitarian political system. Throughout the 1930s the government succeeded in reducing its once large, vocal political opposition to no more than a handful of imprisoned communists. At no point during the 1930s was there any significant dissent from scholars, journalists, or writers, while all prominent leftists had converted (Tenko) to the government line by the early

1930s. Perhaps the best measure of these totalitarian controls was the willingness of all Japanese – women, children, and old men as well as soldiers – to blindly toss their lives away during the war rather than surrender, even when there was no chance of success.

Japan's wartime totalitarian political institutions and thought control were first systematized by the Showa Research Association (Showa Kenkyukai) founded in 1933 by three-time Prime Minister Prince Konoe Fumimaro, and then adopted by the government. In 1934 Tokyo proclaimed the Amau Doctrine which it justified as an Asiatic Monroe Doctrine, and promised to drive out the Western powers and assert a protectorate over China. This would be accomplished by the program of national mobilization and purification announced by an Army Ministry publication entitled the 'Kokubo no Hongi to sono Kyoka Teisho' in October. The Amau Doctrine and 'Kokubo no Hongi' contained the essence of Kita Ikki's program of Japanese fascism; it preached a doctrine of the 'superiority of the Japanese race', Japan's divine right to rule over East Asia, and the need to purge Japan of any liberal or internationalist tendencies, and instead return to the pure essence of Japanese spirit and familism (Kokutai). In 1938 the Showa Research Association published the Principles of Thought for a New Japan (*Shin Nihon no Shiso Genri*) which essentially espoused the idea that the individual's role in life is to blindly follow the state's wishes (kyodoshugi): 'race is a whole that transcends economic classes, and the state is one moral whole which is established on the basis of a race . . . the state must . . . solve the problems of economic classes with its authority and realize a national cooperative body'.[9]

In August 1940 the third Konoe Cabinet achieved these ideals when it dissolved all parties, interest groups, and other organizations into the Imperial Rule Assistance Association (IRAA, Taisei Yokusankai), composed of a hierarchial system of cooperative councils that ranged from the Diet to every corner of Japan. The bottom level of this system were the Neighborhood Associations (Tonarigumi) which were compulsory councils designed to mobilize the local population behind government policies and such ultranationalist ideas as 'Japanism' (Nipponshugi), yamato spirit (yamato damashii), and 'all the world under one roof' (hakko ichiu, or Japan's imperial mission). The tonarigumi's more sinister role was to identify and stamp out all political dissidents. The schools played a similar role in indoctrinating students into the same beliefs.

'Yamato Damashi', however, proved incapable of winning an ever widening war. Formal war with China formally broke out on 7 July 1937, but after some spectacular early victories capped by the capture of the capital of Nanjing, in which Japanese troops may have slaughtered as many as 350 000 civilians, Japan's 'holy war to free China from Imperialism' bogged down into eight years of ineffective campaigns and constant guerrilla warfare.

The constant drain of material and men in China did not deter Japan's imperialist ambitions; it took over northern Vietnam in September 1940, southern Vietnam in July 1941, and launched an all-out offensive against Southeast Asia led by the sneak attack on Pearl Harbor on 7 December 1941. But, as in China, Japan's early brilliant military conquests in Southeast Asia were soon checked and then steadily reversed by the allies. Rather than liberation, Japan's 'Co-prosperity Sphere' brought the region little more than shameless mass exploitation and murder – an estimated 20 million East Asians were killed during the war.[10] Tokyo's reign of terror over the region and its own people was ended with the atomic bombings of Hiroshima and Nagasaki in August 1945, and Japan's subsequent surrender.

POSTWAR POLITICAL DEVELOPMENT

According to its 1947 Constitution, Japan has a parliamentary system of government similar to those of most other parliamentary systems around the world. Japan's political system is unique in only one respect: literally interpreted, under Article 9 of the Constitution Japan abandons its sovereign right of self defense and a military establishment. But in reality, for both Article 9 and Japan's political system as a whole, there is a vast difference between the constitutional ideals on which they are theoretically built and the reality (honne) in which they actually operate.

One of the reasons for this difference between the way things seem and the ways things are in Japanese politics is the fact that the 1947 Constitution was essentially forced on the Japanese by the American Occupation forces. To SCAP, the flaws in the 1889 Constitution were clear, and largely responsible for Japanese militarism and fascism after 1930. In theory the 1889 Constitution made the Emperor an absolute monarch; in reality he was merely a figurehead through which a small élite not even mentioned in the Constitution, the Genro, ruled Japan. They and their successors, however, steadily saw their own power deteriorate throughout the early twentieth century as other groups and institutions became stronger. By the early 1930s the military had emerged as the most powerful group in the system based on the Army and Navy ministers' ability to report directly to the Emperor and thus completely bypass the Cabinet. Since by law the Army and Navy ministries had to be led by active military personnel, the military could force a Cabinet to resign by refusing to nominate one of its own members to fill a vacant seat.

While SCAP's objective was to create a genuinely democratic political system, the Japanese government wanted to maintain the essence of the old authoritarian system. Between November 1945 and February 1946 SCAP rejected several Constitutional drafts by Prime Minister Shidehara's Cabinet, claiming that they simply recreated most of the authoritarian features of the 1889 Constitution. Finally losing patience, SCAP wrote up its own draft and submitted it, in mid-February, to the Shidehara Cabinet which in turn agreed on 6 March to accept it as Japan's new Constitution. On 3 November 1946 the Emperor submitted the new Constitution to the Diet as an amendment to the 1889 Constitution. It was quickly approved by the Diet and went into effect six months later on 3 May 1947.

Under the new Constitution, sovereignty rests with the people, while the Emperor is stripped of all political power and retains merely ceremonial duties as a symbol of Japan. Under the 1889 Constitution only men over 25 years of age had the right to vote; the new constitution expands the electorate to include all men and women over 20 years of age. Citizens are guaranteed all natural rights such as freedom of assembly, worship, and speech. The Diet, as the institution of the elected people's representatives, is designated as the sole budget and law-making power. In addition, the Diet is given the power to impeach corrupt officials, amend the Constitution, ratify treaties, and pass no-confidence votes on the Cabinet, after which new elections must be held.

To date the Diet has never exercised its right of impeachment or constitutional amendments, although it has passed three non-confidence votes and ratified many treaties. Exposures of blatant corruption usually result in the culprit resigning. In a particularly serious corruption case like that of Tanaka, the courts judge, not the Diet. The Diet has been busy ratifying treaties; as of 1980 the Diet had ratified 537 treaties, 369 unanimously and 168 with dissent.

The Constitution has never been amended despite periodic calls by some right-wing groups for the elimination of Article 9 or even a complete rewrite of the Constitution in more elegant Japanese. In

1957 the Kishi government appointed a Commission on the Constitution composed of various legal experts to determine how, if at all, the Constitution should be revised. The committee's report, finally submitted in 1964, announced that essentially the Constitution was perfectly adequate and recommended against any revision. Even if a particularly nationalistic future LDP Cabinet wanted to revise the Constitution, it would need to organize a two-thirds majority of each house, to be followed by a special nationwide ratification vote. Given these difficulties, the Constitution is unlikely to be amended in the foreseeable future.

Passage of a no-confidence vote is a two-step process. First, a vote can be held only if 50 or more Diet members petition for such a vote. Then a simple majority vote allows the Prime Minister the choice of either resigning or dissolving the Diet and calling for new elections. No-confidence votes occurred against the Yoshida governments in 1948 and 1952, and the Ohira government in 1980. In all three cases the Prime Minister dissolved the Diet and called for new elections.

Although Cabinets can stay in power for up to four years before a mandatory election must be held, a prime minister can dissolve the Diet and hold new elections for many reasons. The most common is either to make way for new leadership within his own party, either because of a deal cut earlier or because he has become unpopular, or to augment his party's strength in the Diet following an unpopular act by the opposition parties. Elections must be held 40 days after dissolution and a new Diet convened 30 days after the election. Of the 15 elections held to date, only one (1969) was held after a full four-year term, while the average Cabinet lasted two and a half years.

There are three types of Diet sessions. An Ordinary Session is convened during the final ten days of December, lasts 150 days, and may be extended once. An Extraordinary Session can be called at any time by a petition of one-quarter of the MPs of either house. A Special Session is opened 30 days after an election, during which the representatives elect the Prime Minister and other Diet officers, assign committees, and determine the Diet calendar. The length of an Extraordinary or Special session is determined by a vote of both houses.

The Prime Minister and a majority of the Cabinet must be from the Diet and be civilians. In addition to being able to dissolve the Diet any time, the Prime Minister can also remove unwanted ministers. The Prime Minister's responsibilities include coordinating Cabinet policy-making, administering such agencies as the Defense Agency, Administrative Management Agency, Imperial Household Agency, and Hokkaido Development Agency, preparing the national budget, and submitting to a weekly question-time before the House of Representatives.

The Diet is a bicameral legislature with a lower House of Representatives and an upper House of Councillors. There are currently 511 House of Representative members from 130 multimember districts, each of which contains from three to five members, who serve a maximum four-year term. Although there is no limit to the number of times someone can be re-elected, candidates must be at least 25 years old. The House of Councillors has a membership of 252 members who serve six-year terms, half of whom stand for election every three years. In each election there are two types of seats: 76 seats from the 47 prefectures and 50 seats nationwide. Since 1983 the House of Councillors has been elected on the basis of proportional representation where the electorate votes for a party rather than individuals. The House of Representatives is more powerful for three reasons: (1) its version of a similar bill passed by both houses becomes law; (2) if the House of Councillors fails to take action within 60 days on a House of Representative bill, it automatically passes; and (3) the budget is first submitted to the lower house. Essentially the House of Councillor powers are, at most, the ability to delay House of Representative actions.

The two houses are administered by a speaker and vice-speaker of the House of Representatives and a president and vice-president of the House of Councillors. All the officers are elected by a simple majority of their respective houses. Their duties are to make committee assignments in proportion to party seats in the House, and they may vote in case of a tie. The officers work through a secretariat in each house which administers everyday activities, the National Diet Library, and the two secretaries allocated to each Diet member.

The Diet is organized along a committee system. There are usually 18 House of Representative and 16 House of Councillor standing committees. Of the 18 House of Representative committees, 14 correspond to the 14 ministries, while the other four include budget, audit, house management, and discipline committees. In addition, there are usually seven or eight special committees appointed each session for issues not covered by the standing committees. There are also Joint Committees formed of ten members from each House to handle special problems; to date there have been 28 Joint Committees. Each committee has a board of directors (rijikai) that assists the chairman; the composition of members is normally proportional to party strength.

Bills are relatively simple to sponsor. An ordinary bill requires a petition of 20 members in the lower house and only ten in the upper house. A budget bill, however, requires 50 sponsors before it is submitted to a committee. After a bill is submitted, the committee has the right to call any minister or other witnesses, hold secret or public hearings, and then pass, amend, postpone, or reject the bill. Approved bills are sent to the house for a vote. A house can vote with a quorum of only 30 per cent of its members, and becomes law with the support of a simple majority. The only limit is that a bill cannot be carried over to a new session if it is delayed, which gives the opposition the advantage of using a wide range of delaying tactics.

The other major institution of Japan's government is the Supreme Court, which has been given the power 'to determine the constitutionality of any law, order, regulation, or official act'. Supreme Court justices are designated by the Cabinet and appointed by the Emperor, while all other judges are appointed by the Cabinet from a list submitted by the Supreme Court. There is a four-level court system with the 15 members of the Supreme Court presiding over the eighth High, 50 District, and 50 Family courts. Judges serve ten-year renewable terms, with a referendum on the judge held during the first House of Representative election following his selection and the first after ten years in office.

The only controversial aspect of Japan's Constitution is Article 9 which states:

> Aspiring sincerely to an international peace based on justice and order, the Japanese people forever renounce war as a sovereign right of the nation and the threat or use of force as means of settling international disputes.

> In order to accomplish the aim of the preceding paragraph, land, see, and air forces, as well as other war potential will never be maintained. The right of belligerency of the state will not be recognized.

Article 9 originated in General MacArthur's messianic interpretation of his mission to demilitarize Japan. Determined to turn Japan into the 'Switzerland of Asia', MacArthur suggested to Shidehara that he include a no-war clause in the SCAP written Constitution submitted to the Cabinet in February 1946. Shidehara agreed, reasoning that the Occupation might soon be lifted if Article 9 could convince the Allies that Japan had completely given up its old militarism.

Japan's political system often operates very differently from the way the institutions are supposed to function according to the Constitution. For example, although the Constitution clearly states that the Diet is the supreme organ of state power, and sole law-making and budget-making authority, in reality the ministries dominate the most important law- and budget-making processes. The Diet merely ratifies decisions made within the bureaucracy and in turn grants additional powers to the bureaucracy to implement its bills. Since 1952 through the present day ministry bills have composed 65 per cent of all bills submitted to the Diet, and over 80 per cent of the ministry bills have become law. In contrast, the political parties have submitted only 35 per cent of all the bills submitted to the Diet, and only 18 per cent of the party bills have passed.[11]

During the early postwar period bureaucratic bills dominated because the ministries had greater expertise and power than the parties. Recently, the LDP Policy Affairs Research Council (PARC) has acquired increasing expertise in virtually all issue areas. Yet ministry bills continue to dominate the Diet although the bureaucrats often have to rewrite the bills according to the needs of the PARC policy bureaux. The Diet remains the supreme ratifier of Japan's political system rather than the center of law-making for which it was originally intended. Likewise, although the Cabinet is supposed to prepare the budget, it is actually the Ministry of Finance which has full budget-making powers and the Cabinet and other ministries must negotiate with the MOF for even the most incremental budget increases.

Although the Prime Minister as the elected head of the Diet is supposed to be responsible for policy-making and decision-making, there is no consensus on his actual powers, and most prime ministers have been passive figureheads rather than active leaders. Most prime ministers try to establish policy goals and climates for their administrations, often by summing them up in slogans, but their actual participation in day-to-day decision-making and long-term policy-making is limited. Prime ministers who attempted to shift Japan's direction either politically or economically, like Yoshida, Tanaka, or Nakasone, were exceptions rather than the rule, and their efforts were largely impeded by a system which discourages personal initiative or dramatic policy shifts.

One constraint on the prime ministers' powers, which is typical of a parliamentary system, is the limited ability to make political appointments. In contrast to the American President, who can make several thousand political appointments to the bureaucracy, the Japanese Prime Minister can only name about 20 ministers and four party officials, including the party's secretary-general. The secretary-general in turn appoints an additional 24 parliamentary vice-ministers, two (one for each house) in the MOF, MAFF, and MITI, and one in each of the other ministries. These vice-ministers are supposed to bridge the ministries and Diet, but have no real policy-making power and serve mainly as prime political channels for the appointees' favors to their constituents and other politicians.[12]

The Cabinet has no more power than the Prime Minister. Article 65 of the 1947 Constitution states that 'executive power shall be vested in the Cabinet' and 'the Cabinet, in the exercise of power, shall be collectively responsible to the Diet'. But the Cabinet has no real power because of the rapid annual turnover of the ministers, whose average length of office is about a year. As a political appointee, the Minister's main job is to ratify policy and budget decisions made below him, and then lobby for their enactment. So the Cabinet is more a collection of ministers than a institutionalized decision-making body.

The Supreme Court is restricted in fulfilling its Constitutional role. There are many reasons for the limited Supreme Court powers. One is cultural: there is no tradition of judicial independence in Japan, and little interest in developing one. This tradition in turn is institutionalized by such things as the policy to limit the number of judges and lawyers. As a result, decisions are reached very slowly, and politics is often more important than precedent in determining the outcome of a case. For example, in 1970 the Supreme Court finally threw out a case first submitted in 1952. Although theoretically the Supreme Court has the power of judicial review, in practice it can not be petitioned on the constitutionality of any abstract law, but only on specific legal conflicts. Lower courts have been known to rule differently on the same case. Elected judges are very susceptible to political pressure. Even if the Supreme Court rules something unconstitutional, the Diet may not enact the appropriate legislation if there is no popular or mass media pressure on the Diet to do so.

Perhaps the most glaring example of the gap between ideal and reality in Japan concerns Article 9 of the Constitution. Although Article 9 clearly states that Japan has renounced its sovereign right to have a military establishment or even defend itself, Japan's Self Defense Force is the third largest in terms of spending in the world. The Supreme Court ruled in its 1959 Sunagawa Decision that, Article 9 aside, Japan has a sovereign right to defend itself and form a security treaty with the United States.

The American Occupation solved many of the political and economic development problems that had plagued Japan since the Meiji Restoration. Yet some problems persisted and others arose despite the barrage of policies that transformed Japan into a nascent liberal democracy. Civil rights made the left-wing parties and labor unions legitimate contenders for power in Japan's political and economic arenas. Meanwhile the purges broke up the prewar élite coalition of aristocratic, military, corporate, bureaucratic, and political leadership. With the aristocracy and military completely removed from power, and the ranks of corporate and political participation considerably thinned, a new constellation of conservative factions emerged to struggle for power in a competitive party system. Finally, although Washington's sweeping economic reforms, continued military procurements, security guarantee, and attempts to reintegrate Japan within a revitalized world economy gave Tokyo a tremendous headstart in developing the country, the government still faced severe problems of economic management, labor unrest, poverty, pollution, and deficient standards of living.

What eventually emerged to resolve these economic and political challenges was an interdependent ruling triad of conservative Liberal Democratic Party (LDP), economic bureaucracies, and corporate world. Chalmers Johnson describes this relationship thus:

> the LDP's role is to legitimate the work of the bureaucracy while making sure the bureaucracy's policies do not stray too far from what the public will tolerate. The bureaucracy, meanwhile, staffs the LDP with its own cadres to ensure that the party does what the bureaucracy thinks is good for the national interest, and guides the business community toward development goals. The business community, in turn, supplies massive amounts of funds to keep the LDP in office, although it does not thereby gain control of the party, which is normally oriented upward, toward the bureaucracy, rather than downward, toward its main patrons.[13]

Leadership within the triad has shifted steadily from the bureaucracy to the LDP as the politicians increasingly became policy experts through long-term participation on 'policy zoku' ('tribes' or associations) in the Diet. Also as Japan's economy has become more complex, conflicts have arisen between different legs of the triad as well as between different corporate sectors, LDP factions, and ministries. Despite the relationship's growing complexity and inner-conflicts, the triad of LDP, economic ministries, and corporate world still dominates Japanese politics and economic policy-making.

Yet significant political development has occurred despite the continued domination of the political system and most policies by the governing triad. LDP popularity steadily diminished from its height of 63.4 per cent of the vote in for House of Representative candidates in 1958 to 48.6 per cent in 1979, although in the 1980s LDP voter support rose to 49 per cent in the 1986 election. In part this decline reflected the emergence of moderate opposition parties like the DSP and CGP; voters who had previously voted LDP as the 'lesser of two evils', now had a moderate alternative. Paradoxically, the LDP decline also reflected Japan's rapid economic growth; prosperity allowed voters to examine quality of life issues involving environmental or consumer issues, which the LDP had neglected.

The LDP's comeback throughout the 1980s parallels the neo-conservatism affecting all democratic industrial countries as they enter a post-industrial age. It is increasingly clear that marxism offers no answers to contemporary problems, and the JSP continues to steadily decline from its height of 35.5 per cent of the House of Representatives vote in 1958 to its most recent low of 17.2 per cent in 1986. Marxism holds little appeal in a society where about 90 per cent of the people consider themselves middle class, or 'middle mass' as Murakami labels it.

The old gap between left and right has been bridged by the center parties; the old politics of ideology and confrontation of the 1950s and 1960s have given way to the politics of pragmatism and joint problem-solving in the 1970s and 1980s. Although they may be quite critical of the LDP during Diet sessions, the mainstream opposition parties – JSP, DSP, and CGP – vote with the LDP on 90 per cent of all bills, and even the JCP votes with the government 70 per cent of the time. This cooperation first began in the early 1970s when the diminishing LDP support made the opposition parties more responsible in anticipation of eventually being invited into a coalition government. Although the invitation never came and the chances of a coalition government seem to recede with each recent election, the cooperation between the LDP and moderate opposition parties continues.

Another reason for the increased cooperation and moderation of Japanese politics is the steady decline of labor union strength. In the 1950s about 50 per cent of all workers were in unions; today union membership has dropped to 28 per cent. The animosity between management and labor in most Japanese industries during the 1950s gave way to cooperation since as increased prosperity undercut the workers' demands and companies set up their own unions to coopt the moderate workers and isolate the radicals. The recent formation of the National Confederation of Private Sector Unions (Rengo), in which all four national labor confederations either will or have already dissolved themselves will deepen this cooperative trend. Rengo is firmly controlled by moderate unions and will coopt the more radical public sector unions once the General Council of Trade Unions (Sohyo) eventually joins.

The most important pillar of LDP popularity is Japan's continued economic growth. The LDP presided over an annual average growth rate of 10 per cent before 1973 and five per cent since, one of the world's most egalitarian income distributions, and highest per capita incomes, which surpassed that of the United States in 1987. Japan became the world's leading financial power in 1985 and is increasingly surpassing America's leadership in technology. Although pollution remains a problem, its levels are down dramatically since the LDP creatively responded to mass popular demands and instituted sweeping pollution controls in the early 1970s. New issues, such as Japan's rapidly ageing population, will arise in the 1990s, but Tokyo will undoubtedly overcome these present and future problems as successfully as it has those of the past.

Regardless of the outcome of these domestic and international challenges, the LDP will continue to rule and Japan's wealth will continue to mount for the foreseeable future. The dynamic virtuous circle of stable conservative rule pursuing growth policies that lead to continued political support and thus further growth will remain unbroken: economic success remains the basis of conservative political success which remains the basis of Japan's economic success, and so on. As in other industrial countries, Japan's electorate is becoming increasingly neo-conservative as mass affluence and pride in Japan's achievements builds. Meanwhile, the opposition will remain fragmented while becoming increasingly centrist. The LDP will continue to coopt the opposition's most popular and economically sound ideas.

The need and ability of government to directly guide economic development steadily lessened as the economy grew increasingly complex and dynamic throughout the 1970s and 1980s. However, the government still plays a decisive role in promoting industrial policies that target strategic high technology industries such as aerospace, micro-electronics, superconductors, or the Fifth Generation computer. Yet the government faces more than technological challenges as Japan moves into the twenty-first century. With the world's most rapidly ageing society, Tokyo must devise policies that provide adequate social security, health care, and leisure facilities for the elderly. Despite their wealth, Japanese still work several hundred hours a year more than the people of other industrial countries. Quality of life issues like leisure time and facilities will increasingly become an important focus of government policy.

Foreign demands on Japan to assume more global responsibilities grow steadily with its wealth and power. Foreign governments are increasingly pressuring Tokyo to genuinely open up its economy, grant massive aid and cheap loans to the developing world, and coordinate its macroeconomic policies with those of the other key industrial countries. In short, the rest of the world is demanding that Tokyo replace its traditional neo-mercantilist policies – which enabled Japan to rise from its pre–1945 poverty to its present position as the world's greatest economic power – with liberal economic policies similar to those Britain and the United States followed during their respective tenures as leader of the world economy. Chapters 13 and 14 will analyze whether or not Tokyo will be able to overcome both these domestic and international challenges with the same flexibility and imagination with which it overcame the poverty and growth problems of the postwar era.

NOTES

1. John Hall, *Japan: From Prehistory To Modern Times*, pp. 22–36.
2. See Roger Hackett, 'Political Modernization and the Meiji Genro', in Robert Ward's *Political Development in Modern Japan*, p. 69
3. Robert Scalapino, 'Elections and Political Modernization in Prewar Japan', in Ward, pp. 271–2.

4. Ibid., p. 272.
5. Ibid., p. 273.
6. Ibid., p. 283.
7. Takeshi Ishida, 'The Development of Interest Groups and the Pattern of Political Modernization in Japan', in Ward, p. 313.
8. Masao Maruyama, *Thought and Behavior in Japanese Politics*, pp. 23–83.
9. Miles Fletcher, 'Intellectuals and Fascism in Early Showa Japan', *Journal of Asian Studies*, Vol. 39, No. 1, November 1979, p. 51.
10. *Japan Times*, 16 August 1986, p. 2.
11. Hans Baerwald, *Party Politics in Japan*, chapter 5.
12. Johnson, *MITI and Japan's Modern Economic Miracle*, p. 52.
13. Ibid.

4 The Economic 'Miracle'

Japan was dragged into the modern world at gunpoint. In 1853 Commodore Perry broke two and a half centuries of Japan's isolation by steaming his gunboats into Edo bay to request that Japan open its doors to the world. Between the Tokugawa's reluctant acceptance and the Meiji coup of January 1868 that overthrew the old regime, Japan's political élite was bitterly divided over how to overcome the Western challenge. A steadily diminishing faction argued that Japan should fight the Western powers; a steadily increasing faction argued that the only sensible path was to accept the humiliating initial loss of tariff and legal sovereignty while embarking on a modernization drive to overcome and eventually surpass the West on its own terms.

The Meiji revolution settled the question; for the next half century, the new dynamic leadership single-mindedly attempted to transform Japan into a modern country. By 1919 Japan's political economy was buttressed with modern mass bureaucratic, political, military, industrial, and educational institutions. Tokyo had carved out a small empire in Northeast Asia, and had not only recovered its sovereignty but was accepted as one of the 'Big Five' powers at the Versailles peace conference.

Yet Japan's modernization was only skin-deep; beneath the façade of modern institutions and impressive industrial development remained powerful traditional psychological and political forces that were pressuring the country to abandon its Western outlook, and recreate a 'total' Japanese state (kokutai) at home and an 'Asia for Asians' led by Japan abroad. During the 1920s the government's legitimacy was steadily undermined by its inability to alleviate a worsening economic crisis of mass poverty, inflation, corruption, and depression. In response, during the 1930s the government gradually incorporated the ultranationalist demands; Japanese armies embarked on a step-by-step conquest of East Asia while the government slowly transformed Japan's nascent multi-party democracy into a totalitarian one-party state dedicated to a divine emperor.

But ultimately, the result was disaster. By September 1945 Japan was in ruins: 25 per cent of its industry was destroyed, while 61 of 62 cities with populations over 50 000 had been leveled by firebombs, leaving over 600 000 civilians dead – only the old imperial capital of Kyoto was spared. The 26 March 1945 firebombing of Tokyo alone killed over 200 000 people; the atomic bombings of Hiroshima and Nagasaki incinerated 140 000 and 48 000 people, respectively. These losses were on top of 2.1 million Japanese killed during Japan's 14 years of aggression in East Asia.

In stark contrast has been Japan's dazzlingly successful economic development since 1945. Its phoenix-like rise from wartime devastation into its current status as the world's greatest economic power has been almost universally lauded as an 'economic miracle' as Japan is rapidly overtaking America's faltering lead to become the world's technological superpower as well. Japanese corporations joust with their American and European rivals for technological leadership in such fields as supercomputers, biogenetics, micro-electronics, aersopace, and robotics. It it estimated that if they maintain their current respective growth rates, Japan's GNP will surpass that of the United States within 20 years, which means that with half the population, Japan's per capita income will be double that of the United States.

Japan's successful postwar economic development raises the same questions as its disastrous prewar development: was it inevitable? If not, what were possible alternative development paths and why were they not followed? Was Japan's development 'unique' or does it offer lessons for others? What are the major reasons for Japan's 'economic miracle'.

Most Japanese sum up the secret of their country's success as simply the result of 'hard work'. But this is clearly a secondary factor at best. The people of most countries work just as hard as the Japanese, yet few of those countries have developed as successfully as Japan.

Japan's rise to economic superpower status is a result of several equally important reasons. First of all, Japan's postwar development was built on over a century of determined pre-1945 modernization efforts. Although many of its cities and industries were destroyed, Japan's modern industrial, technological, and educational system remained intact. Three additional factors account for Japan's economic success. If any one or more of these factors had been missing, Japan's development would have been significantly different: slower, less equitable, and much more unstable.

Perhaps the most important of the postwar factors was a constructive rather than punitive Allied Occupation. The Occupation's demilitarization and democratization policies purged Japan of most of the prewar institutions and practices that had contributed to the militarism and fascism of the 1930s. This was followed up by sweeping economic reforms that set the stage for Japan's later dramatic growth rates. it is extremely unlikely that Tokyo, left to itself, could have ever achieved similar reforms or results.

But the 'economic miracle' did not occur in a vacuum. An open, expanding world economy was equally vital to Japan's development. Although the Allies had constructed the basis for such an economy with the Bretton Woods agreements of 1944, it was not until the Korean War that the global economy really took off. Neighboring Japan with its still underutilized factories and labor was the chief beneficiary of the billions of dollars of wartime procurements. The Korean War inaugurated an era of rapid Japanese and global economic growth that continued unimpeded until the 1973 oil shocks.

From 1950 to 1973 Japan's economy expanded at an average rate of ten per cent a year, over twice the global rate. Why did Japan's growth outstrip that of any other country during this period? Even after the oil shocks, Japan's economy has continued to expand an average five per cent a year, a rate better than any other OECD country and exceeded only by the 'little Japans' of East Asia – South Korea, Taiwan, Singapore, and Hong Kong – which, to varying extents, emulated Japan's development strategy. This rapid growth erupted from two dynamic, interrelated relationships: government-business cooperation that created and implemented rational macroeconomic and industrial policies, and management-labor cooperation that created and implemented long-term corporate strategies designed to win market share and destroy their rivals. These different factors behind Japan's economic 'miracle' will be explored in two sections, the first analyzing the pre-1945 development while the second concentrates on the Occupation reforms. Japan's postwar economic miracle was not inevitable. The second section will first examine the alternative policies Washington considered for Japan, showing how different its political economic development would have been if they had been strictly followed. It will then examine the specific Occupation reforms that set the stage for Japan's later rapid and equitable growth. Since other chapters explore the policies and politics of Japan's economic 'miracle' in detail, this chapter ends with the Occupation in 1952.

PRE-1945 DEVELOPMENT

Like Germany, which began its modernization efforts about the same time, Japan benefitted from being a 'late early developing' country. Tokyo was lucky to be able to embark on its vast industrialization effort at a time when technology was relatively simple and easy to master, and when competition in world markets was relatively low key. Japan could avoid the setbacks and mistakes of early industrial countries like Britain, the United States, and France, while enjoying access to the relatively open and expanding world economy that London had expended such vast economic and diplomatic efforts to create in the nineteenth century.

Woe to those countries which achieved independence after 1945. They are attempting to accomplish in a generation what countries like Japan and Germany achieved over a century of trial and error. Industries and firms in the less developed countries face a frenzied struggle to keep up with product cycles that have been cut to as little as a year when the average cycle was ten years just a decade ago, and to enter markets that are already dominated by huge Japanese, American, and European multinational corporations. Considering these development obstacles, the real economic 'miracles' can be found in small newly industrializing countries (NICs) like South Korea, Taiwan, Singapore, and Hong Kong which have not enjoyed all the benefits that countries like Japan and Germany enjoyed.

Japan has not only had 130 years in which to industrialize, but also benefitted from almost 1500 years of pre-modern development which laid the foundations for its rapid modern take-off. By the time Japan was dragged into the world economy in 1854, it already had a unified state, extensive economic infrastructure, close, cooperative government-business ties, and scores of dynamic merchant houses.

Although the Tokugawa regime is usually credited with creating a relatively unified and uniform national political economy in the early seventeenth century, it may actually have delayed Japan's economic take-off. Two and a half centuries of Pax Tokugawa was certainly a relief after the century of constant warfare and political fragmentation that preceded it, but the isolation policy (sakoku) imposed after 1640 cut Japan off from a flourishing trade developing throughout East Asia and one which Japanese merchants were poised to dominate.

Although the decentralized feudalism of the Ashikaga era (1338–1573) eventually broke down into a century of warfare, it had also stimulated the development of a dynamic trade both within Japan and with East Asia, since decentralized political power was synonymous with decentralized economic power and the entrepreneurship that goes with it. This proved a boom for the economy as the Ashikaga began to grant trade licenses to all who asked to make up for their lack of revenue from the provinces. As a result, Japan became a major regional maritime power during this era as both trade and pirate ships ranged the seas off East and Southeast Asia. By the end of the era, sizeable Japanese communities had been established as far away as the Philippines and even Thailand, where samurai provided an élite bodyguard for the king. Although smuggling and piracy had gone on for centuries, trade with China officially began with the Chinese Emperor's acceptance of tribute from the 'king' of Japan in 1401. After this time, Japanese exports included refined copper, sulfur, fans, screens, painted scrolls, and swords in return for strings of cash, of which over 50 000 strings were received in 1454 alone.[1]

This influx of foreign currency was an important aid to the economy since the government had given up minting in the Heian era. Soon most taxes were collected in Chinese coins and lumps of gold and silver, rather than grain. A money economy led to the development of a nascent banking class as enterprising village warehouse merchants, sake brewers, or temples became money-lenders. The trade in goods and ideas was just as important as the influx of coins in stimulating the domestic economy. Agricultural production increased dramatically as new crops and farming and irrigation techniques were used on both old and reclaimed lands. Increased wealth from trade and agriculture boosted demand for such industries as silk, hemp, linen, paper, dyestuffs, lacquer, and vegetable oils. Transportation and communication improved throughout the era as shipping and packhorse companies emerged to meet the demand for goods and services. Former sleepy villages on these trade routes were transformed into dynamic commercial centers. But eventually, almost all these commercial enterprises came under some form of government control. Guilds (za) first emerged in the mid-thirteenth century as monopoly rights to sell or manufacture products were granted by such patrons as local monasteries, lords, Daimyo, or the Shogun himself.

Japan's economy developed even more rapidly in the century of trade with the West after the Portuguese first arrived in 1543. Such European products as firearms, textiles, glassware, clocks, and tobacco became extremely popular throughout Japan and a source of wealth to those Daimyo fortunate enough to serve as middlemen in the trade. Competing fiercely among themselves, the Portugese, Spanish, and Dutch further unified trade in East Asia and opened up vast opportunities for dynamic Japanese merchants and entrepreneurs.

Perhaps the most important Western impact, however, was the introduction of muskets, cannon, and mass military tactics. Armed with this modern military technology, Oda Nobunaga and his successors, Toyotomi Hideyoshi, and Tokugawa Ieyasu were eventually able to destroy their rivals, disarm the peasants, and unify the country. The hundreds of small castles which had enabled local lords to fend off their rivals were reduced to rubble by mass armies armed with modern cannon and muskets. Only vast fortresses manned with thousands of troops armed with cannon and muskets could withstand a modern seige.

Nobunaga was not only a brilliant military strategist, but an excellent economist who clearly understood the dynamic relationship between wealth and military power. He unified much of the country as early as 1573 and began imposing on his realm a uniform system of coinage, weights and measures while abolishing the barriers and guilds which had impeded the free flow of trade. His reforms led to rapid economic growth within Japan and trade with East Asia. After Nobunaga's assassination in 1582, Hideyoshi continued the unification policy but died in 1598 before it was completed. It was only with Ieyasu's decisive victories at the battles of Sekigahara (1600) and Osaka castle (1614) that Japan was finally unified.

The Tokugawa era (1600–1868) systematized the political, economic, and social developments of the previous Ashikaga era that would serve as the foundation for Japan's rapid modernization during the Meiji period. The centralization of political power as Edo and the requirement that each Daimyo, his family, and followers spend at least six months a year there (sankin kotai) formed the basis of the national economy. These annual migrations to and from Edo spread wealth and innovation along the national highways leading to the provinces. Each of the roughly 200 Daimyo was allowed one castle town in his province (Han) which rapidly became a vibrant regional trade center. By the late Tokugawa era Edo had a population of one million, Osaka and Kyoto about half a million each, and altogether about 10 per cent of the population lived in cities of over 10 000.[2]

The Tokugawa tried to enforce a rigid Confucian class system with the samurai at the top followed by the peasant and artisan classes, all sitting atop the merchants at the bottom. Merchants were despised because, unlike the peasants and artisans, they did not make anything but only traded the products made by others. But despite their low status the merchants became increasingly wealthy as the economy expanded, and the samurai increasingly dependent on the merchants for loans to support their lifestyles as inflation ate away their rice-based revenues. This was the origin of the symbiotic relationship between government and business that persists through today and has been such an important factor behind Japan's dynamic economy.

With unity, peace, and centralized power, the samurai's role changed from fighting wars to administering the country. Japan's élitist, efficient modern bureaucracy and its role in regulating and developing the economy evolved directly from the conversion of samurai into salaried bureaucrats during the Tokugawa era. The Tokugawa bureaucrats became just as adept at managing the range of monopolies and guilds that re-emerged during this time, as MITI and other ministry officials are at regulating today's 500 or so cartels; contemporary politicians are just as dependent on the corporate world for money to finance their re-election to the Diet, as the samurai were on the merchants to fund their elegant lifestyles.

The merchant houses originated as itinerant peddlers, money-lenders, sake brewers, or textile retailers and gradually increased the size of their operations. By 1761 Japan's urban economy was dominated by over 200 merchant houses with an average value of about 200 000 gold ryo (with one ryo equal to one koku, the equivalent of most Daimyo in wealth). The guilds (za) which had originated in the Ashikaga period expanded rapidly in size and diversity. The samurai originally tried to control their own han warehouses and trade, but increasingly sold the privileges to enterprising merchants whose quarters were located alongside the castle walls. With its port and central location, Osaka became the core of the economy. Eventually about 130 warehouses arose to handle the rice and other commodities. A nascent banking class arose to handle an increasingly money-based economy. By the end of the era, 255 han and 21 localities had issued over 1600 varieties of currency equal to 24 million yen (1 yen was equal to 1 Mexican dollar at the time).[3]

These developments were undercut, however, by the policy of isolation (sakoku). The Tokugawa regime knew well that foreign trade created wealth, and wealth in turn could be used to create power. Fearing that the outer provinces would use trade to eventually challenge their rule, the Tokugawa limited all trade to Nagasaki and Hirado as early as 1616, forbad any Japanese from traveling abroad in 1635, and finally limited all foreign trade to the Dutch and Chinese at Nagasaki in 1641. But by restricting trade, the Tokugawa restricted Japan's economic development. If the merchants had been allowed to continue their rapidly expanding trade throughout East Asia, Japan might eventually have attempted to protect its foreign markets with an empire, thus dramatically changing the course of world history. At the very least, trade would have relieved the 20 recorded great famines that ravaged Japan during this period – inflation, over-population, and poor harvests led to over 1600 peasant uprisings in the 250-year period.

One additional important pre-modern development was the emergence of mass education. It is estimated that by the mid-nineteenth century almost 50 per cent of the male and 15 per cent of the female population could read and write. The samurai were educated by the 270 Han schools and 375 related academies, while the merchants attended the 1400 private schools, and the peasants and artisans the over 10 000 temple schools.

Despite these developments, by the early nineteenth century Japan's economy was reeling from inflation, famine, a bloated bureaucracy, huge debts, and recession. Unable to overcome these economic challenges and the foreign threat after Perry's gunboats steamed into Edo Bay in 1854, the Tokugawa regime steadily lost support and was quickly overthrown by the coalition of Satsuma, Choshu, Tosa, and Hizen in January 1869. The new Meiji regime then embarked on a systematic modernization drive under slogans like 'wealthy country, strong military' (fukoku kyohei), 'Western Technology, Japanese spirit' (wakon yosai), and 'civilization and enlightenment' (bumei kaika).

In one generation, Tokyo successfully created modern mass bureaucratic, political, military, industrial, and educational systems, all based on foreign models. The government sent the 48-man Iwakura Mission to the United States and Europe during 1872–73, ostensibly to negotiate treaty revisions, but also to examine those countries' 'courts, prisons, schools, trading firms, factories and shipyards, iron foundaries, sugar refineries, paper plants, wool and cotton spinning and weaving, silver, cutlery, and glass plants, coal and salt mines'.[4] Ito Hirobumi stated his mission's goals clearly in a speech before the city fathers of Sacramento: 'We come to study your

strength, that, by adopting widely your better ways, we may hereafter be stronger ourselves . . . We shall labor to place Japan on
an equal basis, in the future, with those countries whose modern
civilization is now our guide'.[5] In addition to its foreign missions,
Japan hired foreign advisors – about 3000 between 1854 and 1890 –
to guide all aspects of its development drive including creating a
constitution, educational system, agriculture railroads, military, and
legal system. The advisors were sent home as soon as Japan had
absorbed the knowledge.

Japan's industrialization program was highly successful. Since the
merchants lacked the requisite capital or technological expertise, the
government itself built such industries as steel, railroads, shipbuilding, armaments, and telegraphs, and then once they were established
sold them to private investors for as little as one-tenth of their cost.
Industry was largely financed by agriculture, which was squeezed
tightly through high taxes. Although these nascent industries were
at first dependent on massive imports of intermediate capital goods
such as machine tools and special types of equipment or raw
materials, these products were eventually produced in Japan. After
founding and developing these industries, the initial heavy hand of
the state gradually relaxed. Japan's industrialization did not really
take-off, however, until massive procurement orders for the Russo-
Japanese war began to flow in after 1904. By the early twentieth
century Japan had developed both a relatively open economy and a
high degree of industrialization.

Japan's economic growth was export-led and dependent on foreign
markets and sources of raw materials. Japan traded not only with
its Northeast Asian empire of Taiwan and Korea, but throughout
East Asia, as far away as North America and Europe, and even
Africa and Latin America. China, however, became Japan's most
important trading partner, and the source for most of Japan's coal,
iron, and cotton fibres, and the market for over half of Japan's textile
production.

Whether imperialism aids or distorts a colonial power's development remains a controversial issue. Some argue that overseas expansion stimulates domestic industries by providing access to captured
markets, and cheap foreign resources and labor. Others argue that
development would be much quicker and more stable if the enormous financial, human, and material resources required to carve out
and manage an empire were instead invested at home. Japan's first
phase of imperialism (1872–1922) probably aided the country's devel-

opment since it not only stimulated domestic economic growth but also resulted in the reversal of the unequal treaties with the West, while its second phase clearly brought about the destruction of Japan's 80-year modernization drive.

On paper, Japan's industrialization efforts seemed an overwhelming success by the early twentieth century. The watershed in this shift from a predominantly agrarian economy to an advanced industrial economy in little more than two generations was reached when machine-made products first edged out agricultural goods to become more than half of all exports in 1905. This industrial output poured from a dual economy of huge holding companies (zaibatsu) which subcontracted with tens of thousands of small- and medium-sized companies. Although the big four zaibatsu – Mitsui, Mitsubishi, Sumitomo, and Yasuda – are the most famous, altogether there were at least 52 zaibatsu capitalized at more than five million yen each, holding altogether 38 per cent of all national capital.[6] From the Meiji coup to 1930, Japan's urban population more than doubled, including two million people in Tokyo, and one million in Osaka, while the total population rapidly increased from 35 million to 55 million.

Little of the benefits of Japan's remarkable economic growth throughout the period trickled down to most people. The reverse side of these statistics was mass urban and rural poverty stimulated by the dual economy, over-population, inflation, low wages and lack of significant health, labor, or welfare legislation. By 1920, rural tenancy had surpassed 50 per cent. These domestic economic problems were multiplied by the depression and subsequent waves of protectionism that swept the world after 1929. The depression hit rural areas particularly hard, with prices of rice and silk reaching their lowest levels since 1897. Malnutrition was widespread and in some particularly hard-hit regions peasants even sold their daughters into prostitution for a little extra money.

In the early 1930s, however, Japan's takeover of Manchuria plus Tokyo's abandonment of relatively liberal economic policies and embrace of mercantilism began to alleviate some of this economic hardship. Starting in 1932, Finance Minister Takahashi Korekiyo followed a policy of heavy industrial expansion, deficit spending, and predatory trade practices that made Japan the first country to recover from the depression. The Major Industries Control Law (1931) allowed the government to rationalize industries through mergers and cartels, making the zaibatsu and smaller firms more streamlined and competitive in world markets. The government combined this with a severe devaluation of the yen and abandonment of the gold standard. As a result, exports doubled between 1932 and 1936, while the economic base shifted dramatically from light to heavy industry; in 1931 heavy industry was 33.7 per cent of GNP and light industry 66.3 per cent, by 1935 the figures were 47.6 per cent and 52.4 per cent, respectively, and in 1938 heavy industry composed 60.8 per cent of GNP to 39.2 per cent for light industry.[7]

In the late 1930s and early 1940s, the government enacted a series of laws giving it increased control over the economy. Shortly after the aborted February 1936 coup, the government was reorganized into a Cabinet Advisory Council which included four representatives from the military, three party men, two from finance and business, and one from foreign affairs, which presided over a Cabinet Planning Board of 20 men whose mission was to coordinate national policy. The National General Mobilization Law of March 1938 gave the Cabinet dictatorial powers, including the ability to bypass the Diet at will, command all sectors of the economy, and mobilize all resources, equipment, and labor as it desired. That same year, the Materials Mobilization Law allowed government the power to allocate any human or material resources to factories. The Major Industries Control Act (September 1941) divided the economy into 22 mandatory industrial control associations run by the appropriate ministry with the power to limit or channel production, prices, or quotas. The Ministry of Commerce and Industry was converted into the Ministry of Munitions in 1943 with the goal of creating a superagency powerful enough to make and implement plans affecting the entire economy.

Although these laws and institutions sound powerful, in reality Japan's wartime economic mobilization was characterized by mismanagement, poor coordination, inter-agency conflict, piecemeal controls, and little overall planning. For example, as late as 1944, 55 per cent of all weapons were still produced in the private sector.[8] The old zaibatsu bitterly resisted these new controls to the war's end. Still, Japan's economy was relatively more totalitarian than Germany's, which did not begin to centralize planning until 1942. But most importantly, many of the institutions, policies, and industries had been established that would serve as the basis of Japan's postwar development.

THE OCCUPATION REFORMS

The Occupation reforms were as revolutionary in restructuring Japan's political economy as the Meiji reforms had been almost 80 years earlier. Although the Occupation of Japan was supposed to be a joint Allied responsibility, most of the Occupation troops and administrative staff were American. The Occupation administration was officially called the Supreme Command for Allied Powers (SCAP), and was led by General Douglas MacArthur. MacArthur's brilliance as both a general and administrator was colored by a powerful messianic egoism, and he strongly influenced many important policies, particularly Article 9 of the Japanese Constitution renouncing the sovereign right to have a military force. Although SCAP ruled Japan indirectly through the Japanese ministries, sovereignty was transferred to SCAP for the Occupation's duration (1945–52). In theory, SCAP would issue various policy directives and the bureaucracy would implement them. In practice, however, the bureaucracy would tailor or even obstruct SCAP policies if they conflicted with Japanese élite interests, and many times SCAP had to exert considerable pressure to push through controversial reforms. Despite its enormous powers and responsibilities, however, SCAP was ultimately responsible to the Joint Chiefs of Staff in Washington.

United States government planning for the Occupation of Japan began as early as August 1942, developed steadily over several years, and eventually included dozens of committees and hundreds of individuals throughout the wartime bureaucracy united behind the goal to develop a policy that would prevent Japan from ever again posing a threat to world peace. From the start policy-makers were divided over what policy could best accomplish this objective. Three groups – hardline, moderate, and soft – emerged with each claiming its policy could best prevent a revival of Japanese militarism. Yet if any one of these three policies had been selected and strictly followed, Japan's subsequent political economic development would have been vastly altered.[9]

The hardline policy would have had the severest consequences for Japan's economy. The hardliners formed a strong and vocal group which included Treasury Secretary Henry Morgenthau and State Department China hands, and was supported by the Allied governments and exiled East Asian representatives.[10] Their objective was to harshly punish Japan for its militiarism by destroying all its war-making capabilities and turning it into an agricultural country with an economic level of 1926–30. This would be accomplished by dismantling all heavy industry and most related light industries which would then be sent abroad as reparations. In addition, all foreign trade would be cut off, thus forcing Japan to put all its energies into agriculture. Politically, there would be trials and purges of all war criminals, including the Emperor. The imperial system would be dismantled and replaced with a democratic form of government. There were no provisions for American aid or land and labor reforms.

The short-term results of this policy would have been catastrophic: Without aid there would have been mass starvation, epidemics, and social upheaval.[11] The economic structure would have soon resembled that of present day Guatemala or Honduras with most people engaged in agriculture and the rest in small craft industries while small middle and wealthy classes sat atop the mass poverty. Despite the restrictions some trade would eventually have emerged but Japan would have suffered chronic balance of payments deficits. With the trauma over the loss of the Emperor and absence of land or labor reforms the masses eventually would have embraced socialism as the answer to their severe economic and social problems. With the right thoroughly purged and no military to repress the left, a government of socialists and communists committed to an agarian communist development model would have soon been elected.

As a result Japan today would have had an economic and political structure similar to that of Burma or Albania – autarkic and unaligned, concerned chiefly with feeding, clothing, and caring for its poverty-stricken masses, while its economy would be plagued by the problems of inefficiency, waste, corruption, and apathy characteristic of all socialist countries.

Composed of New Deal advocates in both the government and SCAP, the moderate group was guided by idealism and altruism. They maintained that an extensive program of demilitarization and democratization was the best way to prevent a revival of militarism and make Japan a peaceful, responsible member of the world community. Specific steps to this end included massive aid, and widespread political, economic, and social reforms. While the zaibatsu would be dismembered and its heavy industries sent abroad as reparations, Washington would help build up Japan's light industry through subsidies and opening American and Asian markets to Japanese products. Although war criminals would be purged, the

Emperor would be retained as a symbol of the nation while a democratic constitution would transfer sovereignty to the people.

As a result, the present economic structure, income distribution, and standard of living would probably resemble that of contemporary Taiwan. Without a heavy industrial sector exporting such important items as steel, petrochemicals. automobiles, and ships, Japan's economic growth would have been much lower than its historical rate. Politically, without a heavy industrial sector to rely on, the conservative party would have been far more conciliatory and centrist. Moderate factions of both the conservatives and socialists might eventually have joined to form a strong centrist party oriented to both growth and distribution. While Japan would not be as wealthy as it is today, the quality of life for most Japanese would probably be much better than now.

The soft line policy experts were led by State Department Japan experts who were willing to collaborate with Japan's wartime leaders. The promotion of Japan's access to world markets was seen as the best means of ensuring no rebirth of militarism. There were no plans for labor, land, or zaibatsu reforms, nor would there have been any reparations. Likewise, Japan would have been allowed to keep its imperial system and Meiji Constitution while purges and trials would have been largely limited to military leaders.

If followed, this policy would have allowed the continuation of the prewar inefficient heavy industrial sector, lop-sided economic growth, and inequalitarian income distribution. Without the zaibatsu reforms Japanese industry would have remained a 'cordial oligarchy' characterized by the aimiable division of markets at all times and lack of product innovation rather than the 'cut-throat oligarchy' of product innovation and fierce competition during periods of economic expansion (through continued cartelization during downturns) that it is today.[12] Without strong competitive pressures growth would have been significantly less in both quality and quantity than the historic rate. Without land or labor reforms a mass consumer market would not have developed, while the gap between the wealthy élite and poverty-stricken masses would have been as bad as ever. Japanese politics would have polarized while the prewar repression of the left continued. Today, politically and economically Japan would probably resemble countries like Mexico or Brazil, without benefit of their rich natural resources.

Fortunately, none of these plans became the dominant policy. Japan's present highly developed political economy is a result of a largely fortuitous combination of the best aspects of all three plans. SCAP's policies passed through three distinct phases. The first phase lasted from the first arrival of the Occupation in September 1945 and continued up through 1947. It concentrated on policies designed to demilitarize and democratize Japan. The second phase, the so-called 'reverse course', evolved during 1947 and into 1948 as Washington now realized it had to build up Japan economically as part of its global containment policy against the Soviet Union. By making Japan the 'workshop of Asia', Washington could achieve its inter-related goals of strengthening the world economy and containing communism. The third phase began after the outbreak of the Korean War in 1950 when Washington tried to make Japan a military as well as economic power in East Asia.

The initial Occupation policy was a combination of moderate and hardline elements. Demilitarization involved the hardline policy of purges, trials, and reparations while MacArthur was instructed 'not to assume any responsibility for the reconstruction of strengthening of the Japanese economy'.[13] The State Department Pauley Mission to Japan in the Fall of 1945 agreed with the hardline position that Japan's economic level should be reduced to that of 1926–30. The purges were mostly directed against military and zaibatsu leaders while the economic ministries were left intact. This resolved the pre-1945 struggle for control of the economy between the corporate world and bureaucrats in favor of the latter while bringing a new generation of more dynamic leaders to the former. Democratization, however, involved the moderate program of generous aid, land, labor, and zaibatsu reforms, and the creation of a democratic consti-tution. Together these elements of both moderate idealism and hard-line punitive policy radically overhauled Japan's political economy by providing the basic structural reforms that were essential to later economic growth.

Massive aid was the prerequisite for the other reforms. Because of severe shortages of food, medicine, clothing, transportation, building materials, and fuel Japan faced the spector of mass starvation, epi-demics, and social unrest. Without aid a large percentage of the population might well have perished while the rest would have been so preoccupied with day-to-day existence that there would have been little energy left to contribute to national reconstruction. Between September 1945 and December 1951, the United States provided $2.118 billion worth of aid that enabled Japan to move beyond this subsistence level of existence.[14] Part of this aid helped repatriate over six million Japanese stranded overseas after the war and filled the balance of payments gap until Japanese exports revived. As important was aid targeted to such basic industries as electric power, shipbuilding and coal mining.

Land and labor reforms were vital to transforming mass rural and urban poverty into the present '90 per cent middle class society'. In 1945 as much as 50 per cent of the population was rural and in desperate need of land reform. Farm tenancy had risen steadily throughout the Meiji era as industrialization was financed by squeezing the peasants until they fell into debt and lost their land to creditors. By 1945 as much as 70 per cent of all peasants were either partial or full-time tenants paying rents in kind of as high as 50 per cent. Conditions were so bad that peasants were often forced to sell their daughters into industrial employment or even prostitution.[15]

SCAP targeted land reform as a key element of democratization and pushed it through despite persistent resistence by the Japanese government. Still it was not until October 1946 that the government finally agreed to enact a law strong enough to bring about real reforms. Even then the Ministry of Agriculture refused to implement land reform until SCAP issued a directive allowing it no choice. Despite these delays, by 1949 about 88 per cent of the land was cultivated by its owners, and by 1953 the percentage of total agricultural income that went to rents had been reduced from 16.6 per cent before 1945 to 0.2 per cent. These new incentives were combined with new technology to cause huge productivity increases that enabled Japan to maintain an 85 per cent food self-sufficiency up through the late 1970s despite a 30 per cent increase in population.[16]

As a result, the poverty-stricken, exploited, resentful peasants of 1945 quickly became mass consuming farmers with a solid stake in the system. The LDP had largely remained in power throughout the postwar era because it had the farm vote solidly tied up in gerrymandered Diet districts that favored rural areas. A virtuous circle emerged between LDP rule and economic growth: continued conservative rule has allowed the LDP to concentrate on promoting the industrial policies that have fueled growth and the subsequent prosperity in turn has kept the LDP in office so that it can continue those successful policies. Ironically, if left to themselves, the conservatives would not have enacted any significant land reform. The resulting discontent would have caused the rural districts eventually to vote socialist. In the long run the conservatives would have been shut out of power, thus radically changing the course of Japan's postwar political and economic development.

Labor reforms also proved to be important contributions to building a mass domestic market and took away leftist programs that the conservatives would not have implemented on their own. The plight of laborers had become as desperate as that of farmers with factory workers in May 1946 earning only 54 per cent of what it cost to live, teachers 52 per cent, and lower civil servants only 37 per cent.[17] Like land reform, Japan's government and business also severely resisted labor reforms and only after continued SCAP pressure enacted three laws that radically changed labor's working conditions and bargaining power. The Trade Union Law of December 1945 guaranteed labor's right to organize, engage in collective bargaining, and strike. The Labor Relations Adjustment Law of September 1946 provided labor relations boards at both the national and prefectural levels to mediate any disputes. Finally, the Labor Standards Law of March 1947 set the minimum standards for work hours, vacations, restrictions on female and child labor, safety, sanitation, sick leave, accident compensation, and other workplace concerns.[18]

These labor reforms both strengthened and weakened the political left. Union membership had never reached half a million before the war, and unions were abolished during the war, but by 1949 over seven million workers out of a total industrial workforce of 14 million were enrolled in more than 35 000 unions, virtually all of which were coopted to support left-wing parties. Yet SCAP simultaneously weakened the left by taking the issue of labor reform away from them. In addition, SCAP's 'red purge' from 1949 to 1951 caused union membership to sag to around 5.5 million. Although most union members supported the left, their primary concern was wage increases and job stability. With a base level of 100 in 1955, wages rose from about 20 in 1946 to 80 in 1952, helping to build a mass domestic market in which Japanese corporations could exploit economies of scale, thus lowering costs and improving quality.[19]

SCAP's attempt to break up the zaibatsu and deconcentrate industry was another vital reform that fueled Japan's later economic dynamism. The Anti-monopoly Law of April 1947 was designed to break up the family-owned holding companies that Washington believed had contributed to Japanese militarism. The Law prohibited all trusts, cartels, interlocking corporate directorates, agreements in restraint of trade, and other monopoly arrangements. To this end SCAP created a Holding Company Liquidation Commission to confiscate all zaibatsu stocks and sell them to private investors, and a Fair Trade Commission to regulate industry. This policy was initially highly successful: by 1951 83 zaibatsu holding companies had been broken up and some 5000 companies forced to reorganize themselves financially, which meant some 7.57 billion yen worth of stocks had been resold to smaller investors.[20]

The second part of SCAP's zaibatsu reform involved the Elimination of Excessive Concentration of Economic Power Law enacted in December 1947 which was designed to break up individual companies thought to have too much control over the market. Although 1200 firms were initially identified, this number was reduced to 324 because of severe Japanese and some American protests that this would gut the economy. In the face of this protest SCAP eventually announced that the program was complete after only nine companies were actually dissolved.[21]

With the zaibatsu reforms Japan's economy enjoyed the best of all possible worlds. The dissolution of the holding companies freed Japanese firms from the often stifling conservative controls of the old zaibatsu families while SCAP's abandonment of the efforts to dissolve individual companies kept the powerful individual firms intact. The old zaibatsu quickly reformed into new dynamic industrial groups (keiretsu) organized around banks rather than holding companies. Japanese industry was thus transformed from the 'cordial oligopoly' of pre–1945 to its 'cut-throat oligopoly' since.

Another vital American contribution to modern Japan was the rationalization of government economic policy-making and implementation. Before 1945, the military, bureaucracy, and zaibatsu had struggled for control over the economy. But SCAP's elimination of the military and break up of the zaibatsu left the bureaucracy in undisputed control. This power allowed an 'economic general staff' within the bureaucracy led by MITI and the MOF to create and implement the rational macroeconomic and industrial targeting policies that have fueled Japan's rapid growth ever since.[22]

SCAP's purge of over 200 000 individuals in both the bureaucracy and industry succeeded in eliminating much of the old conservative leadership, thus allowing a new generation of talented and visionary leaders to take their place. But the purge was not evenly distributed across Japan's political economy. The military bureaucracy was completely purged while most of the zaibatsu leaders and many of the political leaders were similarly barred from continuing their respective careers. In contrast only about 1800 civilian bureaucrats were purged – over 70 per cent of whom were from the now abolished Home Ministry which had housed the notorious kempeitai (Japanese Gestapo). Only 42 officials were purged from the Ministry of Commerce and Industry (which later became MITI) and only nine from the Ministry of Finance.[23] Thus there was a strong continuity between the prewar, wartime, and postwar leadership of the economic ministries. This is an example of SCAP policy being more important for what it did not do than for what it did; SCAP naively believed the economic ministries had been apolitical during the war.

The enactment of the 1947 Constitution was the final and most significant pillar of SCAP's democratization policy. The declaration of a democratic constitution was preceded by several important steps that swept aside much of the remaining wartime totalitarian controls. A SCAP directive on 4 October 1945 abolished the wartime Imperial Rule Assistance Association and simultaneously removed any restrictions on all political, civil, and religious liberties, freed all political prisoners, and allowed the formation of political parties. On 1 January 1946 the Emperor renounced his divinity over public radio and later traveled around Japan showing the people first hand that he was not a god. The peerage was abolished except for the immediate royal family. Although SCAP had forced the government to agree to the basic framework of a democratic constitution as early as March 1946, it did not become law until 3 May 1947. Enacted as an amendment to the 1889 Meiji Constitution, the 1947 Constitution abolished the old system of absolute monarchy and erected a parliamentary democracy in its place.

Again the Japanese government would have been incapable of enacting basic constitutional reforms without SCAP's continual pressure and guidance. Between November 1945 and February 1946 the Shidehara government submitted several drafts of constitutions, all of which were rejected by SCAP as simply modified versions of the Meiji Constitution. Finally, in exasperation during late February SCAP drew up its own version and gave it to the government, which finally rubber-stamped it on 6 March 1946. Without a firmly established democratic political system, Japanese politics could have been as volatile, unstable, and repressive as that of South Korea.

By mid-1947 SCAP had pushed through basic structural reforms of Japan's political economy that were essential to creating a democratic society and providing the basis for later rapid growth. But the deepening Cold War with the Soviet Union forced Washington to change its policy from demilitarization and democratization to an emphasis on revitalizing Japan's economy and reintegrating it within the world economy. The 'reverse course' aimed to make Japan the 'workshop of Asia' and key defense bulwark against the Soviet Union in the western Pacific.

SCAP now concentrated on overcoming specific economic problems afflicting Japan by forcing the government to pursue rational policies and creating new institutions to formulate and implement those policies. The biggest economic problem of the immediate postwar period was hyperinflation. With 1934–36 as 100, the index of wholesale prices skyrocketed from 350 in 1945 to 20 876 in 1949 while Retail prices in Tokyo rose from 308 to 24 337.[24] Although this inflation was a great help to those in debt – particularly the zaibatsu – it was a disaster for most Japanese, whose real wages plummeted during this time. The hyperinflation also threatened to price Japan out of world markets.

The Japanese government was chiefly responsible for this hyperinflation since it continued to pay off its war debts to the zaibatsu and other economic interests. From the end of the war until 24 June 1946 when SCAP ordered these payments stopped, the government paid out some 26.6 billion yen to the war contractors, amounting to one-third of the total Japan had spent for military purposes between September 1937 and August 1945.[25] But a month after SCAP's decision, the payments were resumed through the newly created Reconstruction Finance Bank (RFB). The government covered these debts by printing money: by January 1949 there was 12 times more money in circulation than there had been in August 1945.[26]

SCAP issued repeated calls to the government to adopt such measures as wage and price controls and a balanced budget, but these calls were ignored by the government. The politicians received most of their funds from the corporations, and if they cut off the flow of money to industry, their own funds would eventually dry up. Again, as in all other areas of Japan's political economy in desperate need of reform, the government and politicians put their own short-term needs before the country as a whole and were thus incapable of enacting the far-reaching reforms necessary to overcome these problems.

Finally, in February 1949 a State Department mission led by Joseph Dodge arrived in Tokyo to submit an extensive program designed to cut the hyperinflation and stimulate genuine economic growth. The key measures included ordering the government to balance its budget, establish a single exchange rate, and create new institutions to guide economic development.

The 'Dodge line' proved a tremendous success. Through forced fiscal responsibility the budget deficit of 160 billion yen in 1948 became a surplus of 260 billion in 1949, while new issues of currency increased by only 20 billion yen in 1949 compared to 100 billion yen the previous year. Although the percentage of government expenditures to GNP rose slightly between 1949 and 1951 – from 51 per cent to 53 per cent – it plunged dramatically to 34 per cent of GNP in 1951 as a result of continued government austerity and genuine economic growth. Statistically economic growth declined from 40 per cent of GNP in 1948 to 11 per cent in 1949, but the former figure was fictitious because it was largely based on increased American aid and government subsidies to industry. Real wages actually rose 35 per cent in 1949.[27] These reforms set Japan's fiscal and monetary system on a firm basis and established the tradition of small, lean government and balanced budgets that continued for the next 20 years.

As important was the creation of a single, fixed exchange rate for the yen that would promote exports. The rate of 360 yen to a dollar was set at the point where all major industries could export profitably.[28] The yen became increasingly undervalued over the next 22 years up to 1971 when the Nixon administration finally forced its revaluation, and proved a powerful subsidy to Japanese exports and non-tariff barrier against competitive imports.

Dodge also presided over the establishment of a number of government institutions designed to help develop the economy. The old Ministry of Commerce and Industry was revamped in 1949 to become the Ministry of International Trade and Industry (MITI). Dodge provided MITI with two laws that were its most powerful industrial policy tools up through the 1970s. The Foreign Trade and Exchange Control Law of 1949 allowed MITI to control all foreign exchange and allocate it to industries it had targeted for development. The Foreign Investment Law of 1950 prevented most foreigners from investing in Japan unless they were willing to give up the repatriation of their profits. Unable either to invest or trade freely in Japan because of such barriers, foreign firms resorted to selling their technology to Japanese firms. But all technology imports had to be approved and allocated by MITI, giving it vast additional powers to develop strategic industries. Between 1950 and 1968 Japanese firms paid $1.4 billion for over 10 000 technology licensing agreements with foreign firms. This was a tremendous bargain for Japanese industry since it avoided the huge R & D costs and was able to jump right into production. It is unlikely that major industries such as automobiles, electronics, computers, petrochemicals, synthetic textiles, or electrical machinery could ever have developed without MITI's industrial policy-making and implementation powers.[29]

During that same visit Dodge also allowed the anti-monopoly laws to be revised so that temporary cartels and increased concentration of industries were allowed while no laws were enacted which specified what ratio of equity to capital a bank loan must have or that prevented cross-sharing between banks and firms. These new rules allowed MITI to help reorganize the former zaibatsu firms into the modern, efficient keiretsu system built around banks rather than holding companies. The typical keiretsu would consist of a bank, a number of companies involved in various government-designated growth industries, and a trading company to promote its exports.

In 1951 Dodge reappeared in Japan to create several new financial institutions dedicated to promoting Japanese industries. The Export Bank and Japan Development Bank were founded with American aid of 15 billion yen and 10 billion yen, respectively. That same year the Fiscal Investment and Loan Plan (FILP) was created with capital drawn from postal savings accounts. Government subsidies to industries channeled through financial institutions such as these were a vital boost to development and comprised anywhere from 19 to 38 per cent of all capital raised by industry up through 1961. With such institutions under its control, MITI was able, for example in 1956, to supervise the distribution of over 169 billion yen while its annual budget was only 8.2 billion yen.[30]

Washington's sponsorship of Japan's reintegration within the world economy went hand-in-hand with the Dodge reforms in revamping Japan's economy. Triangular trade between the complementary economies of the Untied States, Japan, and Southeast Asia was seen as the first step to bringing Japan back into the world economy. The access of Japanese firms to the world's largest market allowed them to establish huge economies of scale with which they could lower prices and raise quality. But in order to complete the third leg of the triangle – Japan-Southeast Asian trade – the United States had to overcome bitter European resistance to Japanese exports to the region. The Europeans viewed the region as their own market and feared the revival of Japanese prewar unfair trade tactics and Southeast Asia's eventual incorporation into a new 'Co-prosperity Sphere'. Washington continually pressured the Europeans to open up their colonial markets while tying American aid to the region to purchases of Japanese goods. Even after the Occupation ended the United States continued its role of sponsoring Japan's reintegration within the world economy. After three years of resistance by other members Washington finally convinced GATT to accept Japanese membership in 1955; similar reluctance in the OECD was overcome by 1964. Both organizations' members were concerned about continued unfair Japanese trade practices. Japan was allowed membership in both GATT and the OECD only after agreeing to stop its neo-mercantilism. As will be seen, the members of those organizations are still waiting for Japan to comply with its earlier promises.

But this trade did not really take off until after the Korean War broke out in June 1950. American procurements alone in 1950–52 totaled $1.565 billion, and $5.6 billion for the whole decade, or 37 per cent and 11 per cent, respectively, of all foreign exchange for the two periods. These procurements helped boost Japan's industrial production index from 90 in 1950 to 140 in 1953. Japanese exports expanded vigorously at this time, too, increasing 270 per cent between 1949 and 1951.[31] All this set off a virtuous economic circle whereby more production led to greater economies of scale which in turn lowered prices and raised quality, the profits of which were reinvested in new capital and technology to create a better comparative advantage, and so on. United States military procurements continued to have a diminishing stimulatory effect on Japan's economy. Between 1960 and 1967 Vietnam War procurements totaled a further $2.646 billion, and procurements continue through today although their impact is now insignificant within the vast Japanese economy.[32]

Ironically, even the reparations Japan was forced to pay turned out to be a boost for its economy. Early on SCAP resisted the demands of the different East Asian countries which totaled more than Japan's entire existing assets. Tokyo eventually reached reparations agreements with 11 East Asian countries and sent over $1.5 billion dollars worth of either grants tied to purchases of Japanese products or outdated equipment that made the recipient dependent on Japan for spare parts. Regardless, the reparations became an excellent export subsidy for Japanese industry and advanced its penetration of East Asian markets.[33]

Although Washington had been pressuring MacArthur to encourage Japanese rearmament before 1950, Article 9 always prevented

SCAP from forcing the issue. After the Korean War broke out, however, MacArthur forced Prime Minister Yoshida to create a 75 000-man National Police Force. A Japan with a military force as strong as its economy was seen as vital to containing the Soviet Union and its allies in the Far East. The price for the restoration of sovereignty to Japan was Tokyo's agreement to conclude a military alliance with the United States. As a result, on 2 September 1951 Tokyo signed a peace treaty with the Western allies (the Soviet bloc countries refused to sign the treaty), and a security treaty with the United States. The Occupation ended six months later, but American bases remained in Japan to guarantee its security.

CONCLUSION

Japan's growth into an economic superpower was not inevitable – its present, deepening economic power is based on a series of previous development policies followed by several different regimes over a period of half a millenium. If the leadership of any of those regimes had followed different economic policies, Japan's current economic structure and level could be significantly different. How different would Japan and the world be today if the Tokugawa had opened up rather than withdrawn from the world or Japan had not gone to war in the 1930s?

The seven-year American Occupation was the most important of all the regimes to rule Japan. The American Occupation was immensely successful in achieving almost all of its major aims. Politically, Japan was transformed from a totalitarian system theoretically under a divine emperor with absolute power into a parliamentary democracy with human rights guaranteed for all. SCAP's land, labor, zaibatsu, and administrative reform policies laid the foundations for Japan's 'economic miracle'. As has been seen, it is unlikely that Japan's government could have achieved any of these far-reaching political or economic goals by itself. In fact, SCAP reforms were often implemented in the face of fierce resistance by the ruling élite. In retrospect, Japan's economic 'miracle' is based on the Occupation policies that set the stage for its dramatic economic development since.

NOTES

1. John Hall, *Japan: From Prehistory to Modern Times*, p. 122.
2. Ibid., p. 210.
3. Ibid., p. 209–20.
4. Marius Jansen, 'Modernization and Foreign Policy in Meiji Japan', in Robert Ward's *Political Development in Modern Japan*, p. 153.
5. See Roger Hackett, 'Political Modernization and the Meiji Genro', in Ward, pp. 65–97.
6. Marius Jansen, 'Changing Japanese Attitudes toward Modernization', in Ward, op. cit., p. 75.
7. Richard Rice, 'Economic Mobilization in Wartime Japan: Business, Bureaucracy, and Military in Conflict', *Journal of Asian Studies*, Vol. 38, No. 4, August 1979, p. 695.
8. Ibid., p. 693.
9. See Tasuo Uchino. *Japan's Postwar Economy*, 1983.
10. See Robert Wolfe, *American's as Proconsuls: United States Military Governments in Japan and Germany, 1944–52*, for details on the different policy schools.
11. Grant Goodman, *The American Occupation of Japan*, p. 15.
12. Chalmers Johnson, *MITI and the Japanese Economic Miracle*, p. 178.
13. Lawrence Redford, *The Occupation of Japan*, p. 290.
14. Goodman, op. cit., p. 15.
15. Redford, op. cit., pp. 130–2, 149–51.
16. Ibid.
17. Kazuo Kawai, *Japan's American Interlude*, p. 161.
18. Redford, op. cit., p. 173.
19. Ibid., p. 286.
20. Ibid., p. 236, Kawai, op. cit., p. 147.
21. Goodman, op. cit., p. 18.
22. Johnson, op. cit., p. 49.
23. Kawai, op. cit., p. 143.
24. Redford, op. cit., p. 70.
25. Ibid., p. 50.
26. Kawai, op. cit., p. 178.
27. Redford, op. cit., p. 79, Johnson, op. cit., p. 208.
28. Ibid., p. 79.
29. Redford, op. cit., p. 127.
30. Johnson, op. cit., pp. 208, 203.
31. Ibid., p. 199, Redford, op. cit., pp. 290, 287.
32. Johnson, op. cit., p. 200.
33. Takafusa Nakamura, *Japanese Economic Growth*, p. 31.

5 The Corporate 'Miracle'

Japan's corporate world seems to have achieved a productivity and managerial 'miracle' as profound as 'miracles' affecting Japan's political and economic development, and an increasing flood of books, articles, and television shows annually appears attempting to analyze the 'Japanese challenge' of this 'corporate miracle'. Most of these reports conclude that American and other foreign firms must either adapt the 'Japanese corporate model' or face a continual decline. What is the Japanese corporate model? Is its emergence a miracle as many argue? And regardless of whether it is a miracle or not, how does Japan's obvious corporate vitality relate to this rather ominous sounding threat called the Japanese challenge?

The last two questions are interrelated. Certainly Japan's economic transformation would not have been complete without the development of a distinct Japanese managerial style that maximized worker productivity and product quality, and a Japanese corporate strategy that stressed a long-term effort to continually develop new and better products at a cheaper price, with which to flood the world's markets and devastate any rival companies. And Japan's dynamic corporations are clearly part of the Japanese challenge.

But the most important aspect of the Japanese challenge has been the ability of the Japanese government, LDP, and corporate world to work together since the early 1950s to create and implement rational industrial policies that target strategic industries for development and fuel growth rates double the average of their democratic industrial rivals. Rational industrial policies are the major reason for Japan's transformation into the world's most dynamic economic superpower. Other industrial countries are thus challenged either to follow similar means in an attempt to emulate Japan's success or else fall further behind economically and technologically. There is nothing any more 'miraculous' about the development of Japan's corporate culture, than there was about Japan's economic and political development. All three areas developed rapidly from a fortuitous combination of favorable internal and external factors.

What then is the Japanese corporate model? Two of the more popular books that present models of Japan's corporate culture are William Ouchi's *Theory Z* and Pascale and Athos' *The Art of Japanese Management*.[1] These two books describe an ideal 'family-

113

like' corporate world in which worker harmony prevails based on such institutions as lifetime employment, seniority-based advancement, and bottom-up decision-making. Other books, such as Robert Cole's *Japanese Blue Collar*, William Zimmerman's *Doing Business with the Japanese*, and Jon Woronoff's *Japan's Wasted Workers*, paint a less ideal vision of what it is really like to work for a Japanese corporation, revealing that, among other things, bitter conflicts often swirl beneath the seemingly harmonious surface, or higher productivity is bought not just with quality control circles but at high human costs including high-speed production lines, unpaid overtime, and a minimal family life. This chapter will analyze Japan's corporate culture in two sections; the first untangles the ideals from the realities of Japan's corporate culture while the second analyzes the relative successes and failures of Japanese firms when they attempt to recreate their corporate culture abroad.

IDEALS AND REALITIES

Any proper analysis of Japan's corporate culture must carefully weigh the ideals against the realities. Although the largest Japanese companies do try very hard to live up to the 'Japanese corporate model', they can afford to do so in part because of several special advantages they enjoy that their counterparts in other industrial countries do not have. From the 1950s and through the 1970s, Japanese corporations had access to huge amounts of low cost capital supplied by the Bank of Japan via their keiretsu banks; since then most Japanese firms use internal savings for most of their capital needs. Regardless, unlike their foreign rivals, Japanese firms have not had to depend on volatile stock markets for their finance. As important continues to be the web of import barriers and huge export subsidies that have simultaneously allowed Japanese corporations freedom from significant foreign competition at home and the price edge over their corporate rivals in foreign markets. These advantages are further boosted by countless official and unofficial price, production, technology and market cartels. Thus, Japanese corporations can well afford to take a long-term outlook in terms of profit and market share while their foreign counterparts are dependent on volatile stock markets for much of their funds, and without government support are bashed by Japanese dumping.[2]

But even with these special advantages, only about 27 per cent of

Japan's workforce enjoys lifetime employment. Japan's dual economy, with its highly efficient corporate world floating on a sea of small- and medium-sized corporations, is another special advantage that foreign corporations do not have. Toyota produces more cars than Ford with only one-seventh the number of workers because it and other Japanese manufacturing companies rely on small- and medium-sized companies to supply most components. During recessions large corporation can afford to retain their lean workforces while cutting back orders from their suppliers. It is the small- and medium-sized companies whose workers do not enjoy employment security and benefits that suffer during recessions. There is a dual economy in terms of productivity as well. According to a 1981 Economic White Paper, there is a huge productivity gap between the most highly efficient large firms and the most inefficient small companies – 88 times in Japan compared to 41 times in Germany and only 14 times in the United States. With American productivity measured at 100, Japan's overall productivity falls far short at 88 per cent.[3]

Yet, despite all these advantages, most Japanese corporations still fall short of achieving the Japanese corporate ideal. First of all, 'lifetime employment' is not actually lifetime. In most companies workers must retire at an average age 57.8 while the average male life expectancy is about 74 years. The company's lump retirement payment and monthly government social security checks are not enough to sustain a worker and his family for the rest of their lives so most must find a 'second career' after retirement. Most end up running small 'Mom and Pop' retail outlets which, with government protection, have become an important form of indirect welfare as well as another huge import barrier protecting Japanese industry.

Even without 'lifetime employment', most companies do not guarantee employment until the official retirement age. During periods of recession and yen strengthening many companies force out older, less efficient workers with 'golden parachutes' of either larger retirement payments or sinecures in smaller companies tied to the corporation. As Japan's economy is slowly opened to increased foreign competition, Japanese companies are increasingly experimenting with limited forms of merit advancement systems parallel to the traditional seniority-based advancement system.

Another myth is that Japanese workers enter an established firm directly after high school or college graduation. For firms with 1000 to 4999 employees, for example, only one-third of male blue collar recruits are new graduates while the remainder have had experience in other firms. The number of employees quitting their first company is extremely high, with turnover rates for male workers in large firms in their early 20s averaging 20–25 per cent.[4] So large numbers of Japanese workers reject the 'harmonious, family atmosphere' of the big companies for a variety of reasons including an inability to fit in, lack of advancement opportunities, unfulfilling work, or better opportunities elsewhere.

Yet another myth is that the 'lifetime employment' system is an inherited characteristic of Japanese culture and society. In reality, lifetime employment first emerged after World War I when, during the rapid take-off of Japan's industry, a few larger firms attempted to secure an increasingly limited supply of skilled workers by offering them guaranteed employment and other benefits. Until then workers were hired and fired according to company needs, as in any other industrial country. But working conditions remained generally abysmal and labor-management relations were strained up to the war's end whether the company had a lifetime employment system or not.

Working conditions only began to improve during the Occupation when SCAP pushed through three key labor reforms that forced firms to fulfill minimal overtime, sanitation, and safety standards. Although SCAP's labor reforms and purges had simultaneously coopted most of the Left's demands while eliminating their leadership, management-labor relations remained strained throughout the 1950s in most industries and firms. Most companies instituted some form of lifetime employment system to secure an increasingly limited supply of skilled workers as the economy rapidly expanded, yet most industries continued to be plagued by strikes for better working conditions and wages.

Management won two huge strikes at the end of the decade that led to the collapse of radical control over most trade unions. Management's defeat of a three-month strike led by leftist leaders in the steel industry in 1959 destroyed radical control over the steel union. In a union election following the strike, moderates overwhelmingly won out over the radicals and have remained in control ever since. A similar shift occured following the end of a 300-day strike at the Mitsui Company's Miike Mine in 1960. The Mitsui strike represents the last real attempt by radical factions to control the unions. With the two most powerful unions broken it was clear to all workers that cooperation rather than confrontation was the only viable alternative. Since then most private unions have been solidly in control of moderate factions.

Thus by the early 1960s most large firms had developed harmonious management-labor relations and guaranteed lifetime employment. Management alleviated any remaining discord through the traditional Japanese tactic of dividing and conquering the opposition by coopting the moderate workers with enterprise unions which gave *Union* them opportunities for faster advancement and benefits than the trade unions. Eventually, virtually all the workers drifted over to the enterprise union as it became apparent that it was the only advancement track. In 1984 12.5 million workers or 29.1 per cent of all workers were in unions, virtually all in enterprise unions.[5] Japan's rapid economic growth itself diminished much discontent as wages rose almost as fast.

Overall the number of working days lost through industrial disputes per 1000 employees in Japan during the 1980s is less than one-quarter the number 30 years earlier. In the five-year periods 1955–59, 1960–64, and 1965–69, the numbers steadily declined from 254 per year, to 177, and finally 107, respectively. Japan, however, experienced an upsurge of strikes during the early 1970s as a result of economic slowdown following OPEC's quadrupling of oil prices in 1973. Between 1970 and 1974, the number of working days lost per 1000 employees rose to 151, but dropped dramatically to only 69 in 1975–80. In comparison during 1975–80, the number of work days lost per 1000 employees in the United States, Britain, and West Germany averaged 389, 521, and 41, respectively. Between 1981–85 Japan's rate had dropped to a miniscule 30 compared to 130 in the United States, 440 in Britain, and 50 in West Germany.[6]

These caveats aside, what are the main pillars of the Japanese corporate model? Although it is clear that no Japanese corporation guarantees its workers 'lifetime employment', Japanese workers in large firms do enjoy much greater job security than their counterparts elsewhere. Ideally, blue-collar and white-collar workers are hired straight out of high school and college, respectively, and remain with the company until their retirement some time after age 55. Advancement proceeds according to a seniority-based step-by-step 'escalator system'. Workers are never laid off during recessions, but are instead reassigned elsewhere within the company and kept busy cleaning or servicing plant and equipment.

The advantage of lifetime employment for the company is a committed workforce that can concentrate on doing its job without fear of being fired in recessions. In particularly hard times, workers will even allow their benefits to be cut back as long as their job security is guaranteed. With most large firms using seniority systems, the longer a worker remains in the company, the less likelihood he will jump ship since he would have to start out towards the bottom of the escalator in another company despite his skills. Of course, if a worker's freedom to move elsewhere diminishes with his age, his dedication to his company becomes questionable since he has no choice but to give himself completely. Thus, large companies rarely lose skilled workers from either recessions or attrition, and save time and money that foreign companies spend in large retraining programs.

There are some significant disadvantages to lifetime employment as well. The seniority system rewards loyalty and not competence. At the lower levels of the escalator highly skilled, creative, or productive workers are generally promoted at the same rate as poorer quality workers. Thus, there is little incentive to excell. At the higher escalator levels where the job pyramid begins to narrow, competition begins to become fierce as workers scramble for fewer jobs. Patrons battle each other to push their followers into key positions. Connections, not worker quality, become the key to advancement, causing considerable acrimony. But this structural trade-off of the advantage of a loyal workforce versus the disadvantage of not enjoying the full potential of its best worker's skills, is relatively mild compared to the side-effects elsewhere of maintaining this seniority, non-market system. Corporations often need government protection during recessions so they do not have to lay off workers. The subsequent informal import barriers through 'administrative guidance' and cartels mean higher prices to consumers and even greater disadvantages to foreign firms battling for miniscule shares of Japanese markets.

But job security is not enough to account for the high productivity that characterizes Japan's largest corporations. If job security and promotion is a given, there is no incentive for workers to work hard. So Japanese managers place a constant emphasis on promoting a corporate *esprit de corps* that wrings increased productivity out of workers. Unlike most foreign managers which view workers as mere 'factors of production' to be used and disgarded as needed, Japanese managers value employees as 'total human beings'. Workers are constantly pushed to consider the company a huge extended family that is concerned with the welfare and happiness of all its members. Managers appeal to the traditional values of groupism, obligation, loyalty, hierarchy along patron-follower lines (sempai-kohai), and hard work that have already been deeply socialized in most Japanese by family and school.

Employees are continually socialized in these ideals through both formal and informal means, and this socialization often begins even before the candidate is formally hired. For example, with the tightening labor market and continual economic expansion, the competition among firms for Tokyo University graduates is becoming increasingly fierce. In 1953 the government ruled that no firms could actively recruit students until after the first of October, six months before graduation. But this rule was widely ignored, and as the labor market tightened throughout the 1960s and 1970s some firms were recruiting as early as 18 months before graduation. The Ministry of Labor unsuccessfully attempted to tighten its rules in the late 1970s, and a 'gentleman's agreement' in 1986 among the largest firms to refrain from interviewing before 6 September and hiring before 1 October monitored by Nikkeiren has also been equally ignored.

Some firms have actually gone so far as to place their recruits under virtual house arrest. As of 8 September 1988 the Ministry of Labor had received 474 complaints of recruit violations involving 154 firms, of which 95 included 'daily detainment' whereby the recruit was required to visit the company up to ten hours a day but was allowed to go home at night, and 131 cases of actual overnight detention.[7] Although these recruitment 'techniques' sound similar to tactics employed by weird cult groups like the 'Moonies', they definitely help socialize employees into such corporate values as total devotion to the firm at all costs.

Formal training is far less controversial but no less intense. It usually lasts at least a year for new graduates, while it is somewhat *training* shorter for those with experience in other firms. In addition, every five years blue-collar workers attend short courses designed especially to increase their skills. Workers are usually divided into five ranks from the lowest at fourth class, up through third, second, first, and finally master class. Large firms also open these training courses to their subcontractors. In 1979 82.0 per cent of all Japanese firms gave some form of special training to their workers ranging from an average of 57.6 per cent for firms of 30–99 workers to 98.2 per cent for firms with more than 1000 workers.[8] Both blue- and white-collar workers are generally taught to learn by observing and emulating their more skilled seniors. Team work is seen as the key to higher productivity, and workers are continually admonished not to let down their team by slacking off.

But this technical training is only part of the socialization process. Perhaps even more important is the socialization of the new employees into the corporate culture so that they consider themselves part of something greater than themselves. Daily group songs, exercise, and management pep talks reinforce the ideals of the company as a 'family' and source of security and primary identity for all its members. But this socialization process does not end at the formal quitting time. Employees are encouraged to drink with their colleagues after work, play golf with them on week-ends, take after-hours company classes, and, in short, spend virtually all their waking hours in some company activity including commuting. Personal fulfillment and identity can be achieved only through hard work through one master – the company.

The advantages to Japanese companies of this continual socialization process are clear: the creation of a highly skilled, dedicated workforce. But the personal costs of this 'family style company' are huge and not immediately apparent to most foreign observers. With the company the central concern of their lives, employees have little family life. Employees are often on the way to work by seven in the morning and it is still considered somewhat shameful for husbands to come home before ten o'clock at night. Week-ends are often taken up with overtime work, golf, or other company obligations, leaving fathers with little time to spend with their wives and children. Although the company attempts to socialize employees so that they view these sacrifices as natural rather than invasions of their free time, many employees privately complain about being coerced into doing many things for the company against their own interests. With almost all large companies using the escalator system, individuals must remain in their company even if they are unhappy. Psychologically, Japan's corporate culture creates a spectrum of neurotic disorders ranging from stress to nervous breakdowns. One sign of this is the fact that there are more muscle relaxing drugs sold in Japan than anywhere else. The constant emphasis on serving the firm above all creates a highly xenophobic we-them mentality where workers transfer their frustrations to their competitors outside the firm.[9]

The extent of this 'quiet desparation' was revealed by a 1987 survey by the All-Japan Federation of Electric Machine Workers' Union comparing the work attitudes of Japanese and American electronics workers.[10] On a scale of one to five with five the highest, the American workers displayed a significantly higher level of satisfaction with their company and work than their Japanese counterparts in such areas as overall satisfaction 3.6 (American) to 2.9 (Japanese), job security 3.8 to 3.5, the ability to communicate with management 3.9 to 2.9, participation in corporate decision-making 3.0 to 2.5, and relations with their superiors 3.9 to 2.9. Regarding support for new machines, 52.2 per cent of the Japanese passively replied 'we have no choice' while 65.8 per cent of the Americans responded with active support. Almost two-thirds, or 63.8 per cent of the Americans said they wanted 'to put their best efforts toward the company' compared to only 29.2 per cent of Japanese workers. Only 5.6 per cent of Americans said 'I don't have much feeling for the company' compared to over a quarter, or 27.4 per cent of the Japanese. Only 1.0 per cent of Japanese workers felt they were very close to decision-making compared to 10.7 of Americans, while 44.9 per cent of Americans said they were 'fairly close' compared to only 28.5 per cent of Japanese.

But this 'quiet desperation' within Japanese firms extends to management as well.[11] A 1988 survey of Fortune 500 firms in Japan and the United States by the Nihon Keizai Shimbun revealed that American managers were twice as satisfied with their jobs as their Japanese counterparts. Nearly 80 per cent of American managers said they were either 'very satisfied' or 'satisfied' with their jobs compared to 41 per cent of Japanese managers, while only 14 per cent of Americans were merely 'somewhat satisfied' compared to a staggering 42 per cent of Japanese managers. Some 48 per cent of American managers and only 31 per cent of Japanese managers thought they had 'more loyalty' to the company than their colleagues. Looking back five years, 63 per cent of American managers and only 33 per cent of Japanese felt their lives had 'become better'. In analyzing the survey, the Japan Economic Journal concludes that 'Japan economic success many have been built on the backs of a contingent of unhappy company managers'.[12]

These findings explode the myth that the Japanese corporate culture produces a 'family' atmosphere in the hearts and minds of its members – in fact it reveals just the opposite. The only finding that did correspond to the common image was the relative job mobility in the two cultures with only half of Japanese workers having ever changed jobs compared to the average three jobs held by American workers. The relative freedom to choose a suitable workplace may be an important reason for the widespread satisfaction among American workers and deep dissatisfaction among Japanese.

Closely connected with the constant socialization process is the largely harmonious labor-management relations found in most Japanese companies. With the enterprise union system union whereby leaders eventually become managers, the biannual bonuses based on company profits given to all employees, and the lifetime employment system which requires continual growth to support it, management and labor interests are virtually identical. Corporate heads often claim that their first obligation is to their employees, and their second obligation to the company stockholders. In this system, strikes become mere rituals during the annual 'Spring offensive' (shunto) that rarely take more than a day with workers later making up the lost hours through unpaid overtime work. Settlements are usually reached well before a strike takes place; the strikes are allowed to give the public the illusion that the workers have power.

These cooperative labor-management relations give Japanese companies an enormous advantage over their often strike-ridden foreign rivals. The disadvantages of weak labor unions are the inability of workers really to protect their rights when they are violated. Although Japanese workers are known for their flexibility in giving up benefits and wages when their company is experiencing financial difficulties, this is rarely from free choice. Generally speaking, the enterprise leaders have their eyes set on eventually attaining a high company management position, not on the needs of the workers they supposedly represent. For example, when Sumitomo heavy industry in 1983 abandoned its central Tokyo location for a 'green-field site' far off in the suburbs, its employees were asked to make two major sacrifices. First, since they were now located in the countryside they had to give up their Tokyo work allowances even though most employees had to commute daily as much as an hour more each way. Second, they were asked to give up compensation for every hour beyond 20 hours of overtime a month since arch-rival Mitsubishi had recently enacted a similar program. The employees privately complained bitterly about these 'exploitative' measures, but when asked why the union did not fight these new policies, laughed at the suggestion claiming the union was completely powerless and was used to control rather than represent the employees.[13]

Another characteristic of the Japanese corporate model is 'bottom-up' decision-making (ringi seido) whereby virtually all the employees have at least some say in forming corporate policies. A policy proposal originates at the section level of the firm which is the most closely involved with the relevant issue. The section reaches a consensus among itself and then circulates the proposal among the other sections in the division, which in turn debate its merits, add their own suggestions, and pass it elsewhere. After all relevant sections have debated and approved the proposal, with modifications if necessary, it is then sent up to the division management for ratification. Once a consensus is reached within the division, the proposal is then sent to other divisions where the same procedure takes place. The final proposal is then sent to the company president for final ratification. 'Bottom-up' decision-making calls for a leadership skilled at forging a consensus rather than pushing through ideas of its own. Top management are thus not decision-makers but decision-ratifiers and consensus builders. The key leaders in the system are the section (kacho) and division (bucho) level managers.

The advantage of the system is that everyone participates, at least nominally, in the decision-making process. Since consensus involves 'unanimous' agreement, everyone is considered responsible for the decision's consequences. Thus, once a decision is made, everyone is prepared immediately to begin implementing it. But there are disadvantages as well. The process is very time-consuming, and Japanese companies often lose some business opportunities to foreign firms that practice a quick 'top-down' decision-making style. In addition, the endless meetings and discussions involving virtually everyone at one time or another tend to undermine productivity as employees are pulled from everyday activities. Consensus decision-making tends to lead to more conservative decisions or 'group think' in which all tend to go along in the later stages of a decision even in the face of evidence showing the decision may not be in their best interests. This bottom-up decision-making style is most common in the older keiretsu companies and less common in entrepreneur style companies in which the founder often uses a top-down method.

The final distinct characteristic of Japan's corporate culture is the long-term orientation the company takes towards things like market share, quality-control, and research and development. Large Japanese firms are able to take a long-term outlook because, unlike their foreign rivals, bank loans and retained earnings rather than volatile stock markets provide the bulk of their finance, while a range of informal cartels and trade barriers protect their domestic markets, and the government often assists their research and development through industrial policies. With a secure financial, market, and research and development base, Japanese firms can well afford to look long term.

Another important aspect of Japan's corporate culture is the range of shop-floor techniques that attempt to squeeze the most productivity out of personnel and equipment. Quality control (hinshitsu kanri) circles, suggestion boxes, and the discretion to make changes or even stop the assembly line if a defect is noted, encourages all workers to fulfill the Japanese corporate ideal of zero defects. This is based on the common sense idea that it is cheaper to prevent a problem in the first place rather than repair it later, and the statistically proven fact that a 2 per cent reduction of defects leads to a 10 per cent improvement in productivity. Quality-control circles are characteristic of most big corporations: over 90 per cent of the firms listed on the stock exchange and nearly two-thirds of the largest firms (those with more than 5000 workers) have active QC circles, but only one-sixth of the smallest firms (under 300 workers) have active QC circles. These quality-control circles are a tremendous boost to productivity as well as a worker's sense of self-worth. For example, in 1982 Toyota received over 1.9 million proposals from its 60 000 workers, of which it incorporated over 94 per cent into its production system.[14] In addition to quality-control circles, Japanese workers are generally better trained and experienced than their counterparts elsewhere. A Japanese worker's typical career will cover about three dozen different work positions while an American worker's will cover only a dozen. Thus, through work experience alone the average Japanese worker is probably three times more skilled than the average American worker.[15]

Firms use equipment just as efficiently as workers. The 'just-in-time delivery' system (kanban) whereby parts are produced only when they are needed significantly reduces inventory costs. Only 3 per cent of the personnel in Japanese companies are devoted to inventory compared to 12 per cent of the employees in American companies. On average, Japanese equipment is newer and better maintained than American equipment. The average age of machine tools in the United States was 20 years compared to 10–12 years in Japan, which last two to three times longer than American machine tools because they are better cared for. The Japanese have been much more active in using robots to improve productivity: in 1981 there were 67 435 robots in Japan compared to only 4100 in the United States, 11420 in West Germany, and only 371 in Britain.[16] Finally, Japanese research and development is oriented to applied rather than basic innovations on the assumption that it is much cheaper to improve rather than create technology. At least 40 per cent of all Japanese research and development costs go into process or equipment improvements, which in turn dramatically boost productivity. The result of all these measures is the creation of high-quality products at cheap prices.

How 'unique' are these characteristics of Japanese companies? In his book *In Search of Excellence*, Dale Peters shows that the most successful American companies employ many of the same personnel, quality-control, and research and development techniques as Japanese companies do. It may well be that most of the characteristics of the 'Japanese corporate model' may simply be ones that any progressive corporation will employ for sound economic reasons. Ideas like quality-control circles, just-in-time delivery, and giving worker's more freedom to innovate originated with American management theorists in the 1940s and 1950s. For example, the Union of Japanese Scientists and Engineers annually presents two W. E. Deming Awards, one for advances in management theory and the other for actual productivity or management advances. Deming is an American management theorist whose revolutionary ideas about boosting productivity were largely neglected by American corporations but avidly emulated by Japanese firms after his first visit to Japan in 1954. As the world becomes increasingly interdependent and competitive, corporations will increasingly have to follow the more positive aspects of the 'Japanese model'.

However, because of things like anti-trust laws most foreign firms will be unable to copy some distinct advantages enjoyed by Japanese firms. One key advantage is the protective political economic environment in which Japanese firms operate. For example, the horizontal and vertical sub-contracting and distribution keiretsu, the widespread use of price, market, production, export, and technology cartels, and the practice of buying based on long-term relationships rather than price are all generally distinct to Japan. The ability of Japanese firms to take a long-term approach to investments results to a large extent from relying on bank rather than equity financing; banks are concerned with long-term debt servicing while stockholders are obsessed with quarterly profit margins. No country's bureaucracy plays a more constructive or active role in guiding economic development than does Japan's. Through administrative guidance the ministries carefully manage the overall economic environment and specific industries and firms within it to optimize economic growth and development, and give Japanese firms every advantage possible over their foreign competitors.

Thus, Japanese firms have become notorious for such practices as a 'lazer-beam' approach to foreign trade whereby they 'dump' their products at prices well below production costs in order to drive their foreign rivals out of business, whereupon, after capturing huge market shares, the Japanese firms then raise prices to recoup the earlier losses caused by dumping. Thus, for Japanese companies profits are a long-term objective based on market shares and large volumes rather than the short-term financial juggling to please stockholders that is particularly characteristic of American firms. The long-term outlook of Japanese companies is systematized by a series of continually evolving plans based on six month, one year, five year, and ten year orientations.

The difference between corporate strategies is clearly revealed in surveys of Japanese and American executives. Given a list of eight corporate goals, Japanese managers rated growth, particularly increases in market share (1.43) the most important, followed by return on investment (1.24) and new product ratio (1.06), while capital gains for stockholders (0.02) were considered the least important. In contrast American executives considered returns on investment (2.43) the most important, followed by capital gains for stockholders (1.14), while increases in market share (0.73) trailed far behind on the priority list. However, both American (0.04) and Japanese (0.09) thought the quality of work conditions was unimportant.[17]

As if these advantages were not enough, Japan's corporate world also benefits from a range of psychological advantages as well. The school system and mass media continually socialize the public with the image that Japan is 'a small, poor, unique country beseiged by foreign rivals' that must 'export or die', and that foreign firms do not sell more in Japan because they do not try hard enough and anyway their products are of inferior quality. This nationalistic outlook is reinforced by a school system that fosters extreme forms of obedience and conformity, and an examination system that emphasizes countless hours spent at memorization rather than creativity, thus providing Japanese business with a dedicated, docile workforce. The hierarchial university system is peaked by Tokyo University, whose graduates move into the ministries, LDP, and top corporations. No other country comes close to matching Japan's 'old boy network' (dokyusei) based on school ties, amakudari, and marriage.

Another advantage is Japan's largely 'free ride' on aid and defense. Although Japanese aid is the highest in volume, it is also the OECD's highest percentage of aid tied to purchases of Japanese goods and service – thus servicing as an export subsidy rather than genuine aid – and at 0.31 per cent is the fourth lowest as a percentage of GNP. Japan's per capita defense spending is the industrial world's lowest as well. While Americans pay over $760 dollars per capita on defense, Britains $572, French $483, Germans $405, Italians $155, Swedes $455, and Swiss $154, Japanese spend only $98. Of the 18 OECD countries, Japan's ODA ranks 14th.[18]

In addition to enjoying these important environmental advantages, Japanese corporations have some distinct characteristics that would be difficult for foreign firms to emulate. In Japan, contracts are based more on mutual understanding and adjustments than legal obligations; the typical Japanese business contract runs two or three pages while Western contracts can be as long as 100 pages. In no other country is bottom-up decision-making as widespread as in Japan. Finally, no other country's corporate culture involves itself as deeply in its employees personal lives as do Japanese firms.

JAPANESE DIRECT FOREIGN INVESTMENT

In their book, *The Second Wave: Japan's Global Assault on Financial Services*, Richard Wright and Gunter Pauli present a six-step strategy whereby Japanese corporations conquer overseas markets.[19] According to Wright and Pauli Japanese firms have successfully followed this strategy in textiles, consumer electronics, steel, automobiles, and semiconductors. The first step involves intensive market research and the identification of key underserved product niches usually at the lower end of the market. The next step is to form a joint venture with a foreign firm to gain access to the technology and knowledge necessary to develop products for that niche. This is followed by mass producing the products and selling them through extensive domestic distribution channels in Japan. During this time the government provides a web of import barriers to prevent foreign rivals from seizing part of the market. After establishing large economies of scale which reduce prices and improve quality the firm then 'dumps' its product in the targeted foreign market through a carefully constructed foreign distribution system and marketing strategy. Under this barrage of cheap priced imports the affected foreign firm then runs to its government for protection. Often long after the Japanese firms have seized huge market shares in the product area, a 'voluntary export restraint' (VER) or 'orderly marketing agreement' (OMA) setting up formal import quotas is struck between the foreign government and Tokyo. With its now dominant market share, the Japanese firm then raises prices to recoup losses encurred from its earlier dumping offensive, and uses the windfall profits to invest in higher-value-added products, with which the same procedure is used to capture those niches as well. During this time the Japanese firm sets up factories in the targeted country to allay continued criticism of unfair trade tactics. During the final stage the Japanese firm buys up its by now severely weakened rivals and the takeover is complete.

Over the past quarter century, considerable criticism has been focused on the intermediate stage of corporate strategy – the waves of Japanese dumping in selected industries. But recently, with Japan's powerful yen and need to recycle its huge payments surpluses, attention is increasingly shifting to the latter stages of the strategy – the impact of Japanese foreign investments. Between 1951 and 1986 Japanese firms set up 36 927 overseas operations worth $83.649 billion. In 1986, the top five recipients of accumulated Japanese foreign investments were the United States with $25.290 billion, Indonesia a distant second at $8.423 billion, followed by Panama $6.440, Brazil $4.587, and Australia $3.621.[20] Japanese foreign investments are worldwide. As of 1982, the largest amount – 33.7 per cent – was in Asia and Oceania, followed by 28.7 per cent in North America of which 26.3 per cent was in the United States, Latin America 16.7 per cent, Europe 11.6 per cent, and 9.4 per cent in the Middle East and Africa.[21]

Until the late 1960s MITI used the Foreign Exchange and Foreign Trade Control Law (1949) to keep both Japanese foreign investments and foreign investments in Japan to a trickle. But between 1967 to 1973, five amendments to the law loosened MITI's grip over foreign investments in either direction. With the increasingly large payments surpluses after the mid–1960s, the government increasingly encouraged and guided Japanese investments abroad to help relieve any upward pressure on the yen's value. Japanese foreign investments in heavy industry were particularly encouraged to 'houseclean' the country of heavily polluting firms which by the 1960s had given Japan the reputation of being the most polluted country on earth. Finally, firms themselves were eager to invest overseas in search of cheaper labor and land, and to secure markets and resources increasingly protected by foreign governments. Chernotsky characterizes Japanese foreign investments as essentially 'defensive measures to relieve pressure on the domestic economy and to assist in the realization of key economy policy goals. It is also an integral part of Japan's enduring 'export or die' philosophy . . . It seems predicated largely on the need to acquire direct access to raw material supplies to support industrial activity, to secure established and additional markets for the sale of Japanese products and to enhance further the country's worldwide competitiveness'.[22]

Much of the first wave of Japanese foreign investments in the 1970s were targeted towards Asia and other Third World countries (64 per cent), and mining and manufacturing (63 per cent). With capital and foreign experience still relatively scarce, most Japanese investments were joint ventures with indigenous or other foreign firms. For example, in 1972 only 41 per cent of Japanese ventures in Asia were majority owned.[23] As Japanese firms acquired more experience and capital they began increasingly to assert either majority or sole ownership over their foreign venture. Throughout the 1980s Japanese investments shifted from labor-intensive manufacturing or resource extraction ventures in developing countries to value-added manufacturing and service industries in developed countries. With huge pools of capital at their disposal, Japanese firms are now buying up foreign firms, plants, and real estate to avoid the expense and time of developing green field sites or distribution systems. The United States with its huge market, skilled, largely non-union workforce, sophisticated infrastructure, and high technology is increasingly the target of choice for Japanese investors. By late 1983 Japanese firms had set up 334 manufacturing ventures in the United States, of which they had either sole or majority interest in 309. These ventures included 479 separate factories employing 73 000 workers.[24] With its internal barriers scheduled to drop in 1992, a wave of Japanese investments in service and manufacturing industries is also sweeping Europe.

Whether they have set up an overseas operation in a developing or developed country, Japanese firms have had considerable problems trying to duplicate the corporate culture that serves them so well in Japan, and have also become the target of considerable criticism for their business practices. Japanese firms in developing countries are subject to the same complaints that swirl around any multinational firm – they transfer prices by manipulating account books, disrupt the balance of payments by importing high priced intermediate goods, soak up indigenous capital and repatriate it, do not transfer technology, or corrupt and coopt local élites.[25] But Japanese firms are also criticized for many practices unique to their corporate culture. For example, Japanese firms employ four times more expatriates than other multinationals. Yoshino writes that 'with the exception of jobs relating to labor and personnel, Japanese managers tended to occupy almost all key positions. In addition, positions below these were often staffed by Japanese junior managers'.[26] Taira exposes the 'shadow management' where real decisions are made and then announced through the president who is often a native but merely a figurehead.[27] Taira's analyses of Japanese investments in Thailand are true in any country, developed or developing: 'the formal organization displayed by the organization chart tells little about how the firm is run and an informal organization behind the formal façade where actual decision-making and implementation take place. If the formal positions are filled by Thai nationals, the Japanese may still be in charge through their exclusive informal network – a shadow organization'.

Japanese firms are also criticized because their escalator system pays far less than other multinationals. Taira writes that 'Euro-American firms are generally looked up to by all Thais as the best employers in Thailand. This means that Thai workers are looking for the opportunity to move to Euro-American firms'.[28] Thus Japanese firms have trouble retaining a skilled workforce since the best move on to American or European firms. Those that remain are less likely than their counterparts in Japan to endure what they see as exploitative practices. Taira points out that 'Japanese firms in Thailand are more prone to labor disputes than other foreign firms', and quotes a Japanese manager expressing envy at the success of Euro-American firms in problem-free personnel management.[29]

Japanese attempts to transfer their corporate culture to Europe and North American have also had mixed results. Their greatest success has been in promoting productivity. For example, the Sony television plant in San Diego has a higher productivity rate than similar factories in Japan, and other Japanese firms have enjoyed similar successes elsewhere.[30] Japanese have had no trouble outproducing their foreign rivals. The joint venture between Toyota and GM at Fremont California has a higher productivity and quality rate than any GM factory, although a recent book by two former workers argues that this was achieved simply by speeding up the assembly line and playing off workers against each other.[31] It is estimated that by 1991, while the Ford plant in Britain is using 45 000 employees to build 550 000 cars, the new Nissan plant will employ only 4500 people to build over 200 000 automobiles.[32]

Part of this productivity comes from state-of-the-art technology, but most is simply using the best Japanese and Western management techniques. Quality circles, just-in-time inventory, and zero defect techniques are mandatory in all joint ventures, company exercise and singing is optional, the assembly lines are faster than Western lines yet below the excessive speed of Japanese lines, while Western values of family, leisure, and vacation are respected. Japanese firms are very careful to hire predominantly young, inexperienced people who have not picked up any bad work habits elsewhere. For example Nissan choose 500 out of over 30 000 applicants for its British plant.[33]

Generally speaking, most factory workers prefer Japan's corporate style which treats them like human beings and encourages their imput to Western style management, which may pay more but treats them as mere factors of production. But Japan's corporate culture has been far less successful in using Western managers. Leah Nathan conducted an extensive investigation of some of the 25 000 American managers now working for Japanese managers and concluded that 'by large they seem to be an unhappy and demoralized lot. The Japanese need American executives' expertise to sell their products in the United States and are willing to pay top salaries to get them. But in company after company, the Americans complain about a system of subtle and debilitating discrimination in which they are treated as necessary but inferior outsiders – without the authority to get things done and without upward mobility . . . Japan's vaunted management methods, while generally successful on the factory floor, are a dismal failure in the executive ranks. . . . American managers have to contend with the traditional xenophobia of the Japanese and their belief in their own superiority'.

One problem is that the qualities that make a good American manager – creativity, risk-taking, decisiveness – are the antithesis of the Japanese values of team work, conformity, and consensus. But the biggest problem is the self-fulfilling prophecy that Japanese expect Westerners to have loyalty only to themselves, and thus do not trust them with enough information or decision-making power, and instead milk them for their expertise. As a result, there is a quick turnover of American managers which reinforces Japanese perceptions and behavior. Closely connected with this is the centralized decision-making structure of Japanese firms whereby all criticial decisions on things like pricing, production, or marketing, are made in Tokyo. Nathan points out that 'every American manager has a Japanese counterpart – or 'shadow' – who officially serves as the communications liaison with the company in Japan but whose real job is to watch over the American and get headquarters approval for decisions made . . . the actual decision-making cuts out the Americans altogether'. The 'shadow' is often caught between loyalty to his superiors in Tokyo and sympathy for his American colleagues.

Japan's corporate culture clearly does not create the magical realm of harmony and happiness either in Japan or overseas that so many writers try to portray. In fact it produces just the opposite. The escalator system of pay and advancement, and corresponding lack of interfirm mobility, produces a loyal, quiescent workforce. Workers have little choice so they simply endure the long hours and lack of leisure in hopes their conformity will be eventually rewarded with further advancement as the pyramid increasingly narrows toward the top. But, as the survey of consumer electronics workers reveals, outward calm often masks deep inner disatisfaction. The strength of Japan's corporate culture is clearly its ability to manage the highest level of productivity from both people and machines. But the production of high quality, cheap products is only one advantage Japanese firms have over their foreign rivals. The success of Japanese corporations cannot be separated from the cozy domestic environment of cartels, amakudari, and import barriers, and an increasingly prosperous, continually expanding world economy.

Perhaps the ideal corporate situation is neither Japanese nor Western, but combines the best of both. Japanese investments in Europe, North America, and other developing countries have created a largely productive, satisfied workforce despite strong signs of a frustrated indigenous management, while firms like IBM, Hewlett Packard, Motorola, and Black and Decker have long been following similar management strategies that leave both management and workers productive and happy. Regardless, Japan's corporate culture is an important pillar of its overall economic power.

NOTES

1. For other ideal views see articles like Akira Kubota's 'Japan: Social Structure and Work Ethic', *Asia Pacific Community*, no. 20, Spring 1983; Kenneth Kiyuna, 'Japanese and American Companies, *Asian Affairs*, vol. 10, no. 2, Summer 1983; Tsung-I Dow, 'The Meaning of Confucian Work Ethic as the Source of Japan's Economic Power', *Asian Profile*, vol. 11, no. 3, June 1983; Hem C. Jain, 'The Japanese System of Human Resource Management', *Asian Survey*, vol. 27, no. 9, September 1987; Robert Ozaki, 'The Humanistic Enterprise System in Japan', *Asian Survey*, vol. 28, no. 8, August 1988 for ideal versions.
2. Tomoko Hamada's 'Corporation, Culture, and Environment', *Asian Survey*, vol. 25, no. 12, December 1985, provides a concise overview of these advantages.
3. Ibid., p. 1218.
4. Kazuo Koike, 'Human Resource Development and Labor-Management Relations', in Kozo Yamamura and Yasukichi Yasuba (eds), *The Political Economy of Japan*, p. 296.
5. Ibid., p. 313.
6. International Labor Office, *Yearbook of Labor Statistics* (various issues).
7. *Far Eastern Economic Review*, 22 September 1988.
8. Koike, op. cit., p. 300.
9. See William Zimmerman's *Doing Business in Japan* for more details.
10. *Japan Economic Journal*, 13 August, 1988.
11. *Japan Economic Journal*, 11 February 1989.
12. Ibid.
13. 1983 interviews.
14. Ibid., p. 15.
15. Koike, op. cit, pp. 291, 304, in Yamamura.
16. Zimmerman, *Doing Business in Japan*, p. 191.
17. Sato, op. cit., in Hoshino, p. 36.
18. OECD statistics, 1988.
19. Richard Wright and Gunter Pauli, *The Second Wave: Japan's Global Assault on Financial Services*, p. 86.
20. *Japan 1986, An International Comparison*, Keizai Koho Center, p. 56.
21. *Jetro*, White Paper on Foreign Markets, 1984.
22. Chernotshy, op. cit., p. 69.
23. Ibid., pp. 69–71.
24. Duane Kujawa, *Japanese Multinationals in the United States*, pp. 11–39.
25. See William Nester, *Japan's Growing Power Over East Asia and the World Economy: Ends and Means*, for a full discussion.
26. M. Y. Yoshino, *Japan's Multinational Enterprises*, Cambridge, Massachusetts, Harvard University Press, 1976, pp. 167.
27. Koji Taira, 'Colonialism in Foreign Subsidiaries: The Lesson from Thailand', *Asian Survey*, vol. 20, no. 4, April 1980, p. 390.
28. Ibid., p. 391.
29. Ibid., p. 394.

30. See Jon Woronoff, *Japan's Commercial Empire*, for details.
31. Jane Slaughter and Mike Parker, *Choosing Sides*, reviewed in the *International Herald Tribune*, 1 February 1989.
32. *Independent*, 11 February 1988.
33. Ibid.
34. Leah Nathans, 'A Matter of Control', *Business Month*, September 1988.
35. Ibid., p. 49.
36. Ibid., p. 50.

Part II
Japanese Policy-makers

6 Bureaucracy

The bureaucracy's power over policy-making and the economy has clearly diminished since the bureaucratic-dominant corporatism of the 1950s and 1960s. Yet the bureaucracy remains an immensely powerful actor in policy-making and implementation. Of the other OECD countries, only France's bureaucracy plays a larger role in guiding economic development, while no liberal democracy's bureaucracy has been more effective in leading economic growth. What are the sources of the bureaucracy's power? How is that power manifested?

Perhaps the most important source of bureaucratic power is tradition. Japan's bureaucracy has played a central role in Japanese politics for over 1500 years. Based on Chinese institutions and imperial sanction, the bureaucracy's role has been to serve the interests of the nation as a whole. It has closely regulated the economy since the Heian era, and during the Meiji period it was the bureaucracy which played the lead role in dragging Japan into the modern world by creating such modern political and economic institutions as the conservative political parties, zaibatsu, and the 1889 constitution. Before 1945 the bureaucracy ruled without virtually any accountability. Although the bureaucracy's formal powers were limited by laws and procedures, 'administrative guidance' (gyosei shido) gave it enormous informal power to force through policies affecting virtually all aspects of the economy and society.

After 1945, the bureaucracy largely escaped SCAP's widespread purges and reforms. Although Article 15 of the 1947 Constitution discusses the importance of public service, the bureaucracy remains élitist and above the people. The word for bureaucrat – kanri – still retains its prewar meaning of an official whose authority flowed from and loyalty was directed to the Emperor. The attitude of the of the typical bureaucrat is still summed up in the phrase 'kanson minpi' or 'revere one's superiors and despise the people'. Despite these authoritarian attitudes and arbitrary power, part of the bureaucracy's power lies in its alleged 'neutrality' (kokkateki churitsusei) and 'specialist competence' (tekkakusei). Unlike the politicians or businessmen, bureaucrats are still seen as generally working for the country as a whole.

'As 'children' of the bureaucracy, the conservative party and corporate world have only recently acquired enough political and economic autonomy to offset the bureaucrat's power. Stockwin writes that 'up to the 1970s the most influential part of the system of government was bureaucratic . . . the role of the party in power by comparison with that of the government bureaucracy was rather weak, though it has notably increased during the 1980s'.[1] Alan Rix writes that 'the economic ministries . . . have developed complex and far-reaching mechanisms for translating policy into achievement, and have built a bureaucratic citadel within the state founded on a set of premises about national directions . . . bureaucrats are powerful in Japanese policy-making because of the limitations of other formal participants (the cabinet, the Diet, and the LDP), and the reliance by the LDP on the expertise and information of the bureaucracy'.[2] Bureaucrats are well aware of the power they continue to weild over Japan. A recent opinion poll indicated that a staggering 96 per cent of Japanese bureaucrats thought they were 'very' or 'rather' influential in policy-making compared to only 85 per cent in Britain and 75 per cent in the United States; 80 per cent of Japanese bureaucrats thought that the civil service was more important in policy-making than the parties or Diet compared to only 21 per cent in Britain and 16 per cent in the United States.[3]

Japan's bureaucrats have retained their power through a range of both legal and extralegal means. The bureaucracy's legal powers – often written by the ministries themselves – give them tremendous power over the system. For example, over 110 laws give MITI vast powers over the economy and most industries, including such powers as foreign exchange and investment controls, creating and administering cartels, import barriers, and export subsidies. Laws are drafted in very vague language giving the empowered ministry vast discretion to interpret it in any way they see fit. But as Japan's neo-mercantilist trade and industrial policies come under increasing foreign scrutiny and criticism, the ministries' powers of administrative guidance (gyosei shido) have become correspondingly more important. Administrative guidance is the ability of a ministry unofficially to coerce industry to follow a particular policy be threatening to withhold certain subsidies or opportunities. This pressure always occurs behind closed doors and is thus generally impervious to foreign criticism. The ministries, business, and LDP all prefer administrative guidance because there is no paper trail leading to foreign charges of unfair trade practices; it is an excellent non-tariff trade barrier because if nothing is written, nothing can be proved. Administrative guidance comes in the form of notifications (tatatsu) containing rec- ommendations (kankoku), which are only sent after intensive dis- cussions between the concerned ministry and industries. These noti- fications contain highly detailed 'advice' about such specific things as price, production, or export levels.[4]

The bureaucracy's policy-making and implementation power is further enhanced by the retirement (amakudari) of bureaucrats into high paying positions in private and public corporations and the LDP. For example, from 1970 to 1980, 173 ex-bureaucrats from the Ministry of Finance became executives of private banks and trust and stock companies, as well as government-related financial organ- izations like the Japan Development Bank and other public corpor- ations. In 1966 retiring MITI bureaucrats joined, among other com- panies, Yawata Steel, Shell Oil, Mobil Oil, and Hitachi Shipping; others from the Ministry of Transportation joined Iino Shipping Lines, Kawasaki Steamship, Morita Steamship, Meitetsu-Tokyo Sightseeing Bus, and Toyonaka Taxi; and still others from the Minis- try of Construction joined Sato Industry, Taisei Construction, Kajima Construction, and Fujitagumi.[5] These ex-bureaucrats retain their links with their former ministries, and keep a close eye on the organization they retired into, whether it be a private or public corporation or the LDP.

Government ministries and agencies further augment their power over policy-making through a variety of means. White Papers are issued to educate those involved with the ministry's policies. Infor- mation about certain planned projects is sometimes leaked to gener- ate public enthusiasm. Petition Groups (chijodan) of interest groups are mobilized to lobby key politicians, businessmen, and other bureaucrats for support. Bureaucracies further enhance their policy- making powers by setting up 'advisory councils' (shingikai) composed of prominent politicians, businessmen, academics, media leaders, and occasionally labor or opposition party representatives. Although they are created with much fanfare, advisory councils have no real power and simply serve as public relations fronts for the ministry to which they are attached. The real work is conducted by the numerous committees and subcommittees (kondankai) that work feverishly behind the scenes.

The economic ministries fight as much among themselves as with the politicians or businessmen over policy. The primary economic ministries are the Ministry of Finance (MOF) and Ministry of Inter- national Trade and Industry (MITI), holding general responsibility for macroeconomic and industrial policy, respectively. Other ministries, however, are increasingly trying to carve out jurisdictions over specific economic sectors and issues. Most of these other ministries favour strengthening the web of trade barriers over the industries under their control: the Ministry of Agriculture, Forestry, and Fisheries (MAFF) has always dominated policy-making in the areas under its jurisdiction – it continues to support high subsidies for farmers and high trade barriers against foreign agricultural, forestry, or fishery products; the Ministry of Health and Welfare (MHW) has consistently favored barriers against foreign medical equipment and pharmaceuticals; the Ministry of Transport (MOT) supports a web of barriers against foreign airlines and automobiles; and the Ministry of Justice (MOJ) barriers against foreign lawyers. The Ministry of Foreign Affairs (MFA), on the other hand, has generally been more internationally oriented, but has no domestic support and plays a weak role in policy-making. It is said to be becoming increasingly nationalist as foreign pressures build on Japan to accelerate its market-opening steps. The Economic Planning Agency (EPA) plays a relatively neutral role in policy-making. Its role is to publish five-year plans setting general economic goals and expectations. Before 1952 the EPA was the powerful Economic Stabilization Board, which was then renamed the Economic Deliberation Agency and largely stripped of its powers, and received its present name in 1955. Its power is limited; it serves as a consensus-making clearing house for the other ministries rather than a policy-making center.

Each ministry is fiercely conscious of the need to protect and expand its own powers at the expense of its rivals. One means of expanding influence is detaching personnel to the various agencies where the battles among the ministries are often conducted on a smaller scale. The EPA is traditionally the most important arena for these conflicts, particularly between MOF and MITI representatives. The economic ministries also enhance their respective power by maintaining intelligence networks through Japan's political economy and even abroad. For example, MFA, MITI, and the MOF generally battle for influence over most international issues, and each of them maintains their own overseas communications network: MFA with the regular foreign office cable system, MOF through the telex system of the Bank of Tokyo, and MITI through the telex system of JETRO. Even something as relatively mundane as the annual growth estimates are shaped as much by turf battle strategies as careful economic analysis. The three main economic bureaucracies,

MITI, MOF, and EPA, have conflicting interests with regard to growth estimates, and thus their estimates reflect their interests. The MOF holds out for lower figures so the ministries will not request as much money; MITI calls for the highest in order to enhance its own power over the economy, and the EPA's estimates are somewhere in between. There are variations to this pattern, however. MITI pushed for a low estimate in 1974 reasoning that a gloomy economic estimate would help reduce oil consumption. In 1962, when Japan was attempting to secure a loan from the IMF, all three presented low growth estimates hoping it would help secure the loan.[6]

Paradoxically, another very important source of the bureaucracy's power is its relatively small size. By being 'lean and mean', Japan's bureaucracy is much more efficient in its daily operations, in part because with less money to spend it must be much more careful about how the money is used. Less money makes potential recipients much more compliant than a situation in which the bureaucracy is seen as a money tree that simply needs to be shaken. Japan has the smallest government of all the OECD countries. In 1985 Japan's government spending was 33.5 per cent of GNP compared to 38.5 per cent in the United States, 49.0 per cent in Britain, 52.2 per cent in West Germany, 54.0 per cent in France, and 64.1 per cent in Sweden. The number of Japanese government employees including education and the military is just over five million at present; a level of 45 per thousand of population compared to 109 in Britain, 83 in France, 82 in the United States, and 76 in West Germany.[7]

The size and composition of Japan's government has changed little over the past three decades. In 1955 there were a total of 40 ministries, agencies, and major commissions, and only 45 in 1982. In the same period, the number of bureaux rose from 80 to 114 and public authorities (tokushi hojin) nearly tripled from 33 to 94, although it has fallen from a high point of 113 in 1967.[8] There are 12 ministries (sho) including the Ministry of Agriculture, Forestry, and Fisheries (MAFF), Ministry of Construction (MOC), Ministry of Education (MOE), Ministry of Finance (MOF), Ministry of Health and Welfare (MHW), Ministry of Foreign Affairs (MFA), Ministry of Home Affairs (MHA), Ministry of International Trade and Industry (MITI), Ministry of Justice (MOJ), Ministry of Labor (MOL), Ministry of Posts and Telecommunications (MPT), and Ministry of Transport (MOT). In addition to the ministries there are a range of other administrative units including, among others, the Management and

Coordination Agency (MCA), which was created by combining the former Prime Minister's Office and Administrative Management Agency, Imperial Household Agency (IHA), Defense Agency (DA), Economic Planning Agency (EPA), Environmental Agency (EA), National Land Agency (NLA), and Science and Technology Agency (STA). In addition, there are over a hundred public corporations ranging from huge government monopolies such as the Japan National Railways (JNR) and Japan Tobacco and Salt Corporation (JTSC) to smaller, more specialized companies like the Japan Housing Corporation (JHC), Japan Highway Corporation, and Japan Railway Construction Corporation (JRCC) used for regional development or the Overseas Economic Cooperation Fund (OECF) which administers much of Japan's foreign aid program. The national bureaucracy in turn cooperates with and dominates with money and personnel the local governments of 47 prefectures and 3300 towns and villages. Altogether, Japan's bureaucrats number about 5.5 million of which one million are in the national bureaucracy, another one million in the public corporations, 3.3 million in the local governments and a quarter million in the Self Defense Force (SDF).[9]

Another seeming paradox behind the bureaucrat's power is the weakness of its leadership. The average tenure of cabinet ministers is less than a year, although ministers at MITI, MOF, MFA, and Chief Cabinet Secretary last about five to six months longer than most other ministries. The reason for this quick turnover is the constant need to placate the various LDP factions with leadership positions. Because of their short tenure, few ministers have any opportunity to shape policy, but instead simply assume the role of leading turf policy battles with other ministries. Thus, there is tremendous policy continuity while the political impact on the ministries is minimal.

The weakness of the politically appointed ministers and vice-ministers contrasts with the expertise and intelligence of the professional officials. The selection system guarantees that some of Japan's brightest people join the bureaucracy. For example, during 1977 about 53 000 people took the Higher-level Public Officials Examination, of which only about 1300 passed, a ratio of one passer to every 41 applicants.[10] Many of the bureaucrats are Tokyo University graduates, with the best coming from its Law School. Tokyo University, or Tokyo Imperial University as it was then known, was established on 1 March 1886 by an Imperial Ordinance with the goal of training Japan's élite, particularly its future officials, and it has still unofficially retained that role despite its 'democratization' during the Occupation. The Tokyo University 'old boy network' (todaibatsu) extends throughout Japan's political economy, further cementing ruling triad solidarity.

The bureaucrats are divided between career and non-career officials. While Non-career Officials settle down to become experts in one section, most Career Officials become generalists by moving each year from one section to another (sotomawari, going around the track). The career officials are the true élite within the élite. For example, in the MOF only 400 out of 60 000 employees are career officials. The careerists are in turn divided between 'administrative officials' or generalists (jimukan) and 'technical officials' or specialists (gikan), based on the member's university studies. Only the Ministry of Construction promotes technical officials to the vice-minister level; generalists are in the fast track in all the other ministries. Most bureaucrats spends their entire career in one ministry and develop an extreme loyalty to it. With this background, the bureaucrats natural sense of élitism, mission, and intelligence is reinforced by their socialization into their particular ministry, the role in promoting their ministry's interests, and their constant turf battles against other ministries.

Advancement is generally based on seniority (nenko joretsu), although as bureaucrats near the top of the job hierarchy, competition becomes very fierce as different patrons (sempai) try to appoint their followers (kohai) into a dwindling number of positions. When one man from a class becomes a vice-minister, all his remaining class-mates immediately resign. The new vice-minister's first duty is to find lucrative jobs for his class-mates in the LDP, businessworld, or public corporations (amakudari). Perhaps because of amakudari, outright corruption such as bribery is relatively limited within the bureaucracy. By performing favors for the business or political world while in office, the official accumulates many debts that can be called once he leaves the ministry. Amakudari into private and public corporations, local government, and the LDP strengthens and extends the hand of bureaucracy. Most MITI officials parachuted into the industries they were regulating while many MOF officials ended up in either the banks or the LDP.

The transition from the bureaucratic-led corporatism of a generation ago to the neo-corporatism of today has obviously meant a corresponding decline in the bureaucracy's power over economic policy-making and implementation. As Japan's economy becomes more complex and prosperous, and as the LDP's policy-making expertise grows, the bureaucracy's role will further diminish. Yet, this is a relative drop from an extremely powerful position. Japan's bureaucracy will remain far more powerful and effective in implementing rational macroeconomic and industrial policies than its counterparts in the West.

NOTES

1. J. A. A. Stockwin (ed.), *Dynamic and Immobilist Politics in Japan*, pp. 17–18.
2. Alan Rix, 'Bureaucracy and Political Change in Japan', in Stockwin, p. 63.
3. Ibid., p. 66.
4. See Chalmers Johnson, *MITI and the Japanese Miracle*, for an in-depth study of these and related issues.
5. Rix, op. cit., in Stockwin, p. 42.
6. John Campbell, *Contemporary Japanese Budget Politics*, p. 74.
7. See John Horne, 'The Economy and the Political System', p. 153, and Rix, p. 65, in Stockwin.
8. Ibid., p. 65.
9. Jon Woronoff, *Politics the Japanese Way*, pp. 108–9.
10. Johnson, op. cit., p. 57.

7 Liberal Democratic Party

Conservative parties have ruled Japan for all but nine months since 1945. Since the conservative Liberal and Democratic parties merged to form the Liberal Democratic Party in 1955, the LDP has continually ruled Japan. Although frequently described as neither liberal, democratic, nor a party, the LDP has been overwhelmingly successful in performing a political party's central role of aggregating the support of related interest groups into a winning electoral combination, and then representing their interests through government policies. The LDP has two interrelated power bases: a virtually impregnable electoral base built on agricultural and small- and medium-sized business support, and a vast sea of finance from the corporate world. Corporate money is channeled to key voting blocks which continue to re-elect the LDP to office, enabling them to continue pushing the growth policies that benefit all. Within the LDP, powerful political patrons rather than issues bind the half dozen factions that constantly compete for plum positions in the Cabinet or party. This balance of power among the factions prevents any one-man rule while ensuring the widest representation of party interests.

The LDP's economic growth policies have brought Japan prosperity, a relatively equitable distribution of income, and global power. The electorate has responded by continually giving the conservatives just enough votes to dominate government. The LDP has at times clung to, and more recently maintained its power base by following pragmatic policies and backing off from controversial issues like constitutional revision, which would alienate many voters. Although conservative, the LDP has been a classic 'catch all' party: it coopts popular political ideas of the opposition such as the environmental or welfare issues, pushes through appropriate legislature, and then basks in the political credit for its efforts.

Why have the conservatives and the LDP ruled for so long, what is the basis of their support, and how do they represent that support in office? What role does the LDP play in policy-making? How has the LDP changed and how has it stayed the same over time?

Four sections address these and related questions. The first section gives an overview of conservative rule throughout the postwar era

145

discussing the major policy objectives, political conflicts, and electoral results, while the next two sections focus on LDP factionalism and organization, respectively. The final section will focus on two LDP leaders – Tanaka and Nakasone – as case studies of the many ways in which Japanese politicians struggle, win, hang on to, and ultimately lose power.

POSTWAR CONSERVATIVE RULE

LDP roots extend back to the emergence of the two conservative parties, the Seiyukai and Minseito, in the mass freedom movement of the 1880s; the Seiyukai eventually became the Liberal Party, and the Minseito the Democratic or Progressive Party. The prewar conservative parties were generally considered political pawns for zaibatsu interests with the Seiyukai fronting Mitsui and the Minseito Mitsubishi. The two conservative parties along with all other interest groups were dissolved into the Imperial Rule Assistance Association in 1940.

In 1945, amidst all the turmoil surrounding the war devastated cities, economic collapse, rapid re-emergence of the JSP and JCP, and foreign Occupation, no one could have forseen the continual conservative party rule and dramatic economic growth experienced by Japan since. For the Occupation's first year and a half, SCAP ruled through many of the pre–1945 political élite, whose governments exerted most of their efforts towards derailing SCAP reforms. Prime Minister Naruhiko Higashikuni, a general and cousin of the Emperor, headed the first postwar Cabinet in the two months following Japan's surrender. Under SCAP pressure, he was replaced in October by the less conservative Baron Kijuro Shidehara, who in turn ruled until May 1946. Like the Higashikuni government, Shidehara's dragged its feet on writing and then implementing a liberal constitution and economic reforms. But despite his Cabinet's attempts to obstruct SCAP's democratization policy, most reforms were beginning to take effect by the time he left office.

Japan's first postwar election to the House of Representatives was held on 10 April 1946. The purge had eliminated many prominent politicians from both the Liberal (Jiyuto) and Progressive (Shimpoto) parties, allowing many bureaucrats to enter politics and take their place. In addition to resuming their old struggle, the two conservative parties faced competition from dozens of small parties and independent candidates that had arisen following SCAP's declaration of civil rights. The Liberal Party won with 141 seats out of a possible 464, while the more heavily purged Progressive Party captured only 94 seats. Together the conservative parties composed a little over 50 per cent of the vote. Of the opposition parties the Japan Socialist Party (JSP) did almost as well as the Progressives, with 92 seats. The other two national parties – the Japan Communist Party (JSP) and the agrarian-oriented Cooperation Party – took five seats and 14 seats, respectively. Independents and smaller parties were important winners in this first election, capturing 81 and 38 seats, respectively.

On the whole, Japan's first postwar election was a dramatic success with a wide participation of parties and individuals. Unfortunately, SCAP chose the Liberal Party's moment of triumph as the time to purge its leader Ichiro Hatayama – a strange lesson in democracy! As a result, the party reins were passed to Shigeru Yoshida, a former career diplomat, with the understanding that he would relinquish power when Hatoyama was eventually allowed to return to public life. The major result of Hatoyama's purge was the Liberal Party division between Hatoyama's 'pure-politician' faction (tojin ha) and Yoshida's 'ex-bureaucrat' faction (kanryo-ha). Hatoyama and his followers had worked their way up through prefectural and municipal assemblies, and were considered more parochial and less intelligent than the ex-bureaucrats who had graduated from Todai or one of the other imperial universities. Yoshida quickly staffed the Liberal Party ranks with former bureaucrats including such future prime ministers as Ikeda and Sato.

Yoshida proved to be surprisingly skilfull at walking the tightrope between the conflicting demands of SCAP and Japan's competing élites. The Liberal Party ruled for five and a half of the Occupation's seven years, and was the more right wing of the two conservative parties; it supported both SCAP and the Constitution while the Progressive Party, in contrast, was at times critical of both SCAP and the Constitution. Yoshida's first year in power, however, was undistinguished as SCAP continued to push through reforms while the economy remained plagued by problems of hyperinflation, and shortages of goods and housing.

Against this background the labor union movement became increasingly militant and called a general strike for 1 February 1947 to protest the dismal conditions. Although Yoshida's government was spared the confrontation when SCAP banned the strike at the last moment, in the 25 April 1947 election the JSP edged out both the Liberal and Progressive parties with 143 seats compared to 131 and 121 seats, respectively, for the two conservative parties. The independents and smaller parties lost heavily with their support falling to about 5 per cent of the vote each, while the Cooperation Party won 29, the new People's Cooperation Party 14 seats, and the JCP four seats.

As a result, JSP leader Tetsu Katayama formed a coalition government with the Democratic Party (Minshuto – formally the Progressive Party), and the Cooperation Party. But, split by heated factional and ideological debates, this left of center coalition proved incapable of governing. Unable to resolve the question of which industries to nationalize, Katayama resigned in February 1948 and was replaced as head of the coalition by Democratic Party leader, Hitoshi Ashida. The Ashida government also failed to manage the myriad of problems confronting it and, following the arrest of the leader of the JSP right-wing faction, Nishio Suehiro, for illegal campaign contributions, resigned in October 1948.

Mass disillusionment over the coalition's failings led to a landslide victory for Yoshida's Liberal Party in the January 1949 elections. The Liberal Party received a clear majority of 240 seats or 56 per cent of the total, and continued to hold a majority in the October 1952 election with 240 seats or 51 per cent of the total diet seats. The timing of both elections was very fortunate for the Liberal Party which came to power before the Dodge Line took effect, and then rode the Korean War economic boom.

The opposition remained fragmented and ineffectual. Throughout this time the JSP and Democratic Party remained discredited by their lackluster role in the coalition government. The JSP split into two parties – one ideological and one pragmatic – in October 1951. Meanwhile the JCP, whose Diet seats had leapt from four to 35 following the October 1949 election, followed a Moscow directive to engage in subversion in January 1950. SCAP immediately purged the JCP and in the 1952 election the party received no Diet seats.

Aside from presiding over Japan's economic take-off, Yoshida skilfully negotiated both San Francisco treaties that simultaneously restored Japan's sovereignty and guaranteed its security. Although he was criticized by many for agreeing to form a National Police Reserve of 75 000 men after the Korean War broke out and for agreeing to eventually assume most responsibilities for Japan's security in its treaty with the United States, Yoshida actually got the best deal possible in both regards. Washington had pressured Yoshida to form a 350 000-man army, but, citing the continued need for Japan to devote itself to economic reconstruction and mass anti-military sentiments, he held out for less than a quarter of that amount. Given the Korean War and global Cold War, Washington would not have allowed Japan to sign a peace treaty without the assurance that it was firmly tied to the Western alliance via a security treaty. By signing the peace treaty Tokyo agreed to renounce its former imperial ambitions in return for receiving all economic and political freedoms, including the option of casting off the Occupation reforms if it so desired.

But at the height of Liberal success and opposition disarray, the party faced an internal struggle that tore it in two. With the end of the Occupation the purgees including Hatoyama, who wanted back his old position as Liberal Party head, returned to politics. But Yoshida refused to give up his position and in the April 1953 election his Liberal Party won only 199 seats or 42 per cent of the total, while Hatoyama's Liberal Party won 35 seats or 7 per cent of the total. The Democratic Party captured 76 seats while the left- and right-wing socialist parties won 72 and 66 seats, respectively. A series of scandals through 1954 involving government subsidies to the ship-building industry further discredited the Liberal Party. Hatoyama's faction defected to the Democratic Party in November 1954 and when Yoshida finally resigned in December, Hatoyama took his place as prime minister. In the February 1955 elections the Democratic Party took 185 seats while the Liberal party's seats tumbled to 112, their lowest level since 1945. The left- and right-wing socialist parties picked up additional strength with 89 and 67 seats, respectively. The JCP managed to capture two seats while other small parties and independents took only 12 seats.

Japanese party politics had clearly consolidated around the two conservative and two socialist parties. Throughout 1955 the corporate world tried to mend the split between the two conservative parties. In January it began to funnel its massive political funds through the Economic Reconstruction Forum rather than each party. But the animosities between Yoshida and Hatoyama still burned too fiercely to heal.

Meanwhile the socialist parties were trying desperately to mend their own split, and in October 1955 the two reunited after long, tough negotiations. After this, fearing an eventual socialist electoral victory that would undermine Japan's economic growth and political stability, the corporate world redoubled its efforts to pressure a conservative party unification. As a result, the two conservative parties joined hands to form the Liberal Democratic Party (LDP) a month later. In the decade following the war, Japanese politics had steadily shifted from a free-wheeling multi-party system into a solid two-party system.

Although Hatoyama's government did not last long, he did achieve two important conservative goals. SCAP had attempted to democratize education by decentralizing it around locally elected school boards and replacing the indoctrination centered around emperor worship with civics classes stressing individualism and civil rights Hatoyama's Cabinet recentralized education under a powerful Education ministry with the power to approve all textbooks, and made the local school boards appointed rather than elected positions. In addition, he restored diplomatic relations with the Soviet Union.

He was succeeded in December 1956 by Tanzan Ishibashi, who in turn resigned two months later because of ill-health and Nobusuke Kishi took over the Cabinet. A controversial leader, Kishi had served in Tojo's wartime Cabinet and was later jailed by SCAP as a Class A war criminal. Kishi tried to complete the efforts of both the Yoshida and Hatoyama Cabinets to reverse the Occupation reforms. Attempting to build on Yoshida's 1952 Subversive Activities Bill directed against the Communist Party and 1954 Police Bill which recentralized police administration, Kishi introduced the Police Duties Law in 1958, which would have further strengthened police powers to control dissent. That same year he also attempted to restore the prewar 'ethic' classes to education. But the JSP led a nationwide coalition of groups concerned that Japan was reverting to its authoritarian past, and both Kishi's police and education measures failed to pass the Diet.

Perhaps because of these controversies, the LDP lost ten seats in the May 1958 election, ending up with a total of 297 seats, while the JSP increased its strength from 153 seats to 166. The JCP's presence fell to only one seat while 13 independents remained in the Diet. This election marked the electoral heights for both parties. The LDP has never surpassed its 57.8 per cent of the electoral vote, a percentage which dropped steadily each following election to a low point of 44.6 per cent in 1979. Since then it has steadily risen to its most recent height of 49.4 per cent in 1986. In contrast to the LDP's slowly diminishing strength until the late 1970s, and dramatic rise in electoral support since, has been the JSP's steady decline from 32.9 per cent of the vote in 1958 to 17.2 per cent in 1986.

A major reason for this difference in the fortunes of the two parties has been their differing degrees of unity. In 1959, in protest against the JSP's continual leftward drift, the right wing under Suehiro Nishio defected to form the Democratic Socialist Party (DSP). Since then neither socialist party has fared well. If added together, the 1986 electoral support for the two socialist parties of 23.6 per cent of the vote is a still considerable drop from its height in 1958. In contrast, the LDP has managed to hang together despite severe strains caused by powerful antagonistic personalities and a series of periodic scandals. The most serious challenge to LDP unity came in early 1976 when a progressive faction broke off to form the New Liberal Club (NLC). Although the NLC won 17 Diet members in the May 1976 election, its strength had fallen to six a decade later in the July 1986 election, after which its members dissolved back into the LDP.

Another reason for the differing fortunes of the two parties has been the LDP's consistent pragmatism and the JSP's continuing obsession with marxist ideology. Kishi was the last LDP leader until Nakasone to promote such elements of the right-wing agenda as education and constitutional revision. Kishi's most controversial action, however, was his handling of Diet approval for a revised Security Treaty in 1960. Negotiations for a revised treaty began in 1958 as Kishi tried to increase Japan's independence without weakening America's defense commitment. But the left, encouraged by its victories against Kishi's attempts to further centralize education and police powers, rallied against the revised security treaty. In February 1959 a People's Council for Preventing Revision of the Security Treaty was formed as an umbrella organization to lead the campaign. Foreign and domestic political developments stimulated widespread support for the movement. International tensions caused by the extension of the nuclear arms race to space, the Berlin Crisis, the shooting down of America's U–2 spy plane over the Soviet Union, and the cancellation of a proposed summit between Eisenhower and Krushchev caused widespread fears among Japanese that they could be dragged into a nuclear war between the superpowers. The March 1959 verdict of the Tokyo District Court in the Sunakawa case (although later overturned by the Supreme Court in December), which declared the presence of American troops was incompatable with Article 9 and cast doubt on the constitutionality of the Security Treaty, further enflamed resistance against the Security Treaty revisions.

The anti-revision coalition became increasingly militant. Led by the JSP, JCP, Sohyo Trade Federation, and All Student Federation (Zengakuren), demonstrators began a virtually constant protest in front of the Diet beginning in November 1959 and tried to prevent Kishi from leaving for Washington in January 1960 to sign the treaty. Meanwhile, the opposition parties continually tried to disrupt Diet proceedings. Failing to pass the Treaty in the House of Representatives on 26 April, Kishi was forced to extend the regular session in order to have it ratified by Eisenhower's arrival on 19 June. But the opposition continued to resist ratification until Kishi called for their removal by the police. With their absence the LDP quickly voted first to extend the regular session and then ratify the Treaty. But opposition grew even more heated as many feared Kishi was attempting to overthrow the Diet. The mobbing of Eisenhower's press secretary on 10 June convinced Kishi to call off the President's visit. Still, the House of Councillors ratified the Treaty on 19 June and four days later Kishi resigned.

The opposition's energies seemed to have been exhausted by the long struggle and final passage of the Treaty, and somewhat mollified by Kishi's resignation. Political passions quickly died, as the new prime minister, Hayato Ikeda, followed a low posture in both domestic and foreign policy. Despite, or perhaps because of the serious political conflict, in the November 1960 election the LDP received its largest Diet membership yet – 296 seats, while the JSP and DSP together took 145 and 17 seats, respectively, losing four seats from their high point after the 1958 election. LDP strength slipped to 283 seats in the November 1963 election, with most of the seats going to the DSP, who increased their strength to 23 seats.

There were no real emotional issues during the early 1960s. In fact, Ikeda's 'income doubling within ten years plan' was simply a slogan designed to take people's minds off politics. In reality, Japan's growth-oriented economic policies had changed little from those originally formulated under the Occupation, and growth continued to average a spectacular 10 per cent a year. Yet Ikeda's slogan nicely captured the spirit of Japan's growing prosperity and international acceptance since the early 1950s. Although Japan's international status received boosts in the mid-1950s, when it joined the United Nations and GATT, its membership in the OECD – the rich countries' club – and Tokyo's hosting of the Olympics in 1964 jointly symbolized Japan's coming of age.

In November 1964 Ikeda had to resign because of ill-health and

Eisaku Sato, Kishi's younger brother, became prime minister. While presiding over the high growth policies of his predecessors, Sato took a more active role in foreign affairs, reflecting Japan's rise to become the world's third largest economic power after the United States and the Soviet Union. His accomplishments included the 1965 restoration of relations with South Korea, his November 1969 success in getting President Nixon to agree to return Okinawa to Japan by May 1972, and the negotiation of an agreement advantageous to Japan during the 'textile wrangle' of the late 1960s.

Japan's steady economic growth and political stability in the two decades after 1950 were undercut by a series of shocks during the late 1960s and early 1970s. In 1968 and 1969 Japan's universities faced growing unrest and disruptions similar to those of other countries at the time. The passage of the Universities Control Bill in August 1969 gave the police enhanced powers to suppress demonstrations and dissident groups. An even greater challenge was posed by the worsening air, water, and noise pollution that accompanied economic growth. Confronted with a grass roots anti-pollution movement, court decisions against polluting firms, and increasing international criticism of Japan's horrible pollution, the Diet passed 14 bills in 1970 that attempted to bring the problem under control.

Although the opposition parties increasingly followed politics of cooperation rather than confrontation, their ranks swelled throughout the 1960s. Japan's multi-party system, or 'one and a half party' system (so-called because of continued LDP domination), expanded further during the 1967 election as the Clean Government Party (CGP – Komeito), the political arm of the Sokka Gakkei Buddhist sect, emerged to capture 25 seats. LDP Diet strength declined to 277 seats, followed by the JSP with 140 seats, the DSP with 30 seats, and the JCP with five seats. Each party's strength reflected the relative strength of its main backers. Financially, the LDP was mostly dependent on the corporate world, while farmers and small and medium-sized businesses supplied most of its electoral support. The JSP and DSP depended largely on the two labor federations, Sohyo and Domei, for their respective financial and vote-mobilizing support. The CGP via the Sokka Gakkai and JCP competed for the same pool of floating voters, who were generally unattached to any large support organization, of lower socio-economic status, and had received few benefits from Japan's rapid economic growth. The CGP and JCP dramatically increased their strength in the 1969 election, receiving 47 and 14 seats respectively as they became adept at moderating their positions and mobilizing the more disaffected members of Japanese society. They expanded their support at the expense of the JSP, whose strength plunged to 90 seats while the DSP gained one seat with 31 seats in total.

But these shocks of university unrest, environmental protests, and the steady deterioration of LDP Diet and electoral strength were overshadowed by new economic challenges of the early 1970s. Although the two Nixon 'shocks' were predominantly psychological, they were powerful enough to cause Tokyo to re-evaluate both its economic and foreign policies. In August 1971 President Nixon announced his New Economic Policy, which included measures to float the dollar. This was a blow to Japan, whose prosperity rested in part on an increasingly undervalued yen throughout the 1950s and 1960s. Sato succeeded in skilfully negotiating a limited revaluation of the yen in December 1971, long after the other industrial countries had agreed to revalue their currencies. Unfortunately, Sato did not survive the second Nixon shock – Washington's announcement of the restoration of relations with China. Although there had been widespread support within Japan for better relations with China, Sato continued to resist such pressure and continued to follow America's policy of non-recognition. Sato resigned in July 1972 and was replaced by Kakuei Tanaka.

Although, unlike his two predecessors, Prime Minister Tanaka at first proved to be a dynamic, popular leader, he was soon bogged down in managing a succession of crises, three of which were of his own making. Shortly after entering office the Tanaka government took the popular step of recognizing China. Despite this new China policy, LDP Diet strength fell to 271 seats in the December 1972 election, its lowest level since the merger of the two conservative parties in 1955. The JSP strength rose to 118 seats while that of the DSP and CGP was halved to 19 and 29 seats, respectively. In contrast, the JCP more than doubled its share to 38 seats, its highest level yet.

Tanaka's next move, his bold plan for the 'Reconstruction of the Japanese Archipelago', which involved decentralizing industry and taking people away from the crowded Tokyo-Osaka corridor to growth centers elsewhere, ended up being abandoned. The plan unleased a speculative boom that rapidly drove up prices in the targeted areas, and, in addition, was subject to widespread criticism that many of Tanaka's cronies in the construction industry were given advanced warning and other advantages in the project.

Tanaka's April 1973 plan to replace the multi-member districts with single-member districts was similarly criticized and rejected by the Opposition parties, which feared the new system would allow the LDP to completely dominate the Diet. Then, the oil embargo and quadrupling of oil prices following the 1973 October War between Israel and the Arab countries battered Japan's economy with double-digit inflation and negative growth. Adding insult to injury were the mass anti-Japanese demonstrations that greeted Tanaka during his tour of Southeast Asia in January 1974. The final blow, however, was struck by the monthly journal '*Bungei Shunju*' which in October 1974 published the first in a series of investigative articles exposing Tanaka's shady financial dealings. After foreign newspapers picked up the investigation Japan's daily press also began reporting on the allegations. Tanaka resigned the next month citing ill-health.

The two largest LDP factions led by Takeo Fukuda and Masayoshi Ohira battled each other to a draw over the prime ministership. Instead the faction leaders compromised and made Takeo Miki, the progressive leader of the LDP's smallest faction, the next prime minister. Miki attempted to reform both the LDP and Japanese politics, but his anti-corruption legislation failed to pass the Diet. In February 1976 a United States Congressional sub-committee investigating the Lockheed Corporation listened as executives revealed having channelled millions of dollars worth of bribes into Japan so that the government would buy Lockheed airplanes. Tanaka himself was accused of taking a $2 million dollar bribe. Miki began a relentless investigation that resulted in Tanaka's arrest in June. Six LDP Diet members defected in disgust to form their own party – the New Liberal Club (NLC).

The LDP lost 22 seats in the December 1976 election, bringing their total down to 249. Of the opposition parties, only the JCP lost seats, falling to only 17 while the JSP, DSP, CGP and NLC won 123, 29, 55, and 17, respectively. The opposition's Diet ranks were swelled by the addition of 20 new urban seats to overcome the increasing population difference between rural and urban electoral districts. Many believed that eventually the LDP would have to form a coalition government with the NLC or DSP.

As the new prime minister, Fukuda presided over an era of revived economic growth and diminished LDP political power as the chairmanship of several Diet committees were led by Opposition politicians. He managed to divert American and European protests against Japan's swelling trade surpluses by promising to open

Japanese markets. In August 1978 Tokyo signed the Sino-Japanese Treaty of Peace and Friendship, expanding trade relations between the two countries. Despite his success in overseeing the resumption of Japan's economic dynamism, Fukuda lost out to Ohira in the November 1978 LDP presidential election when Tanaka, who remained in the Diet despite the indictment against him, threw his faction's weight behind the latter.

Ohira tried to depart from the Cabinet's traditional dependence on the ministries for advice on policy-making and legislation. He created nine special advisory committees around various issues confronting Japan, most of which did not submit their policy advice until after Ohira had left office. The government also successfully managed Japan's recovery from the second oil crisis of 1979. Despite these successes, the LDP did poorly in the October 1979 election, with their Diet strength dropping one seat to a total of 248 seats. The opposition continued to battle each other for the same share of seats with the DSP, CGP, JCP, and newly formed Social Democratic League (SDL) increasing their totals to 35, 57, 39, and two, respectively, and the JSP and NLC seats dropping to 107 and four respectively.

As economic growth surged ahead, the LDP factions continued to battle behind the scenes. On 16 May 1980 the JSP presented a no-confidence motion in the Diet citing continued LDP corruption, defense spending increases, and rises in public utility charges. The non-confidence vote passed when the Fukuda, Miki, and Nakagawa factions abstained from voting, and Ohira resigned. He died of a heart attack on 12 June and the LDP, perhaps because of a large sympathy vote, won an overwhelming victory at the polls on 22 June, carrying 284 seats. The Opposition losers were the DSP which dropped to 32 seats, the CGP whose seats fell dramatically to 33 seats following a corruption scandal involving the head of the Sokka Gakkai in 1979, and the JCP which ended up with 29 seats. JSP seats remained the same at 107 while the NLC and SDL earned 12 and three seats respectively.

Tanaka, the 'king-maker', threw his huge faction's support behind Zenko Suzuki, the successor to head Ohira's faction, as the compromise choice for prime minister. Trying to reverse the big government spending programs that had proliferated during the 1970s, the Suzuki Cabinet pledged to undertake administrative reform with the goal of eventually balancing the budget without tax increases. To this end the government proposed eventually selling off such major government corporations as the Japan National Railway, Nippon Telephone and Telegraph, and the salt and tobacco monopoly. The Suzuki Cabinet also began what would be seven stages of market opening measures designed to offset the complaints from Japan's trade partners about Japanese trade barriers. Finally, Suzuki agreed in 1982 to a Washington request that Japan be responsible for defense of its sealanes up to 1000 miles from its shores.

In what is generally regarded as part of the deal cut with the other faction leaders when he took office, Suzuki resigned in October 1982 and Yasuhiro Nakasone was chosen to replace him, again with the solid backing of the Tanaka faction. Nakasone proved to be the opposite of his often colorless predecessors. Striving to promote a new image for Japan as a leader among nations, Nakasone concentrated on foreign policy issues during his almost five years in office. Starting with a visit to Seoul and Washington in January, Nakasone attended a variety of bilateral and multilateral conferences or hosted foreign leaders in Tokyo throughout the year, impressing most foreign observers with his internationalist style.

Despite his efforts, however, the LDP suffered a setback in the December 1983 election, receiving only 250 seats. Although by expending huge amounts the Tanaka faction was the only LDP faction not to lose any members, the LDP defeat was considered to have been a reaction against his October Court conviction of taking a 500 million yen bribe from Lockheed over ten years earlier. The opposition JSP took 111 seats, the DSP 38, the CGP 58, the NLC 8, and the JCP 26.

Undeterred, Nakasone continued actively to promote his diplomatic initiatives abroad and administrative reform at home. Popular support for his style and 'policies increased steadily after the 1983 election and reached a height with the landslide victory of July 1986, in which the LDP received 304 seats out of the 512 seat lower house. The JSP seats dropped to 86, the DSP down to 26, the CGP 57, and the JCP picked up one seat to total 27. The NLC dropped from eight to six seats and ended up reuniting with the LDP.

During Nakasone's tenure Japan's huge trade and current account surpluses mounted steadily and it replaced the United States as the world's banker. Nakasone used skilfull diplomacy built around his 'Ron-Yasu' relationship with President Reagan and a series of highly publicized but largely cosmetic 'market-opening steps' to allay foreign demands that Japan give more to and take less from the world economy. The official Maekawa Report of Spring 1986 called on the

Japanese to open up not just their markets, but their minds to the rest of the world. Unfortunately, the report was severely criticized by virtually all important economic and political voices – clearly indicating that the Japanese are not yet ready to abandon the neo-mercantilist policies and outlook that have brought their country such vast wealth.

With the smashing 1986 victory and continued high popularity ratings behind him, the LDP bent its rules that limited a party president to only two terms and allowed Nakasone to stay in power up through October 1987. He might have stayed in office longer had his support not plunged in Spring 1987 after he attempted to push through a controversial tax policy that, among other things, would have introduced a Value Added Tax to Japan.

Nakasone announced that he would step down in the Fall and by late summer three contenders – Noboru Takeshita, Kiichi Miyazawa, and Shintaro Abe – had clearly emerged to battle for the party presidency and prime ministership. With the three unable to cut a deal among themselves, Nakasone stepped in as king-maker, choosing Takeshita because, among other things, he headed the LDP's largest faction.

For a colorless, traditional rural politician like Takeshita, Nakasone would have been a tough act to follow in any event. When Takeshita was chosen it was generally believed that as a compromise choice he would step down after two years in office. His only success was the November 1988 passage of the tax reform bill – the same bill that had led to Nakasone's eventual fall proved to be a pyrrhic victory for Takeshita as well, as widespread resentment at the new VAT broke out after it was implemented on 1 April 1989. Other than passing the tax bill, Takeshita's government continued the successful efforts of its predeccesors in managing the growing foreign demands on Japan to open its markets and give more to the world economy. Takeshita's last year in office was plagued by continual revelations of the Recruit scandal in which 159 members of Japan's élite – including members of all the opposition parties except the JCP – benefited from manipulating the stock market.[1] Eventually over 20 members of the élite were forced to resign their respective positions, capped by Takeshita himself announcing his resignation in May 1989 after it was revealed that he had concealed some Recruit contributions.

Takeshita's successor, Sosuke Uno of Nakasone's faction, was free of any Recruit entanglements but in his second month in office was embarrassed by 'pillow-talk' revelations from a former mistress. This sex scandal coming on the heels of the vast Recruit scandal, imposition of the Vat, Tokyo's promise to liberalize the domestic cattle and orange industries, and failure of consumers to enjoy any benefits of the high yen led to a disasterous defeat by the LDP in the 23 July House of Councillor elections in which the opposition parties received a majority for the first time since 1947. Uno resigned, and was eventually replaced with Toshiki Kaifu, a squeaky-clean, undistinguished member of the Takeshita faction. Kaifu attempted to mollify angry women voters by appointing women to the Environmental Ministry and Economic Planning Agency. He is considered yet another caretaker prime minister who will preside over the government until the scheduled summer of 1990 House of Representative elections.

FACTIONS

LDP factions are informal groups of Dietmen, held together by ties of political convenience, money, and personal relations, and led by a potential or current party president. Factions have such innocuous sounding names as Tanaka's 'Thursday Club' (Mokuyokai). These factions in turn spawn a host of smaller groups and organizations such as study groups to assist policy-making and dummy companies to launder funds. Their number fluctuated between 11 and five from the 1950s to the mid–1980s. As of Spring 1989, the 422 LDP Diet members, with 299 in the House of Representatives and 143 in the House of Councillors, were divided among six factions: Takeshita (121), Abe (89), Nakasone (87), Miyazawa (87), Komoto (30), and Nikaido (14). In addition, there were 14 nominally independent Diet members, who were in fact closely aligned behind the scenes with one faction or another.

A range of cultural, historical, and institutional forces accounts for the importance of factions in Japanese politics. According to Hans Baerwald, factions are not only the essence of LDP politics, but the 'core of that country's politics'.[2] Culturally, small groups are the basis of Japanese society. To be anyone or to go anywhere, the individual must be a member of a group (batsu); groups are the basis of every individual's identity and the building blocks of Japanese society. There is a hierarchy both within and between groups, composed of patron-follower relations in which the former gives protection and support to his followers, in return for the latter's undying loyalty and dedication. Groups can be relatively large – such as the zaibatsu (financial groups), gakubatsu (school groups), or kanbatsu (bureaucratic groups), or very small – keibatsu (family) group or a patron and a few followers.

Historically, factions within the Liberal Party can be traced to early 1946 when the recently purged Hatoyama handed over the party's reins to Yoshida, who promised to return control of the party as soon as Hatoyama was rehabilitated. Yoshida, an ex-bureaucrat, packed the party with skilled leaders from the ministries, thus splitting it between the dominant bureaucrat fraction (kanryo) and minority party faction (tojin). The party was further split when Hatoyama returned in 1952 and Yoshida refused to relinquish power. During the first presidential election after the Liberal and Democratic parties merged in 1955, the LDP was composed of eight formal factions, four from each former party. These factions in turn allied themselves into two large factions – a largely bureaucratic mainstream faction (shuryu-ha), and a largely party regular anti-mainstream faction (hi-shuryu-ha). By the 1960s, these eight factions had merged into five factions. But the traditional distinctions between mainstream and anti-mainstream factions have since disappeared as each faction became a broad mix of former bureaucrats and politicians. In 1989, although the faces changed, the balance of power among the factions was preserved in the Takeshita, Uno, and Kaifu Cabinets.

Factions have persisted for several important institutional reasons. The strength of one's faction and one's seniority within the factions are the major requirements for holding positions within the Cabinet or party hierarchy. Seniority is based on the number of times the Diet member has been re-elected. Factions dominate appointments to Cabinet and party posts, most particularly in the selection of the party president. Each faction leader submits the seniority list of his faction to the Prime Minister, who in turn allocates the political plums according to a range of political pay-offs and alliances. There is a quick turnover in ministers to give each faction an opportunity to reward its members. Factions are also important in the distribution of party funds, and sometimes intraparty ideological disputes. While there are many examples of factions taking the key role in policy-making, particularly foreign policy, they are rarely influential in routine policy-making. Factions also compete fiercely for new recruits. This competition is exacerbated by the multi-member electoral districts in which LDP candidates often run against each other as fiercely as against the opposition parties.

For several reasons, no faction has ever represented a majority of LDP representatives. Perhaps the most important reason is that there is a balance of power system among the factions whereby smaller ones often form alliances to prevent any single one from becoming too large. But another reason is that the larger a faction the greater the possibility of a split since the rungs of seniority, position, and patronage rewards correspond to the membership numbers. As former Prime Minister Kishi said, 'politics is money': the more money the more access to power, and the more access to power and the patronage it provides the more money and recruits a faction attracts, and so on. Yet, this brings up a dilemma in which, although larger factions generally attract more funds, their very size means members must wait a long time to climb up through the ranks to high party posts. So the medium-sized and even smaller factions are still able to gain new recruits.

The faction's most important role is to serve as the vehicle for landing its leader into the position of LDP president, and thus prime minister. No one could become party president without a powerful faction behind him. Since 90 per cent of the convention delegates are Diet members, the candidate which can forge the strongest alliance of factions will win. The six current factions vary according to the length of their lineage and success in securing powerful party and Cabinet positions. The most successful faction was Yoshida's original ex-bureaucrat faction which has in turn been led by Ikeda, Sato, Tanaka, and, currently, Takeshita. The next most successful faction was Hatoyama's, which in turn has been led by Kishi, Fukuda, and currently Abe. Following Ohira's death, Suzuki took over his faction, and became both president and prime minister. The two smaller factions – Nakasone's and Komoto's – each supplied one prime minister, Nakasone and Miki, respectively, while Nikaido's faction broke away from the Tanaka faction in 1986.

Seniority within a faction determines who is eligible for a Cabinet, party, or Diet committee leadership position. Faction members are ranked by the number of times they have been re-elected to the Diet. If a Diet member moves from one faction to another, he loses his seniority. The only exceptions to this seniority rule occur when an older member is passed over because of ill-health, or younger member is promoted over his seniors' heads because of his experience as a former bureaucrat. Only 40 per cent of the ministers are reappointed to the Cabinet. To serve the demands of the seniority system, Cabinet turnover is very quick, the average term of a minister being only 278 days.

There are both negative and positive aspects to the factionalism within the LDP and other parties.[3] Factions encourage corruption and money politics since they are the best vehicles to power and money. With access to power being the major concern, issues tend to take a back seat. Politics is shaped by personalities and money rather than issues; in-depth policy debates are avoided to maintain factional unity and attract new members. Faction leaders decide such issues as party policies and candidates behind closed doors. Leadership positions, particularly that of the Prime Minister, are weakened since in reality leadership is shared among the faction leaders. Shifts in the balance of power among the factions give the illusion of change, without its reality. The continued LDP rule and the multi-member districts mean that the most serious rivalry is between factions rather than with the opposition parties.

Most analysts, while acknowledging these negative aspects of factions, generally argue that, on balance, the factions strengthen Japanese democracy. Factional rivalry brings a dynamic, pluralistic atmosphere to the LDP so that it is almost a mini-party system in itself. Since the power of the party president and prime minister rests on such a restless, shifting balance of power, the leader must be responsive to the prevailing public mood. Such recent prime ministers as Tanaka, Miki, and Nakasone reflected anti-bureaucrat, anti-corruption, and nationalistic moods, respectively. Power is thus diffused and pluralistic. The Japanese have never experienced a cult of personality; although Nakasone based much of his success on the strength of his charisma, he has been the exception rather than the rule in Japanese politics. Thus, despite being in power for over 40 years with the likelihood of remaining in power for the forseeable future, the ruling party is largely democratic and adapts its policies to popular moods.

PARTY ORGANIZATION AND POLICY-MAKING

The LDP leadership is centered on the President, Secretary-General, PARC Chairman, and Executive Council Chairman. Since the party president simultaneously serves as prime minister, the post is the pinnacle of political achievement and patronage, and is thus fiercely contested. For 20 years, from 1958 to 1978, the President was selected at a national party convention by an election among all LDP Diet members and 47 prefectural representatives, with the winner decided by a majority vote. If there was no majority vote, a run-off was held between the two top vote getters.

In reality, the convention merely ratifies the choice previously negotiated in a 'smoke-filled room' among the faction leaders. The choice was determined by the faction leader who was most adept at distributing huge sums of money and patronage among the delegates. Although faction members would remain loyal to their candidate, a faction would rally behind a particular candidate for the right price. As might be expected, the richest candidate generally won. The press estimated that at the 1972 Convention between five and ten billion yen changed hands among the 478 delegates, an amount which averaged between \$40–80 000 per delegate.[4]

Despite the openness and vast amounts of cash involved in Japanese 'money politics', there are certain hazy limits that if surpassed leave a politician vulnerable to censure. Factions recruit new members through the money they provide. New candidates running for office must spend as much as \$800 000 a race, while established older candidates seeking re-election must spend at least \$600 000, of which as much as 25 per cent comes from the faction leader. Any new ambitious candidate generally chooses between the LDP factions which do not have a representative in his district, since factions will not endorse more than one candidate per district to avoid interfactional strife. Although the public remains relatively tolerant of the openness with which vast sums of money are exchanged for national and party elections, Japan's corruption toleration threshold does have an ill-defined limit. Each decade seems to present a new corruption scandal, from the Denko Showa scandal of 1947 to the Recruit scandal of 1988–89.

Of these scandals, the Tanaka affair had the farthest reaching effect on the LDP. Prime Minister Tanaka was forced to resign in November 1974 after the monthly investigative magazine *Bungei Shunju* revealed the workings of his political machine. Fearing that the bad press about the scandal would cause the LDP to lose badly at the next election, the party élite chose Takeo Miki, leader of a small faction, as a compromise choice for president and prime minister after Tanaka's resignation. Known as 'Mr Clean', Miki had always been harshly critical of Japanese money politics and seemed the ideal choice to offset the scandal's effects. The party élite assumed they would be able to prevent any attempts by Miki to promote political reforms.

But with public opinion solidly behind him, Miki was able to push through a reform program that the other faction leaders were eventually forced to support. The key reform involved the tenure and selection of the party president. From now on a president could serve no more than two consecutive terms. Any Diet member could run for the presidency if he presented a petition to the secretary-general signed by at least 20 of his colleagues. In order to 'democratize' the presidential selection, a primary system was created in which all the LDP Diet members, prefectural representatives, and party members were allowed to vote. In this general election, one point was counted for every 1000 voters in each prefecture (1525 in 1978), with the top two vote getters splitting points. The ballot was by mail and sent to party headquarters. The second vote was limited to Diet members who chose one of the top two candidates.

Unfortunately, these attempts to democratize the party largely failed while factional infighting actually became even more bitter; the new system simply extended factional rivalries from the national to the local level. Each faction scrambled to sign up new members devoted to their candidates, and as a result, in 1978 alone party membership grew from 300 000 to 1 500 000 members, a total greater than all the opposition parties combined. In contrast, the combined membership of the opposition parties was 670 000, of whom 400 000 were in the JCP. Over 80 per cent of the new members were already in individual LDP politicians' support groups (koenkai), while most of their membership fees were paid for by the factions. Some 'members' did not even know they were in the party, although that often did not stop their ballot from being used for one of the candidates. The new system also increased the dependence of the factions on the corporate world since so much money was required to win the primary. In the old system, factions had generally respected each other's districts, but the new system stimulated them to invade each other's districts in the mad scramble for new voters.

The first test of the new system came in 1978. Three weeks before the primary election, polls showed that Fukuda was well ahead with 52 per cent of the vote compared to Ohira's 30 per cent, Nakasone's 12 per cent, and Komoto's 4 per cent. Fukuda was so confident that he promised to withdraw his candidacy if he failed to win the primary. This gave Tanaka the opportunity he had been waiting for. Tanaka hated Fukuda and poured massive amounts of funds into

Ohira's campaign coffers, which were in turn used to buy up the block votes of the other factions. As a result, Ohira won the primary with 55 0891 votes or 748 points compared to Fukuda's 472 503 votes and 638 points. Nakasone and Komoto got 200 000 and 89 000 votes, and 93 and 46 points, respectively. Fukuda then fulfilled his campaign promise of withdrawing from the convention vote if he lost the primary, and Ohira won by default.

Because of the enormous expense and uncertainty of the new system, the party leaders agreed to prevent any future primaries at all costs. The LDP élite has reverted to its backroom selection process and thus no primaries have been held since 1978. In 1981 they revised the system to make it more difficult for candidates to run. Now a presidential aspirant needs the support of 50 Diet members before he can be considered a candidate, and a primary is held only if four official candidates are running: contests between three or fewer candidates are resolved at a party convention.

After the President, the Secretary-General (kanjicho) is the most important LDP post. The Secretary-General administers the party's everyday business, coordinates fund-raising, selects candidates for other party positions, and is a stepping stone to the party presidency. Of the last nine presidents, only Suzuki did not serve as Secretary-General. The respective chairmen of the Executive Council and PARC occupy the next highest party positions. They work closely together to guide policy-making in the party and Diet. All the LDP presidents except Kishi served in at least one of the two posts. The position of vice-president is an optional appointment and largely ceremonial. For the most part it remained vacant until Prime Minister Nakasone appointed Susumu Nikaido, a Tanaka aid, in 1984.

Cabinet portfolios follow just behind the top four party leadership positions as the system's most valued political plums. Generally, the economic ministries such as MITI, MOF, or MOC are considered the prime Cabinet positions – as much for the opportunities they provide to dispense patronage as for their importance in steering Japan's economy. Service in one of these economic ministries or the MFA is considered an essential stepping stone to the top party positions. Eligibility for a minister's portfolio depends on an LDP member having won at least six re-elections to the House of Representatives and served as a parliamentary vice-minister. Three minor Cabinet posts are reserved for House of Councillor members.

Prime ministers generally allocate Cabinet positions to factions according to their respective strength. The Takeshita Cabinet followed this formula very carefully. In November 1987 there were six factions: Takeshita (117), Miyazawa (89), Nakasone (87), Abe (85), Komoto (32), and Nikaido (19), plus 17 nominally independent Diet members who were in fact tied to one of the factions. Of the Cabinet posts, Takeshita awarded five to his own faction, four each to the Miyazawa, Abe, and Nakasone factions, two to Komoto, and one from the independent ranks. Nikaido was unrewarded because of his earlier break from Takeshita's faction. Of the Cabinet posts, 17 went to House of Representative members and the other three to House of Councillors members. Nine of Takeshita's Cabinet had previously served as ministers while 11 were first timers.

Since ministers are appointed for their political value rather than their expertise and serve such short terms, most ministers have few technical qualifications for their posts. This is fine for the bureaucrats which desire a minister who will lead their budget and turf battles while avoiding meddling in their day-to-day operations and policy-making. The rural electoral bias that makes those districts politically more stable is reflected in their over-representation of rural politicians in the Cabinet.

LDP policy-making is conducted through the Policy Research Affairs Council (PARC) which serves as a clearing house for interest groups and bureaucrats; PARC is made up of a Chairman; several Vice-Chairmen; the Policy Deliberation Commission (Seisaku Shingikai or Seicho Shingikai) of 15–20 members; 17 divisions (bukai) that correspond to government ministries and Diet sub-committees; and over a hundred investigative commissions (Chosakai) and special committees (tokubetsu iinkai) established for special problems or policy areas. Some committees are concerned with controversial issues like Constitutional Revision, but most revolve around the ministries. Each division has from 44 (Foreign Affairs) to 155 (Agriculture-Forestry), with an average of 72 members for each of the 17 divisions. Membership is partly assigned and partly voluntary. The Policy Deliberation Committee, with 15–20 members, and the Executive Council with about 30 members, attempt to coordinate the policies submitted by the divisions.[5]

The work of PARC divisions and committees is complemented by the numerous policy 'tribes' (zoku) composed of Dietmen addressing specific issues, of which agriculture (norinzoku), trade (shokozoku), and construction (kensetsuzoku) are the most important. The policy tribes have proliferated and become increasingly specialized since they first emerged in the 1970s. Today, virtually any industry has its own policy tribe which devotes its efforts to promoting and protecting that industry from international competition. Dietmen are usually members of only one policy tribe and generally become quite knowledgeable on the subject. Far less substantial are the Dietman's Leagues (Giin Renmei, domei) which include members from all parties and are oriented around a specific interest or policy area. Dietmen are often members of dozens of these leagues, some of which are organized for a short time, while others are long-standing. The leagues do not require more time than it takes for the Dietman to sign the attendance list, plus attending the annual convention of the sponsoring business group. These groups often sponsor Member's Bills (not endorsed by the Cabinet) which stand a chance of success when the opposition Dietmen are in the League.

Despite the LDP's growing policy-making role, it is the bureaucrats who have the first and last say in determining the policy agenda and shape of the issues. They not only initiate legislation but carefully guide it through the LDP and Diet committees to the final vote in the Diet. According to Baerwald, the bureaucrats 'stage manage most of the proceedings. It is they who have prepared the questions and it is they who provide the answers either by having briefed the minister or by answering the questions themselves. Only rarely have these carefully prepared, staged productions broken down. There is very little prospect that the bureaucrat's dominant influence will lessen in the near future. Government officials will continue to draft the vast majority of legislative bills'.[6]

By whatever means it uses, the LDP has been very successful in pushing its bills through the Diet. For example, in the 36th Diet Session from July 1980 to November 1983, 446 bills were presented to the Diet. The Cabinet sponsored 269 of which 240 or 89.2 per cent passed while individual Diet members or the opposition sponsored 177, of which 47 or 26.6 per cent passed.[7]

Both the LDP presidents and rank-and-file are highly educated. Of the prime ministers, only three did not graduate from the élite schools – Takeo Miki from Meiji University, Zenko Suzuki from Fisheries Polytechnic, while Tanaka's highest education was junior high school. The percentage of university graduates among LDP diet members has steadily increased from 69 per cent in 1955 to over 85 per cent today, of which about 30 per cent were Tokyo University graduates.

The occupation of the Diet members is more varied. In the 1980s local politicians have comprised 26 per cent of the rank and file, bureaucrats 20 per cent, businessmen 16 per cent, and LDP staff members 19 per cent. This represents a slight shift in the LDP composition since the 1950s when bureaucrats represented about 30 per cent of all LDP Diet members, while staffers had virtually no positions at all. In the House of Representatives, the percentage of ex-bureaucrats holding LDP seats has averaged about 26 per cent from 1955 up to the present. The ex-bureaucrat presence in the House of Councillors has been even higher, varying between 32 per cent in 1977 to a height of 40 per cent in 1974.

Although the percentage of ex-bureaucrats in the LDP has declined slightly their influence remains powerful. Up through the early 1980s, ex-bureaucrats composed about half of the senior party and Cabinet position, a percentage that has declined to about one-third at present. Ten of the 17 postwar prime ministers were former bureaucrats. In Nakasone's third Cabinet formed on 28 December 1985 six out of 21 ministers were former bureaucrats.

As the seniority system lengthens, it will become increasingly difficult for former officials to parachute down into influential LDP positions as they did in the past. Generally speaking, an LDP Diet member must now be re-elected seven times to be considered for a Cabinet post. Most of the new ex-bureaucrats were middle-ranking officials. Bureaucrats will continue to hold a disproportionate share of power within the LDP. The middle-ranking officials who enter politics retain their patron-client network in their respective ministries which can be used to the LDP's advantage. Although most bureaucrats are generalists, they still know far more about policy issues than the average politician; their skills will remain in high demand despite the rise of the zoku (policy 'tribe').

Perhaps the most interesting change of all within the LDP has been the rise of 'second generation' (nisei) politicians. About one-third of its Diet members, and almost all the party's youngest legislators are the sons or sons-in-law of former politicians. Many of these nisei start out as private secretaries to their fathers, and then inherit the father's political machine after he retires. Fourteen of the 17 postwar prime ministers were actually linked to the imperial family through marriage. The only exceptions were the JSP Katayama, Ishibashi, and Tanaka.[8]

TANAKA, NAKASONE, AND JAPANESE POLITICAL WARLORDISM

Takeo Tanaka was postwar Japan's most powerful political warlord. Although his tenure as prime minister lasted little over two years – from 1972 to 1974 – Tanaka served as the 'king-maker' of Japanese politics from then until his stroke in 1985. With the largest and wealthiest faction, Tanaka was instrumental in placing the last four prime ministers Ohira, Suzuki, Nakasone, and Takeshita – in office. He succeeded in doing this despite the vast cloud surrounding his exposure as the leading figure in major corruption scandals in 1974 and 1976, which forced his resignation from the LDP in 1978, and his conviction for corruption in 1983.

Of the 17 prime ministers since 1946, none had a more unconventional background than Tanaka. In a classic 'rags to riches' story, Tanaka overcame such handicaps as lower-class origins, an irresponsible gambler father, and a failure to graduate from high school, to become one of the wealthiest and most powerful men in Japan. He achieved this through his high intelligence, hard work, and ambition which earned him the nickname the 'computerized bulldozer'. Characteristically, his road to power began with a favorable, though highly unconventional marriage. He married a divorcee seven years older than himself, who was the daughter of the owner of a medium-sized construction company, soon inherited his father-in-law's company, renamed it Tanaka Construction, and relocated the factory in Korea to escape the wartime bombing.

When the war ended Tanaka returned to Japan rich, and used his wealth to run for office as an independent socialist candidate promising the poor farmers of Niigata prefecture price supports and construction of an economic infrastructure. But after being elected to the Diet in 1946 Tanaka joined the Yoshida faction of the Liberal party and worked closely with the bureaucrats thereafter. From then Tanaka rose quickly through the Liberal and LDP party ranks despite a 1948 arrest for taking a bribe from mining interests to vote against a plan to nationalize the mines. He was later cleared of the charge.

Tanaka was an outstanding political and business leader. His political support group (koenkai), called Etsuzankai, extended throughout Niigata prefecture and excelled at fund raising. Through his connections in the construction world as a businessman and such Cabinet positions as head of MOF in 1962 and MITI in 1971, Tanaka rewarded his supporters by funnelling the country's highest per capita public works funding into Niigata prefecture. His wealth increased steadily throughout this time from a range of ghost companies (yurei gaisha) which speculated in real estate.

With his vast wealth and connections, Tanaka began to form his own faction within Sato's faction in 1970, until with 66 members he formalized his break in May 1972. After becoming prime minister following Sato's resignation later that year, Tanaka's charisma, hard work, and such notable achievements as the restoration of Sino-Japanese relations in 1972 soon earned him a 62 per cent popularity rating. But Tanaka resigned in 1974, ostensibly on grounds of ill-health but in reality because of two major failings. His Plan to Remodel the Japanese Archipelago (Nihon retto kaizo ron) was an attempt to decentralize industry and economic growth away from the Tokyo-Osaka corridor to the prefectures. This reasonable plan was undermined when Tanaka passed on inside information to his cronies, who then bought up property in key locations, leading to a huge land speculation boom that fuelled inflation. The crowning blow, however, was the detailed expose by the monthly magazine Bungei Shunju in October 1974 of the Tanaka machine's corruption, which led to his resignation the following month.

Two years later, Tanaka was hit with yet another corruption scandal, when Lockheed Corporation revealed in February 1976 before the Senate Foreign Relations Committee that it had given a $2 million dollar bribe to Tanaka to ensure All Nippon Airway's purchase of its aircraft. Although Tanaka resigned from the LDP, he continued to head his old faction and used his immense power to put Ohira, Suzuki, and Nakasone in the prime minister's office. Tanaka's influence over the Prime Minister was illustrated following his conviction for corruption on 12 October 1983. Although he promptly appealed the judgement, he forced Nakasone to hold elections in December 1983 to ratify his continued popularity. Although the LDP as a whole lost 36 seats and was forced to form a coalition government with the NLC, Tanaka won a great victory by only losing two members from his faction. His success was built on billions of yen distributed to his followers just before the election.

He received a jolt in Autumn 1984 when a key lieutenant, Susumu Nikaido, ran for the party presidency against Tanaka's choice, Nakasone. But the major blow came in February 1985 when his faction reached an all-time high membership of 121 members. Another key lieutenant, Noburu Takeshita, began to organize a 'study group' (soseikai) or smaller faction (soseikai) within his faction. As a result, Tanaka's faction split into three groups divided between the hardcore loyalists (shimpan giin), Nikaido fence-sitters (fudai giin), and Takeshita rebels (tozama giin). The stress contributed to a stroke Tanaka suffered later that month, which has left him incapacitated.

The Tanaka era of Japanese politics lasted from 1972 to 1985, and had an important impact on the political system. Tanaka upset the stable balance of power among the factions which had lasted from the late 1940s to his assumption of the prime ministership. Despite his early alliance with the bureaucrats in the ministries and LDP, Tanaka led the party's shift from a predominantly bureaucratic leadership structure (kanryo shudo taisei) to a predominantly party leadership structure (to shudo taisei). Tanaka and his successors encouraged the rise of the policy zoku and a greater role for PARC.

This shift in the party's orientation was continued by Yasuhiro Nakasone who became Japan's 14th postwar prime minister in 1982 when he was chosen 'unanimously' by the party leaders to avoid a divisive election. The party had been split between the Tanaka, Suzuki, and Nakasone factions which supported the latter, and the Fukuda and Komoto factions which backed Abe and Komoto, respectively. With the weight of the Tanaka machine behind Naksone, Abe and Komoto soon dropped out.

Ironically, although as prime minister he soon became very popular among Western observers because of his straight-talking, internationalist style, Nakasone's early political career was characterized as shrilly nationalistic, and anti-American. Nakasone was no hero during the war; he served safely in Japan as a pay officer for the navy. But Nakasone tried to compensate for Japan's defeat by several anti-Occupation stunts that earned him a measure of notoriety. Once he publicly raised the abolished Japanese battle flag while another time he marched into SCAP with a letter criticizing the Occupation. Nakasone's anti-Americanism lasted long after the Occupation. As late as 1969 he proposed ending the Security Treaty and revising the Constitution. But starting in the 1970s he became increasingly pragmatic to the point where he was derisively called the 'weathervane', because of his ability to quickly adapt his views to political realities.

As Prime Minister Nakasone was successful in achieving most of his goals. He became a strong vocal supporter of the Security Treaty, and an expanded Japanese role in it. In 1987 he succumbed to Allied pressure, and pushed through a budget which breached the 1 per cent spending cap on defense which had been originally imposed in 1976. He has also publicly talked of Japan acting as an 'unsinkable aircraft carrier' for the alliance. In addition, he helped along the slow shift in public opinion on the need for a stronger defense, and more positive image for the SDF. But rhetoric and symbols aside, the spending increase was not significant and his agreement to share military technology with the United States to date has not yielded anything of significance. Thus, he succeeded in defusing Allied pressure while avoiding any genuine commitment that might undermine Japan's economic dynamism.

Nakasone was equally successful in deterring Western, and particularly American pressure, for Japan to reduce its huge trade surpluses. The seven 'significant market opening steps' were unveiled with great fanfare, but proved to be largely cosmetic upon closer examination. By carefully nurturing a close 'Ron-Yasu' relationship with the American President, he pushed Reagan to derail many retaliatory actions initiated by Congress or his advisors against the web of Japanese import barriers and export offensives.

Nakasone attempted to short-cut the ruling triad by organizing 'wise men' policy groups composed of his advisors to articulate his policy ideas, which were then appealed straight to the public for approval. His popularity reached a height with the 1986 election in which the LDP won 304 of 512 seats in the Lower House – the largest LDP victory ever. Nakasone's faction alone rose from 57 to 79 members. The public liked his virile, presidential style of leadership that seemed to reflect Japan's growing power and prestige in the world economy, and gave him the highest consistent rating for any Japanese prime minister until early 1987. Because of Nakasone's high popularity, his term in office was extended until October 1987 even though an LDP rule formally bars any party president from serving more than two terms. In the decades ahead, however, the LDP two term maximum rule will probably be fairly strictly observed because of the compelling need for a relatively quick turnover of prime ministers to serve the pressures of the seniority system.

But despite these international successes, Nakasone's popularity plunged after March 1987 when he tried to ram an unpopular tax reform proposal through the Diet. The LDP had originally agreed in December 1986 to a reform package that would reduce corporate taxes from 52 per cent to 37 per cent, the highest marginal rate from 70 per cent to 50 per cent, and income tax brackets from 15 to 6 per cent. Although these measures were popular, they were undermined by the rest of the package, which included a 5 per cent VAT tax on consumption, and an end for tax exemptions on interest on deposits in postal savings accounts for all but the retired and female family heads. The small business community and consumer groups joined the opposition parties in opposing the tax reform bill. Within a month of the bill's submission, Nakasone's popularity rating plunged from about 60 per cent to only 26 per cent while 60 per cent wanted him to resign. Although by mid-September his popularity rating had risen to 45 per cent with 37 per cent opposed, the party leaders forced him to agree to an October presidential election.

By mid-Summer, candidates began manuvering for the presidency. From July to Early August, a tenuous alliance between the Takeshita, Abe, and Komoto factions supported Takeshita. By mid-August, however, Abe broke away from the alliance and threw his hat into the ring, and the two candidates became three when Miyazawa announced his candidacy in late August. During late September, Nikaido complicated the race further as he struggled to find the 50 Diet supporters necessary to become a candidate. On 8 October Nikaido finally dropped his effort, thus ending fears of a mandatory election that four candidates triggers, and negotiations were begun among the three remaining candidates.

These three candidates were dubbed the 'new leaders' of the LDP, as they took over the reins of power in their respective factions: Fukuda (aged 81) to Abe (62), Suzuki (75) to Miyazawa (67), and Tanaka (68) to Takeshita (62). Noboru Takeshita was born in Shimane prefecture, the son of a sake-brewer. A graduate of Waseda University, he was first elected to the Diet in 1958, and steadily rose through the ranks under the mentorship of first Sato and then Tanaka.

His bid for the prime ministership began in February 1985 when he set up his own faction – euphimistically called a study group (keiseikai) within the Tanaka faction. In his career he has served as Chief Cabinet Secretary, and minister of MOF and MOC. But his only international experience was to represent Japan at the G–5 meeting in September 1985 in which the five industrial nations present agreed to weaken the dollar. Takeshita represents one of the most rural and conservative areas, and was thus considered the worst candidate by foreign observers.

With 114 of the 445 LDP Diet members in his faction, and the qualified support of the 31-strong Komoto faction, Takeshita was in the strongest position for the presidency. His reputation for fund-raising and behind the scenes negotiations made him pop·ular among older LDP members, but he garnered only 29 per cent of those polled who were eligible to vote in the LDP election. Takeshita's strategy was to push for a straight party vote in which his strength would eventually win out.

Kichi Miyazawa comes from an old political family in Hiroshima, and was related by marriage to both Hatoyama and Suzuki. A Todai graduate, Miyazawa's intelligence and policy-making skills gained him the posts in the EPA, MITI, MFA, Chief Cabinet Secretary, and Chairman of the Executive Council. With his extensive international experience and fluency in English, he was considered the best man to resolve the trade conflicts, and is highly regarded by Washington and Europe. Although he had 89 members in his faction, Miyazawa gained the support of only 23 per cent of those eligible to vote in the LDP election. Unlike Takeshita, Miyazaewa is considered a poor back-stage operator. His strategy was to conduct extensive behind-the-scenes negotiations, horse-trading to receive the support of party elders like Fukuda, Suzuki, Nikaido, and agree to step down in two years in favor of Abe.

Shintaro Abe is from Yamaguchi and, like Miyazawa, a Tokyo University graduate. With his father formerly in the Diet, and with Kishi his father-in-law, Abe had excellent connections on which to base a political career. He started out, however, as a reporter for the Mainichi Shimbun, and turned to politics in the 1960s. He rose through the ranks to serve in such positions as minister of MOAFF, MITI, and MFA, as well as Chief Cabinet Secretary, and Chairman of the Executive Committee. Fukuda turned over the faction to Abe's leadership in 1986. With an 86-member strong faction, no significant enemies, a long-time friend of Takeshita, the backing of 28 per cent of those eligible to vote, and a reputation for being a 'Mr Nice-Guy', Abe seemed on the surface to be a strong candidate. However, he is not considered good at either policy or consensus making, and even his mentor Fukuda expressed doubts over his leadership ability. Abe's strategy was secretly to throw his support behind Takeshita in return for his promise to support Abe in the next presidential selection.

In early October negotiations began among the three in an attempt to choose a party president. In reality these long policy discussions were a smokescreen behind which the three scrambled to tie down supporters and horse trade for Nakasone's support. As the three candidates reached a stalemate in their negotiations over who was to become party president, it became increasingly clear that Nakasone would need to broker the selection. Nakasone wanted negotiations to maximize his influence over the new prime minister and gain the most advantages for his faction. He did not support any candidate for fear of alienating the rest, and agreed to arbitrate only after the candidates agreed to accept his decision without dissent.

Finally, on 19 October 1987, Nakasone, after consulting with LDP elders, selected Takeshita as the new party president. In retrospect, the choice was clear: Takeshita's huge faction and alliance with Komoto, plus Abe's tacit support gave him a majority.[9] In addition, in picking Takeshita, Nakasone paid back the past support of Takeshita and Tanaka for him in 1982, 1983, and 1986. During the party convention on 31 October 1987, the LDP formally selected Takeshita a day after Nakasone's term expired. A week later, during an Extraordinary Diet Session on 6 November 1987, Takeshita was elected prime minister by a vote of 299 of the 498 votes cast in the 512-member House of Representatives. JSP candidate Takako Doi supported by the CGP and the Shaminren came in second with 145 votes, DSP candidate Saburo Tsukamoto third with 27 votes, and JCP candidate Kenji Miyamoto last with 26 votes. In the House of Councillors, Takeshita won with 143 of the 246 votes cast, with Doi, Miyamoto, and Tsukamoto gaining 72, 15, and 12 votes, respectively.

Takeshita quickly formed a government which rewarded the factions and their leaders according to their respective strengths and the deals struck during the campaign. The party leadership positions were carefully divided among Abe as Secretary-General, Masayoshi Ito of the Miyazawa faction as Executive Council Chairman, and Michio Watanabe of the Nakasone faction as PARC Chairman. Among the 20 Cabinet posts, five went to Takeshita, Nakasone, Miyazawa, and Abe got four each, and Komoto two.

Takeshita's traditional leadership clashed sharply with that of his colorful predecessor Nakasone. Takeshita is a classic consensus builder and behind the scenes operator, but his inexperience in foreign affairs, inability to think clearly on his feet, poor speaking ability (he reads directly from speeches), and tendency to continually evade answering questions in the Diet, makes him seem insincere. These characteristics are exacerbated by the vague, almost meaningless slogans he uses to describe his policies. The most frequent slogan is 'Furusato', which can be translated as homeland, hometown, or community. He explains it as bringing the quality of small town life to the nation as a whole. Equally perplexing is his 'new Sincerity', which is supposedly the basis of Japanese foreign policy, in an attempt to harmonize Japan with the world. The term makes one immediately wonder what happened to the 'old sincerity'; is this a tacit admission that such former promises as the market-opening steps were less than sincere?

These slogans aside, Japan's economic and foreign policies did not change at all. The United States continued to be the cornerstone of Japan's foreign policy, trade conflicts were finessed with yet more cosmetic concessions, and defense spending continued to hover just above the 1 per cent of GNP level. Domestically, although battered by the Recruit scandal, the Takeshita government succeeded in pushing through its primary objective, tax reform.

Takeshita may represent the last truly old style Japanese politician. With Takeshita a one-term prime minister, and Miyazawa and Abe damaged from the Recruit scandal, the way is open for a new generation of LDP leaders. Increasingly, the new leaders will reflect the popular desire for more international, articulate leaders who represent an increasingly powerful Japan.

Takeshita's two successors, Uno and Toshiki Kaifu, however, fell short of fulfilling these popular images. Neither succeeded in breaking free of faction entanglements to become a real Statesman.

CONCLUSION

The LDP has made a steady comeback since its electoral nadir of a mere 44 per cent of the vote in 1979. In the 1986 election the LDP received 49.4 per cent of the vote, its highest level since the 1963 election when it captured 54.7 per cent. There are several reasons for the deepening LDP support. Japan's growing prosperity is the most important: 90 per cent of the population considers itself middle class in a country with one of the world's highest per capita incomes. Middle class voters tend to vote conservative. The LDP has steadily broadened its appeal over the past 35 years from a relatively narrow base in rural districts to broad national electoral support rooted in virtually all socio-economic groups. In 1955 the LDP captured 68 per cent of the farm and small business vote, but only 13 per cent of the white collar and 15 per cent of the blue collar vote. In the late 1980s, the LDP continued to capture about 70 per cent of the farm and small business vote, as well as 75 per cent of the white collar and over half of the blue collar vote.[10] Over half the LDP national vote comes from metropolitan areas while only one-quarter is based in towns and villages. The LDP has also made significant inroads among floating voters who have consistently numbered about 40 per cent of the electorate from the 1950s through today and were traditionally mobilized by the leftist parties.

What is perhaps most surprising is that, given Japan's prosperous, contented mass electorate, the LDP does not receive more voter support. Those who support the LDP have risen steadily from 50 per cent of the electorate in 1980, to 54 per cent in 1984, and most recently 59.3 per cent in 1986.[11] Even among university students, traditionally one of the more anti-establishment groups in society, support for the LDP is large and growing. A 1983 survey of University of Tokyo freshmen indicated that while 44.4 per cent had no preference, 28.5 per cent supported the LDP, almost three times the support for the JSP with 10.5 per cent, and four times the JCP support of 6.9 per cent.

Actual electoral support lags behind intellectual support for several reasons including the continued ability of the opposition parties to mobilize blocks of voters. But perhaps the most important is the widespread feeling that while the LDP is the best party to govern, it requires an active opposition to restrain it from excesses like constitutional revision or a large defense build-up. A 1984 Japan Broadcasting poll showed that the population overwhelmingly wanted the LDP to stay in office, but by a relatively narrow margin: 45 per cent favored a narrow LDP majority, 35 per cent a stable majority, and only 10 per cent wanted a coalition government that would exclude the LDP. A 1986 Asahi poll following that year's election revealed that not only 65 per cent of all respondents thought the LDP had won too many seats, but even 53 per cent of the LDP voters agreed, while only 39 per cent thought it was good the LDP had won a landside.[12]

How has the LDP managed to stay in power for so long? The most important reason is Japan's rapid economic growth and prosperity. The Occupation reforms dramatically overhauled the institutions of Japan's economy. This set the stage for the ruling triad to formulate and implement rational industrial and trade policies that boosted Japanese growth in an expanding world economy.

The gerrymandered electoral districts allowed the LDP to stay in power throughout the 1960s and 1970s despite a steady deterioration of voter support. In the 1980s, the LDP has experienced a resurgence of support stimulated by the neo-conservatism sweeping Japan and other countries paralleling their transition into a post-industrial society. In Japan, the most satisfied age group is the young in which over 50 per cent agree that things are going well.

Another reason for the LDP's continued success is its ability to coopt popular opposition party ideas and make them into law. The LDP remains a 'catch all' Party of umbrella organization composed of factions divided by ambition rather than ideology. The LDP's strategy continues to be based on pragmatism and flexibility designed to appeal to urban voters. Meanwhile the opposition parties remain fragmented and unable to come up with any policy proposals with popular appeal. For all these reasons, the LDP will continue slowly to expand its Diet and electoral strength in the decades ahead, enjoying the financial and psychic rewards of guiding Japan's deepening hegemony over the world economy.

NOTES

1. *Farm Eastern Economic Review*, 24 November 1988.
2. Hans Baerwald, *Party Politics in Japan*, p. 16.
3. Ibid., pp. 16–30.
4. Scott Flanagan and Bradley Richardson, *Politics in Japan*, p. 186.
5. Gerald Curtis, *The Japanese Way of Politics*, pp. 120, 211.
6. Baerwald, op. cit., pp. 166, 167.
7. Curtis, op. cit., p. 180.
8. *World Herald Tribune*, 11 April 1988.
9. See Haruhiro Fukui, 'Japan's Takeshita at the Helm', *Current History*, April 1988 for details.
10. Curtis, op. cit., p. 197.
11. Ibid., p. 198.
12. Ibid., pp. 121–30.

8 Corporate World

In the 1980s Japanese corporations rapidly surpassed their rivals in other democratic industrial states to dominate international business. In 1987 Japanese corporations included 15 of the world's 20 largest corporations, and 315 of the world's top 1000 firms. The combined assets of those Japanese firms represented 48 per cent of the total assets of the world's top 1000 firms. In comparison, American firms numbered 345 but held only 32 per cent of the total assets.[1] The world's ten biggest banks, and 17 of the largest 25 banks are Japanese. The combined assets of those leading Japanese banks in 1987 was $1.4 trillion, more than twice the $630 billion assets of the American banks, the largest of which, Citicorp, was only number 27 in the world.[2] It is this huge financial power that allowed Japan to replace the United States as the world's banker in 1985. With foreign reserves of $88.9 billion and net foreign assets of $250 billion in 1988, Japan is now the financial superpower while the United States owes over $450 billion to foreign creditors. Dozens of Japanese corporations like Toyota, Sumitomo, Hitachi, and Sony have become household names throughout the globe from America to Zambia. Countless foreign corporations are studying and trying to implement such Japanese management techniques as 'lifetime employment', 'just-in-time inventory', or the bonus system. A 1987 US Academy of Engineering Report revealed that Japan led in 25 of 34 technologies identified as vital to a post-industrial society.[3]

Since 1945 the corporate world (zaikai) has dominated Japanese politics as thoroughly as it has more recently taken over so many farflung foreign markets. The Federation of Economic Organizations (FEO, Keidanren) serves as the corporate world's political voice, and plays a major role in all important economic policies. Most of the LDP's massive funding comes from corporate sponsors; the LDP reciprocates by cooperating with the ministries to create industrial policies and an overall economic environment perfect for continued rapid economic growth, while individual LDP Dietmen push through measures designed to give major advantages to corporations in their districts. Described as 'corporatism without labor',[4] no other democratic industrial country's corporate world has as powerful as voice in policy-making and the economy as does Japan's. But the immense political power of Japan's corporate world is not just confined to

Japan. Japanese corporations, individually and collectively, are increasingly using their vast financial and market power to influence foreign political systems as well.

How has the corporate world managed to achieve such a powerful position in Japan's political economy? What channels does the zaikai use to influence politics and policy-making? How is Japan's corporate power being translated into political power overseas?

To a large extent, these questions can be answered by examining the web of horizontal relationships within and between the massive industrial groups (keiretsu) that gird Japan's economy, and the vertical relationships between the keiretsu and the sea of small- and medium-sized firms on which they rest. The first section will analyze the zaikai's overall political power while the next two sections will examine the intersecting horizontal and vertical relations within the corporate world, and demonstrate how political power parallels these economic arrangements. The final section will examine the transformation of Japanese corporate power overseas into political power by examining the growing influence of the Japanese lobby in the United States.

DOMESTIC POLITICAL POWER

The corporate world remains one of the three key players that have dominated Japanese policy-making since 1945. Zaikai interests sculpt the national agenda through four national corporate organizations whose political and policy efforts complement each other. The Federation of Economic Organizations (FEO-Keidanren) is the most influential, and represents the corporate world's interests in all relevant policy areas. Its membership includes 117 trade associations with represent virtually every industry in Japan, as well as 839 leading corporations.

Keidanren was founded in 1946 by General MacArthur who wanted to create a democratic alternative to the autocratic zaibatsu that he was trying to abolish. Unwittingly he ended up creating an organization that has surpassed the prewar zaibatsu's power to dominate policy-making. There have been five heads of Keidanren since it was founded in 1946, and this leadership has come entirely from old heavy industries like steel and automobiles. New service industries and older firms with entrepreneurial origins like Sony and

Honda hav. a relatively limited influence within Keidanren despite their growing economic power.[5]

Keidanren is organized into about 30 committees which include general policy, economic adjustment, industrial policy, reform of the government, energy policy, transportation, shipping, fisheries, forestry, industrial technology, small and medium-sized enterprises, environmental policy, agricultural problems, finance, taxation, capital, economic controls, foreign capital problems, industrial capital, economic cooperation, problems with the EC, liberalization, tariffs, and international problems. After achieving a consensus among the relevant industries on a particular issue, and approval by Keidanren as a whole, the committee then lobbies the key ministries, advisory councils, LDP policy bureaux, and politicians to shape the policy. Keidanren reinforces the power of its lobbying efforts with the politicians and bureaucrats by annually supplying trillions of yen to the former and high-paid second careers to the latter. Up through the 1980s, Keidanren openly coordinated how much each firm would pay the LDP. Although campaign contribution laws in the late 1970s limited individual annual corporate contributions to 150 million yen, Keidanren still openly channels about 12 billion yen into LDP coffers each year.[6] Yet, despite this vast flow of funds and other benefits to the politicians, Keidanren has only once directly intervened in party affairs. In October 1955, shortly after the JSP reunited, Keidanren exerted enormous pressure on the conservative Liberal and Democratic parties to shelve their incessant squabbles and unite to prevent the possibility of a socialist election win. As a result, one month later the two parties merged to form the LDP.

The other three national corporate organizations concentrate on more specific but overlapping policy areas. Most Keidanren members also dominate these other organizations, so once a concensus is forged within Keidanren it is relatively quickly mirrored in the others. Although the Chamber of Commerce (Shoko Kaigisho) is supposed to represent all businesses, it is actually dominated by big corporations and serves as a secondary channel for the zaikai in policy-making. The efforts of Keidaren and the Chamber of Commeree in shaping macroeconomic and industrial policies is complemented by the Council for Economic Development (CED, Keizai Doyukai) composed of a small group of business leaders who push more visionary policies designed to assist the transition of both the corporate world and Japanese society as a whole into a post-industrial world. Finally, the Japan Federation of Employees Association (Nikkeiren) represents zaikai interests in all labor-related issues.

For most of its 40 years Keidanren and the other national business federations have generally been able to achieve a concensus on every policy area. But as Japan's economy became increasingly differentiated, consensus on controversial issues became increasingly difficult to achieve. For example, Keidanren has often failed to forge a consensus on 'voluntary export restraints' in various industries. In the 1980s, the automobile and semiconductor industries struck their own deals with MITI after negotiations broke down within Keidanren. Keidanren has recently voiced support for the liberalization of agricultural imports and a streamlining of the inefficient distribution system, but its efforts have been blocked by the farm and small business lobbies which are the most important policy-making players in their respective areas. Keidanren's 'free market' stands on agriculture and distribution emerged only after years of often bitter debate between the industries which wanted to maintain Japan's overt range of import barriers and those which favored dismantling the more obvious barriers to defuse foreign pressure for a genuine liberalization. Keidanren also recently lost a tough battle with the Ministry of Posts and Telecommunications over deregulating the telecommunications industry. Keidanren pushed for a single strong competitor to NTT, while MPT succeeded in creating several weak firms that could be dominated by its godchild NTT. But these setbacks remain a fraction of the zaikai's policy efforts. While it will become increasingly difficult to forge a consensus in specific policy areas, the zaikai will continue to either dominate or influence all policy areas.

The efforts of these four corporate associations are in turn complemented and implemented by the industrial and enterprise associations which in 1974 totaled 22 626 and covered virtually every aspect of Japan's economy.[7] Some of the more prominent are the Japan Iron and Steel Federation, the Japan Automobile Manufacturers' Association, the Japan Electrical Manufacturers' Association, and the Japan Machinery Association. These industry associations provide a forum where corporate and bureaucratic representatives can develop policies for that industry. After agreeing to a specific industrial policy, the industrial association is then used as a channel for administrative guidance in which a ministry, usually MITI, coordinates strategies involving cartels, licenses, tax concessions, investments, and trade barriers.

HORIZONTAL KEIRETSU

The most important reason for the immense economic and political power of Japan's corporate world lies in the tight relations within and between business groups (keiretsu). The typical keiretsu includes a bank and an insurance company which supply much of the group's funds, a trading company to sell many of its products and buy key raw materials or capital goods, and several dozen related manufacturing and service firms. Keiretsu are a postwar phenomena which differ significantly from their prewar zaibatsu predecessors. The zaibatsu were controlled by family-owned holding companies which dictated all investment decisions of the individual firms, and divided domestic and foreign markets, fixed prices, and cooperated politically with other zaibatsu. In contrast, banks rather than holding companies form the hub of each keiretsu. The bank chairs investment decisions within the keiretsu at monthly meetings of the group's company presidents. Another big difference between the zaibatsu and keiretsu is the intensity of competition between big business before and after 1945; Johnson distinguishes the corporate world's prewar 'cordial oligapoly' from its postwar 'cut-throat oligapoly'.[8] Each of the prewar zaibatsu had its own sphere of activity over which it held a virtual monopoly: Mitsui in paper, synthetic dyes, coal and foreign trade; Mitsubishi in heavy industries centered on shipbuilding, marine transportation and plate glass; and Sumitomo in metal manufacturing industries centered on rolled copper and aluminum. These industries formed the focus of each zaibatsu's investments and profits. In contrast, the Keiretsu now compete fiercely with each other in all these industries and scores of others.

The Occupation reforms, later revised by Japan's government, were chiefly responsible for this shift from the inefficient zaibatsu monopolies to the postwar highly efficient keiretsu oligopolies which compete with each other as fiercely as they cooperate. SCAP's zaibatsu reforms included three key elements: the purge of the wartime corporate leadership, the dissolution of the holding companies and break-up of the zaibatsu, and the build-up of bank power.

The purge began in November 1946 when SCAP ordered the removal of the wartime managers of Japan's 200 largest companies. This was followed up by a January 1948 law which banned all members of the ten zaibatsu families and high ranking directors of 240 zaibatsu-related companies from management of these or related firms for ten years. As a result of these two directives, over 3600 managers were purged from the business world.[9] This prompted a managerial revolution as a new generation of managers, more open and willing to innovate and take chances, gained control of each firm.

The anti-zaibatsu program began in August 1946 when SCAP identified 83 companies as holding companies controlled by ten zaibatsu families which owned over 18.4 billion yen-worth of these holding company and family shares, or about two-fifths of the total value of outstanding stock at that time. These stocks were transferred to the Holding Companies Liquidation Commission which in turn sold them to the public. Company employees and local residents were given the first opportunity to buy these stocks with the stipulation that no person was allowed to own more than 1 per cent of any company. By the end of the anti-zaibatsu program in March 1950, individual holdings reached nearly 70 per cent of all outstanding stock.[10]

SCAP's anti-zaibatsu policies did not affect the banks, while other policies gave the banks preferential treatment that reinforced their control of other firms. Although the 1947 anti-monopoly law strictly prohibited intercorporate shareholding and imposed a 5 per cent ceiling on city bank holding of any stock of any single company, SCAP repealed the law against intercorporate shareholding in 1949, and in 1953 the government raised the amount of stock a bank could own in a company to 10 per cent. As a result, intercorporate shareholding increased from 5.6 per cent in 1949 to 15.7 per cent in 1956, while bank holdings in listed companies rose from 9.9 per cent in 1949 to over 20 per cent by 1956.[11]

By the mid–1950s the zaibatsu had been largely reformed into their present bank-centered keiretsu form, and these ties have steadily tightened to the present. Because capital remained relatively scarce up through the 1960s, the banks were in turn dependent on the Bank of Japan for funds. Since the amount of government loans and grants, fed through each keiretsu's bank, depended on the size of the keiretsu's market share in targeted products and industries, each keiretsu established 'one set' of new enterprises in each industry to attract these funds, and competed fiercely to expand its production and range of products. The presidents of firms within each keiretsu meet monthly (shacho-kai) to coordinate overall keiretsu policies such as investments, joint ventures, and so forth. Committees are then formed by representatives of firms directly involved in each specific project to work out the details and implement the policy.

Because of anti-trust laws these President's Clubs are officially informal, but in effect they serve as the policy-making arena for each
keiretsu.

Japan was the only industrial country that relied heavily on indirect
financing to fuel its economy. Between 1958 and 1962 Japanese firms
received as much as 63 per cent of their funds from various kinds of
loans compared to 21 per cent for American firms, 17 per cent for
British firms, and 34 per cent for West German firms. In stark
contrast, foreign firms were mostly dependent on internal sources
for their financial needs – American firms 65 per cent, British firms
62 per cent, and West German firms 55 per cent – compared to
Japanese firms which used internal funds for only 24 per cent of all
their financial needs. While American, British, and West German
firms almost always obey the 50 per cent rule of the equity/asset
ratio, the Japanese ratio remains about 20 per cent.[12] This reliance
on cheap bank loans rather than equity has given Japanese firms a
huge advantage over their rivals since they can concentrate on long-
term goals and investments rather than depend on short-term earnings to please their stockholders, as most Western firms do.

The bank's role in supplying funds to keiretsu members rose rapidly during the 1950s and 1960s, peaked in the mid–1970s, and has
been declining slowly since. As late as 1954, government institutions
supplied as much as 19 per cent of all industrial funds compared to
about 15 per cent from city banks and 10 per cent from long-term
credit banks. But as Japan's economy continued to expand, the
private banks became increasingly important in financing industry
until by 1957 private banks were supplying over 38 per cent of
industrial financing compared to only about 8 per cent from government institutions. The percentage of bank funds to the keiretsu's
total financial needs rose to as much as 45 per cent by the early
1970s but declined to about 20 per cent by the late 1980s as the
prosperity of individual firms allowed them to raise the bulk of their
financial needs from retained earnings.[13]

This relative decline in the dependence of firms on bank loans has
been replaced by the banks' growing power over the firms through
stockholding. As early as 1968 shareholding by keiretsu banks had
climbed to 30.3 per cent of the total outstanding stock by all listed
companies, while crossholdings by other keiretsu companies had
risen to 21.4 per cent. Individual shareholders decreased steadily
throughout this period, from as much as 70 per cent of all outstanding
shares in the late 1940s to only 6.8 per cent in 1983, or only 16.9

per cent of all households.[14] This matrix of crossholdings with over 50 per cent of any large company's stocks controlled by either its keiretsu bank or fellow keiretsu companies made any member virtually immune from outside takeovers. This security allowed managers to concentrate on market share at the initial expense of profits.

There are several reasons why individual investors abandoned the stock market to institutional investors. One was the steadily diminishing level of profits to be made in the market – the ratio of average dividends to the average price of shares for all listed companies has declined steadily from 5 per cent in the early 1960s to 1.5 per cent in the late 1980s. Tax profits paid out as dividends by the entire corporate sector had been around 10 per cent throughout the 1980s compared to about 40 per cent in the United States. But not only is the stock market unprofitable to individual investors, it is also highly risky since insider trading and manipulation of prices is the norm.[15] Transactions like the Recruit scandal in which stocks were sold cheap to 160 prominent politicians, bureaucrats, corporate executives, and newspaper editors before the stocks were publicly listed occur daily. Another important reason is the weakness of individual stockholders. The typical corporate shareholders' meeting lasts about ten minutes and follows the same pattern. When the president, as chairman, proposes deliberation on the annual income statement, a 'meeting man' springs up right away, receives the acknowledgement of the chair, and calls for 'omitting the reading of figures and going immediately to the controller's report'. Collaborators quickly vote for the motion and all the proposals on the agenda are smoothly approved. Other shareholders have no opportunity to speak.[16]

While there are dozens of keiretsu, and each of the 13 city banks is the center of a keiretsu, most of these are in turn related to one of the big six keiretsu: Mitsubishi, Mitsui, Sumitomo, Fuyo, Daiichi Kangyo, and Sanwa. All six were prewar zaibatsu and had reformed into their present keiretsu by the early 1950s. Since then the big six have averaged about 25 per cent of Japan's total corporate assets and 35 per cent of its equity while employing only about 5 per cent of the workforce and representing less than 1 per cent of all corporations.[17] The year 1974 was typical: these six keiretsu together included 174 core firms whose presidents are members of the respective keiretsu president's clubs. These firms represented 21.9 per cent of all Japanese corporate equity and 22.9 per cent of total assets. The big six collectively owned 50–100 per cent of an additional 3095 companies which represented 26.1 per cent of the total equity and 25.3 per cent of the assets; 25–50 per cent of 6302 companies representing 33.5 per cent of equity and 28.2 per cent of assets; and 10–25 per cent of 8476 companies representing 41.0 per cent of total equity and 30.9 per cent of total assets.[18]

In addition to the big six there are dozens of smaller keiretsu. The next three largest keiretsu are also centered on a financial institution: Industrial bank of Japan, Tokai Bank, and Nomura. Many large manufacturing firms are not directly tied into an old keiretsu, but over time have become the centers of their own respective keiretsu, serving the same role that banks do in the larger keiretsu. For example, Nippon Steel, Kobe Steel, Toyota, Yawata, Fuji, and Hitachi are prominent firms that did not rejoin their respective zaibatsu in the 1950s, while firms like Matsushita, Honda, and Sony grew rapidly after the war despite discrimination by the more established keiretsu. All of these firms have formed their own keiretsu, which rely much more on the Long-Term Credit Bank and foreign affiliated financial institutions rather than a specific city bank for their funds. As they have grown they increasingly rely on retained earnings for the bulk of their investment funds while incorporating a wide range of affiliated firms within their respective groups.[19]

Yet these new keiretsu are in turn tied to the older keiretsu. For example, Honda, although usually described as a relatively independent corporation heading its own loosely structured keiretsu, is actually considered part of the Mitsubishi group. Sony has a similar affiliation with the Mitsui group while Sumitomo includes such influential autonomous firms such as Matsushita, Idemitsu Kosan, Toyo Kogyo, Bridgestone Tire, Asahi Chemical Industry, Takeda Chemical Industries, Kubota Ltd., Sanyo Electric, and Komatsu Ltd. Most of these ties were made in the 1950s when these firms were starved of capital and received vital financial infusions from the keiretsu bank. The Hitachi group, composed of 41 companies, is a member of the president's clubs of three different keiretsu – Sanwa (87 member firms), Fuyo (117 member firms), and DKB (85 member firms). Although the financial dependence of these smaller keiretsu on the larger keiretsu has steadily lessened since the 1950s, they continue to cooperate extensively in managing markets, production, technology, and foreign competition.[20]

Although the big six's share of total equity has remained about the same, the keiretsu ties have steadily strengthened as corporate shareholding rose and individual shareholding fell. Today about 70 per cent of any keiretu's outstanding shares are owned either within the keiretsu or related firms, about 10 per cent are owned by other keiretsu, about 5 per cent by foreign investors, and around 15 per cent by individual investors.[21] Financial firms such as banks and insurance firms generally compose about 75 per cent of a keiretsu's corporate investors. A dominant share of each keiretsu bank, in turn, is generally owned by the group's insurance firm. For example, Sumitomo Life Insurance holds 19 per cent of Sumitomo Bank, Yasuda Life Insurance 17 per cent of Fuji Bank, Mitsui Life Insurance 19 per cent of Mitsui Trust Bank, Meiji Life Insurance 24 per cent of Mitsubishi Trust Bank, and Sumitomo Life Insurance 15 per cent of Sumitomo Trust Bank.[22]

These loan and equity ties are further cemented by an understood policy whereby each individual firm first goes to another keiretsu firm to buy needed goods regardless of price, and if unavailable, only then buys from another, related keiretsu. The typical keiretsu includes companies producing steel, ships, electronics, automobiles, and machinery, all of them complementary. This 'buy keiretsu' policy accelerates when one firm within the group is ailing. Other keiretsu members then go out of their way to contribute finance and buy its products. For example, when Toyo Kogyo, the maker of Mazda automobiles, was on the brink of bankruptcy in 1979–80, the entire Sumitomo group switched its auto purchases to Mazda. Toyo Kogyo estimates that the 600-member group purchased 3000 vehicles per year, or 18 000 between 1975 and 1981.[23]

A keiretsu's internal and external transactions are generally coordinated by a huge trading company. In 1981 49.5 per cent of Japan's exports and 59.6 per cent of its imports went through a trading company, and altogether these transactions represented about 30 per cent of Japan's GNP and about 5 per cent of world trade.[24] Of this amount, the respective trading firms of the big six keiretsu controlled about 50 per cent of the exports and 60 per cent of the imports. Because the trading firms buy vast amounts of goods, they allow the keiretsu members huge economies of scale in raw materials and components, as well as the advantages of transfer pricing in foreign investments. In addition, the trading firm's farflung offices act as a vast intelligence network which shares key information on market and investment conditions with other keiretsu members. For example, the intelligence expertise of the big six trading firms is so powerful that in 1977 each keiretsu had detailed information on President Carter's energy policy well before the official announcement.[25] The trading corporations usually serve as the secretariat for major over-seas development projects involving joint ventures, and provide such additional services as handling the paperwork, warehousing, trans-portation, and negotiating on a daily basis with foreign firms and governments. Recently, manufacturing firms are increasingly hand-ling these affairs as they become familiar with overseas markets.

These intricate webs of relations within keiretsu are in turn connec-ted with other keiretsu. The 22 000 industrial associations coordinate the activities of both legal cartels which numbered 422 in 1985 and the countless illegal cartels winked at by the ministries.[26] These cartels include agreements on production, exports, prices, tech-nology, investments, and imports. While Japan's domestic market may seem to be characterized by intense competition, in reality competition is carefully managed behind the scenes to ensure market shares and profits for all the big six keiretsu and their affiliates. Only foreign firms are excluded from the spoils.

These cartels are reinforced by extensive crossharing between kei-retsu; from 5 to 10 per cent of any keiretsu's stock is owned by the other big five keiretsu. For example, Sumitomo Life Insurance is the tenth largest stockholder in Mitsubishi Heavy Industry and Dai Ichi Kangyo is the seventh largest stockholder in Mitsubishi Corporation. Meiji Life Insurance is the fifth largest stockholder in Kubota, NTN Toyo Bearing, and Dai-Ichi Kangyo, the second in Sanwa Bank, the ninth in Yamashita Shinnihon Steamship Company and Mitsukoshi Department Stores, the third in Hitachi, the eighth in Japan Steel Works, and the tenth in Nisshin Steel.[27]

An equally important linkage between keiretsu is loans. Keiretsu like to spread investment risks between their group bank and other banks and financial institutions, particularly when it involves a blue chip firm that could be hurt by 'excessive (free) competition'. Each of the big six trading companies receives extensive loans from either the bank or insurance firm of the other five keiretsu. For example, in 1974, the Mitsubishi trading company owed Mitsubishi Bank 1 470 billion yen, the Bank of Tokyo 981 million yen, Daiichi Kangyo 812 million yen, Mitsubishi Trust and Banking 750 million yen, and Sanwa Bank 613 million yen.[28] Obviously such extensive sharehold-ing and loans would restrict any genuine free competition between the keiretsu while making it extremely easy to cooperate at virtually anytime.

Keiretsu are also extensively linked by joint investments in third enterprises. For example, although Nippon Steel is nominally independent, in reality it is deeply tied to both Mitsui and Mitsubishi, whose financial firms are heavy investors. Meiji Life is the fifth largest investor, Tokyo Marine and Fire Insurance the eighth, and Mitsubishi Bank the tenth. Both the Mitsubishi and Mitsui trading companies supply Nippon Steel with vast amounts of raw materials and cheap credit. These ties go back to 1934 when the two zaibatsu originally merged their own steel firms into Nippon Steel to form a cartel. But the cartel was broken up by the Occupation into the two pre-1934 firms, Yawata Steel and Fuji Steel, which resumed their ties with their respective keiretsu. In the mid–1960s, Mitsubishi and Mitsui again joined their two steel firms to form Nippon Steel. Officially, neither Mitsubishi or Mitsui has its own steel company, unlike Sumitomo with Sumitomo Metals Industries, Dai-Ichi Kangyo's Kawasaki Steel, or Sanwa's Kobe Steel. In reality, Japan's two largest keiretsu, Mitsubishi and Mitsui, share the world's largest steel firm, Nippon Steel.[29]

This vast web of cozy relations within and between keiretsu underlies the seemingly fierce competition that occurs on the surface. Appearances can be deceiving. Mergers and acquisitions, for example, are considered to be a sign of a healthy, free market environment. In 1979 there were almost as many mergers and acquisitions in Japan (1493) as in the United States (1516).[30] However, none of the Japanese takeovers was hostile. Most occurred within the vast ranks of small- and medium-sized firms tied to the keiretsu. No merger or acquisition in Japan occurs without a prior agreement between the stockholders and the unions of the affected firms. The main bank for the affected firms coordinates the negotiations and implements the merger.

VERTICAL KEIRETSU

Almost as important as the horizontal ties within and between keiretsu are the vertical ties between individual keiretsu companies sitting atop two parallel pyramids of small- and medium-sized firms – one composed of manufacturing firms and the other of retailing firms, with both pyramids giving the Japanese keiretsu company an enormous advantage both politically and economically over its foreign competitors.

Unlike the trend toward concentration elsewhere, the amount of small- and medium-sized companies in manufacturing in Japan has actually increased from 53.1 per cent of all manufacturing firms in 1966 to 65.5 per cent in 1981. In 1982 small firms with less than 100 workers employed 36.5 million Japanese, or 68.7 per cent of the entire workforce, while medium-size firms of 100–999 workers accounted for 16.2 per cent and large firms of over 1000 workers 15.0 per cent of the remaining workers. Although they compose over two-thirds of the workforce, small firms only produce half of the GNP in the private sector. In Japan 46.5 per cent of all manufacturing workers are in firms of less than 50 employees while the figure is only 15.2 and 15.9 per cent in the United States and Britain, respectively.[31]

In 1983 85.3 per cent of all small and medium-sized companies entered into subcontracting relations with a larger firm.[32] Although the average number of firms with which small and medium-sized companies have subcontracting relations is four, most have one prime manufacturer (mouke) which enjoys priority production. A comparison of Toyota and Ford reveals the greater reliance of the Japanese firm on subcontracters. Although Toyota produces more cars it employs only one-seventh Ford's number of workers.

There are three types of relations between a large and small company. Any firm which is 50 per cent or more owned by another firm is considered a subsidiary ('child', kogaisha). Parent firms always send their own personnel to manage a subsidiary. An affiliate ('relative', kigyo) is any firm in which the large firm has less than 50 per cent of the stock. Finally, there are vast numbers of small subcontractors in which the parent does not own any stock, but the firm is just as closely tied through its dependence on cheap loans.

Trading companies are an important source of finance for small- and medium-sized firms. With their intimate day-to-day contacts the trading firms are in an excellent position to know who is creditworthy. Acting as a protective cushion between the two, the trading companies borrow vast sums at cheap rates from the banks and insurance firms, and then relend the money to other firms. In 1982 loans from the big six trading firms comprised over 34 per cent of the total commercial credit extended by major corporations.

Mitsubishi is a typical keiretsu. In 1974 its President's Club included 27 firms which held 4.4 per cent of Japan's total equity and assets. Mitsubishi's keiretsu in turn held from 50 to 100 per cent of the stock in 399 firms, from 25 to 50 per cent of the stock in 1070 firms, and from 10 to 25 per cent of the stock in 1460 firms. Mitsubishi Heavy Industry was a major shareholder in over 300 of these firms, of which it held over 50 per cent of more than 40 companies, and above 10 per cent of the rest. Mitsubishi Heavy Industry directly manages those firms in which it owns 50 per cent or more of the outstanding stock. Management includes sending down its own personnel to run the firm in times of difficulties. Mitsubishi Heavy Industry jointly manages with the other major stockholders those firms in which it owns less than a 50 per cent interest.

The relationship between a keiretsu company and its subcontracting firms is mutually advantageous. The large firm shares technology, managerial expertise, cheap loans, and a steady market to the subcontractor in return for a reliable stream of custom-made products made by a cheaper labor that can be laid off in recessions – in contract to the lifetime employment system of the larger firm. Thus, both the large and smaller firms enjoy a long-term, flexible relationship that shares both risks and benefits.

There are disadvantages, however, to Japan's 'dual economy'. Although the starting wages for smaller firms are actually larger than that of the keiretsu firms, overtime their wages average about 10 per cent less, while they lack the range of fringe benefits and job security that the larger firms enjoy. As a result, the large firms tend to receive the best and brightest of employees while the smaller firms pick up the rest. While nearly all the keiretsu company's employees are highly skilled 'intellectual workers', small and medium-sized firms are composed of three groups of workers, each with different types of skills: the 'core' white collar workers with intellectual or technical skills numbering at most only 5–10 per cent, with some semi-skilled workers, and the majority of workers unskilled.[33] Dynamism and innovation are thus concentrated in the keiretsu firms while the smaller tied-firms tend to lack entrepreneurical spirit. Almost 99 per cent of the average 70 000 annual average bankruptcies involve small firms.[34]

As important as the web of subcontracting firms tied to the keiretsu company are the tied-distribution systems. Manufacturers captured huge numbers of small- and medium-sized retailers within their distribution nets by a variety of means including special rebates, loans, and commissions. With a tied distribution system the manufacturer can control marketing, after-sales servicing, rationalize delivery of goods, adapt production quickly to changes in demand, and most importantly have a steady market. As many as 34 per cent of wholesalers are controlled by manufacturers, and they in turn, control as many as 17 per cent of retailers. A good example of tied distribution systems is the consumer electronics industry in which 5000 of 7000 retailers are tied to a major manufacturer and sell only that company's goods.[35] There are disadvantages to the tied-distribution system as well. Because of the lack of competition, Japanese consumers must pay prices for Japanese-made goods that are often twice as high as what foreign consumers pay for the same goods. Foreign manufacturers also lose heavily, since they are either completely shut out of or given only a token share in the tied distribution system while the costs of developing their own distribution system remains exorbitant.

Trading firms comprise a large percentage of the distribution firms. In 1982 there were over 9700 firms that participated in foreign trade, of which about 70 per cent were wholesalers, 28 per cent were manufacturers, and only 2 per cent were department stores. About 600 of these firms were subsidiaries of the big six trading firms, of which Mitsui owned 135, C. Itoh 121, Marubeni 115, Mitsubishi 94, Nissho-Iwai 78, and Sumitomo 73.[36]

Politically, the vast array of small- and medium-sized firms acts as an indirect welfare system by soaking up potential unemployment, which in turn leads many of the sector's workers to vote for the LDP. There are over 50 000 industrial associations representing small- and medium-sized firms throughout Japan. Their political orientation is generally parochial and independent; they will cast their votes for the candidate who can best deliver local benefits. Taxes, labor standards, and environmental problems such as pollution control are among the issues that can politically galvanize smaller firms. The LDP finesses these problems by turning a blind eye to the pervasive tax evasion, lower labor standards, and pollution emission of smaller firms, while more strictly enforcing such laws for large firms.[37]

FOREIGN POLITICAL POWER

Japanese have become experts at manipulating America's political process to their own advantages. The Japanese Embassy in Washington coordinates the efforts of Japan's vast lobbying network which includes 14 diplomatic consulates, seven trade centers, 18 Japan societies, 11 non-profit organizations, and hundreds of private corporations.[38] The Embassy has 80 officials, most of whom are constantly mobilized to sell Japanese interests in Washington while MITI has a huge office in New York.

In 1985 there were 182 Japanese lobby groups in Washington alone, which spent nearly $60 million to advance Japanese interests. It is estimated that there are about an additional 200 unregistered Japanese lobbying groups spending from $50 to $200 million a year. These firms employ several thousand Americans devoted to lobbying for Japanese interests; the draw is huge salaries.[39] The head of the Justice Department Foreign Agent Registration Bureau pointed out that many lobbyists 'are exempt from registration requirements because they do simple legal representation, as opposed to direct lobbying, or are actually employed by exempted domestic affiliates of Japanese companies'.[40] It is estimated that only about 5 per cent of foreign agents actually register.

The ranks of these Japanese lobby groups are filled with more than a hundred former senior American officials including veterans of Congress, the White House, and even the Office of the United States Trade Representative. Representative Howard Wolpe characterizes the Federal Government as 'a finishing school for lobbyists for foreign interests . . . Can you conceive of masses of top administrators and prime minister's staffers in Japan going to work for Americans? It'd be a scandal there and it ought to be a scandal here'. One of the most remarkable switches is former Under-Secretary of Commerce Lionel Olmer, who was once a tough critic of Japan's unfair trade practices, but now represents NTT.[41] Some of the other big name hired guns include Richard Whalen, former special assistant to President Nixon, Stuart Eisenstadt, head of President Carter's domestic policy staff, the former CIA chief Bill Colby, and Richard Allen, former National Security Advisor to President Reagan.

Global USA Inc., with over $1 million in annual fees, is Japan's largest lobbying firm. Its clients include such blue-chip Japanese firms as Hitachi, Komatsu, All Nippon Airways, Fanuc, Yamazaki-Mazek, and Kyocera. The firm is led by Stanton Anderson, a key State Department official in the Nixon administration, William Timmons the chief congressional lobbyist for the Nixon administration, William Morris and Bo Denysk from the Commerce Department and John Nugent from the Energy Department in the Ford Administration. Another prominent firm, Tanaka Ritger & Middleton, is led by William Tanaka, who previously represented the Electronic Industries Association of Japan, the Japanese Automobile Association, and the Japan Tire Manufacturer's Association for over two decades.

By all accounts, Japan's lobbying efforts have been extremely successful. Representative Sander Levin said that 'Judging from the results . . . it's certainly one of the most effective lobbies'. Examples of Japan's immense lobbying power abound. Although it passed the House of Representatives, extensive lobbying, led by Japan's automobile manufacturers, helped kill the domestic content legislation for automobiles in the Senate. Another example is when Japan's electronic manufacturers pressured Speaker of the House Jim Wright to delete a provision imposing a one-year ban on the import of digital audio taping equipment. When Japanese investment houses wanted to persuade the Federal Reserve to allow them to become primary dealers, they hired Stephan Axelrod who formerly served as Federal Reserve chief of staff for policy. The Fed allowed two Japanese securities firms to begin dealing shortly thereafter. When the US semiconductor industry won a complex dumping case, the Commerce Department imposed tough restrictions on imports of Japanese semiconductors. The Japanese responded with an intensive lobbying campaign that included many hired big guns. As a result, the White House forced the Commerce Department to scale back the restrictions to a mere symbolic slap on the wrist.

But the most remarkable display of Japan's lobbying power occurred after June 1987 when it was revealed that Toshiba Machine had sold technology to the Soviet Union that would enable their submarines to run quietly, thus giving them an advantage in the event of nuclear war. It is estimated that the United States must now spend between $30–40 billion dollars to regain its lead over the Soviet submarine fleet. Rightfully incensed at this devious act of treachery the Senate voted 94 to 0 to ban Toshiba from its $2.5 billion-a-year American market.

Toshiba responded with a vast multi-million dollar lobbying campaign that Senator Jake Garn described as the most intense of his 14 years in the Senate. Toshiba acknowledges spending at least $3 million on the campaign and the American companies dependent on Toshiba products spent millions of dollars more. This lobbying blitz was enormously successful as the final version of the trade bill reduced penalties against Toshiba to a slap on the wrist. Toshiba Machine would be barred from United States sales for only three years and its parent company barred from Federal contracts for the same period. The total price tag for all three years was estimated at $200 million rather than the original $2.5 billion a year that would have lasted indefinitely.[42]

Outside Washington, Japanese corporations have been just as successful at lobbying for advantages in America's open political economy. Japan's government and Keidanren have carefully coordinated a massive corporate charity campaign which rose from $85 million in 1987 to $140 million in 1988. This rapid increase is stimulated by efforts by the Foreign Affairs Ministry which sponsored a seminar in Tokyo in April 1988 on public relations abroad attended by over a hundred corporations, or Keidanren's Council for Better Investment in the US designed to advise firms on ways to improve their image.

Japan's huge corporate lobby has become very effective at damage control. For example, when Prime Minister Nakasone remarked that America's economic difficulties were attributable to the low intelligence of American blacks, hispanics, and other minorities, the corporate world stepped in with large, highly publicized grants to a variety of organizations including the United Negro College Fund, the National Association for Colored People, and the Congress of Racial Equality in order to soften any possible black boycott against Japanese products. When Honda was sued for discrimination over hiring practices at its Ohio plant, it settled out of court by immediately hiring some 370 black and women, donated $50 000 to the Clara Hale House in Harlem, which cares for children born addicted to drugs, and started a scholarship for minority students at Drake University.[43]

Hitachi launched a massive public relations campaign after it pleaded guilty to buying stolen IBM secrets in 1983, followed by the embarrassing publication of a 1985 memo ordering distributors to cut prices to destroy their American competitors. First it set up the Hitachi Foundation in Washington in 1985 with an endowment of $25 million targeted on high profile charities, and chaired by former Nixon Cabinet member, Elliot Richardson. Then it promised to buy $350 million-worth of American goods a year and increase production in its United States plants. In addition, Hitachi has set aside 1.5 per cent of its pretax profits to be distributed to local charities by community action committees at each of its American plants. Hitachi has also made large donations to the University of Oklahoma located adjacent to its plant in Norman. These efforts have paid off. Representative David McCurdy of Oklahoma helped Hitachi avoid high tariffs on its imports of computer products while Representative Wes Watkins was roundly condemned by the Oklahoma press when he voted in favor of the Omnibus Trade Bill in 1988.

A number of large corporations are donating large sums of money to key American technological institutes in order to win both a better image and access to key technology and researchers. Hitachi was one of 11 Japanese firms that have so far endowed permanent chairs at MIT, which included $1.5 million in combined grants to its Sloan Management School from Daiichi Kangyo and Mitsubishi. The largest single Japanese gift was $1.5 million to endow a chair in electrical engineering. Nomura has endowed chairs at both MIT and New York University.

Japanese firms have been effective at managing public relations even when they were not directly responsible for their bad image. For example, Flat Rock Michigan convinced Mazda Motor Manufacturing to open a plant in return for a 100 per cent tax rebate for 12 years and a $120 million incentive package. Public criticism began to amount when the infrastructure investments severely strained the local community. Mazda responded by promising to donate $100 000 a year for 12 years, added another $1 million to complete the sewer project, and amidst great fanfare, donated $70 000 to the United Way.

One interesting means of influencing public opinion was the documentary series 'Faces of Japan' hosted by Dick Cavett on PBS in Spring 1986. The series was billed as a 'candid look at the Japanese people . . . produced by an American crew'. However, an investigation revealed that the show was actually produced by TeleJapan, whose president, Junichi Shizunaga, is a key LDP member, and the show was actually funded by 20 Japanese corporations whose efforts were coordinated by keidanren. Both Prime Minister Nakasone and MITI conferred extensively with TeleJapan on both the content and budget for the series. TeleJapan relies heavily on funds from both the government, corporations, and wealthy conservatives like Ryoichi Sasakawa, a suspected former war criminal and organized crime leader. Several of the America crew were forced to quit after TeleJapan constantly overruled them on content.[44]

Japan's enormous power within America's political economy results largely from Washington's dependence on Japan to finance its huge deficit which almost tripled under the Reagan administration. The growing dependence of the American economy on Japan is vividly illustrated by the statement by Robert McElwaine, President of the American International Automobiles Dealers' Association for over 17 years, which represents Japanese automobile manufacturers in the United States: 'We don't feel we lobby for the Japanese. We lobby for 8500 American businessmen'. Those American businessmen sell annually about $30 billion-worth of Japanese cars in the United States. It is estimated that there are 250 000 Americans, earning $4.5 billion annually, directly employed by the imported car industry.[45]

Power, used wisely, begets more power. Clearly, Japan's corporate world has been just as successful in the United States as it has been in Japan in translating a small portion of its economic power into political power, which in turn is used to push through measures designed to further enhance its economic power, and so forth. Japan's corporate power, in turn, is orchestrated by the government as one powerful arm of many in enhancing Japan's interrelated foreign policy goals of economic and military security, rapid modernization, global power, and international recognition of all its accomplishments.

NOTES

1. *Business Week*, 18 July 1988.
2. *Los Angeles Times*, 19 July 1988.
3. Clyde Prestowitz, *Trading Places: How We Allowed Japan to Take the Lead*, p. 76.
4. See T. J. Pempel and Keiichi Tsunekawa, 'Corporatism without Labor', in Philippe Schmitter (ed.), *Trends Toward Corporatist Intervention*.
5. See Gary Allinson, 'Japan's Keidanren and Its New Leadership', *Pacific Affairs*, Vol. 60, No. 3, Fall 1987.
6. *Economist*, 3 September 1988.
7. Kazuo Sato and Yasuo Hochino, *The Anatomy of Japanese Business*, p. 57.
8. Chalmers Johnson, *MITI and Japan's Modern Miracle*, p. 63.
9. Kazuo Kawai, *Japan's American Interlude*, p. 147.
10. Lawrence Redford, *The Occupation of Japan*, p. 236.
11. Sato, op. cit., p. 33.
12. Ibid., pp. 57, 307.
13. Ibid., pp. 61, 254.
14. Masahiko Aoki, 'The Japanese Firm in Transition', in Kozo Yamamura and Yasukichi Yasuba, *The Political Economy of Japan*, pp. 272–7.
15. Ibid., pp. 273–7.
16. Sato, op. cit., p. 287.
17. Ibid., p. 271.
18. Ibid., p. 265.
19. Ibid., p. 256.
20. Ibid., p. 262.

21. Ibid., p. 267.
22. Ibid., p. 127.
23. Ibid., p. 215.
24. Ibid., p. 245.
25. Thomas Young, *Japan's Trading Companies*, p. 62.
26. Higashi, *Internationalization*.
27. Sato, op. cit., p. 181.
28. Ibid., pp. 180, 182.
29. Ibid.
30. Ibid., p. 352.
31. Hugh Patrick and Thomas Rohlen, 'Small Scale Family Enterprises', in Yamamura, op. cit., pp. 332, 336, 338.
32. Aoki in Yamamura, op. cit., p. 283.
33. Kazuo Koike, 'Human-Relations Development and Labor-Management Relations', in Yamamura, p. 323.
34. Patrick in Yamamura, op. cit., p. 373.
35. Sato, op. cit., p. 114.
36. Patrick in Yamamura, op. cit., p. 336.
37. Ibid., pp. 366–70.
38. Prestowitz, op. cit., p. 265.
39. *Japan Times*, 21 January 1986.
40. *Santa Barbara Newpress*, New York New Service report by Cylde Farnsworth, 7 May 1987.
41. *Newsweek*, 22 December 1986.
42. *World Herald Tribune*, 2 May 1988.
43. The following examples are from *Businessweek*, 11 July 1988.
44. *Japan Times*, 14 November 1986.
45. *Santa Barbara New Press*, op. cit.

9 Political Auxiliaries

Japan's policy-making regime has developed from the bureaucratic-led corporation of the 1950s to the present neo-corporatism. Although elements of the bureaucracy, LDP, and corporate world continue to dominate every policy area, the number of actors shaping many policies has not only multiplied both between and within the legs of the ruling triad, but traditional outsiders like the opposition parties and labor are increasingly allowed to participate. This is a natural evolution: as Japan's economy grew more complex and differentiated, the arenas in which conflicts over policy take place and the number of actors in them had correspondingly to expand.

There are two types of political auxiliaries. Political insiders include the mass media, agriculture, small- and medium-sized firms, and consumers. Each is well organized on the national level and has been coopted by the ruling triad; the mass media generally support most government economic policies, and in particular rally around the flag on international trade issues; agriculture and the small business world work closely with the ruling triad in shaping policies affecting their respective sectors; and finally consumers actually support the ruling triad's economic growth and protectionist policies even if it means they must pay higher prices.

The opposition parties and labor unions are generally political outsiders, and remain largely fragmented and ineffectual. Although both the opposition parties and labor federations have steadily moderated their policies and politics throughout the 1970s and 1980s, and support the LDP on most Diet votes, their impact on policy-making remains symbolic at best. Popular reforms they have advocated, such as welfare or environmental legislation, which do not challenge the government's economic growth policies are generally cooped by the LDP, which then takes political credit for the policy.

There are a variety of other political auxiliaries that have played a role in policy-making but have not sustained their political cohesion and influence. Environmental groups had a significant impact on shaping environmental policy in the late 1960s. In classic Japanese fashion these groups started as political outsiders but were eventually cooped by the ruling triad, and then collapsed as a significant political force in the early 1970s after they had achieved most of their immediate goals. The various national groups which lobbied for buraku rights underwent a similar cycle in the late 1950s and 1960s. Their campaign to end discrimination was taken up by the JSP and JCP in the 1950s, and once it became popular was coopted by the LDP in the 1960s, and since then the various buraku groups have had no influence on any policy area. Unlike either the environmental or buraku movements, the women's movement has never had any significant impact on policy. Its efforts to revise women work laws in the mid-1980s were largely unsuccessful.

INSIDERS

Mass Media[1]

The freedom of the press, along with other 'natural rights' like freedom of religion, assembly, and speech, is enshrined in Japan's political system by the 1947 Constitution. Over the past 40 years, unleashed by this right, a vast mass media has emerged to satisfy the reading, viewing, and listening needs of one of the world's most literate populations. Japan has over 180 newspapers with a daily circulation of over 40 million, about a hundred important weekly magazines with a combined yearly circulation of one billion, and about 2000 monthly magazines with a yearly circulation of two billion. In addition, there are 1503 VHF and 9453 UHF television stations, and 1018 radio stations.[2]

Although sometimes called the fourth branch of government, can one make meaningful generalizations about the political influence and orientation of the 'mass media' in Japan or any other liberal democratic country which guarantees 'freedom of the press?' If the press is really free, would not the subsequent diversity of political views make any generalizations about the mass media meaningless?

Apparently most Japanese political groups not only believe there is a monolithic bloc called the mass media, but also ascribe to it vast political influence. A 1980 survey of 11 groups which included business organizations, bureaucrats, LDP members, farm organizations, mass media, intellectuals, labor unions, opposition parties, citizens movements, feminist groups, and the Buraku Liberation League found that almost every group considered the mass media to be the most influential group in Japanese society.[3] The only exception were the mass media which ranked themselves second in importance while asserting that the bureaucrats were the most influential group. While united in their view that the mass media were the most influential force in society, these groups strongly differed over the medias' political orientation. The conservative groups consider the media too far to the left, while leftist groups label the media too far to the right.[4]

Are the mass media Japan's most powerful political force as virtually all believe? Regardless of whether they are or not, do the mass media project one political viewpoint, and if so do they predominantly reflect left, center, or right-wing political views? Are Japan's mass media a monolithic group that is easily labelled?

The second two questions are relatively easier to answer than the first. The mass media are clearly not some monolithic bloc with one political viewpoint. The news magazines reflect a highly diversified readership and orientation. The television and radio stations operate under strict government guidelines that generally forbid any political slant while guaranteeing each candidate equally limited opportunity for appeals during Diet elections.

Given the relative diversity of the magazine industry and apolitical nature of the broadcasting industry, and the immense circulation of the national newspapers any question of undue influence would revolve around the national newspapers. Japan's press industry is remarkably powerful and centralized with a dual structure similar to that of other Japanese industries. While there are about 180 newspapers, over half of those Japanese who read a daily newspaper read one of the big three: the *Ashahi, Mainichi*, or *Yomiuri*, with about 12 million, 6.3 million, and 13.5 million readers, respectively. In addition to the big three, there are two other newspapers with a national circulation: the *Sankei* and the *Nihon Keizai*, with 2.9 million and 3.3 million readers, respectively.[5] Below these nationwide newspapers are three regional or 'bloc' newspapers: the *Hokkaido, Chunichi*, and *Nishi Nihon*, with 800 000, 2 million, and 600 000 readers, respectively. Altogether the eight national and regional newspapers account for about 65 per cent of the total readership. The remaining 90 percent of Japanese newspapers average 150 000 readers and circulate no further than particular cities or prefectures.[6]

The newspaper industry is similar to other industries in the control each major newspaper has over distribution. In 1974 there were 20 908 distribution agencies, of which about 70 per cent were exclusive sales stores that are bound by contract to handle the distribution of a particular newspaper. Each of the national newspapers is the center of its own Keiretsu of other companies. For example, the Yomiuri owns more than a 50 per cent share of 23 companies which include several local newspapers, a television network, travel agency, theme park, orchestra, several junior colleges, and the Tokyo Giants baseball team.[7]

Although a few powerful newspapers dominate the reading habits of most Japanese, do the newspaper majors offer a uniform political outlook? Like most observers, Gibney points that the mainstream papers 'do not differ significantly from one another in their editorials and news coverage'; they differ only 'in matters of degree and emphasis'.[8] A major reason for this uniformity of reporting and views stems from the fierce competition among newspapers for market share. For example, all the mainstream papers proclaim a principle of 'impartiality', and thus neutrality in the rivalry between the LDP and the opposition. But the reason for this adherence to lofty principles results from money rather than ideals. Surveys of the political composition of the big three readership reveal that about 45 per cent support the LDP while about 20 per cent support the JSP, and 10 per cent each the DSP, CGP, and JCP.[9] The mainstream press remains aloof from any party in order to maintain this diverse readership, and thus revenue. Any newspaper that aligned itself with a party could soon lose as much as half of its leadership. For example, the press has continually tried to tip-toe quietly around the scandal-plagued CGP and its parent organization the Sokka Gakkai, for fear of alienating readers affiliated with that religion.

If the press tries to avoid controversial issues to maintain readership, then why do predominantly left-wing groups believe the press is conservative, and right-wing groups believe the press is liberal? Kim argues that the press is both pro- and anti-government. The press established its independence from both the government and opposition parties as early as the middle of the Meiji period, and except for the period of ultra-nationalism, has been largely independent ever since. Yet despite this apparent independence and its frequent criticism of the LDP, the mainstream press has never questioned either the government's economic growth oriented policies or Japan's political economic system.[10] Baerwald agrees, pointing out that the press regularly prints stories that claim 'the Cabinet consists of knaves and fools, that the Diet is riddled with corruption, and that the bureaucrats are more interested in protecting their turf than in governing'. Yes, despite this apparent independence and critical stance, Baerwald goes on to show that on most issues the press is easily coopted by the politicians, bureaucrats, and corporate élite.[11]

A major reason for the press's uniform and generally centrist political outlook is the conformity of Japanese newspapermen. Although polls indicate that the political views of most reporters fall slightly left of center, the group method of reporting along with the general avoidance by newspapers of controversial issues, guarantees that their personal beliefs will not influence their reports.[12] But perhaps the most important means of ensuring conformity is the extensive recruitment and socialization method by which each reporter is made a part of the newspaper 'family'.

The national newspapers use a recruitment process that is almost as demanding as that of the bureaucracy. Applicants must pass a gruelling written and oral exam in which less that one out of a hundred succeed. Unlike the bureaucracy, however, which generally prizes Law Faculty graduates of Tokyo University, the newspapers generally seek a well-rounded individual with a humanities degree from any of the best universities.

The socialization process also parallels that of the bureaucracy or big business. After a brief orientation program lasting up to a month, reporters are assigned to various local bureaux throughout Japan where they will stay for two to three years, followed by a similar two to three year stint at another local bureau. During this time the reporter learns the fundamentals by being employed on all the possible local beats. After returning to Tokyo in the fifth or sixth year, Political Affairs reporters are assigned a specific government agency or political group for five to seven years. After this 'beat' career the reporter is assigned to a specific desk and works his way up through the administration ranks. Managerial ranks are generally filled on the basis of merit; editorial ranks by seniority. Mandatory retirement is at age 55. As in the bureaucratic or corporate worlds, there is no lateral movement between newspapers; almost every reporter works for the same newspaper until retirement. And each newspaper emphasizes the values of loyalty, hierarchy, and conformity.

But the most important reason for the uniform outlook of the mainstream press is its deep dependence on each leg of the triad. The government and bureaucracy control the press through the tight reign they hold over the release of information and the channels through which they release it. A Japanese reporter once anonymously said that to maintain its power the government 'restricts the "right to know." The government only releases information that helps it maintain power, but suppresses information which would hurt it politically'.[13] This perspective is common among reporters;

surveys indicate that 80.1 per cent of all reporters do not think that the 'people's right to know' is fully guaranteed in Japan. Surveys of government officials collaborate this view. Only 33.3 per cent of bureaucrats polled disagreed with the statement that the government may withhold information when its disclosure discredits the government, and only 40.3 per cent disagreed that it could withhold information when its disclosure reveals differences of opinion within the government.[14]

Although every government attempts to suppress unfavourable information to varying extents, no democratic government achieves this as systematically as does Japan. 'Freedom of the Press' in Japan suffers from a range of environmental and internal constraints that inhibit the ability or inclination of newspapers either to actively search for or print as much politically sensitive information as they potentially could.

How does the government restrict information? Despite the appearance of independence, the mainstream press operates within the confines of 'information cartels' similar in many ways to the hundreds of industrial cartels. 'Excess information' is considered as potentially damaging to national interests as 'excess competition'. This attitude is summed up by the common bureaucratic saying: 'people must not be informed, but made dependent on the government's authority' (tami as shirashi o bekrazu, yorashi o beshi).

Press clubs are perhaps the most important means of governmental control. The only significant difference between contemporary press clubs and those before 1945 is the amount of information provided by the government; before 1945 the government was generally miserly with what it provided; since then it inundates the reporters with a daily flood of information that is difficult to digest. Ironically, press clubs originated in the early Meiji era as reporters gathered to exchange information in an attempt to overcome government secrecy; but soon every government ministry and agency had an attached and thoroughly coopted press club.

Both before and after 1945, the government has used these clubs as information cartels whereby it supplies limited information in return for the members' promise not to write anything damaging. If any reporter violates the agreement, he is expelled from the club and his newspaper loses its standard source of information – as well as considerable face. Each press club is composed of 50 to a 100 reporters generally representing the top 20 news organizations. Each government ministry or agency provides a press room and equipment, and a daily late afternoon briefing. Only mainstream news-papers are allowed membership; radical or foreign reporters are automatically black-balled. The press clubs also serve to curb 'excess competition' among newspapers; since each newspaper is given equal access to information, no one is allowed a scoup at the expense of its rivals, and thus an orderly news market prevails. Occasionally, a conscientious reporter may leak a story to an opposition newspaper, but generally no information leaves the confines of the press club. These information cartels are reinforced by the Japanese newspaper system of group reporting, whereby stories are produced by teams of anonymous reporters. Group reporting prevents 'excess competition' within newspapers as thoroughly as press clubs prevent it between newspapers. No newspaperman is allowed credit for his own investig-ative reports, so none bother.

The Japan Newspaper Association (Nihon Sibumkyokai), com-posed of mainstream publishers and editors, occasionally denounces the press clubs for repressing information. But these are merely tatemae denoucements designed to keep up appearances. The Association has the power to live up to its proclaimed ideals by boycotting the press clubs, but no mainstream newspaper wants the 'excess competition' that abolition of the clubs would bring.

In addition to press clubs, the Prime Minister and other leading government officials coopt the mass media by entangling them in a web of social ties through the constant wining and dining of news-paper presidents, managing editors, and editorial writers. During these meetings the officials continually try to get the media to support government policies. Another way in which the mass media are coopted is through token membership in various government coun-cils. The bureaucracy constantly uses the press to float trial balloons or even disinformation.

There are also press clubs associated with key political leaders and factions, and their reporters are coopted even more blatantly than the ministry reporters. Each newspaper's political department (seiji-bu) is linked with a specific LDP faction, and each reporter with an LDP politician. In order to gain any significant insights, reporters must establish close ties with the figure they are assigned to follow. What invariably develops is a classic patron-client relationship in which the reporter receives gifts of information, cash, and other benefits while providing the politician with a certain amount of loy-alty and information. Reporters either end up writing favorable reports about the politician, or at the very least refraining from any critical comments and retaining damaging information.

Kim identifies three stages of growing intimacy between reporters and their politician. First, the reporter 'is allowed to go as far as a guest room near the entrance to the politician's house; as he gains a politician's confidence he may be allowed to enter a living room to talk informally with his news source; and, finally, after a prolonged period of trial he may be allowed to roam around the kitchen to open up a refrigerator at will. Reaching the third stage signifies that he has finally made it; the politician considers him one of his men'.[15] Even if a reporter dared publish a critical article exposing his patron's corruption in an newspaper or magazine other than his own, he would have violated the trust of both the politician and his own newspaper, and his career as a journalist would be destroyed.

Investigative reporting of the kind that revealed the Watergate scandal is virtually impossible in the stifling atmosphere of Japan's mainstream newspaper world. Embarrassing political corruption and scandal stories are generally published by the smaller weekly news magazines, forcing the larger media to follow them up to maintain their image of impartiality and public trust.[16] For example, although reporters were well aware of the background to the 1974 Tanaka scandal, the 1976 Lockheed scandal, the recent Recruit scandal, and virtually every other postwar political scandal, no newspaper dared to reveal its information. The scandals were revealed only after outsiders – the monthly magazine *Bungei Shunju* in 1974 and 1988, and Congressional committee hearings and the foreign press in 1976 – got access to the information. Only after the scandals came to light elsewhere did the mainstream Japanese press pick up the stories and begin running critical editorials.

Karl van Wolferen, the former President of the Foreign Correspondents' Club of Japan, blasts the Japanese media for their consensus-oriented views of news which often neglects critical information and questions that if pursued would give a dramatically different view of reality.[17] He uses the example of the LDP's loss of 36 seats in the 1983 election which the Japanese mass media ascribed to the Tanaka scandal and Nakasone's internationalism. Wolferen points out that in reality the LDP's share of the vote in any election depends on the voter turnout; in almost every election the greater the turnout, the greater the LDP share of the votes. In the 1983 election the voter turnout was a record low and the LDP suffered accordingly. Wolferen points out several other key factors which the Japanese media refused to pursue such as whether the unanimous press predic-tion of a comfortable LDP majority convinced many supporters to say at home, whether the poor party organization which allowed too many LDP candidates to run in many multi-member districts caused a number to lose close races, and why every faction except the Tanaka faction lost heavily – an ironic result considering it was Tanaka's indictment that prompted the election.

Wolferen levels a barrage of very serious charges against the Japanese media: 'relevant questions were not pursued', 'hard put to find, in any other nation . . . a press track record on any issue that is as egregiously bad as the Japanese press has been on the Tanaka phenomena . . . predictions were partly wishful thinking and partly meant to be self-fulfilling prophecies . . . the simplistic slogan 'money politics' was substituted for an investigation into the actual nature of Japanese political power and the reasons for Tanaka's success'. He calls the media's failure to drop its clichés and conduct a serious investigation and analysis of Japanese politics a 'major scandal' in itself, but points out that the 'Japanese media faces a gigantic dilemma. It occupies an awkward place in a society which does not reward those who point out its contradictions . . . Reality in Japan exists on different levels . . . and . . . the institutionalized gap between reality and make-believe passed off as reality plays an important part in the Japanese power game'.

While the press may be manipulated by the the bureaucrats and politicians, surely given their enormous power they are independent of other business interests? On paper Japanese newspapers look extraordinarily free of outside influences. In an attempt to prevent the press from being subjected to outside pressure, the government wrote laws that allow newspapers to restrict the granting of stock to those who are directly connected, and each of the big three news-papers' stock is solely owned by members of those newspapers.

But despite this apparent power and independence, the press is deeply dependent financially on the corporate world. Like other Japanese industries, the newspapers are vulnerable to outside influ-ence because of their high debt-to-equity ratio which in 1973 was 82.2 per cent for all industries and 83.3 per cent for the newspaper industry. The big three average a 95.2 per cent dependency on outside sources to service their debts. This ratio has remained largely the same since. In addition, the newspapers rely on advertisements for more than 50 per cent of their revenues.[18] Thus, it is unlikely that any mainstream newspaper would do anything to jeopardize its dependence on the business world for its loans and revenue. Just as the press clubs inhibit any investigative reporting of government scandals, so the deep dependence of the Japanese newspapers on the business world prevents serious criticism of any particular firm. The press will run critical articles and editorials only after a firm has been indicted. Kim gives some examples of ways newspapers serve their financial patrons: 'massive food poisoning arising from eating at a department store's restaurant go unreported . . . a case of embezzlement at a major bank is ignored', and so on.[19]

Given this web of constraints, what then is the power of the Japanese press? Reischauer writes that the major 'weakness of Japanese newspapers is their amazing uniformity in coverage and treatment . . . they commonly come out with headlines and editorials that seem to be almost paraphrases of each other. As a result, tens of millions of Japanese, intellectually armed with the same television and newspaper news and opinion, sally forth to work each day with the same facts, interests, and attitudes in their heads'.[20]

But in reality, this ability to reach most of society on a daily basis with the same views is the mass media's strength. Japan has had a modern press for over 120 years. During that time it has generally supported two often conflicting goals – democracy and nationalism – at times simultaneously but more often emphasizing one more than the other. Before 1945 the press helped lead three major democratization movements: for civil rights (Jiyuminkenundo) in the 1870s, for constitutional government (Kenseiyogoundo) in the 1880s, and for universal suffrage (fusenundo) in the early 1900s. Yet the press also virulently supported each step of Japanese imperialism from the first calls to take over Korea in the 1870s through the war against the West in the 1940s. Ultimately, these contradictions helped undermine the democracy the press had so vigorously supported, and by the late 1930s the press had been 'nationalized' and turned into a vast government propaganda organ.

This pattern of supporting both democracy and nationalism has continued since 1945, with the press uniformly criticizing any mention of rewriting the Constitution while just as fervently rallying around the flag on international trade issues. The press's pro-democracy orientation was particularly important in the 1950s when the system's democratic roots were still shallow and the LDP with 65 per cent of the Diet seats had the two-thirds vote necessary to pass amendments to the constitution. The press's pro-democracy, anti-violence orientation has also helped soften the policies and tactics of the opposition parties. Thus, overall the press has helped strengthen Japanese democracy since 1945.

Yet the mass media's economic nationalism contrasts sharply with its general democratic orientation. Economic nationalism does not pose the threat to democracy that calls for imperialism once did. But when the press consistently adopts a 'Japan right or wrong' stance on trade issues and denounces any government promise to open markets as allowing a 'second coming of the Black Ships', it unwittingly contributes to the cycle whereby the government makes only cosmetic reforms, which fuels further foreign criticism that Tokyo is insincere and protectionist, which leads to further often bitter negotiations, and new government promises attempting to mask continued intransigence.

Higashi points out that 'the Japanese mass media are . . . always ready to exaggerate even the smallest sign of United States pressure. In the resulting highly charged atmosphere, Japanese government officials and negotiators find it difficult to respond to even the most reasonable United States expectations'.[21] Yet the government is partially responsible for the media's one-sided portrayal of foreign negotiators, since it often claims it was forced to make trade concessions because of foreign bullying, and thus uses the press to stave off foreign demands while justifying its own actions.

De Mente relates a typical example of the press's nationalism and parochialism: 'foreign politicians who go to Tokyo and make what they feel are rational, reasonable, and practical dissertations on Japan's "invisible trade barriers," pointing out example after example, are often stopped cold when a ranking Japanese journalist gets up and says something like, 'Senator, what we really want to hear is what you think about the Japanese people . . .' the journalists go on to write that foreign businessmen have trouble getting into the Japanese market because they are not willing to do things the Japanese way, not because of any barriers blocking their entry'.[22]

Are the mass media the most important political influence in Japan, as ten of eleven significant groups assert? Clearly, the mainstream press has and uses vast powers to shape the minds of its readers on political economic issues, particularly trade. But as has been seen, the mainstream press is heavily coopted and its world view is shaped by the politicians, bureaucrats, and corporate élite. The mainstream press does not initiate policy, but simply serves as a cheer-leader for policies hammered out within the ruling triad.

Agriculture

Over the past 30 years the number of Japanese farmers has dramatically declined, from almost 50 per cent of the labor force in the early 1950s to about 7 per cent or 4.5 million farm households by 1990. Meanwhile the consumption of domestic foods fell from about 90 per cent of all food consumed in the 1950s to about 70 per cent by 1990. Less than 10 per cent of all farmers, and thus less than 1 per cent of Japan's total labor force, are actually full-time farmers. Farming remains a small-scale operation with the average farm size about 1.2 hectares today compared to 1.0 hectare in 1950. When farmland was sold, it ended up chiefly in the hands of developers rather than other farmers.[23]

Yet the political power of Japanese farmers remains undiminished despite this massive decrease in farmers as a percentage of the workforce. Perhaps the most important reason for the farm lobby's continued power is that electoral districts remain firmly gerrymandered in favour of rural districts. Both the LDP and JSP rely on predominately rural districts for almost half of their Diet seats; about 200 of the LDP's 450 Diet seats and half the JSP's 85 seats are from rural districts. Politicians running for the Diet in rural districts devote most of their time to wooing the local farm vote blocs which collectively can make or break a candidate. The farm lobby has warned the LDP that any genuine food import liberalization could result in the loss of 80 seats in the next election. The LDP is thought already to have lost 30 seats through its limited orange and beef liberalization.[24]

Yet, the other political parties are just as vigorous in supporting continued protectionism for Japanese farmers despite the fact that their respective political power bases are largely urban. The opposition parties differ only in the degree of protectionism they advocate. The JSP and JCP both stress food self-sufficiency and expansion of the total farm area. In contrast, the DSP and CGP try to strike a balance between food producers and consumers by arguing for increased productivity on existing farmland. The reason for the unanimous support of all Japanese political parties for protectionism is that 70 per cent of Japanese consumers favor continued high subsidy and import barriers even if it means continued high food prices.[25]

Only the corporate world has supported any genuine gradual liberalization, arguing that high food prices dampen consumer demand

and thus lower prices could boost economic growth.[26] The zaikai points out that the average Japanese family spends about 35 per cent of its income on food while the typical American family spends only 20 per cent. If Japanese could pay international market prices for food they would have at least 15 per cent more disposable income to either save or spend, thus helping stimulate both the domestic and world economy.

The agriculture lobby is as highly organized as that of the corporate world and its structure resembles that of a giant keiretsu. Like the typical keiretsu, agriculture has a central bank, insurance company, and trading company.[27] with $229 billion in assets in 1987, the National Farm Cooperative Bank (Noringinko) is Japan's largest bank after the postal savings system, and serves as the farmer's most important savings and loan institution. With 230 trillion yen-worth of policies in 1987, the National Mutual Insurance Federation (Zenkyoren) is the largest insurance group in Japan. One major reason for its immense wealth is that it is the only organization allowed to write both life and non-life insurance. The National Federation of Agricultural Cooperative Associations (Zenno) is Japan's sixth largest trading company, with sales of $53.6 billion in 1987. As a cooperative, Zenno is exempt from the anti-monopoly law and pays only 27 per cent on its earnings compared to 43 per cent for private industries. With these privileges, Zenno controls 90 per cent of Japan's rice, 70 per cent of its fertilizer, and 80 per cent of its cattle feed trade. But it also trades a range of consumer products, including automobiles and electronic goods.

Zenno sits on top of 48 regional federations which in turn coordinate the efforts of 4,200 local farm federations (nokyo) with a total of about 7.5 million households. Each nokyo is comprised of 50 to 100 families, although only half are actually farm families. The nokyo's farm households are further organized into 'destiny sharing societies' (shuraku) of 20 to 40 farmers. The nokyo serve both economic and political functions. They and their shuraku are farm cooperatives in which members share equipment, labor, and subsidies. They also vote as blocs in elections for the candidate that either is or promises to be the most successful in passing on subsidies and protection once in office. The nokyo are economically and politically 'guided' by Zenno's 380 000 employees, which translates to one official for every nine families. Zenno holds very tight political reigns over the nokyo members by threatening to ostracize (mura hachibu) any farm household which does not support the party line.

Zenno's lobbying arm in Tokyo and even overseas is the Central Union of Farm Cooperatives (Zenchu). Because of Zenno's power, farm policy is largely made politically rather than bureaucratically; it is the LDP's Comprehensive Farm Policy Research Committee, not the MAFF, which is the center of farm policy-making. The MAFF helps initiate and implement policy, but has trouble presenting a united front since its divisions battle each other fiercely over turf issues.

The farm lobby has been enormously successful in achieving its goals of keeping Japanese farms small and numerous through a vast subsidy and import protection program. For example, rice prices rose every year until 1985; it costs Japanese farmers ten times as much as Thailand's farmers to grow a bushel of rice, and Japanese consumers five times as much for the privilege of eating it. Despite enormous foreign pressure spanning years of negotiation, the government still severely protects all significant Japanese farm products, allowing in only token amounts of competitive imports like beef and oranges. Zenno will continue to resist growing liberalization pressure and maintain its enormous subsidy and import protection program for the foreseeable future.

Small and Medium Sized Firms

Frequently neglected in most discussions of Japan's political economy are the small- and medium-sized firms. But the ruling triad cooped these firms as early as 1949, when it re-established the 'control cooperatives' for the small- and medium-sized business sector that originally had been created by the industrial laws of the 1930s. These cooperatives were systemized by the Small- and Medium-Sized Enterprise Organization Law of 1957, and became the main channel of government support to individual businesses or sectors. Since the 1960s workers in small and medium-sized firms have provided a growing percentage of LDP votes.

Distribution firms – retailers, wholesalers, and trading firms – are the largest block of the small and medium firm sector. Japan has over 1.3 million retailers which together employ over five million potential political supporters. In Japan there is one retailer with an average of 3.7 employees for every 68 people compared to one with an average of 7.0 employees for every 120 in the United States, and one for every 160 in both Britain and West Germany. Although there are over two to two and a half more stores per capita in Japan than in the other key industrial countries, the distribution of sales is far greater. In Britain, the top four retailers accounted for a quarter of all sales; in Japan it took the top 200 retailers to capture 27 per cent of all sales. About 92 per cent of all retail outlets are 'mom and pop' stores that account for almost 80 of Japan's sales.[28]

Virtually all these retailers are dependent on a wholesaler to carry inventory and extend credit. In 1982 83 per cent of all retail stock came from a wholesaler, only 15 per cent was bought directly from a domestic producer and only 2 per cent from a foreign producer. There are about 428 000 wholesalers in Japan employing 3.7 million people whose sales were 380 per cent of retails sales. In comparison, West Germany has 110 000 wholesalers employing 1.2 million people with an average 165 per cent saies to retail sales. In other word, the average distribution chain in Japan is over eight times longer than West Germany's. Most wholesalers are themselves small and dependent on other, larger wholesalers. One-fifth had only two employees, and one-quarter had ten or fewer employees.[29]

How did Japan's distribution system become so complex? There are sound political and econorlic reasons for the creation and continuation of Japan's Kafkesque distribution system. The country's small- and medium-sized companies are becoming as important a political pillar of continued LDP power as the farm bloc vote. Since the 1960s the LDP has continually courted the masses of small firms with laws and administrative guidance that protects them from the ravages that a free market would bring, and in gratitude, the sector has increasingly shifted its support to the LDP. In 1960 the LDP secured only one-fifth of voters who worked at small- or medium-sized companies; by 1986 this support had risen to two-thirds of the total.[30]

The distribution sector has become an indirect form of welfare for needy Japanese. The average retirement age from a big firm is 58. No family could survive long on the firm's measly lump retirement payment or the even more miserly monthly government social security cheques, and with the average male life expectancy over 75, most Japanese must begin a second career. Over 70 per cent of the working population is employed in firms without life-time employment systems, and business downturns frequently result in lay-offs. Thus, the relative ease with which someone can open a small retail shop has proved to be a vital lifeline to both retirees and the unemployed, who then return the favor by supporting the LDP.

The LDP created and largely captured this vast pool of voters through a series of laws which provide virtually iron-clad protection to any retailer or wholesaler. The Department Store Law of 1956 empowered MITI to approve new department stores and the expansion of existing ones of more than 3000 square metres in the seven largest cities and stores of 1000 square metres or larger elsewhere. MITI's decision in turn was shaped by the powerful voice of local retailers who would be affected by the new, more efficient store. MITI also had the power to regulate the store opening hours and days, and restricted stores from providing free transportation to customers. MITI's powers were enhanced by the 1974 Large Scale Retailer's Law and subsequent amendments. Under the new law, MITI approved all stores greater than 3000 square metres in the largest ten cities and 1500 square metres elsewhere, and further could 'recommend' that new stores reduce their floor space, postpone their opening, or adhere to earlier closing hours or holidays. A 1978 amendment dropped the approval threshold to any store above 500 metres, about the size of the average convenience store. The Temporary Measures to Adjust Retailing Commerce and the Small and Medium Retail Business Promotion laws of 1981 solidified the system by giving local retailers veto power over new stores larger than 500 square metres.

Ironically, these latest protectionist laws occurred when foreign countries increasingly identified Japan's distribution system as a significant non-tariff barrier to competitive imports. Although about 600 large stores were approved in 1979, the number dropped to an average of 150 stores a year since, with a slight rise to 203 in 1987.[31]

As if these laws were not enough, the government has continually turned a blind eye to anti-trust laws forbidding the creation of distribution cartels. For example, virtually all of the roughly 2000 wholesalers and 5000 of the 7000 retailers who handle electronic consumer goods are tied as an exclusive dealer to one of the 12 major manufacturers. One major reason why Toyota and Nissan enjoy about 70 per cent of Japan's automobile market is the fact that they have tied a similar percentage of automobile retailers as exclusive dealers. Similar tied distribution systems exist for virtually every consumer good produced in Japan, in which the large firm provides cheap credit, technological and managerial expertise, and information to the smaller firm in return for its promise to only sell its patron's goods. The benefits to Japanese firms from these anti-trust loopholes are reinforced by the 'sole agent law' which forces foreign producers to use only one Japanese important agent which has the power to control the distribution, price, and amount of the foreign goods sold. Even if the foreign producer is fortunate enough to find an agent which is relatively untied to one of its Japanese rivals, the agent will be inclined to sell the product as a luxury good with high mark-ups rather than as a mass consumer good.

Almost everyone is satisfied by these arrangements. By supporting these policies the LDP gains access to a vast pool of potential voters; MITI enjoys the power to administer the hundreds of resulting legal cartels and arrangements and wink at the others; and both the small- and medium-sized firms as well as the huge corporations profit from the security of carefully divided markets that prevent 'excessive competition'.

Only two major groups are hurt. Consumers continue to pay inflated prices for goods, particularly foreign goods, despite the doubling of the yen's value between 1985 and 1988. For example, in 1988 Japanese who could afford it had to pay $3452 for an IBM personal computer, $99 for a Black and Decker steam iron, and $62 for Levis that retail, respectively, for $2295, $36, and $32 in the United States.[32] Of course, because of these high prices the vast majority of Japanese consumers buy Japanese goods instead. Thus, foreign producers with a comparative advantage are severely hurt by their inability to penetrate Japan's protected markets within which Japanese producers enjoy enormous undeserved economies of scale. A 1982 MITI survey of 109 large European and American firms revealed that 91 thought Japan's distribution system was 'long and complicated', 53 that it was 'closed off to foreign products', 52 claimed to have 'suffered damages' as a result, and 66 demanded that Japan opened its distribution markets.[33]

The construction industry is another huge realm of small- and medium-size firms that has recently been the subject of foreign claims of protectionism. Japan's annual construction market is huge – 20 trillion yen or $180 billion – all of which is firmly in the hands of Japanese companies. The construction industry is dominated by five corporations which sit atop a sea of tiny firms whose ranks are constantly increasing. About 99 per cent of all construction firms are capitalized at less than 100 million yen and are unable to do more than light construction work. Their ranks tripled between 1960 to 1980 reaching 488 520 that year, and rose to 510 844 in 1987.[34]

These firms are jointly protected the Ministry of Construction and MITI's Small and Medium Sized Enterprise Agency which coordinate the bidding for projects and bail out troubled firms. The bureaucrats in turn parachute into high paying, low stress jobs in the industry upon retirement. About 40 LDP Dietmen are part of the construction zoku, including top faction leaders. Nakasone and Takeshita are literally wed to the construction industry; Nakasone's daughter is married to the crown prince of Kajima Construction, Japan's largest construction firm, while Takeshita's youngest daughter is married to the son of Takenaka Komuten, head of another of the big five construction firms, and his oldest daughter is married to the son of MP Shin Kanemaru, head of the construction zoku.[35]

The government's responsibility is to referee the fierce behind-the-scenes negotiations (dango) that precede the announcement of a construction project. Projects are rotated so that everyone gets a piece of the action. With all the terms worked out beforehand, construction projects and bid winners are usually announced simultaneously. The government coordinated 700 'cooperatives' in 1987 alone. In addition, it pours huge amounts of subsidies into the coffers of small firms – $2.24 billion in 1988.[36] Foreign firms are effectively barred by the catch – 22 requirement that only firms with experience working in Japan can bid on projects, and since virtually no foreign firms have been allowed the experience none are allowed to bid.

The government justifies this protectionism by arguing that 'excessive competition' would result if there were openbidding, with the number of smaller firms quickly dropping from 'over half a million to only several thousand'.[37] The resulting mass unemployment would translate into a severe blow to the LDP's Diet strength. As in the case of the distribution system, the LDP, bureaucracy, and large and small sized firms all benefit enormously from the system. The losers are foreign firms with a comparative advantage, and Japan's economy as a whole which suffers inflated prices and an inefficient allocation of labor, which in turn makes the country even more dependent on its few efficient industries, which must also be protected to ensure their continued efficiency – a self-perpetuating protectionist cycle.

Consumer Groups

Statistically, Japan's consumer groups seem formidable. Although the number of consumer groups and members has steadily declined from its peak in 1974 following OPEC's quadrupling of oil prices and the resulting recession and inflation, there are currently 4385 consumer groups composed of about 30 million Japanese. These groups are organized in hundreds of federations, of which the Japanese Consumers Cooperative Union (Sekiyo), with almost 19 million members, is the largest.[38]

In reality Japan's consumer movement is as fragmented and ineffectual as its labor movement. The label 'consumer group' is largely a misnomer since neither price nor quality of life is the major concern. Japanese consumer groups largely avoid tackling the issues that are the central focus of consumer groups in other industrial countries. Despite Japan's enormous wealth, no consumer groups have made an issue of the reality that consumers must pay exhorbitant prices for tiny, cheaply built apartments or for Japanese goods that are dumped overseas at a fraction of the cost, while they continue to work in conditions of largely uncompensated daily overtime and commuting time, and few vacations. Instead, Japanese consumer groups spend their time either rallying around the flag on trade issue or cloaking themselves in vague, idealistic slogans. For example, one of the goals of the Japan Consumer Union is 'to preserve Japanese culture' while the Japan Housewives Association (Shufuren) stresses the need for 'the abolition of all nuclear arms and general disarmament'.[39]

Japan's consumer groups have been largely coopted by industry. The most notorious example of supporting the policy emphasis on continued economic expansion rather than quality of life is agricultural policy, where Japanese consumer groups – although forced to pay five times the world price for rice, beef, and other goods – have rallied against any liberalization of food imports. Surveys indicate that about 70 per cent of consumers would rather pay higher prices for rice than import it because free trade could be dangerous to the nation's economy. And consumer groups actively campaign for those higher prices. For example, on 11 January 1988, the day before Prime Minister Takeshita was about to fly to Washington, representatives of eight consumer groups joined in a mass demonstration in Tokyo against liberalization. Takeshita used the consumer groups' support to stave off Washington's liberalization demands by saying 'We have to think about the consumer's standpoint' on imports. Even Japanese who prefer free trade deeply resent the efforts by foreign countries to open Japan.[40]

Why would consumer groups, supposedly oriented towards making life easier for all consumers by lobbying for lower prices and greater variety, actually support import barriers and high prices? One important reason is that Japanese consumers have been thoroughly socialized by the government, education system, and mass media to believe that Japan is still a 'small poor country without any natural resources', despite the reality that if is now the world's banker, has one of the world's highest per capita incomes, and is not much more dependent on foreign sources of energy and raw materials than most other industrial countries. Another is an environmental and cultural concern to maintain a green rural countryside. Yet another reason was the dampening effect of a 1978 Supreme Court ruling that said consumers were not entitled to challenge government decisions.

But perhaps the most important reason is that Nokyo, the national agriculture federation, supplies massive amounts of funds to consumer groups.[41] About out-third of consumer groups are actually considered fronts for agricultural interests, and have been highly effective in serving those interests. For example, Nishoren sponsored a nationwide showing of a Nokyo produced film which vividly links birth defects, skin diseases, and rotting food to American agricultural imports. The film asks the question: 'If Japanese consumers are being poisoned, is it good to have open trade with the United States'.[42]

Another issue over which most consumer groups are philosophically if not politically united is the demand that distributors pass on the benefits of the strong yen. Although the yen has doubled in value against the dollar since 1985, manufacturing and distribution firms have been the chief beneficiaries by maintaining the same high prices and pocketing the difference. A recent survey by the Economic Planning Agency revealed that 82.7 per cent of all consumer groups want more exchange profits returned to them. Yet the EPA Director of Consumer Affairs said that 'even though they wanted cheap products, consumer groups did not work hard enough to get what they wanted'. Less than half the consumer groups had actually made any effort to get importers to pass on savings.[43] Ironically, Keidanren has provided the major impetus for cheaper consumer prices.

Unless Keidanren decides to follow Nokyo's lead and start funding the consumer federations, Japan's consumer groups are unlikely ever to become an effective lobbying force for anyone but the farmers. The consumer groups will remain underfunded and thus dependent on hand-outs from any group willing to dispense them, even if that group actually favors higher prices. Other than supporting high food prices, Japan's consumer groups have not won any significant 'consumer' victories and are unlikely ever to do so.

OUTSIDERS

Political Parties

Overview

Since 1945 Japan's opposition parties have dramatically changed their political tactics and orientation from one of confrontation and radicalism up through the early 1970s to cooperation and moderation since. There are many reasons for this steady shift of the opposition parties to the political center. Perhaps the most important has been the growing conservatism of most Japanese voters. Although the LDP steadily lost votes throughout the 1960s to the late 1970s as the electorate became increasingly urbanized and affluent, and thus more concerned with quality of life issues, the LDP has see a resurgence of support throughout the 1980s as Japan shifts from an industrial to a neo-conservative post-industrial society.

During the 1970s the opposition parties became more moderate and cooperative as it appeared they had a chance of forming a coalition government with a steadily weakening LDP. Opposition members chaired Diet committees for the first time, and both the LDP and the opposition (except for the JCP) cooperated in certain policy areas. The LDP agreed to give up its forced votes (kyoko saiketsu) as early as 1972 in order to gain the opposition's cooperation. This pattern of cooperation has persisted as the LDP has regained strength throughout the 1980s. As the electorate becomes more conservative the opposition has to moderate its views and actions accordingly.

The LDP continues to coopt and take credit for popular political ideas proposed by the opposition, thus weakening the identity of the opposition and their ability to gain votes by backing popular issues. The DSP and CGP views on issues differ little from those of the LDP except in defense, and even there the two moderate parties may eventually accept the LDP outlook. For the past ten years the JSP has attempted to create a new image of moderation and responsibility and, although it has moved toward the center, its political support remains stagnant. The JCP remains the pariah party of Japanese politics, even though it is more ideologically flexible than the JSP on many issues.

All the opposition parties except the JCP remain tied to one source of finance and organization: JSP on Sohyo and DSP on Domei until 1987, and both parties on Rengo since, and CGP on the Soka

Gakkai. Meanwhile, the LDP continues to enjoy the virtuous cycle whereby continued economic growth allows huge financial contributions by big business, which in turns keeps the LDP in power allowing it to continue economic growth policies which in turn allows further huge contributions, and so on. As Japanese society becomes increasingly affluent and self-confident, LDP support will steadily expand and the opposition parties correspondingly decline.

Japan Socialist Party (JSP) and Democratic Socialist Party (DSP)
The Japan Socialist Party's (JSP) peak of political influence occurred almost 40 years ago when from June 1947 to February 1948 the JSP under Prime Minister Tetsu Katayama led a coalition government with the Democratic and People's Cooperation parties. Although the JSP won only 26 per cent of the vote in the April 1947 election, it was the largest party in the Diet at the time, with 143 seats. This represented a large jump in support from the April 1946 election when it held only 17 per cent of the vote and 92 seats. The government fell after a failed attempt to nationalize the coal industry, and the JSP promptly joined another coalition government under Democratic Party leader Ashida from March to October 1948. Although the JSP has never participated in a government since, it remains the largest and most significant opposition party despite the steady erosion of its voter support from its peak of 35 per cent in the late 1950s to only 17 per cent today.

In addition to a diminishing appeal among the public, the JSP remains plagued by a deep ideological factionalism whose roots go back to the 1920s shortly after the party was formed. The right wing of the party, the Shamin-kei, generally supported labor-management cooperation and moderate stands on national issues; at the opposite end of the spectrum, the Rono-kei consistently advocated a hard, ideological, confrontational line on most issues, and has been the most anti-American of the two factions; the Nichiro-kei was the center faction which shifted its political support between the Shamin-kei and Roo-kei throughout the postwar era.

These postwar factions publicly re-emerged in late 1949 when the Rono-kei under Imamura pushed for a class-based party emphasizing socialism first and democracy second, while the Shamin-kei under Morito emphasized a mass-based party with democracy first and socialism second. Imamura's faction was deeply influenced by a heavily ideological German marxism dating from the 1920, while Morito's was influenced by British style Fabian socialism and Christianity.

This split became a three-way with the emergence of the Nichiro-kei later in April 1950.

In October 1951 the party formally split into a left-wing JSP composed of the Rono-kei and Nichiro-kei opposing both the peace and security treaties, and a right-wing JSP under the Shamin-kei supporting the peace treaty but opposed to the security treaty. Although the creation of Sohyo in 1951 initially aided the left wing, Sohyo itself split in 1954 with its moderate private sector unions favoring the right-wing JSP and the public sector unions supporting the confrontational tactics and violent strikes of the left-wing JSP, particularly during the mining strikes.

The party was reunited in October 1955 when moderate leaders emerged in both factions, but the deep ideological gap between moderates and radicals remained unbridged. From 1955 to 1959, the JSP was increasingly taken over by the left wing and Sohyo, led by the radical Socialist Association (Shakaishugi kyokai), expounding an extreme revolutionary marxism propounded by Sakisaka Itsuro of Kyoto University. This extremism was exemplified by a statement by Secretary-General Asanuma, the head of the Nichiro-kei, during a trip to China in 1957 when he declared that Japan and China were united against American imperialism. This extremism led to yet another split in 1959 when the moderate wing under Suehiro Nishio completely abandoned the JSP to form the Democratic Socialist Party (DSP).

Jarred by this split, declining voter support, the failure to stop the renewed Security Treaty, and the assassination of Asanumu in 1960, the JSP adopted a policy of gradualism in the early 1960s. New party secretary Eda Saburo of the Nichiro-kei introduced a pragmatic policy of 'structural reform' which downplayed Marxism and advocated a 'vision' of a new Japan with the standard of living of the United States, the social security of the Soviet Union, the parliamentary democracy of Britain, and the peace Constitution of Japan.

However, the Nichiro-kei's moderate orientation was cut short when Sasaki Kozo of the Rono-kei took over the JSP in 1965. From then until 1977, the JSP returned to the confrontational tactics and ideological rhetorical of the 1950s. This Rono-kei/Nichiro-kei split was extended to party intellectual groups when the moderate New Current Society (Atarashii nagare no kai) arose to oppose the Socialist Association which had become deeply imbedded within the JSP leadership. Despite steadily declining voter support, the JSP did succeed in capturing the mayorship of several large cities in the

1970s, including Tokyo and Osaka. A minor split occurred in 1977 when the Social Democratic League (Shaminren) succeeded in electing three Diet members under its label.

JSP moderates finally took over control of policy-making in 1977 and have held it ever since. That year the Socialist Association's attempts to assert complete control over the JSP was defeated after three gruelling party congresses. Finally, at the December congress, Ichio Asukata, a former progressive mayor of Yokohama, agreed to become chairman on three conditions: if the chairman's powers were strengthened, the Socialist Association abandoned its 'Thesis' that the JSP is a revolutionary party that would assume a dictatorship of the proletariat in office, and the chairman be selected by the rank and file.

Atsukata advocated a program of administrative decentralization and local initiatives oriented to solving specific problems, and launched a membership drive which increased the JSP ranks from 40 000 to 70 000 between 1977 and 1980. The JSP took a significant step towards democratization when the party chairman was elected by mass membership rather than the previous method which was confined to party congress delegates.

Yet, despite this shift to the center, the JSP continued to lose voter support and its big city mayorships, and Asukata underwent increasing criticism for his perceived indecisiveness and poor image. He was replaced in summer 1983 by Masashi Iishibashi, with a reputation for his desire for pragmatic reforms and his unalignment with any particular faction, for example, Iishibashi got the JSP to agree to support the JDF as unconstitutional but not illegal, and to cap rather than eliminate the nuclear power industry. Iishibashi shared with Nakasone details of JSP delegations to Pyongyang (1984) and Moscow (1985). He led a delegation to the United States in 1984 which met with Vice-President Bush and attempted to visit South Korea, but was not allowed in. At the December 1985 JSP Congress he attempted to rewrite the party's marxist basis to a more pragmatic one. But he was defeated and resigned in favor of the present president, Takako Doi. Doi, the first woman JSP chairman, has continued Iishibashi's moderate policies.

The JSP is rather loosely organized with no strong central authority; power is defused among a constellation of party factions. The JSP leadership is composed of a chairman, three to four vice-chairman, a secretary-general, a chairman of the Control Commission which is in charge of party discipline, and the chairmen of various branches and committees. These positions are divided up according to faction strength. Like the LDP and other leadership positions in Japanese groups, the JSP chairman is a relatively weak position, whose job is to maintain harmony between the different factions. The Central Executive Committee is supposed to be the decision-making body for the JSP when it is not in Congress, but actually simply acts as the clearing house for the dozens of committees dealing with specific issues.

A party Congress must be held at least once a year; extraordinary sessions can be called. Although Congressional votes and resolutions are non-binding, they do set the general guidelines for party policy. Before 1962 Diet members could be Congressional delegates; since then only local JSP branch officers can be elected to the party Congress. This rule change helped shift the balance of ideological power within the JSP to the radicals, since local party officials tend to be far more radical than the more pragmatic Dietmen who represent them.

Sohyo traditionally provided the main source of funds and personnel. More than half the JSP members of the House of Representatives continue to be labor union officials, mostly of ex-government or public workers, in 1977 reaching a peak of 65 per cent.[44] Sohyo members make up about 70 per cent of the JSP membership. Sohyo raises almost all the JSP's campaign expenses.

Like the other opposition parties, JSP behavior in the Diet has shifted from the confrontational tactics of the 1940s through early 1970s to cooperating with the LDP and other parties since. The JSP capture of Diet committeeships in the mid–1970s as the LDP continued to steadily lose Diet strength, gave the JSP a stake in the system and they responded by treating their new responsibilities with moderation. The party has remained cooperative despite losing more committee positions to the LDP as they regained voting power in the 1980s.

For the last decade, the JSP has become increasingly pragmatic in many broad policy areas and has been willing to work closely with the LDP on certain non-controversial issues. Yet, the JSP remains torn by factionalism, much of it ideological. Conflict is more open than in the LDP because, being out of power, the JSP does not have to worry about losing cohesion as much as the LDP. The JSP is composed of many small factions which, like the LDP, are masked by study group designations. Like the LDP, all individual JSP Dietmen are aligned either formally or informally with a faction as a source of funds and party positions. In addition, each Dietman has his own koenkai that handles fund-raising and re-elections.

The JSP's voter support declined rapidly from 32.8 per cent of the vote in 1958 to 21.4 per cent in 1969, and deteriorated steadily since to a low of 17 per cent in 1986. The diversity of the JSP vote diminished in proportion to its percentage of the total vote. In the 1950s the JSP was a 'catch all' party which enjoyed wide support from a range of groups. About one-third of its supporters were blue collar workers, one-quarter white collar workers, one-quarter farmers, and small firms comprised about 12 per cent. But since then its electoral support from each of these groups has steadily diminished. The LDP, CGP, JCP, and DSP have captured most of the JSP'S former urban strongholds and as early as 1976 60 per cent of its seats were in rural and semi-urban districts. The JSP's strong rural base reflects the fact that public unions are often influential in local areas and support small party machines. In addition, many early JSP Diet members were interested in land reform and still retain the loyalty of their constitutency.[45]

The number of districts in which the JSP runs candidates has diminished greately in the last 30 years. In 1959 the JSP ran multiple candidates in 80 per cent of all districts, of which 20 per cent were successful; in 1979 it ran multiple candidates in only 20 per cent of all districts, of which only 10 per cent were successful. In 1958 eight districts had three JSP members; in 1979 only one district had three JSP members. In the 1980s JSP support seems to have stabilized at around 18 per cent of the electorate of ten million voters, most of whom are middle aged and poor.

Perhaps the most important reason for this decline is the JSP's inability to shed its anachronistic marxist garb and adapt to the tremendous changes that have been overtaking Japan. Curtis writes that 'by the early 1980s the Socialist party had become the most conservative of Japan's parties, unable to break with old policies or articulate new ones, and dominated by politicians who, lacking any hope of capturing governmental power, set their sights on little more than getting themselves reelected'.[46] Unlike its counterparts in West Europe, the JSP remains mired in an obsolete ideological marxism and has not significantly moderated its outlook. The JSP has become increasingly schizophrenic as the party platform and many of its local officials retain a heavy marxist bias while its Dietmen are increasingly pragmatic. The party continues publicly to advocate phasing out the security treaty and the JDF, declare Japan's non-alignment, and to blast the conservatives as the party of monopoly capitalism, national-ism, and militarism. At the same time, the JSP votes for 90 per cent of the government's bills and works cozily with the LDP behind the scenes carefully choreographing things like how much protest time it will get in the Diet.

As a result, the JSP suffers from a chronic poor image among all Japanese – even its supporters. In many ways the JSP is an anachron-ism; it is poorly organized, poorly funded, and faction-ridden, with much of its energies wasted on endless discussions of marxist doc-trine. Its class-based rhetoric sounds increasingly absurd in an afflu-ent country like Japan where 90 per cent of the population considers itself middle class. Even blue-collar workers are increasingly throw-ing their support behind the LDP. The JSP is caught in a vicious cycle whereby the less voter support it wins, the less access it has to funds, and the fewer funds it receives, the less opportunity it has to fund its political campaigns, which leads to a further erosion of support, and so on.

The DSP faces a similar dilemma; its name implies a commitment to radically changing Japanese society, yet the party itself is moder-ate. Thus, those who believe in genuine social change tend to vote JSP or JCP, while those who support DSP policies tend to vote LDP. This dilemma became clear when in September 1987 Secretary-General Ouchi Kengo said the party was prepared to hold policy consultations with the JSP. Until then the DSP had repeatedly made it clear since the mid-1970s that it was prepared to enter a coalition government with the LDP, and the sudden declaration of a willing-ness to work with the JSP showed the DSP's split personality.

Because of this paradox, the DSP remains the smallest of the opposition parties. In its first election in 1960, although only 17 of the DSP's 105 candidates won, this still represented a relatively respectable 8.8 per cent of the vote. But this percentage declined to 7.4 per cent in the 1963 election, and the DSP has hovered between 6 and 7 per cent of the vote since. In the 1986 election the DSP captured 6.4 per cent of the vote and 26 seats.

The DSP largely represents the interests of company workers, but also receives some support from farmers and small- and medium-sized entrepreneurs. Until the creation of Rengo, the DSP was almost completely dependent on Domei for its funding and voter mobilization. Given its moderate orientation and vast resources, Rengo will undoubtedly give the DSP a great deal of financial and organizational support which could increase the party's voter support and Diet members.

Japan Communist Party (JCP)

The Japan Communist Party (JCP) has changed greatly in the 65 years since it was founded by the Commintern on 15 July 1922 in Tokyo. The Commintern wrote its original manifesto and regulations, and created a small Leninist party to lead what was thought to be an imminent revolution designed to destroy Japan's imperial system and impose a 'dictatorship of the proletariat'. Today the JCP is a non-aligned communist party committed to Japanese democracy which regularly captures about 10 per cent of the popular vote.

The metamorphysis from revolutionary to mass party was pressured by periodic repression from without, and bitter ideological conflict from within. The government outlawed the JCP shortly after it was founded, and spent much of the 1920s and 1930s trying to completely stamp it out. JCP members were constantly in hiding, on the run, or in exile, and were bound by Moscow directives that had little relation to actual political conditions in Japan.

The JCP was reborn on 1 December 1945 when Comintern representative Sanzo Nosaka returned from his wartime exile at the CCP headquarters at Yenan to lead the Fourth Party Congress. Two months later Nozaka was named party chairman and set out to create a 'lovable JCP'. Under Nozaka's leadership the JCP steadily increased its Diet strength, from only 6 of 464 seats or 3.7 per cent of the vote in 1946 to 35 seats and 10 per cent of the vote in 1949. JCP strength came largely from former JSP supporters, who steadily deserted the party after the failure of the Katayama government.

But these gains were completely lost after the JSP accepted Moscow's orders in January 1950 to abandon parliamentarism and instead try to overthrow the government. The immediate result was a severe party split between the moderates and hardliners, with the revolutionary policy winning out. In response, MacArthur ordered the JCP Central Committee purged, and all its leadership either fled abroad or went into exile. As a result, the JCP lost all their 35 seats in the 1952 election.

The JCP's slow political comeback was engineered by Kenji Miyamoto who became chairman in 1955. Miyamoto joined the JCP in 1931, and then spent 17 years in prison until his release in 1945 for his role in helping murder a dissident party member in 1933. He became chairman at a time when the world communist movement was experiencing tremendous strains and challenges. Stalin had died three years earlier, relations were increasingly bitter between Moscow and Beijing, and attempts by communist parties in East Germany, Hungary, and Poland to become more independent were smashed with Soviet tanks, causing communists everywhere to question their subservience to Moscow dictates. In 1956 Krushchev's destalinization and Palmiro Togliatti's concepts of poly-communism encouraged Miyamoto to push the JCP to replace its militarism with a popular-front strategy, based on reviving Nozaka's notion of a 'lovable' party. This independence deepened in the 1960s as the JCP first split with Moscow over the nuclear test ban treaty, and then with China in 1966 over demands by Mao that the JCP join an anti-Soviet/anti-American front. As a result, JCP voter support rose gradually during this time from one seat with 2 per cent of the vote in 1953 to five seats with 5 per cent of the vote in 1967.

After the Soviet crushing of the Prague spring in 1968, the JCP complete embraced the Euro-communist model of independence from Moscow. Since then the JCP has become increasingly open. In 1969 it declared it would respect the rights of opposition parties if it ever took over the government; in 1970 party Congresses were opened to the public; in 1972 the JCP hosted the International Conference on Communist Theory which presented a range of possibilities for communist theory and practice; and at the 12th party Congress in 1973 the JCP replaced the word 'dictatorship' (dokusai) with 'regency' (shikken) of the proletariat, renounced violence, and declared there were as many paths to communism as there were communist parties. As a result, the JCP became the second largest opposition party in 1969 with 14 seats and 7 per cent of the vote in 1969, and 38 seats and 10 per cent of the vote in 1972. On the local level the JCP joined coalition governments in Kyoto and Osaka.

At the 13th Congress in 1976, the JCP pushed its liberalization even further when it replaced all Marxist-Leninist references with those of scientific socialism, issued a 'Manifesto of Freedom and Democracy' that lauded such documents as the American Declaration of Independence and French Declaration of the Rights of Man, and asserted a Japanese version of communism designed to address Japanese development problems. This time, however, the JCP went too far. In the elections that year, although they still retained about 10 per cent of the popular vote, the JCP Diet seats fell from 38 to 17 as its radical supporters defected to the JSP, whose seats rose from 118 to 123. The JCP responded to this loss by reinstating some

Marxist-Leninist ideology and downplaying democracy. As a result, the JCP again seized 38 seats in 1979 while the JSP seats fell to 107.

Clearly, the JSP and JCP were caught in a zero-sum-game for the same pool of radical voters, and the JCP has generally played the game better than the JSP. The problem, of course, is that the JCP seems to be caught on an electoral plateau of 10 per cent of the popular vote. If it tries to move toward the center it loses its radical supporters to the JSP while the DSP and CGP continue to retain the moderate vote. The JCP has succeeded in maintaining its political balancing act throughout the 1980s both in terms of Diet seats and votes, and in party policy. The JCP restored relations with Moscow in 1980, but in 1984 denounced both the Soviet Union and United States as imperialistic.

Even in the heyday of 'democratization' in the mid–1970s, liberalization was always more symbolic than real. The JCP remains organized on classic democratic centralist lines whereby the party congresses rubberstamp decisions made by the Chairman Miyamoto, who presides over a Central Committee composed of five vice-chairmen, and policy department heads. Miyamoto has built the JCP membership into the largest of all the Japanese political parties after the LDP, and the third largest non-ruling communist party after Italy and France. The JCP has gone through four membership phases since 1945. An initial rapid growth from about 1000 to 84 000 between 1945 and 1949; followed by a plunge to only 40 000 members after the 1950 purge and loss of its Diet seats in 1952; Miyamoto's moderate line and membership drive after 1958 resulted in a steady membership expansion to 300 0'0 by 1970; since then membership has risen at a slower pace to its current level of 500 000.

Despite its central control, the JCP is a grass roots organization which finds support in a wide variety of professional and community organizations including labor, youth, women, and the 'three great families' (gosanke) doctors, lawyers, and accountants. Women comprise about 40 per cent of the total membership but only 13 per cent of the congress delegates and central committee. Although from 1945 to the mid-1960s, Soviet and Chinese contributions laundered through a variety of front organizations comprised most JCP funding, the party largely abandoned those sources with its independence policy and now relies on sales of its daily newspaper *Red Flag* (Akahata) and other publications for virtually all its finance. Officially, the JCP is Japan's richest party, but only because it is the only party that accurately reports its income and expenses as required by law;

the other parties are estimated to report only about 10 per cent of their funding. The JCP is the only opposition party that is financially independent of any one external source.

Despite its ideological and financial independence, its grassroots efforts and appeal, and attempts to promote a 'lovable' image, the JCP remains an alien party, untrustworthy and autocratic in the eyes of most Japanese. The JCP power-base among the radical and outcast members of Japanese society prevents the party from being accepted by most Japanese; even the other opposition parties shun close ties with the JCP. The JCP will probably remain at its current level of electoral support and Diet strength.

Clean Government Party (CGP)

The Clean Government Party (CGP) is Japan's only genuinely new postwar party, and the only religious-based party. The CGP was born of the Sokka Gakkai religion, which has been the most successful of the hundreds of 'new religions' that emerged in the modern era. Sokka Gakkai was created by Tsunesaburo Makiguchi in 1930 with the intention of reforming Japanese society and the education system along the lines of Nicheren Buddhism. Nicheren was a thirteenth-century Buddhist monk who expounded a very nationalistic form of Buddhism which rejected all other sects and religions. Makiguchi added to Nicheren's beliefs the concept of a 'Buddhist Democracy' in which politics and religion were one, and dedicated to the social welfare of all. Buddhist democracy could only be realized when everyone realized the truth of Nicheren and were converted to the Sokka Gakkai. Thus, followers actively proselytized and attempted to convert others by the 'break and subdue' method (shakubuku) which involved extreme psychological conditioning of the potential adherent. The government, however, viewed Sokka Gakkai as subversive, and the religion was suppressed and its leaders imprisoned during the war.

The ranks of the Sokka Gakkai swelled rapidly after the war, fuelled by the 1947 Constitution's guarantee of freedom of religion, the crusading zeal of its adherents, and the deep need among many Japanese for something to deeply believe in after the devastation of defeat. By 1959 there were almost a million Sokka Gakkai followers. But the religion really took off during the 1960s under the highly influential and charismatic presidency of Daisaku Ikeda; converts numbered seven million by 1969 and rose slightly to around 7.8 million by 1979, a number which has held steady since. One reason for its inability to grow further was the resignation of Ikeda in 1979 as president of Sokka Gakkai and the related religion Nicheren Shoshu, when he was denounced by Doctrinal Study head Hirashima Takashi for his 'god-like' demeanor, misappropriation of funds, and tendency to pour billions of yen into huge assembly halls for his followers.

Although the notion of the inseparability of politics and religion had been present from the Sokka Gakkai's birth in the 1930s, it was not until the early 1950s that its leaders began actively to campaign for public office. In November 1954 a Department of Cultural Affairs was created to promote a variety of political activities and goals, with the prime objective of building a huge national assembly hall for the religion. In the 1955 election, 55 Sokka Gakkai supporters were elected as 'independents' in local elections. Encouraged by this success, the Sokka Gakkai attempted to win on the national level in the 1956 elections, and three of the six candidates it fielded won seats in the House of Councillors. The Komei Political League was created in November 1961 to coordinate the efforts of the Sokka Gakkai's emerging national political presence. In that year the Sokka Gakkai had nine members in the House of Councillors, seven prefectural assemblymen, and 268 city representatives. In the 1962 election, the Sokka Gakkai pushed their House of Councillor representation up to 15 members.

Using the Christian Democratic parties of West Europe as a precedent, the Sokka Gakkai officially created the Clean Government Party (Komeito) in November 1964 with the goals of promoting world peace, the abolition of nuclear weapons and political corruption, humanitarian socialism, and Buddhist democracy. During the next election in 1967, the CGP captured 25 seats in the House of Representatives.

But the growing religious and political successes of the Sokka Gakkai and CGP during the 1960s was undercut by several scandals throughout the 1970s. In 1970 Hirotatsu Fujiwara, a political scientist, attempted to publish an investigative book entitled *'I Denounce the Sokka Gakkai'* in which he exposed Ikeda's efforts to make Nicheren Shoshu Japan's state religion. After hearing about this book, the Sokka Gakkai attempted to suppress its publication by spreading disinformation through the mass media and pressuring the publisher. The book was published, however, and not surprisingly, given the publicity, became a best-seller. As a result, the Sokka Gakkai and Komeito formally split into separate organizations on 3 May 1970, and the CGP has since attempted to recruit non-Sokka

Gakkai adherents to run for election. But the damage had been done and both the Sokka Gakkai and CGP reached a plateau in their number of new converts and political representatives, respectively.

Another controversy occurred five years later in July 1975 when it was announced that the JCP and Ikeda had reached an agreement whereby the former would hereafter tolerate religion while the latter would tolerate communism, and both agreed to denounce nuclear weapons. The CGP was shocked by the announcement since it contradicted both the religion and the party's traditional anti-communism, and undermined the efforts of both to show a more moderate, mainstream orientation. The CGP leadership denounced the agreement as a communist plot to estrange the Komeito and Sokka Gakkai. Under fire from the CGP and from within the Sokka Gakkai itself, Ikeda agreed to repudiate the agreement. But the controversy exposed how tight the ties remained between the Sokka Gakkai and CGP despite the formal split five years earlier, as well as Ikeda's absolutist leadership style.

The Sokka Gakkai and CGP were blasted by several scandals in the early 1980s that further undermined their religion and political gains. In 1980 Masatomo Yamazaki, a lawyer and advisor to the Sokka Gakkai who attended its most sensitive meetings, was paid 300 million yen to keep quiet about alledged improprieties, including Ikeda's secret wiretapping of JCP chairman Miyamoto in 1975. The Sokka Gakkai called in the police, however, when Yamazaki demanded another 500 million yen. This was followed up by an exposé in 1982 that Ikeda had had extramarital affairs with two secretaries who later became CGP Diet members, and his court appearance in 1983 on charges of blackmail and illegal wiretaps.

The CGP's latest scandal broke in May 1988 when two of its House of Representative members – Toshio Ohashi a 20-year member and Yukimasa Fujiwara a 22-year member – harshly criticized Ikeda for turning the party into his 'personal property' and violating the Constitutional separation of church and state. Although the CGP's founding charter limits funds to individual contributions, the Sokka Gakkai annually funnels billions of yen to the party while its members work as 'volunteers' to get out the vote in each election. Fujiwara also asserted the Sokka Gakkai's real membership was only about three million, far less than the 7.9 million claimed. But the core membership of about 500 000 has the utmost faith in Ikeda, and will do anything he says. Thus, other Sokka Gakkai or CGP leaders lack the power to challenge Ikeda's arbitrary rule. Ohashi went so far as to call Ikeda a 'Sutra-chanting Hitler'.[47] Ikeda and his followers dismissed all the charges as simply unfounded personal grudges, and both Fujiwara and Ohashi were denounced as corrupt and expelled from the party.

This most recent scandal has set back the latest CGP attempts to forge closer links with the DSP, JSP, and new labor federation Rengo. The CGP has proposed a plan to cooperate with the other two parties and Rengo in the 1989 House of Councillors' election, but given the latest scandal and the CGP's generally poor image among Japanese, the DSP and JSP are hesitant about committing themselves.

Despite these scandals, the CGP remains an important member of the political opposition. And despite their formal 1970 split, the Sokka Gakkai and CGP are meshed at virtually all levels. CGP and Sokka Gakkai followers are virtually synonomous; the Sokka Gakkai claims to turn out 100 per cent of its followers for elections in which they uniformly vote for the CGP. Polls, however, indicate that only 74 per cent of Sokka Gakkai members vote for CGP candidates. The discrepancy is explained by the fact that CGP candidates do not run in all districts, thus forcing Sokka Gakkai followers to vote for another party. Polls indicate another discrepancy – only 4–5 per cent of all those polled indicate they support the CGP, yet the CGP generally wins about 10 per cent of the vote. Thus, at least half those who support the CGP refuse to admit it because of the scandals and general disregard with which most Japanese view the Sokka Gakkai. The CGP also attracts a large protest vote from independents. Still, it is estimated that only about 10 per cent of those who vote for the CGP are not members of the Sokka Gakkai.

The Sokka Gakkai and CGP compete with the JCP for a similar pool of the bottom socio-economic level of Japan among people who are generally poorly educated, hold dead-end jobs, and lack community or group ties. In 1982 almost 60 per cent of CGP supporters were women, 25 per cent were industrial workers, 21 per cent worked in small businesses, 17 per cent were clerical workers, and 15 per cent were self-employed.

Practically all CGP funds come from the Sokka Gakkai. The religion receives a steady and enormous flow of money from its followers and can mobilize even more funds for specific projects. For example, Ikeda raised over 35 billion yen in just four days in 1965 to construct an assembly hall, and between 1967 and 1977 a further 67 billion yen was collected for similar construction projects. Fund

raising and political mobilization is based on a grass roots organization whereby the religion is organized into ten family cells which
meet almost daily for discussion, which are in turn members of
larger units of 50–100 families, which are organized into districts of
500–1000 families. The Sokka Gakkai also has thousands of neighborhood 'consulting centers' which assist people with their daily problems. Thus, the Sokka Gakkai and CGP have a reputation for problem-solving and action similar to that of the JCP, which operates
its own grass roots organizations. In addition, the Sokka Gakkai
sponsors a range of art, music, youth, athletic, and educational
groups, and funds the Sokka University. Its daily newspaper, the
Komei Shimbun, has a circulation of 860 000, with a Sunday edition
of 1.4 million. The Sokka Gakkai publishes a number of magazines,
journals, and books.

With its funding and constituency ensured, the CGP does not
suffer from the factionalism that plagues other parties. Any divisions
are generally over genuine policy issues rather than personalities.
The most controversial issues are defense-related. Although the CGP
was originally against both the SDF and security treaty, it now favors
the former and would only gradually phase out the latter. This policy
shift caused a great deal of intra-party debate.

The CGP has the lowest percentage of university graduates among
both its Diet and party ranks. It runs candidates in less than half the
House of Representative districts. In the House of Councillors the
CGP has recently followed a 'zone voting' strategy whereby candidates are assigned a zone in which to mobilize their supporters; in
1980 this strategy resulted in nine out of nine candidates winning the
election.

Despite its solid grass roots organization and funding, the Sokka
Gakkai and CGP are unlikely to grow significantly beyond their
current level of religious and political support. The CGP will remain
dependent on the Sokka Gakkai for virtually all its funds and votes.
The Sokka Gakkai remains a religion of the lowest socio-economic
class. As Japan becomes increasingly prosperous, that pool of potential adherents will steadily shrink. Thus, the Sokka Gakkai must find
a way to broaden its appeal. Another obstacle to further growth is
the negative image most Japanese hold of the Sokka Gakkai. In a
1964 poll, over 40 per cent of 1500 asked used the word 'fanatical'
to describe it, only 4 per cent supported the religion, and 39 per
cent had no opinion.[48] Although the survey indicates a large segment

of the population that could be targeted for conversion, the repeated scandals continue to sully the Sokka Gakkai's image.

Overall, the CGP has played a very positive role in Japanese politics. Its mainstream stands on various issues and willingness to cooperate with the JSP and DSP has helped bridge the political gap between left and right. At the same time, it serves as a political watchdog by exposing the corruption of the other parties. The CGP also serves as a counterbalance to the JCP. The two parties compete for the same pool of lower and underclass Japanese; without the CGP the JCP could possibly be twice as large and influential as it now is. Finally, despite the scandals that have frequently rocked the CGP, the party brings the discussion of ethics and values to politics and Japanese society as a whole, offering both a standard and challenge for all.

Labor

Industrial workers have struggled for a voice in policy-making ever since the first labor unions emerged in the 1920s. Before 1945 unions were at first severely repressed, then coopted by the mainstream parties during the 1930s, and finally dissolved in 1940. Since 1945 organized labor's relationship with the political system and corporate world has passed through four distinct phases. The first phase lasted from 1945 to 1950. SCAP reforms following the suppression of unions during the war unleashed a decade of labor militancy. Three Occupation labor reforms gave laborers the hope that they would finally influence policy-making. The 1945 Trade Union Law guaranteed the right of workers to organize, engage in collective bargaining, and strike. In addition it provided for labor relations boards at both the national and prefectural levels to mediate disputes. This reform was followed up by the 1946 Labor Relations Adjustment Act, which specified the procedures for the labor relations boards. The 1947 Labor Standards Law set the minimum standards for work hours, vacations, restrictions on women and child labor, safety, sanitation, sick leave, accident compensation, and other worker's welfare issues.

Union membership had never reached more than 500 000 before the war; during the war they were abolished. But SCAP's reforms led to a proliferation of unions and union members: from virtually none during the War, the number of unions rose to 509 with 380 000 members or 3.2 per cent of the workforce by the end of 1945, shot up to 17 266 with 4 926 000 members or 41.5 per cent of the workforce by the end of 1946 and peaked at 34 688 with 6 655 000 or 55.8 per cent of almost 15 million workers in 1949.[49]

In an environment in which any political party or union could freely operate, the better organized radical factions soon took over the labor movement. From 1945 to 1950 two major national labor federations – the communist controlled Sanbetsu (Congress of Industrial Labor Unions) and socialist Sodomei (General Confederation of Labor) – battled to win the hearts and minds of the unions. In 1947 Sanbetsu had a membership of 4.47 million against Sodomei's 3.01 million. The new radicalism helped elect a JSP-led coalition government from June 1947 to March 1948. This electoral victory was undercut, however, by a setback that occurred several months earlier when SCAP forced the labor movement to call off a general strike scheduled for 1 February 1947.

Yet this was only a temporary setback to labor militancy. Sanbetsu launched a major labor offensive in 1949 when its strike strategy won out over Sodomei's more conciliatory policy. That year there were over 800 strikes amounting to about six million man-days of work lost. The number of labor strikes intensified throughout early 1950 as Sanbetsu joined the JCP in supporting Moscow's January command to abandon its popular front tactics and instead embark on a campaign of industrial sabotage and strikes. SCAP got wind of the Commitern directive and responded with a 'red purge' in which hundreds of JCP and Sanbetsu leaders were arrested. The purge broke the back of Sanbetsu's power, and by 1951 its ranks had declined to a mere 200 000, while union membership as a whole dropped from about seven million in 1949 to 5.5 million by 1951.

This power vacuum was soon filled by the newly formed General Council of Trade Unions (Sohyo), which coopted most of Sanbetsu's predominately enterprise unions as well most of the public, occupation, and general unions. Sohyo and the other labor federations largely set aside political action and concentrated their efforts on collective bargaining for higher wages. In 1955 Sohyo negotiated an agreement among the labor federations to conduct a carefully coordinated annual 'Spring offensive' (Shunto) to wring higher wages from management. Labor union leaders meet several months before the Shunto and work out an agreement over how much of a wage increase to demand and which industries or firms will lead the struggle. Unions in the most successful firms and industries are targeted for the largest wage demands. Other unions then use the wage increases from the successful unions as the opening demand in their own negotiations. An agreement is usually reached and announced by January, and between then and the actual strike date management and labor engage in tough negotiations over the final wage hike. Since an agreement is usually reached well before the strike date, the strike is held for an hour or two for its symbolic effect, followed by an announcement of the agreement. Labor largely achieved its wage targets from the early 1950s to 1973 largely because its demands actually fell below the average 10 per cent a year growth rate.

Yet, despite this conciliatory strategy, labor never recovered the power it commanded in the late 1940s when as a proportion of the total workforce union membership reached 50 per cent. Although by the late 1950s, union membership rose to 6 774 000, this was only 46.2 per cent of the total factory workforce. Although the absolute number of unions and members rose steadily over the next quarter century, union strength continued to steadily diminish as a percentage of the total workforce. In 1966 there were almost 20 000 new unions (52 879) representing almost four million new members (10 146 000), but the percentage of the total workforce dropped to only 34.8 per cent. This percentage remained unchanged over the next decade; in 1975, while the number of unions had risen to 69 333 representing 12 590 000 workers, this remained only 34.4 per cent of the total workforce.

The vast majority of these unions were enterprise unions. In 1948 90.5 per cent were enterprise unions while only 4.3 per cent were occupation unions, 3.4 per cent were industrial unions, and a miniscule 1.4 per cent were general unions. Although the efforts of the left-wing federations had reduced the number of enterprise unions to 85.6 per cent of the total in 1950, while almost doubling the percentage of occupational (7.9 per cent) and general (2.7 per cent) unions, the red purge reversed this trend. By 1960 enterprise unions had risen to 93.6 per cent of the total, while occupation unions had dropped to a mere 1.7 per cent, industrial unions to 3.1 per cent, and general unions to 0.3 per cent.

The unions' power to strike diminished as steadily as their declining percentage of the total workforce. Largely as a result of economic growth, which averaged an annual 10 per cent between 1950 and 1973, the number of working days lost from strikes per 1000 employees dropped steadily: 254 in 1955–59, 177 in 1960–64, and 107 in 1965–69. The number rose to 155 in 1970–74 largely because of OPEC's quadrupling of oil prices, which has cut economic growth in half since, and actually led to a decline in growth in 1974. But

Japan's ability to tighten its belt and then continue to grow at double the rate of the other OECD countries led to a dramatic drop in 1975–80 to only 69 working days lost per year per 1000 workers, and from 1981 to 1985 the annual average was only 20. Of the other OECD countries only The Netherlands has matched Japan's low strike rate of 20, and only Switzerland's record was lower – it had virtually no strikes during the 1980s. In comparison the United States' figure in 1981–85 was 130, West Germany's was 50, Britain's was 440, France's was 90, and Sweden's was 40.

During the early 1970s, two trends pulled most of the teeth from Japan's labor movement. By this time, most companies had thoroughly coopted their workers through enterprise unions. Prosperity moderated the political orientation of the opposition parties; for both the radical parties and unions, the politics of confrontation gradually gave way to the politics of cooperation with the LDP. With the LDP steadily losing its share of the Diet seats with each election, the opposition parties began to moderate their position in hopes of eventually being invited to form a coalition government. The quadrupling of oil prices in 1973, which cut Japan's economic growth rate in half, forced the unions to make even more humble Shunto requests. It was clear that the old labor ideas of class struggle were increasingly irrelevant as prosperity increased.

Despite the growing cooperation between the LDP and opposition parties, both private and public sector unions continued to have little influence on policy-making. The leadership of most public unions remained in the hands of radical leftist ideologues. Yet, without the right to strike, public unions have had no individual influence on public policy. Enterprise unions are naturally moderate in their demands and political orientation since the union's prosperity depends on the company's prosperity. In the escalator seniority system, labor union leaders eventually become middle-ranking company managers, so they will attempt to tow the company line while diluting union demands. Another reason for the impotence of company unions is that their ranks are filled by both white- and blue-collar workers.

Sohyo remained the largest union from its founding in 1951 up through the formation of the labor federation Rengo in 1987. In 1985 Sohyo was composed of 6186 unions with 4.5 million members, of which 2730 unions with 1.5 million members were private and 3456 unions with 2.9 million members were public. Although it adopted a conciliatory policy in the early 1950s, Sohyo's tendency to mask its moderation with harsh marxist rhetoric gave it the reputation of being the most radical of the labor federations. Sohyo continues to provide the bedrock of financial and administration support for the JSP. Over half the JSP Diet members come from Sohyo, causing some to call the JSP the 'political affairs section of Sohyo'.[50]

Domei, or the All Japan Labor Federation (Zen Nihon Rodo Sodemei) was founded in the fall of 1964 of moderate unions opposed to the strict socialism of Sohyo and the JSP. In the mid-1970s, Domei reached a peak membership of 5851 unions, of which 5737 with 2.2 million members were private and 114 unions with 168 000 members were public. But this represented only 17.8 per cent of all union members. Domei remains the chief source of funds for the DSP. The other two national federations until recently included the Churitsuren, or Federation of Independent Unions, which in 1975 was composed of 911 unions with 1.3 million members, or 10.7 per cent of the total, and Shinsanbetsu composed of 78 unions with 65 000 members or 0.5 per cent of the total.

Interestingly, it was the small federation Churitsuren, rather than Sohyo or Domei, which has led the consolidation of the labor movement over the past decade. In October 1976 several unions from Churitsuren organized the Trade Union Council for Policy Promotion (TUCPP, Seisui Kaigi) in an attempt to promote a constructive labor imput into policy-making. The TUCPP included 16 industrial labor federations (two from Sohyo, six from Domei, three from Churitsu, two from Shinsanbetsu, and three from unaffiliated unions). Four more federations joined in 1978. The TUCPP presented its policy proposals direct to the Prime Minister as well as the opposition parties (except the JCP). The LDP welcomed the TUCPP's moderate policies and adopted a number of them.

In March 1979 Churitsu and Shinsanbetsu, encouraged by the TUCPP's success, formed the General Confederation of Trade Unions (Sorengo) which they hoped would act as a catalyst for a unified trade union movement. Domei soon went along and Sohyo eventually accepted the agreement that Sorengo would be led by private rather than public sector unions. In December 1982 Sorengo was replaced by the Private Sector Trade Union Council (Zenmin Rokyo, JPTUC), which was reorganized as the General Confederation of Japanese Private Sector Trade Unions (Rengo) during its sixth convention in November 1987. During the convention Domei, Shinsanbetsu, and Churitsu dissolved themselves into Rengo, forming a confederation of 62 labor organizations with a combined membership of 5.5 million, or about 45 per cent of all union membership. About half of Sohyo's private sector unions have moved to Rengo, and Sohyo had promised to dissolve itself into Rengo in 1990. Sohyo would have declined whether Rengo had formed or not. The government's privatization program of the 1980s in industries like telecommunications and railroads has steadily undermined Sohyo's traditional support. For example, between 1986 and March 1987 membership in the National Railway Workers' Union dropped from 155 723 to 62 000.[51]

There are now three Japanese labor federations, Rengo with 5.5 million members, a truncated Sohyo with little over three million remaining members, and the communist federation Toitsu Rosokon formed in 1974 with two million members which remains dedicated to class struggle. When Sohyo dissolves itself, most of its federations will move to Rengo and the rest to Toitsu Rosokon. In addition, over one third or 37.5 per cent of all Japanese trade unions are unaffiliated with any labor federation. These 21 212 unions with 4.6 million members are virtually all conservative company unions which support either the LDP or DSP.

Rengo has abandoned most socialist ideology and trappings, and has joined the moderate International Confederation of Free Trade Unions (ICFTU). All the opposition parties except the JCP support Rengo. Now that the JSP and DSP no longer enjoy the backing of Sohyo and Domei, respectively, there is pressure for the two parties to join. Altogether, Rengo has accelerated the moderation of the opposition parties and labor movement. Although Rengo is unlikely to arrest the steady decline of the percentage of Japanese workers in unions, which had dropped to a mere 28.2 per cent in 1988, a unified movement will increase labor's power within the policy-making arena. Once Sohyo joins, Rengo may become an increasingly important policy-making actor in labor-related issues.

CONCLUSION

There is unlikely to be any significant change in the composition and policy impact of these 'auxiliary' political actors for the indefinite future. The mass media will continue to rally around the flag on trade and economic issues, while occasionally criticizing specific LDP policy or moral failures. If anything, the media will become more conservative, along with the population as a whole. As the two most important LDP voting blocs, agriculture and the small- and medium-sized business world will continue to dominate policy-making in their respective areas, while having no influence on any other policies. Other than those groups that are fronting farm interests, consumer groups are unlikely ever to play an important policy-making role.

As political outsiders, the opposition parties and labor federations face the same dilemma. The more vociferously they battle for their interests, the less chance there is that the ruling triad will accomodate them. The more they attempt to work within the system, however, the more they must compromise their original interests and accept those of the ruling triad. In return for this 'Faustian deal' they are granted a token rule in policy-making and implementation.

Despite Japan's slow transition to a relatively neo-pluralist system, the ruling triad continues to dominate most policy-making, while the opposition remains largely removed from power or even significant influence. The LDP and bureaucracy dominate all policy-making channels, while the needs of big business remain the dominant issue for policy-makers. This arrangement is likely to continue indefinitely.

NOTES

1. A version of this section appeared in *Pacific Affairs* (April 1989) under the title, 'Japan's Mainstream Press: Freedom to Conform?'
2. Boye De Mente, *Japanese Business Etiquette*, p. 190.
3. Ikui Kabashima and Jeffrey Broadbent, 'Referent Pluralism: Mass Media and Politics in Japan', *Journal of Japanese Studies*, Summer 1986, pp. 329–61.
4. Ibid., p. 355.
5. *Japan 1986: An International Comparison*, p. 70.
6. Jung Lee, *The Political Character of the Japanese Press*, pp. 83–5.
7. Young Kim, *Japanese Journalists and Their World*, p. 8.
8. Frank Gibney, *Fragile Superpower*, pp. 245–85.
9. Lee, op. cit., p. 82.
10. Kim, op. cit., p. 85.
11. Hans Baerwald, *Party Politics in Japan*, 120.
12. Lee, op. cit., p. 114.
13. Kim, op. cit., 92.
14. Ibid.
15. Ibid., p. 175.
16. Kabashima, op. cit., p. 355.

17. Karl von Wolferen, 'Agreeing on Reality: Political Reporting by the Japanese Press', *Speaking of Japan*, Vol. 5, No. 44, August 1984.
18. Lee, op. cit., pp. 76, 78.
19. Ibid.
20. Edwin Reischauer, *The Japanese*, p. 199.
21. Chikara Higashi, *Japanese Trade Policy Formulation*, p. 141.
22. Boye De Mente, op. cit., p. 125.
23. *Japan 1987: An International Comparison*.
24. *Far Eastern Economic Review*, pp. 24–34, 17 November 1988.
25. *Japan Economic Journal*, p. 28, 6 February 1988.
26. *Economist*, pp. 63–4, 3 September 1988.
27. *Far Eastern Economic Review*, pp. 24–34, 17 November 1988.
28. Mitsuo Wada, 'Selling in Japan: Consumer Behavior and Distribution as Barriers to Import', pp. 95–8, in Pugel.
29. Ibid.
30. Gerald Curtis, *The Japanese Way of Politics*, Chapter 5.
31. Helmut Laumer, The Distribution System: Its Social Function and Import Impeding Effects', pp. 257–60.
32. *Herald Tribune*, p. 1, 9 November 1988.
33. Laumer, op. cit., p. 257.
34. *Japan Economic Journal*, p. 1, 13 February 1988.
35. *Far Eastern Economic Review*, p. 5, 7 January 1988.
36. *Japan Economic Journal*, 30 January 1988.
37. *Japan Economic Journal*, 23 January 1988.
38. *Far Eastern Economic Review*, pp. 79–81, 3 November 1988.
39. Ibid.
40. *Japan Economic Journal*, p. 28, 6 February 1988.
41. *Far Eastern Economic Review*, pp. 79–81, 3 November 1988.
42. Ibid.
43. *Japan Economic Journal*, 6 February 1988.
44. Curtis, op. cit., Chapter 4.
45. Ibid., p. 120.
46. Ibid., p. 122.
47. *Far Eastern Economic Review*, 30 June 1988.
48. Ronald Hrebenar, *The Japanese Party System*, pp. 175–7.
49. Most of the following statistics were taken from Kenichi Furuya, 'Labor Management Relations in Postwar Japan'. *Japan Quarterly*, Vol. 27, No.1, 1980, and Koji Taira, 'Labor Federation in Japan', *Current History*, April 1988.
50. Hans Baerwald, *Party Politics in Japan*, p. 7.
51. Curtis, op. cit., p. 216.

Part III
Japan's Neo-Mercantilist Policies

10 Macroeconomic Policies

Up through the early 1980s, the Ministry of Finance (MOF) and Bank of Japan (BOJ) reigned supreme over all macroeconomic policies that affected the economy as a whole. Recently, however, MOF's freedom to pursue macroeconomic policies has been undermined by constant foreign pressure on MOF to liberalize Japan's financial markets, as well as attempts since the September 1985 Plaza Hotel Accord among the Group of Five industrial countries (United States, Britain, France, West Germany, and Japan) to coordinate macroeconomic policy-making with the aim of devaluing the dollar and stimulating world economic growth. In particular, Tokyo has been repeatedly asked to diminish its huge payments surplus with its trade partners, and instead act as an 'engine of growth' for the world economy by shifting its own economy from export-led to domestic-led growth. Japan's government began stimulating domestic growth in late 1987.

Yet, despite these changes, MOF's powers to manage Japan's economy have been only slightly diminished; it continues to pursue essentially neo-mercantilist macroeconomic policies designed to achieve the optimum conditions conducive to Japan's economic expansion. Since 1945, Japan's macroeconomic policies have passed through three distinct phases and are entering a fourth. These policy phases roughly correspond to Japan's transition after 1945 through 'bureaucratic-dominant corporatist', 'corporatist', 'neo-corporatist', and recently nascent 'neo-pluralist' structure of state power and policy-making.

From 1945 to 1949 the MOF and SCAP battled for control over macroeconomic policy-making. SCAP repeatedly tried to convince MOF to follow relatively tight fiscal and monetary policies to help curb the hyperinflation that was further impoverishing most Japanese and preventing Japan's economic recovery. The Young mission of summer 1948 was the latest of several SCAP attempts to convince Tokyo of the necessity to conduct conservative macro-economic policies, but was unable to overcome the entrenched political interests that favored continuing the hyperinflation policies despite private assurances by both politicians and businessmen that fiscal and monetary retrenchment was vital for Japan's recovery. For political reasons, Japan's government followed loose fiscal and monetary poli-

245

cies to fund its corporate financial backers. The government-run Reconstruction Finance Bank (RFB) poured billions of yen into corporate bank accounts, part of which were then channelled to conservative politicians running for office. Since tax receipts were minimal, the MOF funded the RFB by printing money, which in turn stimulated hyperinflation. The government did not worry about hyperinflation because its main backers – big business and farmers – both benefitted from higher prices even though the economy as a whole was devastated by it.

In October 1948 the US Security Council issued Resolution 13/2, which formalized the policy shift from democratization to economic revival concerning Japan. SCAP articulated the new policy in its Nine-Point Economic Stabilization Program issued in December 1948. Joseph Dodge was assigned the task of implementing the Program, and arrived in Japan in February 1949 with the rank of minister as financial advisor to SCAP. The 'Dodge line' imposed a very tight fiscal and monetary regime on Japan that balanced the budget and cut the size of government. The RFB was abolished and government subsidies to big business were suspended to curb inflation. In addition Dodge replaced multiple yen exchange rates with a single exchange rate. Until then the yen had been cheap relative to the dollar for export goods, at rates of 500 to 600 to a dollar, while for imported goods it was valued at about 100 to a dollar. Although this multiple rate helped exports in the short run, it undermined Japan's competitiveness in the long run. With their exports subsidized by the cheap exchange rate, industries were not forced to cut costs and raise productivity. Likewise the expensive import prices for vital raw materials and capital goods further undermined the competitiveness of Japanese exporters. In April 1949 the exchange rate was set at 360 yen to a dollar, which was about 10 per cent lower than the 330 yen to a dollar rate that was widely held to be the appropriate rate.[1]

The Dodge Line inaugurated the second phase of Japan's policy-making, a phase which lasted up through the early 1970s. During this time MOF continued not only to balance the budget and curb inflation through tight fiscal and monetary policies, but was able to give annual tax cuts as tax receipts swelled from the steady economic growth of 10 per cent a year. In addition, the government prevented significant capital inflows or outflows by maintaining strict control over foreign investment in Japan or Japanese investments overseas. This prevented any possibility of foreign control over Japanese industries, while forcing Japanese capital to be reinvested at home. Japanese capital investment was further swelled by strict controls over consumer credit and the narrow range of investment possibilities for households. For a variety of reasons, Japanese households saved their money rather than spent it, and the savings were in turn channelled by MOF and MITI into strategic industries at extremely low interest rates by international standards.

Japan's economy began to undergo changes in the 1960s that resulted in a significant shift in MOF macroeconomic policies by the early 1970s. Japan's average annual growth rates of 10 per cent for almost two decades had transformed the country from poverty to relative prosperity. The Japanese public was increasingly demanding a shift from the government obsession with economic growth at all costs to more emphasis on welfare and the environment. In return for its membership of the OECD, Tokyo had promised to loosen its controls over foreign investment and imports. In August 1971 President Nixon devalued the dollar against other currencies, thus forcing the revaluation of a yen that had become increasingly devalued over the previous 18 years as Japan's economy became increasingly dynamic.

In response to these changes, the MOF began running small fiscal deficits in 1965, and increasingly large deficits after 1972 to stimulate the economy as the saving rate outstripped the investment rate, and to fund a range of new welfare programs. Between 1967 and 1973 Tokyo presented five market opening steps geared towards allowing foreign investors more opportunities in the economy. Finally, after the dollar began to float in 1973, MOF had actively to intervene to prevent the yen from rising to a point that would undermine Japanese exports. During the late 1970s and throughout the 1980s MOF has sponsored a series of small, incremental steps designed to open Japan's financial markets.

The fourth stage of Japanese macroeconomic policies can be dated from the September 1985 Plaza Hotel accord among the five key industrial countries to coordinate attempts to devalue the dollar and stimulate domestic growth. Since that time Tokyo has generally attempted to coordinate its macroeconomic policies with Washington and the other industrial countries, shift its economy from export-led to domestic-led growth, strengthen the yen's value, and further open Japan's financial markets.

Although this new policy shift has somewhat lessened MOF's ability to macro-manage the economy, these changes have proved to be essential for stimulating growth as Japan's economy develops into an ever higher, and more complex information-and-high-technology-based level.

In each of the four phases, meaningful change in Japan's macroeconomic policies almost invariably came from foreign pressure. Vested interests and political constraints impeded these policy shifts even though it was clear that the new policies in each phase would actually stimulate rather than impede the economy, as was popularly feared at the time. Yet MOF has been relatively free to pursue macroeconomic policies within each policy phase's framework. After first discussing the structure and functions of the Ministry of Finance, this chapter will analyze in detail the changes in different aspects of overall macroeconomic policies – monetary, tax, fiscal, investment, and yen, from 1949 up through the present day.

THE MINISTRY OF FINANCE

The most powerful economic ministry, MOF dominates such macroeconomic policies as budget preparation, monetary, fiscal, and tax policy, and, in addition, plays a significant role in such industrial policies as the regulation of financial planning and lending or subsidy policies to specific economic sectors. One important reason behind MOF's power is its ability to maintain a relative independence from politics among both the parties and bureaucracies. MOF is disdainful of both politicians and bureaucrats who appear subservient to narrow political interests. This outlook was exemplified by a former top MOF official who used to welcome new recruits with the warning: 'no matter how busy you are, read a book every day, don't catch the clap, and don't borrow from a loan shark', which roughly translates as 'master your subjects, avoid becoming intimate with the ministries you review, and don't cut deals'.[2] Yet MOF is not as apolitical as it would like to think. Many MOF bureaucrats, for example, have parachuted into prominent positions in private industry and the LDP. For example, in 1974, as many as 17 former MOF officials served in the lower house and eight in the upper house.[3] These former officials are in a position to advance specific interests by tapping into their network within MOF.

MOF is composed of the Budget, Tax, Customs and Tariff, Financial, Securities, Banking, and International Finance bureaus. Responsibilities of the tax, customs and tariff, and budget bureaus are self-explanatory. The other bureaus, responsibilities are more diverse. The Financial Bureau administers the national debt, governmental investment, trust funds, national property, loans to local government, and even housing for civil servants; the Securities Bureau supervises the securities companies and stock markets; the Banking Bureau supervises the Bank of Japan and controls many aspects of commercial banking and the insurance business. Although policy questions are fought out among the different bureaus, the infighting is not considered as intense as in other ministries. The Budgeting Bureau is considered the élite of the élite and its director is always a leading candidate for the vice-minister's post.[4]

Another major reason for MOF's professionalism is the quality of its recruits. From 1966 to 1974, 194 of the 200 who joined the MOF were graduates of one of the three major national universities (Tokyo, Kyoto, Hitotsubashi); and over three-quarters came from Tokyo University, half from the Faculty of Law. By discipline, 134 were trained in law, 61 in economics, and only five in other fields. Although recruitment has gradually become more diverse, the MOF is still dominated by Todai graduates.[5] Every recruit embarks on a series of posts which amount to a seven-year training program. By the sixth year, at age 27, the official will have sole responsibility for the district tax office in a small city. By the seventh year, he is back in Tokyo and then begins to specialize in an area like capital market operations, local government finance, or others. After this seven or eight year period, career paths become less standardized, although advancement still proceeds by seniority. Each official considers himself in competition with the other 25 or so members of his entering class; progressively it will become clear which of them is on the 'success course' (shusse kosu). After 22 or 23 years in the ministry, the most successful become directors of key divisions. The final stage occurs when one of the class becomes a vice-minister, at which time the remaining class members will resign.[6]

MOF's most significant duty involves its preparation of all three government budgets: the general account, special accounts, and government investments. Under the Constitution, the annual budget is supposed to be prepared by the Cabinet, but provisions under the Finance Law assign the responsibility of actual preparation to MOF. The process begins shortly after the beginning of each fiscal year on 1 April, when the various ministries and other agencies begin formulating their budget requests for the following fiscal year. Ministries are required by law to submit no budget 25 per cent higher than that of the previous year. These mini-budgets are submitted to the Finance Ministry by 31 August, after receiving a consensus with the appropriate ministry equivalent among the divisions (bukai) of the LDP Policy Affairs Research Council (PARC).

During September ministry officials appear at the MOF Budget Bureau (Shukeikyoku) to explain their requests to the budget examiners (shukeikan). During October and November the shukeikyoku go over details of each ministry's budget, while high-level MOF officials discuss the total budget size, the size of the yearly tax cut, and other macro-budgeting questions. For about two weeks in early December, a MOF-led ministerial conference meets to ratify, and sometimes modify, the draft budget prepared within the budget bureau. At the same time, the PARC Deliberation Commission (Seisaku Shingikai or Seicho Shigikai) draws up the annual LDP Budget Compilation Program, which is then passed by the party's Executive Council (Somukai) and referred to the Cabinet and MOF before release of the final draft.

The release of the final MOF draft is usually scheduled for late December, but is usually postponed into January, and begins a week of 'revival negotiations' (fukkatsu sessho) during which ministry appeals are heard by the MOF and small supplements are doled out. The Cabinet and MOF then negotiate the final draft and the resulting budget is then ratified by the Cabinet to become the government draft (Seifu-un), and is sent on to the Diet to become law.[7]

Following the Cabinet's endorsement, the budget is sent on to the House of Representatives for debate and passage, first by the Budget Committee and then by the full House, and then on to the House of Councillors for a similar process. If the Upper House does not pass the budget, or if it amends it without the Lower House's approval, the budget becomes law after 30 days. With the single exception of 1972, the budget has not been amended since 1955. The budget debate generally does not concentrate on specific expenditures, but is instead an opportunity for the opposition parties to attack LDP policies. Provisional budgets must be compiled and passed to cover the financial gap before the new budget takes over. In addition, the Diet usually passes two or three Supplementary Budgets each year to cover special fiscal needs that arise.

Politics plays a relatively insignificant role in budget preparation. General elections scheduled during the final budget negotiations put more pressure on the MOF for a larger budget. MOF usually gets around this by delaying the budget's publication until after the election. Since 1961 the LDP's Budget Compilation Program has submitted its own budget shortly before that of the MOF. But the LDP budget is merely a political document without any actual financial figures or spending priorities, and has no influence on the actual budget. The LDP's major role in budget-making is to aggregate interests and throw its weight behind programs with important current political interest.

MONETARY POLICY

Since 1945 Japanese monetary policy has been built on four key goals: (1) to maintain a steady supply of money to the economy as a whole; (2) to maximize household savings; (3) to channel savings into strategic industries vital to Japan's economic development; and (4) to encourage accelerated plant and equipment investment through tax deductions and other exemptions in those sectors.

Regulation of the Money Supply

Although economic growth averaged about 10 per cent a year from 1950 to 1973, there were seven economic boom and turndown cycles throughout the period. The boom years included 1951 (Korean War), 1953 (investment boom), 1956–57 ('Jimmu boom'), 1959–61 (the plant and equipment investment expansion or 'Iwato boom'), 1963 (expansion without a boom), 1967–69 (the 'Izanami boom') and 1973. The BOJ imposed monetary restraints at the height of each boom as the economy threatened to overheat: in 1951, 1954, 1957–58, 1961–62, 1964, 1967 to preserve the balance of payments, and 1969–70, and 1973–75 to curb inflationary pressures.[8]

All of the growth recessions of the 1950s and 1960s were induced by the MOF tightening the money supply in order to prevent the economy from overheating. The recessions would end after the MOF loosed its reins over the money supply. MOF's tight monetary policies alone were unable to deal with the deep recessions induced by OPEC's quadrupling of oil prices in 1974, and since then the government has used both monetary and fiscal policy to regulate the economy. The government imposed a tight monetary policy for two years after OPEC's quadrupling of oil prices, while the Bank of Japan rationed credit through 'window guidance'. Although inflation was initially the second highest of all the industrial countries except

Britain, Japan cut its wholesale inflation rate to 1.9 per cent in 1977, the lowest of the OECD countries, although its consumer price index of 8.1 per cent was about average among industrial countries. Although its growth rate since 1973 has been half its previous level, Japan's economy has still outperformed any of the other OECD countries.

MOF managed OPEC's 1979 doubling of oil prices even more smoothly and successfully than the 1973 oil hike. A tight monetary policy quickly curbed existing inflationary pressures and Japan's economy was soon booming again. Since then MOF has generally followed a relatively loose monetary policy to fuel Japan's continuing economic expansion.

Virtuous Savings/Investment Cycle

Japan's huge household savings rate which in the mid-1980s was still an impressive 25 per cent of GNP is largely a result of government policies rather than cultural factors. Before 1945 Japan had a relatively modest savings ratio comparable to those of other industrializing countries. Between 1890 and 1940 national savings averaged 5 per cent of GNP. By the 1960s, however, Japan's net national savings rate of 25 per cent of GNP was five times larger than that of the prewar era, and the second largest in the industrial world after Switzerland.[9]

This shift from a low to high household savings rate was a direct result of government policies. MOF used a number of means to ensure Japanese householders saved a large portion of their income, including tax exemptions on interest earned by small savers (maruyu seido), and by encouraging households to put their money in the government-controlled postal savings system which payed slightly more than city bank deposits. The postal savings accounts were in turn channelled into the Fiscal Investment and Loan Program (FILP), administered by the MOF, which were then directed into key economic growth sectors. Other government measures that indirectly contributed to the high savings rate include: low levels of social welfare and inadequate social security; inadequate consumer credit and the subsequent need for households to save for such things as homes, their children's education or marriage; without capital controls, however, many Japanese savings might well have leaked out to more favorable investment opportunities abroad – instead savings were bottled up for domestic investment; the general lack of alternative investment opportunities. For example, with its pervasive insider trading, Japan's stock markets remain no place for small investors, and most households put their savings in either commercial banks or post office accounts.

Other factors were of secondary importance. Companies contributed to high savings through their twice-yearly bonus system, and increases in the amount of bonuses. Economic growth allowed real incomes to rise rapidly while prices trailed behind, thus allowing households more money to save. A demographic shift to smaller families also allowed more opportunity to save for the future rather than immediately consume. Finally, there is a general cultural disposition toward frugality and avoidance of conspicuous consumption.

The government's chanelling of these huge savings into corporate investment was one of the key reasons for Japan's rapid postwar economic growth. By maintaining a savings rate equivalent to the investment rate, Japan experienced rapid growth without high inflation. Savings were channelled into industry at the expense of private consumption, housing, or other benefits. Between 1970 and 1977, Japan's percentage of GDP devoted to capital formation averaged 33.5 per cent, compared with America's average of 17.6 per cent, Britain's 19.4 per cent, and West Germany's 23.4 per cent.[10]

Window Guidance

Interest rate regulation and credit rationing have been the most important elements of monetary policy, but by rationing credit to strategic industries via the banks, the lines between macroeconomic and industrial policies became very blurred. The government first set low interest rates after World War II in order to stimulate investments. As the economy continued to rapidly expand, the demand for investment funds quickly outstripped supply, and the BOJ was able to use 'window guidance' (madoguchi no shido) to allocate cheap funds to high-growth sectors. Credit rationing gave the government great powers to shift the direction of the economy. Strategic industries gobbled up virtually all of the cheap loans; until recently, small- and medium-sized firms and consumers either had to do without or borrow at exceedingly high rates. The targets of window guidance broadened steadily from heavy industries like shipbuilding, coal, steel, or petrochemicals during the 1950s to high-technology industries like computers, microelectronics, biotechnology, or semiconductors up through today. Industry associations were important mean: for targeting and allocating funds. Although during the 1980s relatively cheap credit was slowly being allocated to small- and medium-sized firms and consumers, the government continued to maintain artificially low interest rates, and channel the credit to strategic industries.

The BOJ has been able to ration credit because it has consistently controlled interest rates for bank deposits and short-term bank loans through a variety of laws and administrative guidance. The 1947 Temporary Interest Rate Adjustment Law forces private banks to fix the short-term prime rate at a constant margin above the official discount rate. Although the 1947 law grants the government considerable powers, MOF prefers to set interest rates through administrative guidance. Long-term loan rates and bond-issue interest rates are determined by an implicit cartel arrangement among large financial institutions presided over by MOF and BOJ. The cartel is enforced by equally indirect means: for example, a bank lending at a rate higher than what BOJ advocated would have extreme difficulties when it tries borrowing from the BOJ or applies for permission to open new branches. The government and not markets continues to determine the level of interest rates.[11]

Several other laws including the Rules of Financial Institutions' Fund Supplies based on the Emergency Ordinance on Financial measures of 1946 and the Order of Priority in Industrial Loans allowed the MOF and BOJ to channel funds to key industries. According to these laws, the essential industries were mining, metalworking, chemicals, electric power generation, oil supply, and transportation. Private financial institutions could make loans to industries designated as 'important' or 'not urgent' only with the MOF's permission. The BOJ's Loan Mediation Bureau researched the lending requirements of key industries and monitored their funding by private financial institutions. Thus, the BOJ could monitor the funds it lent to banks, especially to city banks.

Most direct controls over private financial institutions disappeared by the mid–1950s. The BOJ withdrew from direct mediation by 1954 and the investigation system was abolished in 1955. Instead, it pursued indirect controls by sponsoring and overseeing cartels such as the Bond Issue Committee, the Financial Institution's Fund Council, and the Industrial Finance Committee among the key private financial institutions. MITI had an important role in channelling funds, too; its Industrial Finance Committee, for example, supervised investment and associated finance plans of major industries.

All these institutions became instruments of government policy and benefited from government information and protection.[12]

In the 1950s and 1960s, window guidance was essential for providing enough funds to strategic industries. Government funds complemented the immature capital markets in supporting some industries that could not have obtained a sufficient amount of funds had capital markets been well developed. By the late 1960s for heavy industry and late 1970s for high technology industries, window guidance had diminished in importance as those industries had developed to the point where increasing amounts of their capital came from retained earnings.

The dependence of both banks and industries on BOJ lessened as their respective financial assets and economic clout grew. For example, the level of financial assets held by both corporate firms and individuals increased sevenfold between 1953 and 1963 and fivefold between 1963 and 1973. This reduced transaction costs, led to a diversified demand for financial instruments, and made financial assets other than bank deposits increasingly important in the portfolios of private investors.[13]

Reliance by big business on bank loans dropped from an annual average of 30.2 per cent of total investment funds in 1973–77 to 17.5 per cent in 1978–82. Japanese corporations have gradually increased the relative share of overseas funds in their total bond financing from 20.8 per cent of all bonds in 1977 to 47.6 per cent in 1982. As a result, competition among banks for prime borrowers has become so fierce that many have reduced their loan rates to levels below the prime rates. Small businesses have become increasingly important customers for banks. In 1974 36.9 per cent of all bank loans were to small businesses; the comparable figure in 1982 was 48.8 per cent.[14]

Although MOF and BOJ controls over the financial world have shifted from direct to indirect control over the past 40 years, their controls are only slightly diminished. While the importance of window guidance has lessened, MOF has kept a tight rein over all changes in financial markets, shaping the direction and degree of change. For example, to protect the administered interest rates and financial institutions Japanese banks are prohibited from using foreign funds in Japan. In addition to controlling interest rates, MOF further carefully regulates the banking world by determining the amount, distribution, and location of each branch office of each bank. Branch offices are an extremely important element in banking business as the number and location of branches crucially affects their fund-raising capabilities. These controls over branch locations, deposit rates and amounts, and interest rates gave MOF immense power over virtually all aspects of the banking world.[15]

Tax Policy

MOF tax policies have been another key element of its macroeconomic policies designed to maximize economic growth. Tax policy has changed dramatically from the progressive policies encouraged by the Occupation to the increasingly pro-business orientation of tax policy up through today. In 1949 a group of tax specialists led by Professor Carl Shoup of Columbia University, arrived in Japan to help revamp the tax system. Although the Shoup mission advocated a highly progressive tax system, the Japanese government passed a watered-down version of the Shoup policy in April 1950. Personal income tax began at 20 per cent for incomes below 50 000 yen, and rose in eight gradations to 55 per cent for incomes exceeding 500 000 yen. The government also inaugurated what would be a series of annual tax cuts.

The central goal of tax policy after 1953 was to achieve a high rate of growth. Tax laws were revised to encourage individual savings and corporate investments. The tax rate increasingly shifted from the progressive structure imposed by the Shoup mission in 1949 to its present regressive structure which places the burden on salaried workers. In 1953 both the wealth tax introduced by the Shoup mission and the capital gains tax for share trading were abolished to encourage more investment in the economy, while a flat 10 per cent tax on all earned interest was imposed to encourage savings. Corporations were allowed a 20 per cent tax exemption for any export-earned profits.

In 1955 three major tax reductions were carried out including an income tax cut, an abolition of the tax on interest income and tax-rate reduction for dividend income, and the reduction of corporate profits taxes to 40 per cent for firms whose profits exceeded 500 000 yen and 35 per cent for those below that amount. The Tax System Examination Commission (zeisei chosa kai) was established in 1955 as an advisory body to the Cabinet to regulate these new policies. Two years later, in 1957, personal income taxes were further reduced and special reductions and exemptions were added. Since the government continually underestimated both the economic growth rate and the growth in tax revenues when they drew up the budget, they were able to grant annual tax rebates which further stimulated economic growth. An annual tax cut of about 2 to 5 per cent of tax revenues occurred most years until FY 1974. Tax rates are reduced with the principle that the tax burden should never exceed 20 per cent of national income.

The basic principle of the Japanese income tax system is comprehensive taxation – in other words, all income categories are combined and subject to the same tax schedule. Direct taxes make up an increasing percentage of national receipts. In FY 1955 the share of direct taxes in national taxes was 51.4 per cent; in FY 1983 it had risen to 70.7 per cent. The tax burden is increasingly shifting to salaried workers. Between 1975 and 1981 the share of taxes from salaried income in total income tax revenues rose from 49.9 per cent to 56.3 per cent, while that from business income dropped from 3.7 per cent to 2.7 per cent.[16] Known as the 10–6–3–1 problem, the portion of income subject to taxation is 100 per cent for salaried workers, 50 per cent for self-employed workers, 30 per cent for farmers, and 10 per cent for politicians. The self-employed and farmers are allowed a myriad of expense deductions while salaried workers are accorded practically none. Almost 100 per cent of salaried income taxes is captured by the government since it is withheld at the source. Since the self-employed and farmers are allowed to assess their own taxes, it is difficult for the tax authorities to capture the entire income. The chances of being audited become increasingly remote since the number of taxpayers is steadily increasing while tax office personnel remain constant. Only about 2–3 per cent of taxpayers are audited annually.[17] This inequality across occupation groups partially reflects interest group politics: small businessmen, farmers, doctors, and other cohesive groups have pressured the government into granting them privileges. Salaried workers, on the other hand, are a huge, unorganized category unable to lobby for themselves. The government has tried three times in the last decade to increase taxes to offset the growing public debt. But the LDP attempts to introduce a general consumption tax in 1979 and 1986 were met with public outcries that forced the LDP to drop the plans. It was only in December 1988 that the Takeshita government succeeded in passing a tax reform bill that extensively simplified the system, closing many loopholes and imposing a 3 per cent value-added-tax.

FISCAL POLICY

Fiscal policy, the use of government spending either to stimulate or rein in the economy, was not an important element of MOF macroeconomic policy until after 1965, when the government began running annual budget deficits. Until then, Japan's government was required by law to balance its budget. The Finance Act, passed in 1947, clearly dedicated the government to achieving a balanced budget, and included a clause prohibiting the issue of long-term national government debt bonds. The 1949 Dodge Plan even prevented the MOF from issuing short-term securities with maturities of one year or less.

The first clear attempt to use fiscal policy to stimulate the economy occurred in 1960, when Prime Minister Ikeda expanded public works spending. As a result, the 1961 budget grew by a record pace of 24.4 per cent larger than the previous year's budget, although it still remained balanced. Increasingly, though, throughout the early 1960s, some businessmen and politicians began to call for bonds to finance needed investment in public works. Although MOF strongly resisted these pressures, the public works section of the budget was steadily increased. Budget growth, however, continued to run behind economic growth through 1965.

It was only after Japan began to run continual balances of payments surpluses after 1965 that the government felt confident enough to begin running budget deficits to help stimulate economic growth. The Finance Act was amended in 1965 to allow budget deficits, after which fiscal policy became increasingly important in Japanese macroeconomic policy. MOF gave in to the demands for bond-financed deficits in order to stimulate the economy, signalling the 'new era of public finance' (zaisei shinjidai).

Despite this policy shift, MOF continued to try to limit the amount of deficit financing. MOF was forced to abandon this conservative fiscal policy and take the government deeply into debt after 1973 for three reasons. First, Prime Minister Tanaka after taking office in 1972 advocated an expansionary fiscal policy to stimulate growth and achieve his 'Plan for Remodelling the Japanese Archipelago', which involved diverting economic growth from the Tokyo-Osaka corridor to regions around Japan. To these ends, Tanaka advocated a 1973 budget 31 per cent larger than that of 1972, and after tough negotiations the final budget was 24.6 per cent higher than in 1972, although public works grew by 32.2 per cent.

The second reason was the dramatic drop in the growth rate after OPEC's quadrupling of oil prices in 1973. Tax receipts dropped just as dramatically, forcing the government increasingly to rely on bonds to cover the deficit. The decline in growth also disrupted the equilibrium between savings and investment. From 1953 to 1973 the government maintained a small surplus on its budget, averaging about 1 per cent of GNP, which further swelled national savings. During the same period private gross fixed investment rose from 15 per cent of GNP to 27 per cent while private savings rose from 11 per cent of GNP to 24 per cent. Thus, generally, there was equilibrium between investments and savings throughout the period. After the 1973 oil shock which cut economic growth in half from 10 per cent to less than 5 per cent a year, private investment fell to an average 21 per cent, below that of household savings, leaving an annual savings excess of about 4–5 per cent of GNP. The increased tendency of firms to finance the bulk of their financial needs by retained earnings also contributed to the savings/investment gap. The percentage of retained earnings in total corporate financial needs rose from 33.8 per cent in 1970 to 76.8 per cent in 1984.[18]

The government made up this savings gap by running annual deficits averaging 5 per cent of GNP after 1974 which increased spending, but in doing so sharply increased public debt from 6 per cent of GNP at the end of 1972 to 37 per cent in 1982.[19] Between 1975 and 1983 annual government deficits averaged 3.9 per cent of GDP. By 1983 the outstanding balance of national debt had grown to 46 per cent of GNP, surpassing that of the United States. In 1985 Japan's total government-debt-to-GNP ration was 52.1 per cent compared to 48.8 per cent in the United States.[20]

The final reason for Japan's greater emphasis on fiscal policy has been the repeated calls by other industrial countries for Tokyo to shift from export-led to domestic-led growth. Throughout the late 1970s, almost every OECD country was running a payments deficit except Japan, yet Japan refused significantly to boost domestic spending or give up its efforts to weaken the yen. Finally in December 1977, the Fukuda government agreed to act as a 'locomotive' of the world economy by stimulating domestic spending, a promise repeated by the Strauss-Uchiba agreement of 1978.

Unfortunately, Tokyo failed to fulfill its promise. By the late 1970s, the government was more concerned with reducing its spiralling public debt than stimulating domestic growth. In fact, the Ohira government tried to push through a tax increase, which would have further dampened domestic demand, forcing Japan's industries to rely even more on export earnings. Without a tax decrease, the Ohira government attempted to deal with the deficit by lowering the ceilings for budget requests by each government ministry or agency. Between FY 1961 and FY 1979, the ceiling had been set at 20 per cent over that of the previous year's budget. In FY 1980, the ceiling was reduced to 10.1 per cent.

The Suzuki administration followed this up by forming a Commission for Administrative Reform in 1981 to find ways to cut government spending. In addition, the Suzuki administration declared that the issuance of deficit-financing bonds would be terminated by FY 1984, which would be achieved by expenditure cuts rather than tax increases. The government has tried to achieve this by privatizing NTT, JNR, and other public corporations while cutting the budget. As a result the rate of increase in general expenditures has slowed from 1.8 per cent in FY 1982, to zero in FY 1983, and to –0.1 per cent in FY 1984.

The Nakasone government continued Suzuki's program of administrative reform but floundered in Spring 1987 when it attempted to introduce a sweeping tax reform policy. The Takeshita administration picked up the reins from the fallen Nakasone government and finally passed a comprehensive tax reform program in December 1988. In addition, after a decade of foreign pressure it has agreed to shift Japan's economy from export-led to domestic-led growth.

Despite the dramatic increase in government spending since the early 1970s, Japan's government remains relatively small, lean, and highly efficient compared to those of other OECD countries. In 1970 Japan's ratio of government expenditures to GNP was only 19.5 per cent compared to 32.9 per cent in the United States, 37.7 per cent in Britain, and 36.1 per cent in West Germany. By 1980, however, Japan's ratio had risen to 33.0 per cent, almost identical with America's 33.5 per cent, although still behind Britain with 42.9 per cent and West Germany with 44.3 per cent.[21] Japan's government expenditures, particularly for welfare, generally lagged behind those of the other OECD countries throughout the 1950s and 1960s but have recently caught up. Japan devoted only 3.7 per cent of GNP to social security in 1955–57 compared to 4.1 per cent in the United States, 6.1 per cent in the UK, and 12.0 per cent in West Germany; in 1974–76 the figures were 7.0 per cent, 10.9 per cent, 11.3 per cent, and 15.4 per cent, respectively; and in 1980 the figures were 10.9 per cent, 11.1 per cent, 11.7 per cent, and 15.3 per cent, respectively.[22]

There has been a large shift in the direction of the FILP investments in the economy. In 1965 the Japan Development and Export
Import banks (which loan their money to private industry) received
19.2 per cent of the total, while housing enjoyed a meager 10.7 per
cent. In 1980 the two banks received only 7.6 per cent, while hous-
ings' share had increased to 25.2 per cent. The largest increases
were in social security benefits, particularly health insurance and
government pensions. The ratio of social security payments and debt
servicing costs to GNP rose from 1.5 per cent and 0.1 per cent,
respectively, in 1965, to 3.2 per cent and 2.9 per cent, respectively,
in 1983. The ratio of total expenditures in the general account budget
to GNP has risen during the same period from 10.9 per cent to 17.9
per cent. About 40 per cent of this rise came from increased social
security payments. Japan's fiscal policy seems to be slowly shifting
from economic growth to quality of life.[23]

YEN

SCAP set the yen at a ratio of one dollar to 360 yen on 25 April 1949.
This exchange rate simultaneously allowed Japan's most important
industries to export competitively while it was strong enough to allow
the importation of capital equipment and raw materials vital for
Japan's industrial development. Although Japan continued to run
current account deficits from then until 1965, Tokyo never considered devaluing the yen to achieve equilibrium; to have done so
would have hurt exports since it would have raised the price of raw
materials and capital goods, and thus hurt the comparative advantage
of Japanese products in world markets. Japan's export-led growth
rates averaging 10 per cent a year in the 1950s and 1960s were, in
part, the result of an increasingly undervalued yen throughout the
period.

The yen's continued undervaluation became increasingly noticeable after 1965 as Japan annually wracked up higher current account
surpluses. Although severely criticized for 'exporting unemployment'
with its undervalued yen, Tokyo resisted all foreign calls to revalue
the yen during this time, even though all the other major industrial
countries had long before revalued their own currencies.

It was President Nixon's suspension of the dollar's convertability
into gold on 15 August 1971 that finally shocked Tokyo into the
realization that a yen revaluation was inevitable. MOF responded

by continuing to maintain the 360 yen to a dollar exchange rate for about ten days after all the states of Western Europe responded by allowing their exchange rates to float. In doing so, MOF enjoyed a glut of dollar sales in anticipation of the eventual rise in the yen, and Japan's foreign exchange reserves increased by $4.6 billion to reach a total of $12.5 billion by the end of August.[23]

At the Smithsonian Conference on 18 December 1971 Tokyo agreed to revalue its currency by 16.9 per cent, bringing an exchange rate of 308 yen to the dollar. But the revaluation of the key currencies against the dollar was not enough to offset America's continued economic troubles, and in February 1973 the industrial countries agreed to abandon the Bretton Woods system of fixed exchange rates and allow the currencies to float in value.

Despite participating in this international agreement for market-determined exchange rates, Tokyo had no intention of allowing the yen's value to be determined by market forces. Despite widespread foreign criticism of its 'dirty float', MOF continued to suppress the yen's value from 1973 through the 1980s through central bank intervention, discount policy, and changes in capital controls. The Bank of Japan, under the guidance of MOF, actively intervened in the exchange market by covertly buying and selling on the spot market. BOJ imposed temporary capital controls in 1974 and 1978 to prevent too great a yen appreciation.

Capital controls remain Tokyo's most effective way to maintain an undervalued yen. The government has steadily lowered its restrictions on capital outflows while largely maintaining its restrictions on capital inflows. Meanwhile, Japanese interest rates are kept artificially low and credit rationed to key Japanese industries, while the market determined American interest rate continued to rise in the late 1970s and 1980s. As a result, foreign investors could not borrow money from Japan at low interest rates which would have raised demand for yen and thus its value. The wide interest-rate differential between the United States and Japan, plus excess liquidity in Japan's financial markets, induced long-term capital outflows from Japan into the United States to take advantage of the high interest rates, boosting them further. At the same time, there was an asymmetry of macroeconomic policy between Washington and Tokyo: the United States followed loose fiscal policies and tight monetary policies while Japan followed tight fiscal and loose monetary policies, exacerbating the flow of money from Japan to help finance America's increasingly huge debts. Thus, the dollar's value rose dramatically throughout the 1980s, despite America's worsening current account deficit.

By the mid–1980s, however, the arm-twisting of the United States and the European Community had resulted in the reversal of many of MOF's policies that had contributed to a severely undervalued yen. The 1980 Law on Capital allowed no institutions other than credit institutions licensed as 'authorized foreign exchange banks' to deal freely in foreign currencies. But this was abolished on 1 April 1984 as part of a new package of liberalization measures. Now exchanges between authorized banks can occur without the mediation of brokerage firms. The 'Report on Yen/Dollar Exchange Issues' issued by an American-Japanese negotiating team in May 1984, required Japan to relax a number of administrative restrictions on its capital market in order to strengthen the international role of the yen. But, like the 1980 'liberalization', the 1984 agreement largely eased capital outflows so that the yen would actually be weakened rather than strengthened.

It was only after the September 1985 Plaza Accord, in which the five key economic powers agreed to take actions lowering the dollar's value, that Japan stopped systematically digging in its heels on a strong yen. Since then the yen has risen almost 100 per cent against the dollar and by Spring 1989 was hovering at around 125–130 yen to the dollar. The yen is now the third largest international currency in volume after the American dollar and German mark.

Yet in relative terms Japan's currency remains severely restricted. Both Japanese government and business resist a greater role for the yen because it would strengthen the currency, thus undercutting Japanese exports and increasing the pressure to accept more imports. Government restrictions on financial transactions continue to impede the growth of yen-denominated trade transactions. Over 80 per cent of the demand for and supply of yen in international currency markets is financial-flow-oriented while only 20 per cent is related to trade. Yen-denominated transactions still account for only about 35 per cent of Japan's exports and about 3 per cent of its imports. By contrast, 60 to 80 per cent of export sales and 30 to 50 per cent of imports of other advanced countries use their own national currencies.[24] If MOF would allow the yen to be used to underwrite trade at a similar proportion as that of other currencies, the yen would quickly rise in value beyond 100 yen to the dollar, and Japan's huge trade and payments surpluses with its trade partners would dissolve into equilibrium.

FOREIGN INVESTMENT

The Japanese government's controls over foreign investment in Japan and Japanese investments overseas was an important pillar of macroeconomic policy. By keeping Japanese capital in and foreign capital out for almost 20 years, Tokyo succeeded in maximizing domestic investments while minimizing foreign ownership of the economy. Japan's foreign investment policy has been an integral part of both its overall macroeconomic policies and industrial policies designed to develop key economic sectors. The Foreign Exchange and Foreign Trade Control Law of 1949 and the Foreign Investment Law of 1950 gave the government vast powers to control trade, investment, and economic development. Foreign investments were allowed only in the form of minority-owned joint ventures with Japanese firms, and only then if they were considered essential for 'the self-support and sound development of the Japanese economy'. Even then MITI strictly regulated the firms' operations and repatriation of profits. By strictly limiting foreign investment for most of the postwar era, Tokyo forced foreign firms to untie technology from their control; since foreign firms could neither sell nor invest freely in Japan, their only opportunity to make money was to sell their technology to their rivals.

Japan achieved article–8 status in the IMF and membership in the OECD in 1964. With the prestige of membership in these organizations, however, came responsibilities. Under article 8 Tokyo promised to guarantee the repatriation of principal and earnings of foreign investment. But Tokyo succeeded in undercutting its promises to liberalize by a variety of means. For example, several large foreign multinationals such as Scott Paper, Kaiser Aluminum, and Olivetti rushed to set up yen-based companies when it became clear that Tokyo would soon achieve article 8 status. Of the 289 yen-based companies that were set up, 95 were established in the last two years of the program. About 161 of the total were wholly owned by the foreign company. Tokyo responded to this surge in investments by quickly eliminating the yen-company route to investment, thus actually limiting investment further rather than liberalizing as promised, despite being severely criticized by foreign governments and the OECD.[25]

Tokyo delayed offering any genuine relaxations of restrictions of foreign investments for three years. During that time it frantically promoted a wide range of mergers and acquisitions among Japanese firms, in the belief that increased size would allow them to better compete against their foreign rivals. Then, between 1967 and 1973, the government offered five liberalization steps which gradually reduced but fell far short of totally eliminating restrictions on foreign investment. The 1967 reforms, for example, offered two categories of industries in which foreign investment would be automatically granted: Category 1 allowed up to 50 per cent foreign ownership while Category 2 allowed 100 per cent ownership as long as it did not involve taking over an existing Japanese firm. Category 1 contained 33 industries, such as consumer electronics and semiconductors, which Tokyo had targeted for development. By forcing foreign firms to form joint ventures at less than 50 per cent ownership, they allowed Japanese firms to acquire foreign technology without foreign control. Many of these joint ventures collapsed shortly after the Japanese firm had mastered the technology and no longer needed the foreign firm. For example, the Caterpillar/Mitsubishi Heavy Industries joint venture and the Bucyrus-Erie/Komatsu joint ventures both collapsed in anger and recriminations in the late 1970s after the Japanese partners had learned all they needed in order to compete internationally.[26] As might be imagined, Category 2 was comprised of industries such as steel, shipbuilding, textiles, and motorcycles in which Japanese firms already had a large comparative advantage. About two hundred other industries remained 'non-liberalized'.

In 1968 Tokyo allowed a limited liberalization of technology imports. Henceforth, the Bank of Japan would automatically approve all technology-import contracts valued at less than $50 000, except for a long list of strategic sectors such as aircraft, nuclear energy, computers, and petrochemicals which the government continued to control as part of its industrial policy. The fifth liberalization step announced in May 1973, completely dropped its 50 per cent category and allowed all industries except five to be considered for 100 per cent foreign ownership, subject to government approval. In 1980 the old Foreign Investment Law was finally repealed and the Foreign Exchange and Control Law was amended. Foreign direct investments are now free in principle, but in reality are still closely monitored with the government reserving the right to prevent any investment that harms national security, the economy, or enterprises in the same sector. In other words, the law remains neo-mercantilist rather than liberal.

Japan's strict controls on foreign investments have been highly effective. New foreign investment in Japan averaged only about

$1–10 million a year in the 1950s, $22–70 million in the 1960s, and $100 million in the 1970s. The cumulative total of all foreign DFI in Japan between 1950 and 1965 did not exceed $270 million, less than half the amount of foreign DFI in West Germany. Although Japan made five foreign investment opening steps from 1967 to 1973, the net increase of foreign investments in the 1970s was only $278 million, while it rose ten times in West Germany to over $2.6 billion. In the 1980s Japan has received over $1 billion a year in new foreign investments.[27] Despite this increasing flow, foreign investment has captured only minor shares of Japanese industry. Foreign firms comprise less than 5 per cent of manufacturing as a whole. Only in petroleum and rubber products do foreign firms have a significant production share, and even that share has declined from 60 per cent and 20 per cent, respectively in the mid–1960s, to about 40 per cent and 10 per cent at present.[28]

Throughout the 1950s and 1960s, MOF used the Foreign Exchange and Trade Control Law of 1949 to obstruct any capital outflows as well, thus forcing Japanese corporate or household savers to invest their money in Japan rather than abroad. Throughout the 1950s and 1960s, there were very few Japanese foreign investments. It was only after Japan began achieving current account surpluses after 1965 that MOF began loosening the restrictions on Japanese foreign investments. Still, Japanese capital outflows trailed far behind exports of goods and services. By 1974, however, Japan had surpassed Britain as a net creditor country in terms of its total net foreign assets; by 1980 its surplus had reached $80 billion; in 1985 Japan surpassed the United States as the world's largest creditor country, and its net foreign assets in 1987 were over $240 billion.

On paper Japan's economy seems wide open to financial inflows and outflows. In 1980 the basis of the Foreign Exchange Law was changed from the principle that all capital flows were regulated in principle, unless stated otherwise, to all capital flows were allowed free movement, unless stated otherwise. The Law codified incremental liberalization steps that had previously occurred. But while free in principle, the Law preserves the government's powers to continue to regulate financial markets. Licenses and notification are required for a wide range of financial transactions, including large foreign exchange and investment. The government reserves the right to obstruct any transaction it deems undesirable. Other transactions include money-lending to foreigners, Japanese direct investments abroad, issuance or offer of subscription of securities at home or abroad, acquisition of immovable properties in Japan by non-residents, and foreign direct investments in Japan. The time within which the government can decide to impede a financial transaction is 20 days; for foreign direct investment 30 days. Both MOF, MITI, and any other ministry under whose jurisdiction the transaction takes place are given the power to obstruct. The Law particularly targets transactions that occur outside an authorized foreign exchange bank.

CONCLUSION

Japan's macroeconomic policies have been highly successful in creating the optimum environment favorable for economic growth. MOF combined classical macroeconomic tools like manipulating the money supply, government spending, and taxes with neo-mercantilist tools such as maintaining a weak yen, curbing household consumption, channelling savings into strategic industries, and restricting capital flows. In many cases, the lines between macroeconomic and industrial policies became very blurred. MOF's most important policies involved carefully regulating the money supply to ensure a steady flow of funds was available to strategic industries and, to a lesser extent, the economy as a whole. To this end MOF followed policies designed to maximize the savings/investment ratio – households were encouraged to save their money, which was in turn chaneled to strategic industries at extremely low interest rates. No other industrial country has been as successful in achieving such a dynamic savings/investment circle.

The tremendous efforts MOF and BOJ put into maintaining a weak yen for almost 40 years are also without precedent in other industrial countries. Tokyo was the last major industrial country to revalue its currency, and since then had used all the means at its disposal to keep the yen undervalued to promote Japanese exports. It has only been since the 1985 Plaza Accord that MOF has joined in with other key industrial countries to revalue the yen.

MOF restrictions on both the outflow of Japanese capital and inflow of foreign capital has also been highly neo-mercantilist. Again Tokyo delayed implementing liberalization policies long after it promised the OECD to do so in 1964. It was not until 1980 that capital flows were made free in principle, although, as we have seen, MOF preserves a range of measures designed to prevent this from becoming a reality.

MOF had no real fiscal policy until after 1965, and it did not become an important part of overall macroeconomic policy until a decade later. However, unlike the other aspects of MOF macroeconomic policies, fiscal policies are steadily shifting in favor of consumers and the elderly through expanded social welfare and infrastructure expenditures. In 1987 Tokyo finally gave in to the demands of the other industrial countries, and shifted its economic policies from export-led to domestic-led growth.

Overall, Japan's macroeconomic policies have changed considerably since 1945, although the most significant changes have occurred only in the last few years. Recent MOF policies to stimulate domestic demand and strengthen the yen are a clear departure from the generally neo-mercantilist, export-led growth orientation of its postwar macroeconomic policies. In addition, MOF has removed most legal restrictions on capital outflows and inflows, although it reserves the right to impose restrictions as it sees fit. These changes parallel the steady shift from the bureaucratic-led corporatism of the 1950s through the mid-1960s, corporatism of the 1970s, neo-corporatism through the mid-1980s, and the slow shift to a future neo-pluralist political economy. Yet, despite these changes, Tokyo's macroeconomic policies will remain focused on enhancing Japan's economic power over the global economy.

NOTES

1. Takafusa Nakamura, *The Postwar Japanese Economy*, p. 39.
2. John Campbell, *Contemporary Japanese Budget Politics*, pp. 20, 51.
3. Ibid., p. 49.
4. Ibid., pp. 43, 49.
5. Ibid., p. 44.
6. Ibid., p. 47.
7. Ibid., pp. 9–11.
8. Nakamura, op. cit., p. 32.
9. Kazuo Sato, 'Saving and Investment', in Kozo Yamamura and Yasukichi Yasuba, *The Political Economy of Japan*, p. 140.
10. John Macmillan, *Japan's Economy*, p. 28.
11. Koichi Hamada and Akiyoshi Horiuchi, 'The Political Economy of the Financial Market', in Yamamura, op. cit., p. 238.
12. Ibid., p. 240.
13. Ibid., p. 246.

14. Ibid., pp. 248, 250.
15. Ibid., p. 244.
16. Yukio Noguchi, 'Public Finance', in Yamamura, op. cit., p. 198.
17. Ibid., pp. 198–9.
18. Michele Schmiegelow, *Japan's Response to Crisis and Change in the World Economy*, p. 104.
19. Ibid., p. 182.
20. Ibid., p. 155.
21. Ibid., p. 176.
22. Macmillan, op. cit., p. 30.
23. Noguchi Yamamura, op. cit., p. 188.
24. Schmiegelow, op. cit., p. 161.
25. Nakamura, op. cit., p. 219.
26. Schmeilegow, op. cit., pp. 59, 49.
27. Ibid., p. 19.
28. Ibid., p. 66.

11 Industrial Policy

Macroeconomic policies are designed to affect the overall economic climate such as the levels of savings, investment, inflation and unemployment by manipulating such things as government spending, the amount of money in the economy, the taxation rate, and the exchange rate. Macroeconomic policies generally reflect the neo-classical economic idea that the government's role in the economy should be minimal, that government should confine itself to managing the money supply and public spending to smooth out economic cycles. Neo-classical economists have a static notion of comparative advantage whereby every country has a different mix of advantages and disadvantages over the goods it can potentially produce. Countries should manufacture what they produce most cheaply while importing everything else. All industries are equally valued: skateboards can be as important to the economy as satellites. Free markets are seen as ends in themselves; by definition, the more markets are freed from government interference, the more the economy will be efficient, productive, and prosperous. This idea was embraced most enthusiastically by early industrializing countries like Britain and the United States, whose industries largely evolved without significant government assistance.

Industrial policies, on the other hand, are government attempts directly to develop specific industries, technologies, or firms through such devices as subsidies, protection from imports, cartels, tax incentives, and others. Industrial policy generally reflects the neo-mercantilist idea that the government should work closely with business to develop the economy as efficiently and rapidly as possible. Neo-mercantilists have a dynamic notion of comparative advantage whereby industries and products can be created rather than inherited. Some industries are considered far more important to economic development than others, and the government's role is to target those strategic industries and supply them with all the advantages they need to develop. Properly managed, the market mechanism is an important means to development the economy. However, neo-mercantilists see development, not markets, as the chief economic goal. Thus, neo-mercantilist economies fall in between neo-classical economies, where the market decides all and command economies, where the state decides all. Late industrializing countries like Germany, France, and Japan, or Newly Industrializing Countries (NICs) like South Korea and Taiwan, have, to varying extents, used industrial policies to develop their economies.

No country has been as successful as Japan in perfecting the use of both neo-mercantilist macroeconomic and industrial policies to develop its economy. Tokyo's economic policy-makers understood well that to rely solely on free trade and markets for development would condemn Japan forever to center its economy on the production of textiles and toys, the only products in which Japan had a comparative advantage in the early postwar period. Instead, the government has attempted to use all means possible continually to upgrade the economy to higher technology-based levels while retaining the older light and heavy industries. The Japanese government has particularly focused on developing such industries as steel and semiconductors, which are the basis of the heavy and high technology sectors, respectively; the government's promotion of a vigorous steel industry from the late 1940s through today in turn helped develop other heavy industries such as shipbuilding and automobiles, just as its promotion of a vigorous semiconductor industry from the early 1970s through today is aiding other high technology industries such as microelectronics, computers, telecommunications, and aerospace.

Although the government is involved in all economic sectors, it has played a particularly strong role in developing infant 'sunrise' industries and protecting senile 'sunset' industries. An infant industry is one that is 'not now internationally competitive, and that would fail to develop without some form of government assistance. But if given assistance, the industry could develop and in its maturity become internationally competitive and viable without continued government support'.[1] James Abegglen and Chalmers Johnson have written extensively about Japan's political economy and its development policies. Abegglen vividly describes the overall economic environment Japan's government attempts to nurture: 'the pattern of competition until recently has been drearily similar. The Japanese entry to a product area begins with a large number of companies attempting initial production. The Japanese market, totally protected from both imports and foreign investment, then grows rapidly. This growth, enjoyed entirely by domestic producers, allows them to bring their costs down to world levels rapidly and without foreign intervention. After fierce domestic competition, a few winners emerge in a strong position. From this protected and substantial domestic base – a virtual fortress – the Japanese competitor moves his troops out into the world market'.[2] Johnson describes in detail some of the specific industrial policy tools the government uses to develop strategic industries: 'On the protective side, discriminatory tariffs, preferential commodity taxes on national products, import restrictions based on foreign currency controls, on the development side they include the supply of low interest funds to targeted industries through governmental financial benefits, exclusion from import duties of designated critical equipment, licensing of imported foreign technology, providing industrial parks for private businesses through public investments, and administrative guidance by MITI and other ministries'.[3] After OPEC's quadrupling of oil prices in 1973, many of Japan's heavy industries, like shipbuilding, petrochemicals, or metal processing, lost the comparative advantage that the government had so carefully nurtured over the previous two decades. Ironically, Tokyo had to bail out these 'sunset' industries by reimposing many of the same cartels, subsidies, and import barriers that had been used to create them in the first place.

All of Tokyo's industrial policies, to varying extents, have been enormously successful in developing Japan from a poverty-stricken, war devastated country into the economic superpower it is today. Perhaps the most important reason why Japan's industrial policies have been so successful, is that they have been largely conceived and implemented bureaucratically rather than politically. Japan's powerful centralized, highly professional bureaucracy has targeted strategic industries for development based on their contribution to the economy as a whole rather than to narrow political or economic interests. The LDP and corporate world have generally followed the ministries' lead in industrial policy-making and implementation. Nevertheless, some policies are conceived for purely political purposes: agriculture is the most glaring example. But these successful policies and arrangements are not the result of any 'miracle' somehow 'unique' to Japan. Other countries – most notably South Korea, Taiwan, and Singapore – have used the same methods based on similar close government-business relations to achieve equally high growth and development.

Industrial policy-making has grown increasingly complex as the economy has developed. MITI used to play a role in industrial policy-making almost as dominant as MOF does over macroeconomic policy-making. That is no longer true. Other ministries, such as MPT, MOE, and MOC, battle MITI for control over specific industrial policies and significant input over others. Likewise, the LDP policy 'tribes' are increasingly sharing policy-making with MITI and other ministries. Although the corporate world continues to try to speak with one voice through Keidanren, each industrial association cooperates or competes with the bureaucracy to varying degrees. Yet, despite these internal dynamics, the pace of change in policy-making has been largely determined by persistent foreign pressure; not just other industrial countries like the United States and West Europe, but increasingly from developing countries and regions like the NICs or the Middle East. Despite these changes, Japanese industrial policy-making remains largely depoliticized.

This chapter will examine in detail Japan's industrial policy-making and policies. The first two sections will discuss the prewar and Occupation legacies, respectively, that helped shape Japan's postwar industrial policy-making. The sections will concentrate on the institutional evolution of the different ministries and organizations involved in industrial policies. The third section will analyze three broad industrial policy tools: cartels, technology, and trade policies.

THE ROOTS OF INDUSTRIAL POLICY: INSTITUTIONS AND POLICIES, 1868–1949

Japan's successful postwar industrial policy-making regime was the result of almost a century of policy-making trial and error, and political struggles among different interests for control over policy-making and specific policies. Between 1868 and 1952 Japan's economy passed through four distinct economic development phases.

The first phase lasted little more than a decade during which the new Meiji élite attempted to develop Japan's economy by directly owning its major industries. But it soon became obvious that government lacked the expertise to run complex modern industries. By the early 1880s Japan's political economy moved into its second developmental phase as the government began selling off its industries to private investors in the hope that the market would be more effective than itself in developing them. Although at first these industries continued to receive continued government subsidies, these gradually diminished and by the early twentieth century Japan's economy was relatively *laissez-faire*.

This largely free-market regime began to dissolve in the mid-1920s as the newly created Ministry of Commerce and Industry (MCI) began the first pioneering attempts at industrial policies targeted at strategic economic sectors. From then and increasingly during the 1930s, the government began a step-by-step process of assuming greater control over the economy, until by the early 1940s it had legally achieved totalitarian economic power. The reality, however, was quite different, since until the end of World War II the zaibatsu resisted all government attempts to achieve total control.

It was only during the Occupation that this tug of war between the zaibatsu and bureaucracy for control over the economy was resolved in favor of the latter. SCAP's decision not only to preserve the bureaucracy, but to bolster its powers with a range of sweeping laws while simultaneously breaking up the zaibatsu, finally gave government the controls over the economy that it had struggled for during the 1930s and 1940s, thus shifting Japan's political economy into a forth development phase.

In his book, *MITI and Japan's Modern Economic Miracle*, Chalmers Johnson analyzes this evolution of Japan's industrial policies from the early Meiji period through to the present day.[4] Although Johnson argues that the first modern industrial policies can be traced to the mid–1920s when the government abandoned its *laissez-faire* policies and began targeting economic sectors for development, he points out that the roots of Japan's industrial policy-making complex can be traced back to the early Meiji era.

On 5 November 1880 Matsukata Masayoshi the new MOF minister, issued the 'Outline Regulations for the Sale of Government-operated Factories', marking a dramatic policy shift from a state-centered towards a market-centered economy. The government sold off many of its pilot factories to private merchant houses like Mitsui, Mitsubishi, Sumitomo, Yasuda, and others at fire-sale prices, and followed up the sales by providing them with exclusive licenses, subsidies, cheap loans, and other privileges. Thus emerged the zaibatsu, each holding a virtual monopoly over huge strategic sectors of the economy.

The following Spring, on 7 April 1881, Matsukata created the Ministry of Agriculture and Commerce (MAC) to guide Japan's economic development. MAC combined responsibilities such as administration of all laws and orders relating to commerce, industry, technology, inventions, transportation, agriculture, and others which had previously been divided among the ministries of Finance, Civil Affairs, Industrial Relations, and Home Affairs. In 1885 MAC's powers over shipping and postal service was trimmed off and given to the newly created Ministry of Communications, while it picked up the powers over mining previously enjoyed by the now abolished Ministry of Industrial Affairs.

Despite this wide range of responsibilities, MAC's role became increasingly regulatory and advisory up through the 1930s. Ties between bureaucracy and business remained generally weak, and Japan's economy was largely *laissez-faire* throughout this period. However, the government still retained control over some important industries, particularly steel: in 1901 the MAC-owned Yawata steel corporation accounted for 53 per cent of the nation's production of pig iron and 82 per cent of its rolled steel. But most of MAC energies were devoted to agriculture which as late as 1914 still accounted for 45.1 per cent of GNP, while manufacturing remained a percentage point behind, at 44.5 per cent of GNP. Although Japanese industry first 'took off' during the Russo-Japanese war, it was not until World War I that the economy really expanded dramatically, and industry became the economy's powerhouse. In the five years between 1914 and 1919 trade expanded from 1.2 billion yen to 4.5 billion yen. During this period Japan enjoyed a trade surplus of 1.3 billion yen, which the government used to pay off all of its foreign debts.[5]

Although Japan's industrial growth had been rapid, it was undercut by a host of problems including mass urban and rural poverty, food shortages, inflation, and conflict between industrial and agricultural interests. The World War I boom was followed by a recession and annual trade deficit that lasted through most of the 1920s, capped by the global depression after 1929. As if this was not enough, most of Tokyo was destroyed by the 1924 great Kanto earthquake, which caused a staggering 438 million yen in damage.[6]

In 1925, in order to deal with these increasingly severe economic problems, the old Ministry of Agriculture and Commerce was divided into the Ministry of Agriculture and the Ministry of Commerce and Industry (MCI). MCI sponsored two laws in 1925 – the Exporters Association Law and the Major Export Industries Law – which were the first steps in creating a comprehensive industrial policy. The laws allowed MCI to form export, production, and price cartels within any export industry. Although there had been a few cartels before then – the Japan Paper Manufacturers' Federation of 1880, the Japan Cotton Spinners' Federation of 1882, and the Japan Fertilizer Manufacturers' Federation of 1907 – the 1925 export laws gave MCI vast and unprecedented legal powers to create and administer cartels in virtually any industry.

But a comprehensive industrial policy dates from 23 May 1927 when a Commerce and Industry Deliberation Council (sogo shingi-kai) was set up under MCI to formulate and implement industrial policies for the entire economy, and a Resource Bureau attached to the Cabinet which undertook the first steps towards genuine economic planning. In 1930 the Temporary Industrial Rationalization Bureau was set up within MCI to draw up plans for such activities as the control of businesses, implementation of scientific management principles, improvements in industrial financing, standardization of products, simplification of production processes, and subsidies to support the production and consumption of domestically manufactured goods. These plans were implemented by powers granted by the Important Industries Control Law of 16 August 1931 which allowed MCI to form price, production, market, member, and export cartels in all key industries. When two-thirds of the firms in a particular industry requested a cartel, MCI would then legalize it, forcing even those opposed to join. Soon thereafter 26 industries had formed cartels of various kinds. MCI control over trade tightened further with the enactment of the Foreign Exchange Control Law of 29 March 1933, which made all overseas transactions subject to approval and licensing of MOF, a law which lasted until 1 April 1964.

During the mid to late 1930s a full range of industry specific laws granted MCI sweeping powers over not just specific industries, but the restructuring of the entire economy. The first industry-specific law was the Petroleum Industry Law of 28 March 1934 which gave MCI authority to control all aspects of the petroleum industry. On 9 June 1937 MCI created the Fuel Bureau, its first industry-specific bureau, to administer the Petroleum law. The next industry-specific law was the Automobile Manufacturing Law of 29 May 1936 which allowed MCI completely to reorganize the automobile industry. MCI's power to deny licensing to unwanted companies proved to be an important industrial policy tool. The government supplied licensed companies (kyoka kaisha) with half their capital needs, and granted them five-year tax and import-duty holidays. Only Toyota and Nissan were licensed while Ford and GM, which had huge market shares because of their comparative advantage, were eliminated. There followed a series of industry specific laws which eventually encompassed virtually the entire Japanese economy: Artificial Petroleum Law (10 August 1937), Steel Industry Law (12 August 1937), Machine Tool Industry Law (30 March 1938), Aircraft Manufacturing Law (30 March 1938), Shipbuilding Industry Law (5 April

1939), Light Metals Manufacturing Law (1 May 1939), and the Important Machines Manufacturing Law (3 May 1941).

On 10 September 1937 the Temporary Measures Law Relating to Exports, Imports, and Other Matters allowed MCI to control all trade, and the manufacture, distribution, transfer, and consumption of all imported raw materials. This was the predecessor of the 1949 Foreign Exchange and Foreign Trade Control Law. MCI created the Trade Link System on 23 June 1938, whereby all raw materials were authorized only for civilian industries that manufactured goods for export and earned more foreign exchange than they spent. The Trade Bureau was organized into departments to administer each market and commodity. Other ministries were also given sweeping powers over the economy. On 10 September 1937 the Munitions Mobilization Law and the Emergency Funds Regulation Law enpowered MOF to direct public and private funds to the munitions industry as needed, and allowed MOF to use administrative guidance to restructure the banking industry.

After 11 May 1935 these laws were administered by MCI and the Cabinet Research Bureau, but on 14 July 1937 the MCI Trade Bureau was made into a semi-attached bureau with military officers serving in policy-making roles. The Trade Bureau was the direct ancestor of the Board of Trade (Boeki-cho) created by the Occupation. Later that year, on 23 October 1937, the Cabinet Planning Board was created to act as an 'economic general staff' for the economy. The Board included a Research Bureau and Resources Bureau, each of which was composed of 'new bureaucrats' (kakushin kanryo) who were imbued with German and Japanese fascist ideology, and used their power to reorient Japan along those lines.

The result was a series of laws that attempted to complete the government's control over the economy. The National General Mobilization Law of 5 May 1938 authorized the complete reorganization of society along totalitarian lines. This was followed by the Price Control Ordinance of 18 October 1939, which allowed government to fix all prices and wages. The General Plan for the Establishment of the New Economic Structure of 13 September 1940 allowed the Cabinet Planning Board to oversee the semi-nationalization of all industries. The Important Industries Association Ordinance of 30 August 1941 created control organs for each industry. All enterprises in an industry were assigned to a 'control association' (Toseikai), comparable to a government-authorized cartel, which was enpowered to allocate materials, set production quotas, and distribute the products of its members. The control associations were headed by a chief officer who was from the largest firm in the industry. By August 1942 there were 21 control associations covering production and distribution for 15 industries. The General Plan for the Conversion and Closing of Medium and Small Enterprises of 12 January 1942 allowed MCI to organize those companies under zaibatsu control. The Enterprises Bureau Law of 17 July 1942 gave the government unlimited power to convert industries to war production. Finally, in 1943, the Ministry of Munitions was created by a merger of MCI and the Cabinet Planning Board in order to administer this vast web of economic controls.

On paper the web of new laws, institutions, and policies created in the 1930s and early 1940s gave the government totalitarian controls over all aspects of Japan's economy; in reality the controls were poorly administered and, like that of wartime Germany, Japan's economy was never completely controlled. All these laws and measures were bitterly opposed in the Diet by most of the politicians and their zaibatsu supporters. The laws worked poorly because of the continuing stand-off between the zaibatsu and bureaucracy. Most of these laws merely added another layer of bureaucracy to the private cartels that had existed since 1931 under the Important Industries Control Law.

Despite this resistance, these industrial policies achieved dramatic economic results. Manufacturing remained mostly composed of light industries until the mid–1930s when these were overtaken by heavy industries like metals, machinery, chemicals, and fuels. Between 1930 and 1940, Japan's mining and manufacturing output more than doubled, while the composition of manufacturing shifted from light industries dominated by textiles to heavy industries like metals, machines, and chemicals. In 1930 heavy industries made up about 35 per cent of all manufacturing; by 1940 it had grown to 63 per cent.[7]

According to Johnson, these wartime controls, associations, and institutions created in the two decades between 1925 and 1945 formed the basis for Japan's postwar economy; the war became a vast proving ground for policies, institutions, and associations that later proved the basis Japan's postwar economic miracle. The wartime mobilization plans were the basis of the Industrial Rationalization Council of the 1950s and the Industrial Structure Council of the 1960s and 1970s, while the role of the 'economic general staff' shared by MCI, MM, and the Cabinet Planning Board during the war was resurrected in MITI in 1949.

Following the surrender, the government quickly renamed the Munitions Ministry the Ministry of Commerce and Industry out of fear that it would be abolished by the Occupation. SCAP not only tolerated the MCI, but continued to strengthen it until it was combined with the Trade Board to become MITI in 1949. On 13 December 1945 the Board of Trade (BOT, boeki-cho) was created as an autonomous bureau attached to MCI, and was given the responsibility to administer the 78 trade associations which were continuations of the pre–1945 control associations. In 1946 SCAP sponsored the Temporary Materials Supply and Demand Control Law (1946), which allowed MCI to control all commodities, and the Economic Stabilization Board (ESB, 12 August 1946) which served as the successor to the Cabinet Planning Board and was renamed the Economic Planning Agency in 1952. The ESB served as the government coordinating body for economic policy-making. In April 1947 SCAP abolished the trade associations and replaced them with four broad government corporations including minerals and industrial products, textiles, raw materials, and foodstuffs, all controlled by the Board of Trade. While the BOT controlled all foreign exchange, using a rate of 130 yen to the dollar for imports and 300–500 yen for exports, the ESB determined the prices.

INDUSTRIAL POLICY PERFECTED: INSTITUTIONS AND POLICIES, 1949–PRESENT

But these SCAP-sponsored institutions proved to be just as inefficient as their wartime predecessors; the economy remained mismanaged and inefficient, undercut by hyperinflation and corruption. SCAP then pushed through rational macroeconomic and industrial policies designed to rebuild Japan's economy. The Nine-Point Economic Stabilization Plan (19 December 1948) called for a balanced annual budget, strengthened tax collection, limitations on RFB loans, improved controls over foreign trade and US aid, and a fixed exchange rate, and were implemented by the Dodge Mission of February 1949.

As important as these policies was Dodge's creation of the Ministry of International Trade and Industry (MITI) on 25 May 1949 by combining MCI and BOT. SCAP further strengthened MITI with a series of laws and responsibilities. Article 3 of the law that established MITI states that it would be responsible 'for (1) the promotion and regulation of commerce and the supervision of foreign exchange accompanying commerce: (2) the promotion, improvement, regulation, and inspection of the production, distribution, and consumption of mineral and industrial goods'. To these ends MITI was authorized to establish an Industrial Policy bureau to devise 'policies and plans related to the overall supply and demand of goods . . . related to commerce, mining, and manufacturing'.

MITI's powers have been strengthened over the last four decades by hundreds of other laws and administrative directives. For example, the Foreign Exchange and Foreign Trade Control Law (FECL) of 1949 gave MITI absolute powers to control trade and allocate scarce foreign exchange to targeted industrial sectors, while the Foreign Investment Law of 1950 gave MITI similar powers to control foreign investment. These two laws were further strengthened when on 1 August 1952 both the ESB and Foreign Exchange Board were abolished and their duties transferred to MITI. The Export Import Bank was opened on 1 December 1951 with 15 billion yen in US aid counterpart funds (the yen proceeds of sales in Japan of US aid products), and the Japan Development Bank on 31 March 1951, again with SCAP provided funds of 10 billion yen from counterpart funds. Although the JDB was actually under MOF jurisdiction, it became one of MITI's most important industrial policy instruments since MITI screened all loan applications.[8]

As in all other areas of Japan's political economy, there is a great difference between where policy-making actually (honne) took place within MITI and institutions set up to give the appearance of policy-making (tatemae). The Policy Concerning Industrial Rationalization published on 13 September 1949 by MITI's Enterprises Bureau, designated the Enterprise Bureau to preside over the Industrial Rationalization Council, which was a clearing house for the plans of 45 committees and 81 subcommittees (kondankai) covering every industry and bringing together several hundred leading industrialists and academic specialists.[9] These committees or Kondankai were the real workhorses of policy-making and implementation.

The Council on Industrial Structure (CIS; Sangyo Kozo Shingikai) was created on 1 April 1961 as the advisory council to the minister of MITI, and is assumed to play a comprehensive coordinating role in policy-making. In reality it is simply a public relations council composed of industrial, academic, labor, consumer, and media leaders designed to popularize MITI policies. The Council has no budget and devotes its efforts to producing 'visions' of future economic development, and is to MITI what the EPA is to the Japanese government as a whole. The real work continues to be conducted in the exclusive kondankai rather than the more accessible shingikai. Generally, a policy would first be devised in the kondankai and then reworked and approved by the appropriate MITI Bureau (Genkyoku). Only then would it move to the Council, which would rubberstamp it before sending it over to the appropriate LDP PARC division for a similar approval process.

MITI and its industrial policy kondankai were empowered by a series of laws. The Enterprise Rationalization Promotion Law of 1952 was the first of 58 separate MITI-sponsored policy laws and 50 administrative directives passed up through 1965 related to industrial and trade policy, that gave MITI enormous, wide-ranging powers to restructure the designated industry. The Law enpowered MITI to provide direct subsidies to firms buying new equipment, plus tax exemptions for all R & D investments. It also authorized designated strategic industries to depreciate the costs of installing new equipment by 50 per cent during the first year. Finally it committed both the central and local government to build the infrastructure – ports, highways, railroads, electric power grids, industrial parks – vital for economic development at public expense, and made them available to these industries.

The formal laws were backed by MITI's powers of administrative guidance, whereby the ministry would issue such things as directives (shiji), requests (yobo), warnings (keikoku), suggestions (kankoku), and encouragements (kansho), and guidance through policy statements (shido yoko), all of which were not legally binding, but were nevertheless followed just as closely by the affected industry. The company knew that although it held the legal right to refuse these requests, MITI had the last word with its powers over such things as licensing, cartels, import barriers, technology-sharing agreements, and other advantages, which it would not hesitate to withhold from recalcitrant companies. During the 1950s administrative guidance was rarely used because most of MITI's orders, permissions, and licenses were then firmly based on explicit industry laws. But from the first limited liberalization steps of the mid–1960s up through the latest today, MITI has had increasingly to rely on administrative guidance to implement its industrial policies.

MITI was not completely successful in pushing through all the legislation it desired. Despite the enormous success of its campaign to weaken the anti-monopoly laws and create a range of industry-specific laws, MITI's 1958 attempt to completely abolish the anti-monopoly law failed when even the corporate world rallied against any further expansion of MITI's powers. The corporate world reasoned it could form virtually any kind of cartel anyway, so it did not matter if a toothless anti-monopoly law stayed on the books. Facing a united opposition, the LDP decided not to even bring MITI's proposed law to a vote. MITI tried again to expand its powers in 1963, when it attempted to push through the Temporary Promotion of Specified Industries Law, which would have allowed widespread mergers throughout industry. Again, faced with a united front of the corporate world joining the opposition parties, the LDP decided not to send the bill before the Diet.

MITI's formal powers peaked throughout the 1950s to the mid–1960s. Its legal powers have diminished steadily from the late 1960s through today as Japan has slowly liberalized various economic sectors in response to continuing foreign pressure. In response to these changes, MITI has increasingly used administrative guidance to implement its foreign policies, while also adapting itself to Japan's growing economic power and impact on the world economy. In May 1971 MITI published 'International Trade and Industrial Policy in the 1970s', which announced a shift in policy means from protectionism to limited market intervention, and the promotion of a shift in policy ends from capital- and energy-intensive heavy industries to high-technology knowledge-intensive industries. This policy shift was accelerated two years later by OPEC's quadrupling of oil prices and the subsequent disruptions of the world economy. MITI published a similar vision in 1980 elaborating on the need to accelerate Japan's development into a post-industrial economic superpower. Despite these 'visions', not much has changed; MITI continues to use its old methods of cartels and protectionism to promote sunrise and ease out sunset industries, while emphasizing more subtle non-tariff barriers which cannot be pointed at easily by Japan's trade partners.

MITI has never been solely in charge of industrial policy-making and implementation. MOF has important controls over a number of industrial policy areas via the BOJ, Eximbank, JDB, and other financial institutions. Since the early 1950s, MITI and MOF have worked together in allocating credit to strategic industries, through the BOJ and city banks. Yet MITI and MOF have not always seen eye to eye on policy despite this almost four-decade partnership. In the early 1950s Bank of Japan governor Ichimada maintained that industrial and export promotion should be based on the industries in which Japan had a comparative advantage,while MITI argued that comparative advantage could be created rather than inherited, and Japan should embark on an industrialization program designed to establish a range of strategic capital- and technology-intensive industries including iron and steel, shipbuilding, petroleum refining, petrochemicals, automobiles, industrial machinery, electronics, and electronic machinery. MITI's plan for managed markets won out over the Bank of Japan's stress on free markets, and Ichimada's successors embraced MITI industrial policies.

Although MITI and MOF generally work together on industrial policy, other ministries are increasingly struggling to take over industrial policy responsibilities in certain sectors: MITI and the Ministry of Posts and Telecommunications (MPT) are battling for control over a variety of high technology industries; MITI and the Ministry of Education jousted over software protection; MITI favors liberalization of agricultural imports, MAFF fiercely opposes it; MITI continues to resist FTC attempts to curb its cartel-granting powers.

INDUSTRIAL POLICY TECHNIQUES

Cartel Policy

Cartels have been a vital part of Japan's industrial policies throughout the postwar era. Schmiegelow writes that the government has 'tolerated, encouraged, and occasionally even coerced thousands of cartels since 1945 to restrict imports, counteract recessions, promote technology diffusion, and restructure industries. MITI and the Japanese public do not share the faith that free market ideologues hold in the market to solve complex economic and social development problems, and therefore do not feel the same anxiety about departures from neo-classical models of the world'.[10] In other words, managed competition is necessary to control the evils of 'excess (free) competition'. This attitude was most clearly summed up in the Enterprises Bureau sponsored Cabinet-level deliberation council on the future status of the Anti-Monopoly Law. The Council's final report issued in 1958 stated that 'the public interest is not best served by the legal maintenance of a free competitive order'. Instead it recommended a new law that would allow MITI openly to coordinate investment and various cartels to overcome 'excessive competition'.[11]

There are currently 42 Japanese statutes providing for as many as 64 different cartel systems. The legal basis for cartels goes back to the 1953 Export and Import Trading Act which allowed price and import cartels, which has since been reinforced by over 20 specific-industry laws. Recently the 1978 Designated Recession Industries Stabilization and the 1983 Temporary Measures for the Structured Improvement of Specific Industries laws further empower MITI to form and administer cartels. The procedure for forming an industrial cartel is simple. The industry federation experiencing difficulties reaches a consensus on the need for a cartel, and then makes a formal request to MITI to do so. MITI agrees, drafts a cartel plan, and then guides the member companies' collusion for the cartel's duration. The number of legal cartels has ranged from 162 in 1955 to around 1000 in the early 1970s, which dropped to 422 in 1986, most of which were composed of small- and medium-sized firms. Countless others illegal cartels were given the wink by MITI and other ministries under administrative guidance.

The first postwar cartel was essentially illegal. On 25 February 1952, a year before the Anti-Monopoly Law was revised, MITI formed the largest textile producers into a production and price cartel through administrative guidance as an 'advice to limit production' (kankoku sotan); it enforced the cartel by threatening to cut off foreign currency allocations to firms that refused to support the production cut-back cartel.

Although this cartel was successful, the FTC had ruled against two other MITI-sponsored cartels, so MITI soon embarked on a long campaign completely to dismantle the anti-monopoly laws, a campaign in which it was largely successful. In April 1952 MITI succeeded in getting the Designated Medium-Small Enterprise Stabilization Act enacted, which gave MITI the power to organize production, investment, and shipping cartels among small- and medium-sized firms experiencing economic difficulties. A year and a half later, in September 1953, after a long struggle against opposition party resistance, MITI succeeded in having the Diet pass a law amending the Anti-Monopoly Law and Export Trade Act, and abolishing the Trade Association Law. The new laws allowed in certain situations recession, technology, investment, production, price, and rationalization cartels, cross-sharing among firms, dumping, and even monopolies. Although the FTC would be consulted, it would largely be up to MITI to determine the situation in which such collusion would be allowed. MITI followed up its rewriting of the anti-monopoly laws with a series of industry-specific laws that gave MITI enormous, wide-ranging powers to restructure the designated industry.[12]

By July 1957 150 cartels of various types were in effect. The majority were export cartels which coordinated the dumping of goods in foreign markets. Japanese dumping, however, had begun as early as May 1953, with industries such as ammonium sulphate, steel rods, cotton weaving, and artificial fibers. Despite repeated foreign protests, Japanese dumping increased steadily with the number of cartels. Most of the industries were dumping goods at prices 20–30 per cent less than the domestic price. Each member received quotas for both the domestic and foreign markets. Although supposedly temporary, these cartels soon became elaborate permanent arrangements.[13]

By 1966 there were 1079 legal cartels in Japan, of which 781 (72 per cent) involved small businesses under the Small and Medium Enterprise Organization Act and related statutes. Another 225 (21 per cent) were created under the Export and Import Trading Act and the Export Marine Products Industry Promotion Act and directly involved foreign trade. By 1982, although the total number of cartels remained 505, the percentage related to foreign trade had dropped to less than 14 per cent (69 cartels), which included export cartels formed to restrict exports at the request of foreign governments.[14]

Although free in principle (tatemae) to decline membership in a cartel, individual firms must in reality strictly conform to any cartel organized in their industry or products. For example, in Spring 1965 the Iron and Steel Federation and MITI agreed on a production cartel for the industry to offset a slump in demand. MITI's Heavy Industries Bureau drew up a detailed plan for the cartel and then the President of Yawata Steel and chairman of the federation, Yoshiro Inayama, met with all the steel company executives to forge a consensus on the specific production and market-share levels outlined by MITI. By July he had achieved an agreement among the cartel to cut production by 10 per cent. On 1 September 1965 the federation and MITI announced the cartel would continue to offset a continuing low demand.

Sumitomo Metals, which had previously invested in new technology designed to give its steel a comparative advantage, had been dissatisfied with the cartel all along and announced on 19 November that it would no longer abide by the agreement. Sumitomo's action was a grave violation of the Japanese value of sacrificing individual for communal interests and directly challenged MITI's industry policy. The Steel Federation immediately responded to Sumitomo's action with the classic Japanese method of dealing with individuals – complete ostracism (Mura Hachibu). Henceforth, Sumitomo would be shunned by all unrelated Japanese industries; banks cut off Sumitomo's credit while industries refused to buy its products. By the end of December Sumitomo humbly admitted defeat and asked forgiveness. On 28 December MITI formally announced Sumitomo's return to the community and the restoration of industrial harmony. The fact that the cartel was not legally sanctioned, but instead organized through MITI's administrative guidance, had made it much more difficult for Sumitomo to resist. As long as there are no enforceable legal norms, MITI and the corporate world are free to organize and operate cartels in any ways they wish.

Not all these cartels went unchallenged by the FTC. MITI and the Petroleum Industry Federation (Sekyu Renmei) organized a cartel of the oil industry following OPEC's 1973 quadrupling of oil price and subsequent industry slump. MITI organized the cartel on guidelines created by the Petroleum Industry Law of 1962. The FTC responded by nurturing two civil suits against the cartel: Japan v. Sekyu Renmei against production restrictions enforced by the Petroleum Federation, and Japan v. Idemitsu Kosan KK against price fixing among the firms. The primary defense was that the firms organized their cartel under MITI's administrative guidance. In 1984 the Supreme Court found the defendants guilty of Anti-Monopoly Law violations and upheld the FTC's assertion that firms are responsible for their actions, even if they act on MITI's advice, but stopped short of holding all collusive activities on administrative guidance illegal. The Court based its ruling on the 1980 amendment to the FECL, which cut back MITI's powers to regulate industry, which seems strange since the cartel had been organized seven years before the amendment was introduced. In retrospect, the political basis of the Court's ruling may have been far more important than any legal arguments. The decision was reached when Japan was under strong pressure from the United States and West Europe to cut back its industrial policies.

Cartels continue to play a dominant role in industrial policies, and are a severe non-tariff trade barrier. Through the 1980s MITI has been active in organizing both 'sunset' and 'sunrise' cartels. The 1978

Designated Recession Industries Recession and 1983 Temporary Measures for the Structured Improvement of Specific Industries laws gave MITI great powers to completely restructure and protect 'sunset' industries. By the mid-1980s, about 20 Japanese industries were officially designated as depressed, and thus allowed to maintain a variety of cartel and anti-trade arrangements. These industries include aluminum smelting, chemical fertilizers, caustic soda, various petrochemicals, lumber, plywood, electric furnaces, paper, soda ash, and synthetic rubber. The total market for such products exceeds $80 billion, yet with the exception of aluminum-ingot and electric-furnace products, import penetration is surprisingly low, usually less than 6 or 7 per cent.[15]

The soda ash cartel provides an excellent example of how cartels can distort the economies of both Japan and foreign countries.[16] Japan is the world's highest-cost producer of soda ash, and at least 40 per cent of its annual 1.2 million MT (metric ton) of soda ash production is inefficient. This means an annual 500 000 MT market opportunity for American producers, the world's low-cost source. Yet despite this, Japanese imports from 1973 through 1980 never exceeded 70 000 tons per year or about 5 per cent of the market, and in many years Japanese soda ash exports exceeded imports.

In 1973, following the liberalization of soda ash imports, the Japan Soda Ash Industry Association formally agreed to prevent any significant soda ash imports. To this end, they, along with seven trading companies and MITI, have continually maintained a price, import, and market cartel. To prevent 'excessive competition' each foreign producer is assigned an import quota and a Japanese trading company to handle it. In 1980 this was 12 000 tons from each of five American producers. All imported soda ash is imported through one dock, which is owned by the Soda Ash Association. The imports are purchased by the Industry Association from the trading companies, and are then resold to Japanese consumers at prevailing prices. Any attempt by the American producers to sell directly to the Japanese consumers is quickly rebuffed with the justification that if allowed it would upset 'delicate relationships' within Japan.

In 1981 representatives of the American soda ash industry asked the Department of Commerce to help them remove Japanese soda ash trade barriers. Citing the need to maintain established supplier relations, reliable supplies, and internal distribution costs, MITI rejected the Commerce Department's request that Japan's soda ash market operate on free trade rather than protectionist principles.

Undeterred, Commerce then filed a complaint in 1982 with the Japan FTC, which agreed to investigate the allegations. A year later the FTC ruled that an illegal import cartel did in fact exist, and ordered it disbanded. As a result, American exports rose steadily throughout 1983, reaching 140 000 MT for the year. In 1984, however, Commerce asked the FTC to investigate rumours that the MITI-sponsored cartel had reformed, this time around a level of 180 000 MT of imports. The FTC has done nothing to investigate these most recent allegations.

Harry First points out that the cartel was formed in 1973, yet the FTC did not investigate it until almost a decade later, and only then after over a year of pressure by the United States. Why?[17] Soda ash is used by a variety of industries including bottle and window glass, soap, crude oil refining, and others. Why did not Japanese consumers of soda ash complain about the cartel as soon as it was formed? Surely, to pay inflated prices would harm the competitive advantage of products that used soda ash. And why were not the American producers able to sell directly to the Japanese consumers?

Obviously, the cartel was not limited to the Soda Ash Association and their trading companies. If Japanese consumers of soda ash had lost a comparative advantage in their products, undoubtedly they would have complained. But those industries were protected as well, and were able not only to limit competitive imports but also to export their own products. As an administrative agency attached to the Prime Minister's Office rather than an independent ministry, the FTC is often pressured to put political goals before its legal responsibilities. Generally, the FTC allows the industry associations to regulate themselves and only steps in when faced with a complaint from a powerful aggrieved party that cannot be ignored.

A cartel involving the chemical fertilizer urea was recently the center of another bitter Japanese-American trade dispute.[18] All chemical fertilizer sales in Japan are controlled by a legal monopoly created by the Chemical Fertilizer Price Stabilization Law. Under this law, almost all fertilizer sales to Japanese farmers must be made through the National Federation of Agricultural Cooperative Associations (Zenno). Once a year Zenno negotiates a price with the various producers, which is then approved and designated as the official price by the Japanese Cabinet.

The Japanese urea industry became vastly overpriced as a result of the oil price rises of the 1970s, and was operating at about half of capacity in the 1980s. A plan under the 1983 Structurally Depressed

Industries Law allowed MITI to revitalize the industry through production and market cartels, while maintaining the existing price cartel. Despite their overwhelming comparative advantage, American urea producers held only about 1 per cent of the market in 1981. Zenno, which handles about 70 per cent of all chemical sales in Japan, imports no urea.

Citing the principles of free trade, the Commerce Department in 1981 asked MITI to open up Japan's urea markets. MITI initially admitted there was a cartel, but later claimed that the policy was due to the need for orderly markets and reliability of supply – an unconvincing argument since Japanese urea producers depend on naphtha imported from the volatile Middle East. MITI did agree to import more urea and allowed foreign producers a 3 per cent market share in 1983.

Not all Japanese markets are as completely defended against competitive foreign products: for example, between 1979 and 1983, aluminum imports rose from 37 per cent to 83 per cent of the market, ferro-silicon from 27 per cent to 65 per cent, and methanol imports have captured a full 100 per cent.[19] Unfortunately, these examples remain the exception rather than the rule.

The Japanese government is currently promoting a wide range of high-technology industries including microelectronics, computers, software, telecommunications, biotechnology, new materials, space technology, and medical equipment, in which cartels play an important role. The Japanese government uses a variety of means to protect its high technology against competitive imports. For example, foreign firms were allowed only a 50 per cent ownership of Value Added Networks (VANs; special telecommunications systems) while Japanese firms were desparately trying to create their own. In order to protect its own nascent aerospace industry, Tokyo refused to buy superior American or European satellites. MITI tried to reduce software protection laws from 50 to 15 years, which in effect would have allowed MITI to force foreign firms to transfer software technology to Japanese firms at terms highly advantageous to the latter. Foreign firms continue to be excluded from government research grants, cartels, and technology-sharing arrangements. Although American and European firms still cling to a comparative advantage in many high technology areas such as satellites, telecommunications, biotechnology, and medical equipment, their lead is quickly eroding, in part because of Japanese protection of their own vast market.

After prolonged, bitter negotiations, Tokyo made concessions in all these areas, though Japan's high-technology industries remain highly protected. While the foreign ownership limits on VANs of 50 per cent were eliminated, other regulations were imposed which continue to give the advantage to Japanese producers. As a sign of 'sincerity', Tokyo did agree in 1987 to buy two American satellites. That same year MITI gave up its attempt to strip foreign software producers of their copyright protection, and has invited token foreign participation on a few government-business councils.

Technology, and Research & Development Policy

Another vital industrial policy tool has been the bureaucracy's role in acquiring technology for Japanese firms. Chalmers Johnson writes that 'before the capital liberalization of the late 1960s and 1970s, no technology entered the country without MITI's approval; no joint venture was ever agreed to without MITI's scrutiny and frequent alteration of terms; no patent rights were ever bought without MITI's pressuring the seller to lower the royalties or make other changes advantageous to the Japanese industry as a whole; and no program for the importation of foreign technology was ever approved until MITI and its various advisory committees had agreed that the time was right and that the industry involved was scheduled for "nurturing" '.[20]

MITI had a strong bargaining position over foreign firms since they could neither freely trade nor invest in Japan; technology licensing was their only means of making money in the vast Japanese market. Thus it could easily force foreign firms to make prices and transfer terms in favor of Japanese firms. MITI also had strong bargaining position over domestic firms. It used its power to defuse technology widely, often by requiring the initial licensee to in turn license the technology to other Japanese firms.

The government sponsored and carefully screened the massive importation of key foreign technology from the early 1950s through today. There were 27 agreements in 1950, 101 in 1951, 133 in 1952, 103 in 1953, and 82 in 1954, a figure which rapidly accelerated thereafter. From 1950 to 1972 Japan received 17 600 licensing agreements for $3.3 billion in royalties involving every modern technology; by 1980 these figures had risen to over 25 000 contracts for $6 billion. This price tag of $6 billion is less than 10 per cent of the annual American research and development budget.[21] In other words, Japan picked up the world's key technologies at fire-sale prices, thus saving hundreds of billions of dollars in R & D expenditures and allowing companies to concentrate on converting these technologies into consumer goods. This massive technology transfer was one of the key reasons behind Japan's rapid postwar economic growth. Foreign technology that could have been used to penetrate Japanese markets was instead used by Japanese firms to penetrate foreign markets.

As a result, according to a 1987 report by America's Academy of Engineering, Japan has technologically surpassed the United States; it is superior in 25 of the 34 critical areas of high technology, including such areas as artificial intelligence, optoelectronics, iron and steel production, new materials, nuclear energy processing, semiconductors, robotics, flexible manufacturing systems, and industrial lasers. In semiconductors alone, the Japanese led in 12 key technologies, are even with the United States in eight, and are rapidly closing the gap in five.[22]

Officially, Japan now exports more technology than it imports by a ratio of 1.76 to 1 in 1984. Only about 40 per cent of these technology exports, however, went to other industrialized countries; 60 per cent went to developing countries and was simply technology Japan had earlier imported and recycled for the needs of poorer countries. In contrast, over 85 per cent of American technology went to other advanced industrial countries with the remainder sent to developing countries. In reality, Japan still imports far more technology than it exports.[23]

One of the most effective means MITI and other ministries used to take foreign technology was their manipulation of the foreign investment laws. Japan's foreign investment policy has been an integral part of both its overall macroeconomic policies and industrial policies designed to develop key economic sectors. By strictly limiting foreign investment for most of the postwar era, Tokyo forced foreign firms to untie technology from their control; as mentioned, since foreign firms could neither sell nor invest freely in Japan, their only opportunity to make money was to sell their technology to nascent rivals.

The Foreign Exchange and Foreign Trade Control Law of 1949 and the Foreign Investment Law of 1950 gave the government vast powers to control trade, investment, and economic development. Foreign investments were allowed only in the form of minority-owned joint ventures with Japanese firms, and only then if they were considered essential for 'the self-support and sound development of the Japanese economy'. Even then MITI strictly regulated the firms' operations and repatriation of profits. Faced with these harsh restrictions, only 101 firms invested in Japan for a total of $59.7 million during the 1950s.[24]

What the government was really after was foreign technology rather than foreign investments, and it used every means at its disposal to obtain it. In October 1956 the laws were amended to allow any foreign firm to set up operations in Japan as long as it agreed not to repatriate any profits. In reality these supposedly unrestricted yen-investments were subject to strict administrative guidance by MITI when it came to key industries. For example, IBM tried to enter Japan as a yen-based company during the late 1950s, but was permitted to operate only under harsh conditions that would eventually strip its products of their existing comparative advantage. MITI Vice-Minister Sahashi made it very clear that the entry price was IBM patents. He told IBM that MITI 'would take every measure possible to obstruct the success of your business unless you license IBM patents to Japanese firms and charge them no more than a 5 per cent royalty . . . we do not have an inferiority complex toward you; we only need time and money to compete effectively'.[25] Faced with this techno-nationalism IBM had no choice but to give in. It sold its key patents as demanded and accepted MITI's adminstrative guidance over the number and type of computers it could market.

Just as the government was instrumental in securing tens of thousands of foreign technology patents vital to Japan's economic development, it has also played a key role in assisting the research and development of specific products and industries. The government's role, however, is often difficult to pin down. Based on comparative statistics, Tokyo's role in assisting private research and development seems far less than that of the other key industrial countries. Only 20.8 per cent of all Japanese R & D expenditures were supplied by the government, compared to 46.6 per cent for the United States, 42.8 per cent for West Germany, 58.0 per cent for France, and 47.7 per cent for Britain. In 1980 the United States government payed about twice as much on R & D efforts than Japan as a percentage of GNP: 1.11 per cent compared to 0.56 per cent.[26] It would seem that Washington plays twice as active a role in assisting private R & D as does Tokyo.

The bulk of American government R & D, however, went to defense – 50.8 per cent of the total compared to only 4.9 per cent in Japan. Instead most Japanese government R & D funding went into agriculture and industry (25.4 per cent) and energy and infrastructure (34.4 per cent) compared to American government funding of 3.0 per cent and 14.2 per cent to these same sectors, respectively.[27] While defense gobbles up huge R & D resources and some of the best and brightest American scientists and engineers, few commercial benefits trickle down to the economy, in complete contrast to Japan's R & D efforts which are concentrated on commercial applications.

Okimoto and Saxonhouse write that America's large government R & D efforts may actually benefit Japan 'if the spillover effects from military to commercial spheres are low or if there are finite supplies of skilled R & D manpower. Of the large industrial states, Japan may be the only one capable of concentrating its finite resources almost exclusively on commercial applications of technology . . . If the Japanese government spends less, it takes more initiative than the U.S. government in microindustrial management through the use of industrial policy. Not only does it identify and target key technologies for Japan's economic future, it also coordinates intra-industry efforts at building a binding consensus within industry and between government and industry'.[28] They go on to argue that there is a difference between technological innovation and its commercial application. The United States has excelled at the former; Japan at the latter. Despite the low ratio of government funding of Japanese R & D, the government plays a key role in ensuring that no Japanese firm gains a monopoly over important technology; instead the government aids the distribution of technology to all viable firms in a relevant industry. Two-thirds of Japan's technological investments are carried out by private sector firms, and almost all of this is oriented towards applied rather than basic research and development.

Trade Policy

Japan's economic growth has been largely export-led throughout the postwar era, with exports at times comprising as much as 60 per cent of its economic growth through the late 1980s.[29] The importance of trade to Japan, however, would not seem obvious if one simply compared its present ratio of trade to GNP, both with its level during the prewar era and with other industrial countries at present. In the mid-1930s, trade comprised about 20 per cent of GNP compared to a relatively steady 12 per cent throughout most of the postwar era and 18 per cent at present. Other industrial states depend far more on trade than Japan: West Germany, Belgium, and The Netherlands as much as 50 per cent of GNP.

Japan's overall trade dependency has not been as important as the types of goods exported. It has been the products of strategic industries carefully nurtured by MITI and other ministries that have comprised the bulk of exports. Just as MOF policies aimed at creating a dynamic savings/investment ratio, MITI has continually sought to create a dynamic trade policy whereby Japan would confine its imports largely to raw materials and key technologies, and its exports to manufactured goods. A web of trade barriers against competitive imports was instrumental in nurturing strategic industries from steel to supercomputers; such techniques as subsidies, dumping, and intelligence gathering were vital to promoting the exports of these strategic industries. These government-provided import barriers and export promotion caused another virtuous circle: with their home market protected and exports subsidized, Japan's strategic industries could soon achieve optimum economies of scale which further brought down prices and made those products even more competitive.

Exports

Japan's government has promoted exports by a variety of means including tax concessions on export income or sales, depreciation allowances for exports, write-offs for the expense of export development, preferential credit terms, comprehensive government export insurance, yen undervaluation, export cartels, dumping cartels, and an undervalued yen. In addition, the MITI-controlled Japan External Trade Organization (JETRO) has played an important role in promoting Japanese exports. Its over 75 offices in 55 countries collect information and assist Japanese exporters in penetrating local markets.

Export subsidies provide an interesting example of how, after continual foreign pressure, Tokyo will change the form yet retain the substance of its industrial policies. Throughout the 1950s and early 1960s, firms could deduct up to 80 per cent of any income earned by exports, quickly depreciate any designated investments for industrial rationalization, exclude strategic machinery from import duties, and deduct royalties paid for foreign technology. In addition the MOF allows a number of special tax write-offs (jumbikin) for such things as bad debts, losses on goods returned unsold, bonuses, special repairs, warranties, overseas market development, overseas investment losses, pollution control, losses due to stock market fluctuations, purchases of computer equipment, foreign sales of patents, copyrights, and royalties.[30]

In 1964, after years of pressure and negotiations, Tokyo finally agreed to fulfill the promises to end all these subsidies that it had made nine years earlier in 1955 when it had originally joined GATT. But MOF simply rewrote the laws so that the subsidies could continue in different forms through even greater accelerated depreciation allowances linked to export performance, preferential lending by the Export-Import Bank, and promotion by JETRO. The Tax Deliberation Council attached to the Prime Minister's office annually revises the tax code in response to the changing needs of its strategic industries. The Council's proceedings are not open to the public.

Government-assisted export offensives (shuchu gouteki yushutsu) are another vital means of industrial policy. The Japanese are said to employ a 'laser beam' approach to trade designed to destroy foreign industries through dumping, take dominant market shares, and then raise prices to recoup their initial losses. In the United States this has happened most prominently in textiles, televisions, steel, automobiles, consumer electronics, VCRs, and semi-conductors. All of these were government-promoted strategic industries.

Dumping is achieved through export cartels whereby all the firms in a particular industry agree to cut prices and dump their excess productions overseas. Despite repeated foreign protests, Japanese dumping increased steadily with the number of cartels. By the early 1970s over a thousand cartels of various types were in effect, the majority of which were export cartels which coordinated the dumping of goods in foreign markets. Most of these industries were dumping goods at prices 20–30 per cent below the domestic price. Each member received quotas for both the domestic and foreign markets. Although supposedly temporary, these cartels soon became elaborate permanent arrangements.[31]

Import Barriers

Import barriers are as important as export subsidies in developing Japan's economy. There are two types of trade barriers, government barriers that directly discriminate against foreign goods, and government-influenced barriers that help protect established Japanese companies from both Japanese and foreign entrepreneurs.

To varying extents virtually every sector of Japan's economy remains protected by import barriers; they vary only in their degree of protection. The government's 115 public corporations ranging from monopolies over salt and tobacco, to public transportation like Japan National Railroads and Japan Airlines, represent a huge, highly protected economic sector. Only recently have some of these public corporations began buying foreign goods. For example, the government telecommunications monopoly, Nippon Telephone and Telegraph, opened up its procurements bidding to foreigners in 1980, but to date foreign manufacturers hold a miniscule 0.5 per cent or $1.5 million of a $3.3 billion annual market.

Japan's heavy industry sector is another highly protected area of the economy. Industries like steel, petrochemicals, metal refining, shipbuilding, synthetic fibers, petroleum refining and others were protected as infant industries during the 1950s and 1960s, and have been protected as senile industries since they lost their carefully nurtured comparative advantage after OPEC's quadrupling of oil prices in 1973. Some of these industries, such as aluminum and low quality steel, have steadily lost their domestic market share to foreign manufacturers.

Agriculture is the most openly protected of all Japan's economic sectors. High tariffs, subsidies, and a government monopoly over sales make Japanese consumers pay as much as five times more than the international market price for rice. Virtually all other agri-business crops are equally protected including citrus, milk, leather, and beef products.

Japan's consumer product markets are protected by much more subtle means including tied distribution systems and domestic cartels. Japanese manufacturers retain virtually 100 per cent market shares of such consumer durables ranging from automobiles to refrigerators to washing machines despite the comparative advantage held by such foreign firms as Hyndai, Whirlpool, or Black and Decker. South Korean televisions and stereos have market shares of less than 5 per cent despite being as much as 50 per cent cheaper than equivalent Japanese products.

Service industries such as banking, travel, insurance, law, telecommunications, or distribution remain another vast protected economic sector. Trade barriers in the service sector can be just as Kafkaesque as in other sectors. For example, the FTC initially rejected foreign complaints against the cartel among Japanese lawyers that restricts the ability of foreign lawyers to practice in Japan, by saying the matter was up to the Japan Federation of Bar Associations to decide.

Needless to say, the Japan Federation of Bar Associations denied any discrimination, and foreign lawyers continued to be refused permission to practice in Japan.

How does Japan's web of trade barriers work? How are they structured? Japan's trade barriers are best understood as a series of concentric walls surrounding specific industries, firms, and products within Japan. The outside walls – tariffs and quotas – are the most visible and easily penetrated. But within those walls are a half dozen others, each more difficult to clearly identify and surmount than the last. Japan's market opening steps, which started essentially in 1964 and have continued sporadically since, have largely concentrated on diminishing the two outer walls – tariffs and quotas – while the government simultaneously strengthened the inner walls.

Japan's average tariff rates are the lowest of the OECD countries: 2.5 per cent for Japan compared to 3.5 per cent in the United States and 4.5 per cent in the European Community. But even in tariffs the government has erected some nasty surprises designed to harm competitive imports. The government practises tariff escalation whereby raw materials receive no tariff while the more refined the import is, the larger the tariff. For example, imported logs have no duty, but if they have been turned into lumber or plywood they receive a considerable tariff. This, of course, is a blatant example of industrial policies designed to maximize Japan's manufacturing base and confine imports to raw materials.

Likewise, although Japan has steadily reduced the number of official quotas, it makes effective use of existing ones to impede competitive imports. In 1962 Japan had as many as 493 official import restriction quotas, but under foreign pressure has steadily reduced the number over the past 25 years until in 1988 there were only 27 items, 22 of which were agricultural goods. Japan's official quotas compare very favorably with the United States (20), France (46), Italy (38), and West Germany (14). In the industrial sector Japan has only five quotas compared to six for the United States, and 27 for France.[32] But Japanese bureaucrats have a crafty way of using quotas to discriminate against competitive imports similar to their use of tariff escalation. For example, American apple jam was first classified as a jam which was not subject to quota. Then after it began to sell and while a Japanese manufacturer was developing a similar product, it was reclassified as a fruit paste purée which was subject to a quota.

Behind these tariffs and quotas are a bewildering series of

government-imposed non-tariff barriers, that Japanese officials in principle claim do not exist. There are a variety of customs procedures that impede imports including a limitation on the number of bonded warehouses that handle imports, not allowing goods to clear customs on bond before duty payments are settled, and a maze of permit procedures that discriminate against foreign goods. To date, the government has still not implemented the part of the 1980 Foreign Exchange and Trade Control Law that requires a transparent import-licensing code.

Government product specifications are another effective non-tariff barrier. For example, any product's model change must be approved first by the government, a process which takes at least 18 months, during which the firm submits detailed plans to the government. This allows the foreign firm's competitors with close connections to the bureaucracy an opportunity to analyze and even copy the desired changes. Another effective barrier that pushed up the prices of imports is the necessity to inspect each product separately rather than by the shipload. For example, the Japanese government inspects each car, while the United States approves each shipload based on allowing Japanese and other foreign automobile producers to certify themselves. Of course, if Washington adopted a similar inspection process for Japanese cars it would be shrilly denounced as 'Japan bashing'.

In 1983, after two years of bitter negotiations, Tokyo agreed to eliminate the protectionist elements of 16 laws that used discriminatory standards and certifications to impede imports. One year later, in 1984, the US Underwriters Laboratory received Tokyo's approval as a foreign-designated testing organization for foreign factories and products. The Department of Commerce estimated that these changes alone would result in more than $5 billion in new annual US sales to Japan.

Unfortunately, according to veteran trade negotiator William Rapp, no significant new sales have emerged despite these changes.[33] Japan's bureaucracy has simply created more subtle means of impeding competitive imports, while foreign products continue to be inspected on a case-by-case basis, even though the Underwriters Laboratory is officially allowed to approve foreign products.

Despite their promise to use US Underwriters Laboratory results, Japanese ministries still do not have a procedure for accepting foreign testing in many areas, including Japanese industrial standards, pharmaceuticals, and medical equipment, and none can do the initial tests of Japan Institute of Science (JIS) marks. Thus, there has been little effective implementation of those standards that have been changed. For example, Tokyo requires that not only all drug testing must take place in Japan, but that pharmaceutical companies must submit the health records of all their executives as part of the approval process. Such a requirement, of course, has nothing to do with the quality of the foreign product but is one more effective means of impeding competitive imports. In areas like telecommunications, foreign firms have so far not been granted access to the ministry's deliberative council in which standards are discussed and set, even though Japanese law now requires such participation for industry-association-standards advisory committees.[34]

The patent office continues to sit atop a huge backlog of foreign patent, trademark, and copyright applications. There are now as many as four times as many patent filings as in the United States, and patent applications can take from four to six years to be processed. Patent applications are open to the public after 18 months, allowing competitors full access to the ideas and procedures of the application, forcing foreign producers to carefully consider the risks of potential loss of their comparative advantage. Japanese firms enjoy a further advantage by being allowed to object to a patent grant before the patent is actually submitted. This causes further delays during which the Japanese firm can perfect its own technology.

Japan's government often goes to ludicrous extremes to bar imports. For example, in the early 1970s Tokyo rejected an American request to sell grapefruit in Japan with the following 'logic': (1) Japanese would not like grapefruit; (2) Japanese tangerine sales (and farmers) would be drastically hurt, an event which might upset the social stability of rural constituencies on which the ruling LDP depended, perhaps leading to JCP election victories; and the ever invoked general plea that (3) Japan was merely 'a small island country with few natural resources' making its way in a cold, cruel world. Japan's negotiators, however, did suggest importing a few grapefruits as a sign of sincerity with the understanding, of course, that no significant numbers could be imported. Another example comes from the early 1980s when the United States was pressuring Japan to open its cigarette market.[35] At that time, American cigarettes could only be sold at 15 per cent of all licensed outlets, and only after being walloped with a 90 per cent tariff. Needless to say, under these circumstances American cigarette firms had managed to capture only 1 per cent of an $8 billion market. Then Finance Minister Michio

Watanabe responded to these complaints by saying that the 'reason we don't smoke foreign cigarettes isn't their high price; it's that they don't taste good'.[36]

Other non-tariff barriers include capital controls, closed financial markets, government procurement, subsidies, and research benefits distributed only to Japanese firms, foreign investment controls in 11 designated industries, and the attitude constantly fed to the public by the ruling triad and mass media that foreign goods are inferior and the only reason they do not sell is that foreign firms do not try hard enough in Japan's wide open markets.

Government-influenced barriers can be as effective as official non-tariff barriers in impeding competitive imports. The government usually dismisses criticism of such barriers as the complex distribution system, restriction on hostile corporate take-overs, amakudari, or the keiretsu system by claiming these are aspects of Japanese culture and thus above reproach. But in all these areas the government has had a strong role in shaping the present system, even if it was not specifically designed to impede imports.

The bewildering maze of the distribution system is an oft-cited non-tariff trade barrier. There are four times more retailers per capita in Japan than in the United States. Large retail outlets hold about 20 per cent of all sales. About 92 per cent of retail establishments are single-line or neighborhood stores, which account for about 80 per cent of retail sales. Over half of these sell food items, often specializing in one product such as meat, fish, or vegetables.[37] These stores are typically family businesses, often opened by men who have retired from a career in business or government, and are undercapitalized and unable to finance inventory.

In a free market, most of these 'mom and pop' outlets would quickly go out of business. But they are propped up by large corporations which seek their economic support while the LDP entices their political support. Keiretsu tie together a vast web of small retail stores through such means as preferential loans, rebates, return privileges, easy credit, promissory notes, and dealer aids. Dealer aids can include management consulting, leisure activities, and formation of channel members social clubs. As a result these outlets generally sell only the products of their corporate patron rather than offering a variety of makes based on price.

Corporations can erect these huge tied distribution systems because the government has imposed strict limits on the size and capacity of new, large retail outlets. Any store of over 500 square meters must be approved by the Japanese government, which in practice means approval by the small stores in the trading area. Since 1980 only about 150 stores per year have been given permission to open.[38] The government supports this vast inefficient system because it serves as an indirect welfare system to support millions of people who might otherwise be unemployed, and supporters of the opposition parties. The LDP is becoming increasingly dependent on the votes of the lower income, urban electorate. In addition, the Sole Agent System allowed by Article 21 of the Tariff Law gives monopoly import privileges to any agent of a foreign producer. As a result of these distribution barriers, foreign manufacturers cannot achieve economies of scale, since they can only sell a small percentage of 'luxury' goods.

The foreign manufacturer's troubles do not end if it tries to buy its way into the system via a joint venture with a Japanese corporation. More often than not the Japanese firm will continue to limit the foreign manufacturer's market share while raking in huge profits from selling the product as a 'luxury good'. The reason for this is that much of the Japanese economy is dominated by the huge keiretsu which include dozens of huge corporations, each presiding over their own manufacturing and distribution hierarchies. Because of the web of cross-share holdings that bind keiretsu and average about 25 per cent of its total outstanding shares, a member company will first buy a needed product from another Keiretsu company. In the unlikely event that it cannot find such a product within the keiretsu, it will then approach another keiretsu. Although supposedly rivals, Keiretsu hold an average 5 per cent of each others stock. Only then if the company cannot find the desired product will it go to a foreign firm. Although Japanese argue that keiretsu are beyond criticism because they are a part of Japanese culture, they essentially exist because the government has refused to uphold the anti-trust laws.

Foreign manufacturers desiring to sell in Japan are also blocked from taking the easiest route to a strong market presence – buying a related Japanese company that already has a skilled staff and distribution system. Unfortunately, hostile take-overs do not occur in Japan. In 1986 Japanese firms took over 44 American firms worth $1.6 billion, while no American firms took over any Japanese firms. If Japan's markets were as free as Japanese claim they are, it would be no trouble taking over most Japanese firms since they have such a low ratio of net worth to assets. Again because of the web of cross-sharings both within and between keiretsu, and the rampant insider trading in Japan's stock markets, Japanese companies may be vulnerable to take-over on paper, but virtually impossible to take over at any market price.

Amakudari is yet another non-tariff barrier that can discriminate against imports since the bureaucrats will protect the firms they will potentially parachute into. The government could stop this practice but it provides unemployed bureaucrats with lucrative jobs and disperses their expertise into the economy. Some foreign firms which have invested in Japan are beginning to hire former bureaucrats to offset the advantage of their rivals.

Between 1981 and 1987 Tokyo sponsored seven 'significant market opening steps' that made Japan 'the world's most open economy'. How far have these much-publicized liberalization steps gone towards actually creating a market in which international comparative advantage rather than connections determines the amount and types of goods sold? In 1984 the US government estimated that the removal of most Japanese trade barriers could result in up to $15 billion a year of new US imports within three years of implementation, and criticized much of each new market opening package revealed by Tokyo as simply rewordings or slight enlargings of promises made in earlier market opening steps.[39] The same report pointed out that the United States had at least a 20 per cent comparative price advantage in such goods as telecommunications, agricultural products, satellites, tobacco, services, finance, pulp and paper products, fruit, livestock and leather, computers, computer parts, computer peripherals, heavy electrical machinery, medical and diagnostic equipment, aluminum refining, petrochemicals, urea manufacturing, ferosilicon, cardboard paper, ammonia, phosphoric acid, copper, naphtha, caustic soda, processed foods, and fertilizer, yet had an average 5 per cent market share in all these goods. Trade Representative Brock added that 'there are 8 to 10 depressed industries; we have a better product at a better price in each of those industries'.

Japan's 'significant market opening steps' date from 1961 when the Cabinet Council for the Advancement of Trade Liberalization was created. Johnson vividly describes the crisis atmosphere that accompanied even the severely limited liberalization steps of the early 1960s: 'The press prattled on endlessly about the "second coming of the black ships," "the defenselessness of the Japanese islands in the face of attack from huge foreign capitalist powers," and "the readying of the Japanese economy for a bloodstained battle between national capital and foreign capital" '.[40] The rhetoric has not changed at all in the quarter century since; Japanese still greet everyone of Tokyo's trade concessions, however insignificant or however just, as yet another example of 'Japan bashing' by the United States or Western Europe against a 'poor, defenseless Japan'.

Japan's markets remain largely protected even after 25 years of 'liberalization'. Trade barriers will continue to be important parts of industrial policies designed to develop sunrise and protect sunset industries. Tokyo will also continue to discuss its markets in contradictory terms; while claiming Japanese markets are the world's most open, in the next breath Japanese justify barriers because Japan is a 'small, poor, resourceless country' dependent on world trade for vital imports. While all countries have trade barriers, Japan's have been the most intricate, the least transparent, and the most successful in aiding its economic development.

CONCLUSION

Japan's industrial policies have been hugely successful. Its GNP developed at an average rate of 10 per cent a year between 1950 and 1973, and about 5 per cent a year since. From 1955 to 1972, out of 25 industries, Japan steadily narrowed its productivity gap with the United States in every industry except petroleum. In 1955 the United States had a technology lead in all but one industry – rubber and plastic products. In fields like non-electrical machinery, electrical machinery, motor vehicles, other transport equipment, and precision, the difference was huge. By 1972 Japan had surpassed the United States in eight industries, and was within ten percentage points in seven others.[41] In 1987 Japan's per capita income surpassed that of the United States to become the world's second highest after Switzerland.

What have been the costs of this rapid and largely egalitarian economic growth? The costs to the Japanese have been relatively limited. The government concentrated on economic rather than social growth, so that while Japan's standard of living rose rapidly , its quality of life as measured by such indices as commuting time, pollution, parks, leisure time, and purchasing power has in many respects got worse or stayed at the same low level relative to that of other OECD countries. While foreign consumers have benefitted from increasingly inexpensive, high-quality Japanese goods, foreign countries that did not use industrial policies to promote their industries have lost hundreds of billions of dollars in sales because of Tokyo's industrial policies.

But these industrial policies have in many ways distorted Japan's own economy. MITI's allocation of money, protection, and technology to the firms with the largest market shares stimulated all firms in that industry to throw themselves into an orgy of capital investment and production, which brought down prices as they achieved economies of scale. The problem was that in economic downturns, the industry suffered from excessive production and competition. Each firm refused to cut back its production or raise prices on its own for fear its competitors would take advantage of this and expand their own market share. So MITI had to form production, market, or price cartels among the affected firms for the down-turns' duration. Meanwhile, the firms dumped their excess production overseas. These cartels only begat more cartels, since firms had no incentive to curb their investments in more production capacity. Thus, firms responded not to consumer demand, but to market share with their rivals.

Yet Japanese would argue that these 'unfortunate' results were a small price to pay for industrial policies that transformed Japan from a poverty-stricken, war-devastated country into the world's most dynamic economic power. But in the zero-sum game of neo-mercantilism, the success of Japanese producers and subsequent boost in GNP translates into the failures of foreign producers and losses to their respective economies. Tokyo's neo-mercantilist industrial policies will become more subtle, but no less successful in solidifying Japan's hegemony over the world economy..

NOTES

1. Thomas Pugel, *Access to Japanese Markets*, p. 210.
2. James Abegglen, *US-Japan Economic Relations*, p. 33.
3. Chalmers Johnson, *MITI and Japan's Modern Economic Miracle*.
4. Ibid, for details see chapters 1–4.
5. Ibid., p. 90.
6. Ibid., p. 97.
7. Ibid., p. 157.
8. Ibid., p. 209.
9. Ibid., p. 216.

10. Schmiegelow, op. cit., p. 280.
11. Ibid.
12. Yamamura, *Economic Policy in Postwar Japan*, pp. 58–9.
13. Ibid., pp. 60–70.
14. Schmiegelow, op. cit., p. 280.
15. William Rapp, 'Japan's Invisible Barriers to Trade', in Pugel, p. 24.
16. For a full discussion of the Soda Ash cartel see ibid., pp. 27–30.
17. Ibid.
18. Ibid. pp. 32–3.
19. Ibid., p. 32.
20. Johnson, op. cit., p. 67.
21. Takahasa Nakamura, *The Postwar Japanese Economy*, p. 450.
22. Clyde Prestowitz, *Trading Places: How We Allowed Japan to Take The Lead*, pp. 76, 27.
23. Dan Okimoto and Gary Saxonhouse, 'Technology and the Future of the Economy', in Kozo Yamamura and Yasukichi Yasuba, *Japan's Political Economy*, p. 393.
24. Terutomo Ozawa, op cit., in Pugel, p. 148.
25. Ibid., p.148.
26. *Japan 1986, An International Comparison*.
27. Ibid.
28. Okimoto, op. cit., in Yamamura, pp. 406–19.
29. Rapp, op. cit., in Pugel, p. 23.
30. Johnson, op. cit., p. 234.
31. Yamamura, op. cit., pp. 60–70.
32. Pugel, op. cit., p. 47.
33. Rapp, op. cit., Pugel, p. 35.
34. Ibid., p. 41.
35. Thomas Pepper *et al*, *Japan's Competitive Edge*, pp. 77–8.
36. Ibid.
37. Douglas, op. cit., in Pugel, p. 108.
38. Ibid., p. 108.
39. Rapp, op. cit., Pugel, p. 22.
40. Johnson, op. cit., p. 252.
41. Pugel, op. cit., p. 212.

12 Foreign Policy

Japan's foreign policy goals have been remarkably consistent since Commodore Perry dragged Japan into the world political economy in 1854 – only the means have changed. For almost 140 years the government has single-mindedly attempted to achieve for Japan four interrelated goals: (1) military and economic security; (2) rapid modernization; (3) East Asian and global power; and (4) international recognition of all Japan's accomplishments. The means to achieve these goals, however, were dramatically different before and after 1945: mercantilist and imperialist before; neo-mercantilist since. Military and technological defeat – by Perry's gunboats in 1854 and the atomic bomb in 1945 – were the stimulus for both foreign policy eras as Japanese leaders became obsessed with reversing both the cause and the humiliation of these defeats.

Throughout the late nineteenth and early twentieth century, the government succeeded in achieving all four goals. The Meiji leaders built up a powerful military and economy strong enough to defeat first China (1895) and then Russia (1905), and carve out a northeast Asian empire in the process. The Western powers rewarded Japan's modernization and imperialism by renouncing the 'unequal treaties' imposed after 1854 which had stripped Japan of its sovereignty, and accepting it as a member of the Great Power club. Britain started this process by forming an alliance with Japan in 1902. Japan's effort to gain international acceptance for its growing power in East Asia and the world economy reached a height in 1919, when Tokyo was designated one of the 'Big Five' powers responsible for drawing up and implementing the Versailles peace treaty. Japan's international security, status, and power were further strengthened during the 1920s as Tokyo played a leading role in the League of Nations, the Washington and London arms reduction pacts, and the Kellogg-Briand pact, whose signatories renounced war. Unfortunately, Japan threw away all these gains after its conquest of Manchuria in 1931, as it rejected the League of Nations attempts to create a peaceful and cooperative world community, and instead embarked on a step-by-step conquest of East Asia. Japanese imperialism, which resulted in the deaths of an estimated 20 million East Asians during Tokyo's 14 years of aggression after 1931, was finally defeated with the atomic bombing of Hiroshima and Nagasaki in August 1945.

In the 45 years since, Japan has been overwhelmingly successful in overcoming the physical and psychological devastation of defeat and achieving all of its four interrelated goals. Today, Japan has surpassed the United States as the world's most dynamic economic power; 35 per cent of America's huge debt is now serviced by Japan, meaning a continually growing shift of vast economic resources from the former to the latter. Although America's current account deficit with Japan peaked at $60 billion in 1986, it has averaged about $50 billion since, despite a massive devaluation of the dollar.

An increasingly interdependent world is becoming increasingly dependent on Japan's vast financial, technological, and corporate power; the more dependent the world is on Japan, the greater are its military and economic security. Although there are considerable mixed feelings around the world over the means Tokyo used to achieve its goals of global power, modernization, security, and acceptance, almost everyone agrees that its accomplishments are astonishing and Japanese industrial policies, corporate strategy, and industrial structure could serve as economic development models for other countries.

These accomplishments are largely a result of Tokyo's single-minded focus for the past 45 years on neo-mercantilist foreign and domestic policies. The basis of Tokyo's accomplishments has been a close relationship with the United States, which has provided for Japan's security by shielding it under its nuclear umbrella and continually sponsoring Japan's economic development and reintegration into the world community. Thus, Japan's goals were achieved by a virtuous cycle whereby international acceptance of Tokyo's membership in the continually expanding world economy at once guarantees Japan's military and economic security and gives it the opportunity to further expand its economic power, which in turn deepens its international status and security, and makes it even more powerful.

Since 1945 Japan's foreign policy has passed through three phases in which the government used slightly different tactics to achieve its goals. During the Occupation (1945–52) the government made the most of its subordinate relationship with Washington to set the basis of its neo-mercantilism; all Japan's resources were mobilized for economic development while Tokyo allowed only a token rearmament. The vast restructuring of Japan's political economy during the Occupation blossomed with a GNP growth rate which averaged 10 per cent a year during the economic miracle phase (1952–73), when Japan developed from a war-devastated third world country into an economic superpower whose corporations captured markets through-out the world. OPEC's quadrupling of oil prices in 1973 plunged the world into an era of economic stagnation and inflation from which it is only now emerging. Although because of its great dependence on imported energy and resources to feed its economic furnace, Japan was initially the hardest hit of all the industrial countries, it soon recovered and has averaged almost 5 per cent GNP growth since, the highest of all the OECD countries. Tokyo achieved this by following a policy of comprehensive security from 1973 on, a strategy designed to minimalize its dependence on foreign resources and markets by diversifying them and in turn making them dependent on Japanese finances and technology.

FOREIGN POLICY UNDER THE OCCUPATION (1945–52)

In the summer of 1945 Japan's government clung to delusions of ultimate victory over the West, despite three years of continual defeats in which, one by one, its armies and navies were destroyed, the vast conquests of its newly won East Asian and Pacific Empire were torn away, and its cities burned to the ground by endless waves of B–29 bombers. The government had mobilized Japan's population of 60 million people to meet the pending Allied invasion with human wave attacks in which 'Japanese spirit' would destroy the West's material power. Although millions of Japanese would die in the attacks, Japan would ultimately win. But the atomic bombing of Hiroshima and Nagasaki convinced a majority of the Cabinet that even Japanese spirit could not defeat America's power to split the atom, and on 15 August Japan surrendered.

Yet, despite this devastating defeat, Japan's leaders had not given up their dream of achieving the interrelated goals of economic and military security, modernization, and international acceptance of Japan's growing power over East Asia and the world economy. But while the ends remained the same, the means were changed. Imperialism was completely discredited as a means to these ends; from now Japan would rise to greatness by concentrating its energies and resources on economic development, while rejecting militarism. Only in this way could defeat be turned into victory. Prime Minister Yoshida captured this new strategy succinctly when he said that Japan's destiny 'was to be a global power, and the expansion as well as the security of the state was best guaranteed by close alliance with the dominant Western power in Asia and the Pacific . . . just as the United States was once a colony of Great Britain but is now the stronger of the two, if Japan becomes a colony of the United States it will eventually become the stronger'.[1]

Tokyo was fortunate that its goals generally coincided with those of Washington. America's postwar policy was to recreate a prosperous, expanding world economy in which issues would be resolved through cooperation in the United Nations rather than through force. To this end the United States attempted to demilitarize and democratize Japan, and make it a responsible member of the world economy. As the Cold War broke out between the United States and Soviet Union in 1947, Japan was identified along with Germany and Britain as one of the three key economic powers that had to be kept out of Soviet hands. Thus, Washington shifted its policy emphasis from Japan's democratization to its economic revival.

Theoretically, the Supreme Command for Allied Powers (SCAP) under MacArthur had vast powers over Japan during the Occupation. In reality, since it ruled Japan through the bureaucracy and elected governments, Japan's leadership had considerable success in adapting SCAP directives to Japanese political realities and goals. Charged with implementing SCAP directives, the bureaucrats had wide leeway to change Washington's policies when they conflicted with those of Tokyo. For example, the bureaucrats considerably weakened and delayed SCAP's land, labor, and zaibatsu reforms. Meanwhile, Yoshida, who was prime minister for five and a half of the Occupation's seven years, was highly successful in diluting Washington's efforts to push Japan's rearmament or to completely cut off its trade with China. By the end of the Occupation, Japan had undergone sweeping economic and political reforms that laid the basis for its economic dynamism.

Japan's economic revival and reintegration with East Asia and the world economy, however, resulted from a combination of Washington's massive economic and diplomatic efforts, as well as luck. Washington wanted to turn Japan into the 'workshop of Asia' by developing triangular trade between Southeast Asia, Japan, and the United States through a division of labor whereby Washington supplied technology and capital, Tokyo intermediate and consumer goods, and Southeast Asia raw materials. But Japanese manufacturers had little success penetrating Southeast Asia during the 1940s since the region was desperately undergoing reconstruction and independence struggles as the colonial powers of Britain, France, and Holland reasserted their former control. Imperial preferences and deep-seated anti-Japanese sentiments among Southeast Asians kept Japanese exports to a minimum.

Japan's trade with Southeast Asia and the world economy only took off with the Korean War, which Yoshida described as 'a gift from the gods'.[2] Allied war procurements from Japan boosted GNP almost 50 per cent alone in 1950, and set off a virtuous circle of foreign demand for Japanese products, leading to economies of scale and capital with which to buy vital foreign resources and technology, which in turn lowered prices and increased demand further – a process which has continued up to the present. Japan's export boom was further stimulated by Tokyo's promotion of export subsidies, cartels, and import barriers for its key industries. As early as 1952, the Europeans were complaining about Japan's 'unfair trade competition. . . . unethical use of . . . industrial designs and trademarks, and excessive Japanese government aid to shipping, shipbuilding and other industries connected with exports'. Yoshida did not deny these accusations, but instead attempted to deter them by suggesting the classical neo-mercantilist device of dividing markets and fixing prices: 'where competition between them might seem unavoidable, British and Japanese manufacturers should cooperate in developing markets through a judicious arrangement of the outlets and types of goods to be reserved for each country'.[3]

This has been Japan's standard trade policy up to the present: government and business extensively cooperate to capture overseas markets through export 'dumping' offensives; after the affected industries protest and gain their government's support, Tokyo then negotiates export quotas that secure the captured market shares, thus enabling industry to raise prices and recoup its initial profit losses caused by the dumping; finally the Japanese exporters gradually widen their market shares against the severely weakened foreign producers, thus dominating the particular market and vastly increasing their economies of scale with which to lower prices and assault even tougher markets elsewhere. By 1952 Japanese industry and trade had rapidly rebounded thanks to this combination of government-aided export offensives built on the earlier Occupation reforms, American sponsorship in the world economy, and the Korean War procurements boom.

Another highly successful area of Tokyo's foreign policy was regaining Japanese sovereignty at minimal cost. In the late 1940s Japan's leaders faced a dilemma: Tokyo desired a peace treaty from all the allies that would ensure Japan's return to sovereignty and allow it to concentrate on economic growth with its security guaranteed by others. But this type of security agreement actually led to the stationing of foreign troops in Japan, and the United States would only sign a peace treaty which assured that Japan would stay in the West, while the Soviet Union and China were against such a treaty.

At first Tokyo tried to gain a security guarantee through the United Nations, but rejected this option by mid–1947 when it had become obvious that the UN was ineffective. Later that year, Prime Minister Katayama asked Washington to guarantee its long-term military security. But the United States was divided over its security policy toward Japan at this time. Tokyo and MacArthur used Article 9 as an excuse to prevent any Japanese rearmament, while Washington's policy was to ally only with countries that were prepared to defend themselves. In 1949 Washington began strongly pressuring MacArthur to rearm Japan, which he resisted until the Korean War broke out in June 1950. After the North Korean attack, MacArthur ordered Yoshida to create a 75 000-strong National Police Reserve. Yoshida tried to resist, claiming that this would harm the economy, lacked public support, and would reopen the scars of defeat, but finally gave in. Washington made it clear that any peace treaty restoring Japan's sovereignty had to be accompanied by a security treaty tying Japan firmly to the West. Although Japan's leadership was severely split over the wisdom of signing a security treaty with Washington, Yoshida realized this was the best means of achieving Japan's security and development policies, even if it meant poor relations with the Soviet Union and China, which refused to accept the treaties. Japan had no choice: Washington would not accept an independent, neutral Japan that could possibly shift to the Soviet camp.

The peace and security treaties were simultaneously signed in September 1951, and became effective six months later on 28 April 1952. Tokyo's concessions included allowing US bases and a gradual rearmament in return for shelter under America's nuclear and conventional military umbrella. Yoshida successfully walked the tightrope between American pressure to rearm and Japanese opposition to rearmament. This was the best deal possible for Japan, since its independence and security were guaranteed, while its economy was boosted by billions of dollars of American procurements and continued access to the vast American market.

Japan's relations with China were yet another area where skillful diplomacy allowed Tokyo to maintain both its economic and military security interests. For Washington, Japan's relations with communist China presented a deep dilemma. On the one hand it was argued that Japanese trade could moderate China's leadership and pull it away from dependence on the Soviet Union. On the other hand, it was feared that if Japan became too dependent on China, Tokyo would be pulled into the Soviet bloc. Yoshida realized that China's revolutionary passions would eventually subside and it would become a moderate member of the world community. Trade would thus simultaneously serve Japan's economic and security interests by mellowing China. Washington tried to force Japan to cut off its China trade after the Korean War broke out in 1950, but it secretly continued through a variety of front companies. Yoshida was also forced to sign the Japan-Taiwan Peace Treaty on 18 April 1952, but did so only after limiting Japan's recognition of the Koumintang regime to the area directly under its control. Finally, Secretary of State Dulles forced Yoshida to sign the 'Yoshida Letter' condemning China for its excesses, but calling for future relations if China became moderate. Like the security treaty, the Taiwan treaty was the best under the circumstances – Japan continued to trade with the two regimes, while both China and Taiwan renounced their demands for reparations.

Despite being constrained by foreign rule, Tokyo was highly successful in achieving a basis for many of its goals during the Occupation. Japan's economy underwent massive economic and political reforms vital to its economic dynamism. Joint Washington-Tokyo efforts to promote exports and reintegrate Japan with Southeast Asia and the world economy took off with the outbreak of the Korean War. The peace and security treaties allowed a sovereign Japan military and economic security within a world economy protected by America's nuclear umbrella. Japanese companies continued to profit from the China trade despite the official diplomatic cut-off.

FOREIGN POLICY OF THE ECONOMIC MIRACLE (1952–73)

During Japan's 'economic miracle' development phase, Tokyo identified and perfected the policy of maintaining a low profile on all political issues while pouring all its resources and energies into economic development. Although in reality, Tokyo's attempts to 'separate politics and economics' (Seikei Bunri) proved difficult, since foreign economic problems caused by Japanese neo-mercantilist policies soon become political problems, on the whole Tokyo was highly successful in convincing others and even itself that such a separation was possible. With its sovereignty returned and security guaranteed, Tokyo built on the SCAP's sweeping political and economic reforms by concentrating on rapid economic growth and international recognition of its achievements. But Tokyo faced a dilemma: Japan's economic growth depended on neo-mercantilist policies of maximizing exports and minimalizing imports, but these policies conflicted with Japan's desire to join the international organizations that would fuel its economic growth – to join these organizations Japan would have to give up its neo-mercantilist policies.

Tokyo finessed these dilemmas in two ways. First it continued to rely on Washington to persuade other countries to allow Japanese membership in key international economic organizations. Meanwhile, it continually made promises to open its economy while in reality making only cosmetic reforms and continuing its neo-mercantilist policies. As a result Japan was allowed into international economic organizations without having to pay the full membership costs. For example, Japan joined GATT in 1955 by promising to open its markets to foreign exports, but after joining, it built up an even more elaborate web of tariff and non-tariff barriers. Tokyo followed the same policy when it joined the OECD in 1964. It promised eventually to liberalize but negotiated 18 reservations with the OECD which allowed it to keep its trade barriers. In fact, Tokyo actually increased its restrictions on foreign investments after it joined the OECD, and only began a slow process of opening after 1967, which even today has not been completed. Thus, Japan enjoyed all the economic and psychological benefits of membership in international economic organizations without having to pay any significant costs.

Bilateral trade relations were handled in a similar fashion. Foreign complaints about unfair Japanese trade practices were dismissed as 'misunderstandings' or 'settled' with cosmetic 'market opening steps' that left the trade imbalances unaffected. For example, American officials had periodically complained about Japan's neo-mercantilist trade policies since the Japanese invasion of 'dollar blouses' in the mid–1950s had hurt American textile producers. At the Hakone Conference in 1961, five United States Cabinet secretaries met with their Japanese counterparts in an attempt to resolve complaints by

American producers that they were being hurt by Japanese import barriers and export offensives. The Japanese countered these charges by claiming that these were mere misunderstandings and the American producers simply were not trying hard enough in either market. Instead, the Japanese demanded that the United States buy more from Japan to offset America's $1 billion trade surplus. The Americans countered that while there was a trade surplus, American procurements in Japan had an overall payments surplus and thus the Japanese had nothing to complain about. But while the Americans presented a logical and documented argument, the Japanese did not change their policies.

This pattern has continued through today. Japan's trade negotiators continually repeat the refrain that Japan's markets are the world's most open and foreign producers do not sell more in Japan because their goods are inferior and they do not try hard enough. In response to foreign accusations of dumping, the Japanese dig in their heels until threatened with retaliation, and then negotiate 'Orderly Marketing Agreements' (OMAs) or 'Voluntary Export Restrictions' (VERs) that solidify the Japanese producers' huge market shares captured through dumping. This pattern has been repeated with such products as textiles, televisions, steel, automobiles, semiconductors, and VCRs with the United States, European Community, and other countries.

Another successful aspect of Japan's neo-mercantilist foreign policy during this period was its ability to resist the revaluation of the yen until the last moment. In 1949 SCAP had set the yen at a ratio of 360 to the dollar to boost Japanese exports. The level was selected because it was the point where all major industries could be competitive in world markets. For the next 21 years, until Tokyo was finally forced to revalue the yen, its currency became increasingly undervalued as Japan's economy became more powerful and successful. Although by 1971 Japan had become the world's second largest economy, Tokyo refused to consider revaluing its currency, despite the fact that it was the only major industrial country that refused to do so. Meanwhile, the United States suffered increasingly severe trade and payments inbalances as the yen became steadily undervalued. Finally, in August 1971 President Nixon imposed import tariffs to force Japan and other countries to revalue their currencies. But while the other countries accepted their currency revaluations, Tokyo spent $4 billion in currency markets attempting to prop up the dollar. It was not until December of that year that Japan finally agreed to join the other industrial countries and revalue its currency. The yen was revalued 16 per cent to a new fixed rate of 308 to the dollar. In February 1973 President Nixon took the United States off the gold standard, thus forcing all major currencies to float against the dollar.

Japan's 'economic miracle' of an average 10 per cent annual economic growth was largely achieved during this period because its trade partners allowed Japan to continue its neo-mercantilist trade and industrial policies. Japan joined and enjoyed the membership of key international economic organizations while paying minimum costs; it brushed aside foreign complaints about export dumping and import barriers; it maintained an undervalued yen until long after the other industrial countries had revalued their currencies. Tokyo achieved all this through its skilfull foreign policy of first denying neo-mercantilist policies, then making cosmetic gestures to deflect foreign criticism while continuing those same policies in a more subtle or controlled way.

During this period, Japan succeeded in replacing the United States as the dominant economic power in East Asia. By the mid-1950s triangular trade between the United States, Japan, and East Asia was solidly established; by the mid-1960s Japanese producers had taken over either the first or second largest market shares of every East Asian country. Between the mid-1960s, when Tokyo first began to lift its capital controls, and 1973 the total amount of Japanese direct foreign investments in East Asia had risen from virtually nothing to surpass that of the United States. With a balance of payments surplus after 1965, Japan could afford to lift its capital controls to take advantage of cheap labor and resources, and growing markets overseas. Japanese DFI was also an excuse to 'house-clean' Japan by exporting heavy polluting industries.

Tokyo achieved its long-standing goal of becoming the dominant economic power in East Asia by a sustained neo-mercantilism that employed a variety of means that went beyond export offensives and import barriers. One of the most important means of ousting its American and European rivals from the region was through economic aid. Tokyo mastered the art of using foreign 'aid' as a highly effective and subtle export subsidy by tying any aid to purchases of Japanese products.[4] Tied foreign aid captures markets in the recipient country thus increasing the economies of scale for the targeted Japanese industry, enabling it to cut prices and be successful in third markets. Aid was also tied to the use of Japanese companies in infrastructure projects or extraction industries. Aside from boosting Japanese industry, and thus the Japanese economy, tied aid also boosts Japanese security since it makes the recipient dependent on Japanese equipment, technology, capital, and expertise.

Japan's first postwar aid was in the form of reparations to some of the countries it had devastated during the war. Article 14 of the Peace Treaty had required Japan to pay reparations, but the amount would be determined by negotiations between Japan and the recipient. Eventually, ten East Asian countries – Burma, the Philippines, Indonesia, South Vietnam, Cambodia, Laos, Malaya, South Korea, Singapore, and Thailand – received reparations, while China and Taiwan abandoned their claims in an attempt to win favor with Japan. The total reparations bill of $1.5 billion during the 1950s amounted to less than 0.2 per cent of Japan's GNP during this time, but proved to be an excellent boost for Japanese exports since all reparations were tied to the purchase of Japanese goods and services.[5]

Starting with an initial outlay of $50 million in 1955, Tokyo has steadily increased its general aid outlays up through today. By 1965 Japan's total aid amount had risen almost ten times to $490 million, and by 1973 had reached $5.8 billion, or 1.42 per cent of GNP. This seems like an impressive amount until it is realized that Tokyo included direct foreign investments and tied aid in the total. In 1973 Japan's Official Development Aid (ODA), was only 0.21 per cent of GNP compared to an OECD average of assistance and multilateral aid of 0.40 per cent of GNP. In 1969 48 per cent of Japan's total aid went to Southeast Asia, and almost 90 per cent to all of Asia, while Latin America received 5.9 per cent, Africa 2.5 per cent, and other regions 1.4 per cent. Aid went hand in hand with trade. The more important a developing country's markets or resources to Japan's economy, the larger Tokyo's aid package to that country. The most outrageous attempt by Tokyo to send aid to Southeast Asia occurred during Prime Minister Kishi's tour of the region in 1957, when he promised large-scale technical and industrial assistance tied to purchases of Japanese goods and services. He neglected to tell the recipients or Washington that the aid would actually come from the United States. Washington quietly refused Kishi's later request for money.[6]

Japan boosted its economic presence in East Asia by participating in a range of regional organizations including the Colombo Plan (1954), ESCAFE (1955), the Bandung Conference (1955), and Asian and Pacific Council and Asian Parliamentarian's Union (1966). But Tokyo's most important regional political initiative was its creation, leadership, and financial contributions to the Asian Development Bank (ABD) in the mid-1960s.[7] Japan has used its membership in all these organizations as a means to expand its economic presence in the region, either by directly selling its goods and services, or by collecting information on economic conditions that would later be passed on to Japanese companies. During this period, Tokyo ignored the region's most important organization, the Association for Southeast Asian Nations (ASEAN). Japan preferred to deal with these countries on a bilateral basis, and thus undercut any negotiating power they could achieve by working together.

During the late 1960s and early 1970s Japan began to economically tie together Northeast Asia as firmly as it had Southeast Asia. Tokyo finally restored relations with South Korea in 1965, after agreeing to extend Seoul $500 million in 'aid', refusing out of pride to call it reparations. Tokyo quickly followed President Nixon's May 1972 trip to Beijing by restoring relations that September. Although trade with both countries boomed after the restoration of diplomatic relations, it was built upon the vigorous trade that had developed since 1945 despite the absence of formal ties. In 1972 the United States restored Okinawa to Japan as part of the textile restraint agreement worked out between Tokyo and Washington two years earlier. Thus, by 1973 Japan had developed deep economic and political ties with almost every East Asian country, supplanting America's former domination of the region.

Throughout this period, despite all these economic and political successes, Tokyo maintained its resistance to Washington's attempts to force it to play a stronger defense role. Although Yoshida agreed to create the 75 000-man National Police Reserve force in 1950, he continued to resist Dulle's calls for its conversion into a 350 000-man military establishment. Yoshida finally agreed to convert the national police into a 180 000-man National Self Defense Force (SDF) in 1954, but only in return for signing a Mutual Defense Assistance Agreement on 8 May 1954 in which the United States essentially agreed to pay for its establishment. Tokyo's Basic National Defense Policy of 1957 was its first attempt to define the role of the SDF in light of the conflict between Article 9 banning any military establishment and its security treaty with the United States. The policy limited self-defense to Japanese territory, declared that Tokyo had no obligation to defend the United States, and refused to permit any nuclear weapons on Japanese soil. The SDF's tentative legal status was strengthened by the Supreme Court ruling in the Sunakawa Case in 1959 that Japan as a sovereign state has an inherent right of self-defense.

The Kishi government reinforced the essentially free ride it was getting from the United States on defense by its signing of the Treaty of Mutual Cooperation and Security on 19 January 1960, which made any American use of troops in or from Japan dependent on prior consultation with Tokyo, while it resisted Washington's attempts to get a Japanese commitment to regional defense. The massive demonstrations that greeted Kishi's attempts to ratify the treaty in the Diet were subsequently used by Tokyo over the years to justify its low defense expenditures when pressured by Washington for increased spending.

Japan's military security largely rests under America's nuclear umbrella. Yet this did not deter the Sato government from announcing its four-point anti-nuclear policy in January 1968 by which Japan will: (1) not possess, produce, or allow nuclear weapons in its territory; (2) be committed to global disarmament; (3) continue to rely on America's nuclear deterrent; and (4) develop nuclear energy for peaceful purposes. Although these were the principles (tatemae) of Japan's nuclear policy, the reality (honne) was quite different. Tokyo and Washington made a secret agreement in 1960 that allowed the transit and storage of nuclear weapons in Japan, an agreement that only came to light after former Ambassador Reischauer's 1982 confession.

Japan's foreign policy of the economic miracle was highly successful in almost every regard. During this time Japan became an economic superpower while continuing to enjoy essentially low cost if not 'free' defense, economic, and political rides. Tokyo mastered its neo-mercantilist strategy of trying to separate – or at least create the illusion of separating – economic from political issues; it continued to concentrate the bulk of its energies and resources on developing the economy, promoting exports, and minimizing competitive imports, while also minimalizing its real defense, aid, and political contributions to the world economy.

FOREIGN POLICY OF COMPREHENSIVE SECURITY (1973-PRESENT)

During the early 1970s Japan was hit with a number of economic and diplomatic shocks that caused its policy-makers to re-evaluate its so far successful policy to minimize diplomatic initiatives while concentrating on economic expansion. Nixon's three 'shocks' – the dollar's devaluation in 1971 and float in 1973, the 1972 restoration of relations with China, and 1973 threat to embargo the export of soybeans – all shook the traditional confidence that Tokyo could rely on the United States. Japan's generally free economic and military ride seemed to have increasingly large hidden costs. The biggest blow, however, came with OPEC's 1973 quadrupling of oil prices, which caused Japan's economic growth to decline for the first time since the war and unleashed double-digit inflation. Finally, the fall of Indochina to communism in 1975 symbolized the decline of American influence in the region.

All these events reinforced a growing sense of vulnerability among Japanese, and the realization that Tokyo would have to work more actively to secure its own interests, even if it meant at times taking a stand different from that of Washington. OPEC's oil price increase finally exposed the illusion that Japanese leaders had until then been so successful in promoting: that economic issues could be separated from political ones. Tokyo only succeeded in reversing the Arab oil producers export embargo by agreeing to break with Washington and support the condemnation of Israel. At the same time the government embarked on a policy of diversifying and stabilizing its overseas sources, energy conservation, greater use of domestic resources, alternative energy development, energy research and development, and stockpiling. As a result of these efforts, Tokyo has reduced its dependence on Middle East oil from about 80 per cent of total oil imports in the early 1970s to 46.6 per cent in 1986, while oil from Iran and Iraq represents only 6.3 per cent of Japan's total oil supply.[8]

Thus was the policy of comprehensive security born. Although the label would not be coined until 1980, when Prime Minister Suzuki formally endorsed the proposals of a special committee on the subject, the policy of defining security in a broad sense of economic well-being and invulnerability to disruptions as well as traditional military security, and the active use of diplomatic, economic, and cultural initiatives as well as a strong military defense to guarantee comprehensive security, quickly emerged in response to the oil embargo. Perhaps the key economic element of comprehensive security is the diversification of foreign sources of energy, raw materials, and markets in order to minimize the impact of any country's or region's cut-off or dramatic price increase. At the same time, Tokyo would use economic and diplomatic efforts to make specific foreign sources dependent on Japanese sources of capital, goods, technology, and services, thus minimizing the chances that any trade disruption would be attempted. Foreign aid would be increasingly targeted to key resource countries like Indonesia or Brazil, or regions like the Middle East. Tokyo would increasingly get involved in controversial issues like the Palestinian question or the Iran-Iraq War. The government would double its efforts to lead Japan from a heavy resource-consuming industrial society into a post-industrial society based on clean, light resource-and energy-intensive high-technology and information industries. Meanwhile Japan would continue to shelter under the United States' nuclear umbrella and enjoy largely unhindered access to the vast American market.

A key aspect of comprehensive security is foreign aid. Although most of Japan's aid remains tied to the purchase of Japanese goods and services, and its grant component of 86 per cent is well below the OECD average of 99 per cent, in 1989 Tokyo did become the largest aid donor in sheer volume with $10 billion earmarked compared to $8.7 billion by the United States. At the June 1988 Toronto summit meeting, the Prime Minister promised to double Japan's aid by 1992. Although Tokyo continues to use the formula of dividing its aid in a ratio of 70 per cent to Asia, and 10 per cent each to Africa, the Middle East, and Latin America, it has shifted some of its aid to 'strategic' countries like Turkey, Egypt, or Sudan in cooperation with the United States.

Tokyo has increasingly acted as the diplomatic go-between or even spokesperson for developing regions. At various times to varying degrees Japanese diplomats have attempted to mediate the conflicts between North and South Korea, Vietnam and ASEAN, Israel and the Arab countries, and Iran and Iraq. These efforts, while largely unsuccessful diplomatically, have proven very advantageous economically as Japanese firms continue to trade with both sides. But, of course, this profitable strategy was perfected during Japan's 'two Chinas' policy during the 1950s and 1960s.

Another interesting diplomatic initiative is Japan's attempts to act as spokesperson for East Asia. Japan has been East Asia's dominant trade partner and has held over one-third of all DFI with almost every country in the region since the mid–1970s. After the fall of Indochina to communism in 1975, Tokyo began actively to support ASEAN in an attempt to fill some of the diplomatic and aid void left by the reduction of America's regional role. During a 1977 visit to ASEAN's annual prime ministers' meeting, Prime Minister Fukuda promised $1 billion in aid to five regional projects and increased economic cooperation while promising never to become a regional military force. Each subsequent prime minister or foreign minister has made a trip to the annual ASEAN meeting armed with promises of aid and cooperation. At the June 1988 Toronto summit meeting of the seven leading industrial nations Takeshita attempted to speak on behalf of East Asia against American and European protectionism while his entourage hinted broadly that Tokyo was considering an East Asian trade zone to counter those of North America and the European Community. Thus, Takeshita skillfully shifted East Asian criticism of Japan's continuing trade surplus and closed markets to the United States and EC who have trade deficits with the region while their markets are largely open.

Japanese diplomacy has been equally sophisticated in managing its continual trade conflicts with the United States and Europe. While the export offensives and import barriers continue, Tokyo has made it much more difficult to trace these to the government. The government's seven 'significant market opening steps' of the mid–1980s made Japan's tariffs the world's lowest and put its quotas on an average with those of other OECD countries. Japan's government, business, and mass media now trumpet Japan as having the world's most open economy; foreign producers do not sell more in Japan not because of non-tariff barriers, but simply because they do not try hard enough; they are beaten out in third markets not because of dumping cartels by Japanese producers, but again, because they do not try hard enough.

The reality of course, is far different from Japan's official rhetoric. Tokyo's succession of market opening steps has been largely cosmetic; where the reductions have been substantive, as in the case of tariffs and quotas, they have largely been replaced by more subtle but no less effective non-tariff barriers. Japan's trade surplus with the United States rose from $500 million in 1973 to $8 billion in 1980 and $68 billion in 1986; its surplus with Europe rose from about $500 million to $20 billion in the same period. Although a high dollar in the 1980s did play an important role in the dramatic jump in its trade surplus with the United States from $8 billion to $60 billion in six years, the most important factor behind Japan's huge trade surpluses with virtually all its trade partners was the perfection of Tokyo neo-mercantilist trade and industrial policies.

The same gap between image and reality continues in defense policy. The National Defense Council in 1976 seemed to advocate a stronger policy when it called for defense increases large enough to repel a small invasion by holding out for a few days until American forces came to the rescue. Yet, at the same time, the government capped military spending to no more than 1 per cent of GNP, thus undercutting the promise for a stronger defense. In the 1980s statements by the Suzuki and Nakasone administrations likewise seemed to indicate that Japan was beginning to take a significantly stronger role in its own defense; in 1981 Suzuki agreed to defend sealanes up to 1000 Miles from Japan, while Nakasone agreed in 1983 to share Japanese defense technology with the United States and breeched the 1 per cent spending increase level in 1987. But to date Japan's navy has not been significantly increased to fulfill its increased sealane defense, only three insignificant technology transfers have occurred, and the 1987 defense spending budget increased to only 1.004 per cent of GNP. Cynics point out that the only Japanese technology transfers were to the Soviet Union, not the United States, when Toshiba sold top secret technology to Moscow that will enable the Soviets to make their submarines run silently – an advantage that will cost the United States an estimated $30–40 billion to overcome.

Since 1973 Tokyo's comprehensive security policy has been enormously successful. It has entangled the world in a web of products, investments, and finance spun from Tokyo to the point where retaliation for Japanese unfair trade would inevitably cost much more than it was worth. It is clear where Japanese interests lie in terms of trade and foreign investments. In 1986, of its total international trade of $335.6 billion, 35.7 per cent was with North America, 16.4 per cent with Western Europe, 21.2 per cent with Southeast Asia, 6.6 per cent with the communist bloc, 4.6 per cent with Oceania, 4.7 per cent with Latin America, and 2.5 per cent with Africa. Japan's foreign investment patterns also clearly show its primary interests. In 1986 Japanese firms invested $22 billion overseas, of which 46.8 per cent went to North America, 21.2 per cent to Latin America, 15.5 per cent to Europe, 10.4 per cent to Asia, 4.4 per cent to Oceania, 1.04 per cent to Africa, and only 0.2 per cent to the Middle East. These investments joined the accumulative total between 1958 and 1986 of $105 billion, of which 35.3 per cent was in North America, 20.6 per cent in Asia, 19.2 per cent in Latin America, 13.7 per cent in Europe, 4.9 per cent in Oceania, 3.5 per cent in Africa, and 2.3 per cent in the Middle East.[9] Thus, one-third of Japan's trade and investments are tied to North America, and over 60 per cent with the Pacific Basin as a whole. The twenty-first century may well be the 'Pacific century' dominated by Japan that many analysts predict.

CONCLUSION

Since 1945 no other major industrial nation has been as successful as Japan in achieving its foreign policy goals of military and economic security, international predominance and prestige, which have remained the same since the mid-nineteenth century. The means to achieve these goals, however, changed markedly as pre–1945 imperialism and mercantilism gave way to neo-mercantilism. The comprehensive security policy since 1973 is simply a more sophisticated version of the policy of attempting to separate politics and economics that first arose early in the Occupation. Tokyo may have heightened its diplomatic profile in some non-controversial areas, but it continues to attempt to cloak its neo-mercantilism by 'consciously avoiding international controversy, maintaining a low posture and limiting its public statements to platitudes'.[10]

Many Japanese leaders have been candid in describing Japan's neo-mercantist policies. Former MITI Vice-Minister Naohiro Amaya argues that the United States and Soviet Union are 'samurai' states while Japan continues to follow a 'merchant' role. The advantage is that while the world appears to 'belong to the samurai . . . in reality it is owned by the merchants'.[11] But for 'a merchant to prosper in samurai society, it is necessary to have superb information-gathering ability, intuition, diplomatic skill, and at times the ability to be a sycophant (gomasuri noryoku)'. According to Amaya, Tokyo has consciously followed a strategy of maximizing Japan's wealth by at times going so far as to 'beg for oil from the producing countries, grovel on bended knee before the samurai', and, it might be added, accept things like 'honorary white' status to increase the profits from its South Africa trade despite Tokyo's declared principle of being against racism.

Masataka Kosaka, one of Japan's foremost political scientists, argues that Japan should continue its neo-mercantilist strategy despite having already achieved enormous wealth, power, and prestige. According to Kosaka, a neo-mercantilist nation 'has wide relations with many alien civilizations, makes differing use of various different principles of behavior, and manages to harmonize them with each other'.[12] For Kosaka benefits flowing from the strategy whereby Japan 'simply takes advantage of international relations created by stronger states' and enjoys 'the advantages of being an ally and the benefits of non-involvement' far outweigh the 'hypocrisy' (gizen) of the strategy and the fact that it 'is not a popular role in the international order, since it is regarded as selfish and immoral'.

As Kosaka suggests, Tokyo's omnidirectional diplomacy (zenhoi gaiko) has been increasingly criticized by Japanese and foreign analysts alike with such terms as a deliberate strategy of 'missing the boat' (nori-okure), 'value free diplomacy' (issai no kachi handan no shinai gaiko), 'unprincipled foreign policy' (musesso gaiko) or – in even less flattering terms – 'kow tow diplomacy' (degeza gaiko), and the 'diplomacy of cowardice' (okubyo gaiko) of 'an international eccentric' (kokusai-teki henjin). But while Tokyo has continually sought to maintain as low a political profile as possible, this strategy has been anything but value-free since it is unashamedly aimed at enhancing Japan's wealth and power in the world political economy, even at the expense of its earstwhile allies. Former Foreign Minister Kiichi Miyazawa put it well when he described a 'foreign policy lacking in moral principles' in which the 'only value judgements we can make are determining what is in Japan's interests'.[13] Yet Miyazawa and other Japanese leaders justify Tokyo's continued neo-mercantilism on the grounds that Japan is 'a special country' (toku-shu kokka). It remains to be seen whether Japan's budding economic hegemony and the accompanying growing demands that Tokyo take greater responsibility for managing and contributing to the world economy will modify or exacerbate its neo-mercantism and sense of superiority.

NOTES

1. John Dower, *Empire and Aftermath*, p. 307.
2. See Shigeru Yoshida's *Memoirs* for a full discussion.

3. Ibid., pp. 119–20.
4. See Takeo Hasegawa's *Japanese Foreign Aid* and Alan Rix's *Japan's Foreign Aid* for details.
5. All aid statistics, unless otherwise marked, are taken from the OECD annual report on foreign aid.
6. Frank Hellman, *Japan's Postwar Foreign Policy*, p. 68.
7. See Dennis Yasutomo's *Japan and the Asian Development Bank*.
8. Muthiah Alagappa, 'Japan's Political and Security Role in the Asia-Pacific Region', *Contemporary Southeast Asia*, vol. 10, no. 1, June 1988, p. 48.
9. Ibid., pp. 19–21.
10. Kenneth Pyle, 'The Future of Japanese Nationality', *Journal of Japanese Studies*, vol. 8, no. 2, 1982, p. 225.
11. Ibid., p. 249.
12. Ibid., p. 251.
13. Ibid., p. 226.

Part IV
Japan and the World into the Twenty-First century: Nationalism or Internationalism?

13 Psycho-Social Internationalism or Nationalism?

The April 1986 Maekawa Report called on the Japanese to open not just their markets, but their minds to the outside world. According to the Report, responsibility should accompany power; as an economic superpower Japan must start giving as much at it takes from the world economy. But Japan should 'internationalize' as much for self-interest as altruism. For example, when it trailed in the technological race it could afford merely to copy and improve on the technological efforts of others. Now that it is slowly nosing ahead of the United States as the world's technological leader, Japan must become as creative in basic research as it has been in applied research. Internationalization thus may in part include education and research and development reforms that encourage creativity and innovation.

Sensible as this mild message seems, its call for internationalizing Japan was immediately denounced across the political spectrum as an attempt to dilute Japanese culture and undercut economic growth. Yet several years later many of the more concrete goals which the Maekawa Report called for are slowly being achieved: financial markets are creaking open, more trade barriers are crumbling, hordes of Japanese are travelling overseas, and more foreign aid is being dispensed. 'Internationalization' (kokusaika) is on everyone's lips, although no concensus has emerged as to its meaning.

Generally speaking, interpretations of internationalization fall into two camps. According to the mainstream view, internationalism is merely disguised nationalism. For businessmen, being an 'international man' (Kokusaijin) in an 'international age' (kokusaijidai) means simply becoming more adept at understanding foreign languages, customs, and markets in order to sell more. For bureaucrats and politicians it means mastering the art of international public relations (tatemae) to cloak Japanese neo-mercantilism (honne). Japan's 'ten market opening steps' of the 1980s provide an excellent example. While tariffs and quotas were reduced a web of less visible non-tariffs barriers remained to repel competitive imports.

However, a small but possibly growing minority want Japan to genuinely internationalize: to follow the lead of North America and Western Europe and not only significantly reduce trade barriers but start running trade deficits with poorer countries, allow in large numbers of refugees and foreign workers, dramatically increase and untie foreign aid, and take the diplomatic initiative in tackling global problems such as environmental decay, Third World debt, famine, and disease. According to these adherents, internationalization means the convergence and opening not only of political and economic systems, but a convergence and opening of people's minds; genuine internationalization must be as psychological as it is institutional.

It remains to be seen whether most Japanese will continue to view internationalization as simply a smoother way to promote Japan's national interests or eventually see it as involving a genuine opening and giving to the world. Genuine internationalization faces immense psychological and institutional barriers. Although Japanese society had undergone enormous changes over the past 40 years as it rose from mass poverty to mass affluence, there has been tremendous continuity beneath all the changes. The traditional Japanese hierarchical 'we-them' dichotomy between themselves and the outside world remains not only intact but may actually be strengthening.

An individual's way of seeing himself, his culture, and his place in the world is shaped by many influences. This chapter explores some of the interrelated psychological and social forces that shape the world views of Japanese, and serve to obstruct any genuine internationalization. Perhaps the two most powerful psychological and institutional barriers to internationalization are the 'Nihonjinron' phenomena and school system, respectively. The first section will examine the extremely influential phenomena of 'Nihonjinron', or the vast and increasing flood of publications penned by Japan's leading social scientists that promote the view that Japanese people and culture are unique and inherently superior to the rest of humanity. An important subcurrent of the Nihonjinron literature is focused on an extremely revisionist version of Japanese history in which among other things, Japan's conquest of China and Southeast Asia after 1931 are increasingly seen as progressive, while its defeat and the Occupation reforms are seen as negative.

An examination of Japan's school system will follow. One of the most important socializing forces in an individual's life is his schooling, and Japan's school system is carefully constructed to internalize individuals with the core values of groupism, hierarchy, and conformity. These values are considered one of the pillars on which Japan's successful corporate culture rests. Although among other things the Maekawa Report called for the internationalization of Japan's school system, it is extremely unlikely that any major reforms will take place that promote individualism and internationalism rather than traditional Japanese values, and thus undercut Japan's corporate and political culture, and economic growth.

Japan's hierarchical world view is mirrored within Japanese society itself. Both individuals and groups are arranged in a social ladder in which one must bow to those above and in turn are bowed to by those below. In the postwar era, minority groups and women have struggled to break out of their traditionally inferior position within Japanese society. Yet, despite some superficial changes, the status and opportunities for minorities and women remain low in a still extremely stratified society. Genuine psychological and institutional internationalization is unlikely when Japanese society itself remains hierarchically structured.

NIHONJINRON

Internationalism, in part, flows from the idea that all people share a common humanity beneath their often dramatically different cultures and socio-economic levels. Internationalists attempt to transcend the limitations of national culture to achieve a deeper understanding and interaction with their fellow human beings elsewhere. Obviously, the prevailing Japanese view that they are members of a 'pure, unique, and inherently superior race', along with the idea that every nation is ranked in a pecking order according to its particular economic and cultural dynamism in which Japan is now 'Number One', are powerful psychological barriers to any genuine internationalization.

Although many analysts have commented on the 'Japan as Number One complex' which steadily intensifies alongside Japan's growing economic power, no one has explored this phenomena as thoroughly as Peter Dale. In his book *The Myth of Japanese Uniqueness* Dale explores the flood of literature called Nihonjinron which attempts to explain what it means to be Japanese.[1] The output has been enormous and is increasing: from 1946 to 1978 about 700 titles on the theme of Japanese identity were published, with the total rising 25 per cent between 1976 and 1978 alone, and has easily doubled since.[2] Yet, Nihonjinron is not a recent phenomenon – the first works were published in the Meiji period. Although the literature includes any writing on the 'Japanese soul', no matter how specious, it is centered on and shaped by Japan's leading social scientists. According to Dale, it would be 'as if virtually all English or American intellectuals for the last 100 years had been preoccupied with the clarification of the essence of English or American culture as a central research focus'.[3]

Dale dismisses the bulk of the nihonjinron as 'merely the intellectual fast food of consumer nationalism' and points out that 'little of what contemporary Japanese scholars write and publish in Japanese could be published intact in a literal English translation without becoming the butt of amazement and even ridicule abroad'.[4] For example, one highly respected Japanese neurologist wrote a best-seller on the Japanese brain, which apparently is 'unique' among human brains. According to Dale the content is thoroughly ultranationalist, and through 'conceptual counterfeiting' its adherents simply 'rephrase extreme right wing notions in terms of a modish jargon borrowed from foreign disciplines of analysis, thus safeguarding and preserving the earlier totalitarian theorums under the impenetrable alias of an ostensibly value-neutral empirical sociology or psychology . . . the nihonjinron often merely recycle, in scientific garb, the ideological forms of the past'.[5]

The central element of Nihonjinron is the notion that the Japanese race, in contrast to all other 'mongrel races', is 'pure, unique, and inherently superior to all others'. Nihonjinron writers constantly contrast 'We Japanese' (ware ware nihonjin) with the rest of the world, and liberally use such expressions as 'unparalleled' (rui no nai), 'not in other countries' (takoku ni nai), Japanese 'superiority' (yohodo sugurete iru), or 'absolute uniqueness' (zettaiteki tokushusei) to illustrate their claims. Another important tenet is a hostility to any non-Japanese perspectives on Japan – only Japanese can understand what it means to be Japanese. Accordingly, 'genuine Western scientific methods are rejected and replaced by intuition wrapped in pseudo-scientific garb'.[6] Foreign analysis is dismissed as inadequate since Japan is 'difficult for foreigners to understand' (gaijin ni totte wakarinikui). In fact, any criticism of Japan, no matter how well argued, is immediately dismissed by most Japanese as 'Japan-bashing' or anti-Japanese.

What follows is a severe stereotyping of Japanese and Westerners based on what Japanese would like to think they are rather than on any empirical evidence. For example, Japanese are emotional (wet) and Westerns rational (dry); Japanese are peaceful and foreigners aggressive; Japanese care about others while Westerners are selfish and individualistic; Japanese love nature and are spiritual; Westerners exploit nature and are materialistic; Japanese communicate through silence (haragei) and subtlety while foreigners are talkative; Japanese bend rules to human situations while foreigners rigidly adhere to cold principles, and so on. Of course, foreigners familiar with Japan can immediately think of numerous examples of Japanese behavior which completely reverse these central tenets of Nihonjinron. But then, as Dale points out, few Western social scientists would concern themselves with such glaring and baseless stereotypes.

But although one is tempted simply to dismiss Nihonjinron as empty pop culture, Mouer and Sugimoto point out that the very 'heavy involvement of the academic community and of the political and business establishment in promoting such images . . . at home and abroad' makes it vitally important for understanding the reality behind the images of Japanese policies.[7] In other words, although analysts cannot take the ideas of Nihonjinron seriously, it is imperative that they understand why most Japanese fervently believe in Nihonjinron, and the economic and political consequences of those beliefs.

Why do most Japanese unquestioningly accept the specious and often downright silly stereotypes of Nihonjinron? Perhaps the most important reason is that with their hierarchical, Darwinian view of the world, Japanese see their enormous economic success as flowing naturally from their own moral and cultural superiority. Takeshi Sasaki, a professor of political science at the University of Tokyo, puts Japan's 'number one complex' in perspective by arguing that the new nationalism is strongly influenced by Japan's traditional feelings of inferiority to the West, feelings that have largely disappeared with the 'relative decline in U.S. economic power . . . It has now become the central concern of Japanese nationalism to speak about Japan's supposed "superiority," as the country is becoming increasingly free of its past inferiority complex vis-à-vis America'. Sasaki finds this new nationalism particularly virulent among young Japanese who have grown up in relative affluence and believe in Japan's 'unique cultural, racial superiority'.[8] Polls indicate a steady swing in the Japanese perception of their relative position in the world. In 1953 a Ministry of Education survey indicated that only 17 per cent of people (aged 20–24) regarded Japanese as superior to Westerners. Twenty years later a 1973 poll showed 31 per cent considered Japanese superior while only 8 per cent thought Japanese were inferior to Westerners.[9] In 1984 80 per cent of those polled in two Tokyo wards thought the Japanese were 'one of the greatest races in the world'.[10] Although these results are alarming, the very question itself is very revealing of Japan's essentially hierarchical world view. It is difficult to imagine any self-respecting pollster venturing a similar question elsewhere without immediately being branded a racist.

Closely connected with this attitude of superiority is, as Mouer and Sugimoto point out, 'an extremely negative attitude toward other cultures . . . (including) the denigration of other cultures and the people who live in them'.[11] They go on to give examples such as Japanese sex tours to Asia, the treatment of Asian entertainers in Japan, and the open use of insulting words like 'keto' (hairy barbarian) when speaking of Westerners. These racist attitudes were most clearly revealed by Prime Minister Nakasone's September 1986 remarks that America's economic difficulties could be attributed to the low intelligence of blacks and hispanics. Chikara Higashi writes that most Japanese completely agreed with Nakasone and those 'who faulted him did so mostly for voicing his opinion, not for having it'.[12] Japanese xenophobia is deeply embedded. A 1986 EPA survey of 3000 people between the ages of 15 and 74 revealed that 71.7 per cent were against foreign workers, 73.3 per cent against international marriages, 60.0 per cent were against Japanese children being educated abroad and more foreign DFI in Japan, 73.8 per cent were against overseas assignments for themselves, and 50.1 per cent against renting living space to foreigners.[13]

One of the reasons for this continuing xenophobia among Japanese is their refusal honestly to confront Japan's war crimes. Although the Japanese military were responsible for the slaughter of over 20 million East Asian civilians between 1931 and 1945 in ways that rival the Nazis in scale and barbarity, Japanese are socialized to see themselves as the victims rather than the victimizers during World War II. Psychologically Japanese increasingly feel that the war began with Hiroshima and ended with Nagasaki, and anything the Japanese military did in the 14 years before was simply something all soldiers do in war, and, regardless, should be forgotten. This attitude was nicely summed up by Emperor Hirohito who, during South Korean President Chun's visit to Tokyo in 1983, said: 'there was an unfortunate period between our countries earlier this century which should not be repeated'.[14]

The government has led the attempts to whitewash Japan's war-time past in three main areas: the remembrance of the atomic bombings, school textbooks, and the mass media. Each year's anniversary of the atomic bombings is greeted with increasingly elaborate ceremonies but underlaid with hypocrisy. For example, representatives of the surviving victims (hibukusha) are brought before the cameras each year to tell their horror stories while they continue to be discriminated against the rest of the year in terms of employment, housing, education, and marriage. Like the Nazis during the war, the Japanese employed forced foreign labor to man the factories and mines, and over 100 000 Koreans were present in Horoshima and Nagasaki during the bombings, of which number 20 000 Koreans, or one-ninth of the total number of victims, were killed. The Japanese government has not only refused to give health compensation to the 18 000 Korean hibakusha, but has refused to erect a monument to those Koreans who died inside the Nagasaki peace park, and only conceded a small memorial outside the park after a long campaign.

Only about one-quarter of the Japanese civilians who died during the war were killed by the atomic bombs. In fact, more Japanese – about 200 000 – were killed during the Tokyo fire bombing in March 1945 than from both atomic bombs, yet they are largely forgotten. Logically it would make more sense to commemorate those who died in Tokyo and elsewhere since they died in vain – the war continued – rather than those who died from the atomic bombs which finally brought the war to an end. But to commemorate those who died in the conventional bombing might remind other East Asian countries of the millions of their own civilians who died from Japanese conventional bombs, bullets, or bayonets. To Japanese, the value of the atomic bombs was not that they brought the war to a quick end and saved possibly millions of lives in the long run, but that the experience 'purified' the nation of any collective sense of guilt for Tokyo's 14 years of aggression.

Revising the high school textbooks has been another means of reinforcing the martyr-scapegoat mentality among the Japanese people. Textbook controversies date back to 1965 when the noted University of Tokyo historian Saburo Ienaga sued the Ministry of Education for its unconstitutional censorship of school textbooks. Despite the lawsuit, which remains unresolved, the government hardened its revisionist views throughout this time. Ienaga reveals that 'In the 1970s I could write more freely on the massacre at Nanjing. In 1980, the ministry suddenly wanted me to write: "Many people died in the confusion after the battle." "[15] The controversy remained largely a domestic issue until the summer of 1982 when the Japanese press incorrectly reported that the Ministry of Education had made sweeping revisions of the next year's textbooks which whitewashed Japan's responsibility for the war. The governments of South Korea, China, and ASEAN condemned the changes. China was particularly incensed – the government threatened to cancel the upcoming Suzuki visit while mass anti-Japanese protests broke out in several cities. Although the government was severely split between the Foreign Ministry, which favored a conciliatory stand, and the Education Ministry, which condemned foreign interference in Japan's domestic affairs, eventually Suzuki apologized and promised there would be no more revisions. Another controversy broke out in the summer of 1986 when the Japanese press correctly reported that the Ministry of Education had approved a textbook prepared by the National Council for the Protection of Japan which cast doubt on whether the Nanjing massacre even took place. The text said that research 'is continuing in order to establish the truth.' The report unleashed another chorus of diplomatic protests which was only quelled when Nakasone flew to Beijing to apologize.

Nakasone himself became the center of controversy when East Asian governments protested his official August 1985 visit to Yasukuni Jinga where the war dead, including war criminals, are enshrined. He refrained from any more official visits while prime minister. The following year, in September, Nakasone had to dismiss his Education Minister Masayuki Fujio after he publically whitewashed the Japanese colonization of Korea. Prime Minister Takeshita also had reluctantly to accede to foreign protests to fire his head of the Land Agency, Seisuke Okuno, when he used the old 'ABCD Encirclement' argument to justify Japanese imperialism after 1930, arguing that Japan was simply 'acting to protect itself against the white race that had turned Asia into a colony . . . Japan fought the war in order to secure its safety'.[16] Takeshita himself professed the same sentiments during the Emperor's funeral, when he claimed Japan was not the aggressor during the war. He recanted several weeks later only after sustained protests from China, South Korea, and other East Asian nations. Ienaga warns that 'without pressure from abroad we would not be able to write the truth at home'.[17]

The head-in-the-sand, revisionist attitudes of Japanese toward their past contrasts sharply with those of West Germany, whose school system and mass media honestly teach their country's role in

World War II. This sensitivity led to the resignation of the speaker of the Parliament, Simon Jenninger, on 11 November 1988 after his speech was apparently misinterpreted as being pro-Nazi. Simon Wiesenthal, the Vienna based Nazi-hunter described Jenninger as 'a friend of the Jews and a friend of Israel', and his resignation as 'a big tragedy'.[18]

Finally, the mass media have helped shape a great deal of the 'Japan as victim' sentiment solidifying in Japan. Buruma identifies a distinct double standard of film scenes considered 'too shocking to be seen'. He contrasts the Japanese attempts to censor newsreel footage depicting the Nanjing massacre from the film *The Last Emperor* with Japanese films depicting fictional atrocities against Japan: 'Japanese audiences are quite used to seeing scenes of American violence. Indeed, scenes of GIs – preferably black – raping Japanese girls in films about the Occupation are as common as shots of Big Ben when the action shifts to London'.[19]

Denys Blakeway described the frustrations he endured trying to negotiate an eventually aborted BBC-NHK series on World War II when the BBC's attempts to present a balanced view of the war were continually undercut by the Japanese, who refused to deal with anything showing Japanese atrocities. Although the standard estimation of the number of Chinese civilians massacred by the Japanese around Nanjing is 200 000, and the Chinese recently revised the number to 350 000 over a one-month period, the Japanese 'made it clear that there could be no cooperation if we insisted on examining such contentious and dangerous questions'. 'If the precise figures are not known,' we were told 'then we should ignore the matter . . . the past is too much for many people to bear . . . if it is revealed too harshly we would not be able to guarantee public order in the streets.'[20] The Japanese presented the same feelings when discussions of other controversies, such as the Bataan death march and treatment of POWs, came up. Blakeways recounted similar Japanese attitudes in preparation for a recent NHK program when it was decided to use the testimony of a Filipino woman who was thought to have been maimed in a Japanese bombing attack. But Blakeways reveals that when it was learned to the horror of the Japanese that the women had been brutally maimed and disfigured not by bombs but by a 'savage and bestial Japanese bayonet attack' on her and others 'recording was stopped. Embarrassed executives hurriedly returned the woman home and the projected broadcast was cancelled. Instead the usual moralizing about the horrors of Hiroshima and Nagasaki

was transmitted. While bombing could be accepted as a horror per-
petrated by both sides . . . the bayoneting of civilians was a crime
for which only the Japanese were notorious. It was better by far to
ignore the matter completely'.[21]

But of course the 'new nationalism' is nothing new. Japan went
through a similar cycle between 1854 and 1945 when feelings of
superiority were first humbled by Perry's gunboats and were then
rapidly transformed into feelings of inferiority throughout the late
nineteenth century as Japanese became clearly aware of the West's
immense power. Much of the motivation behind Japan's intense
effort to modernize was fuelled by the drive among Japanese to
reverse their humiliating 'inferiority' and become a 'superior' country. But, unfortunately, equality bestowed by such early twentieth-
century events as the alliance with Britain, reversal of the unequal
treaties, and Great Power status at Versailles was not enough. A
relatively positive nationalism turned into a virulent ultranationalism
during the 1930s as Japan strove to drive out the West and become
the supreme Asian power. Japan's élite justified its aggression with
the belief that the 'pure, unique Japanese race' was being encircled
by the West.

Lucian Pyle identifies a 'scapgoat/martyr syndrome' or 'siege mentality' (rojo shinri) whereby Japanese see themselves as a martyr
nation being scapgoated or 'bashed' by others. This attitude seems
to be alive and well.[22] Today Japan is besieged by 'Japan bashers'
who are scapegoating it for their own failure to develop. Just as
Japanese militarism was justified to destroy the Western encirclement, Japanese neo-mercantilism through dumping and trade barriers is similarly justified. Of course, although there is considerable
foreign criticism of Japan's trade practices, in reality it is the foreigners who are being 'bashed' with Japan's huge trade surpluses.
Kumon Shupei describes the myths of Nihonjinron as a vicious circle
whereby the 'stronger the criticism and censure from outside, the
more unanimous and firm becomes the reply of self-assurance from
inside. The present psyche of the Japanese is almost on the verge of
being pathological.'[23]

Ian Buruma has explored in depth the institutionalization of
Nihonjinron. He points to the semi-official Japanology Institute
started in 1985 in Kyoto with a government grant of $130 000. In
Nakasone's words, the institute's purpose is 'to establish Japan's
identity once again'.[24] Buruma identifies many pre-1945 ultranationalists affiliated with school, including Kitaro Nishida and Iwao

Takayama, whose views seem little changed from the past – Takayama writes that 'Faith in and preservation of the National Essence (kokutai) is the highest virtue of the Japanese people', while Nishida argues that 'the Japanese emperor system should apply to the whole world'.[25] Another influential affiliate, Soicihi Watanabe, who has written some very popular anti-semitic works on his claims of a Jewish conspiracy against Japan, writes that 'a mystical view of blood purity is necessary to preserve national unity and identity'.[26] To understand the Institute's significance, Buruma asks us to imagine 'say, a Munich school of German scholars gathered around Helmut Kohl, who place themselves in the tradition of such Nazi thinkers as Julius Streicher or Alfred Rosenberg'.[27]

Another important right-wing pressure group is the National Council to Protect Japan (Nihon o mamoru kokumin kaigi), which was formed in 1981 and is chaired by former UN Ambassador Toshikazu Kase. The Council is Japan's most influential right-wing group and includes an array of leading political, business, and media élite. Its ability to mobilize citizens behind various issues at a grassroots municipal, village, and provincial level has been particularly effective. This organization is mirrored in the Diet by the Association to Consider the Fundamental Issues of the State (Kokka Kihon Modai Doshikai), formed by junior LDP members in July 1986.

Most Cabinet and Diet members try publically to avoid associating themselves with the more extreme views of these organizations that the Constitution be revised to drop Article 9 and elevate the Emperor to a more powerful position, and it is extremely unlikely that the LDP would run on an ultranationalist platform. Yet, as in the 1930s, while these right-wing groups remain relatively small and will probably never form a Cabinet, their ideas increasingly color the overall political atmosphere and the country's view of itself and the world in highly nationalistic terms. Buruma points out that former Prime Minister Nakasone and other political leaders frequently sprinkle their speeches with such ultranationalist terms as 'pure racial state' (tan itsu minzoku kokka). 'Japanese race' (Nippon minzoku), and 'racial self-determination' (minzoku jiketsu).[28]

These beliefs have an adverse effect on Japan's relations with the rest of the world. Mouer and Sugimoto write that with the Japanese belief in their uniqueness 'economic conflicts of interests can always be dismissed as either cultural misunderstandings or as ethonocentricism on the part of foreign negotiators. Accordingly the responsibility for conflict resolution is shifted to the foreigners'.[29] But this belief in Japanese uniqueness is not simply confined to Japanese. Mouer and Sugimoto argue that the Japanese government and business 'actively promote these false images of Japan abroad "as a convenient negotiating tactic . . . a mystique is created in which Japan is hidden in mist . . . (making) it easier for Japanese to parry the approaches of foreign negotiators'.[30] Dale agrees, pointing out the 'extension of the images packeted by the Nihonjinron to external markets . . . has been seen as an indispensable device for bolstering Japan's national security'. The Japanese see any possible future 'economic war' as a 'war of cultures' in which the way foreigners interpret the Japanese mind will prove decisive for the outcome. The country's international success will hinge . . . on its ability to convince a sceptical outside world of the uniqueness of its racio-cultural traditions'.[31]

There is good evidence that Tokyo's attempts to school foreigners in the 'myths of Japanese uniqueness' are paying off. For example, under a 1979 agreement between the two countries, Australia promised to supply sugar to Japan for a certain price.[32] Several months after the agreement was signed the bottom dropped out of the world sugar market and the Japanese negotiators immediately pressed Canberra to scrap the old agreement by arguing that in Japanese culture contracts were unimportant and 'amae' allowed a partner to get out when it experienced difficulties. When the Australians were reluctant to abandon the agreement they were accused of imposing a rigid, ethnocentric concept of contract on Japan that was insensitive to cultural relativism and give and take among friends. The Australians bought the argument and signed a new agreement highly advantageous to Japan. But the expediency of Tokyo's cultural arguments was revealed a year later when strikes delayed Australian iron-ore shipments and Canberra used the Japanese concept of contract to urge patience. With the tables turned, Tokyo's response was to condemn Australia for not honouring its contracts, and the Japanese ended up buying elsewhere. Another example of Tokyo's successful use of its 'unique culture' myth to avoid international responsibility was its refusal to accept more than a token amount of refugees in the 1970s and 1980s, when other industrial countries were accepting tens or even hundreds of thousands – it was argued that taking in refugees would weaken Japan's purity. The other industrial nations did not pressure Japan on the issue. Tokyo's public relations offensives and symbolic gestures have been highly successful in persuading

Western nations to ease the pressure on Japan to accept more international responsibilities in trade, aid, and other issues.

THE SCHOOL SYSTEM

Japan's school system has been an enormous success by almost any measure. For example, out of 24 countries Japanese students scored either first or second in almost every area of the 1982 Second International Survey of Mathematics Achievement.[33] Between 1960 and 1985 the proportion of the high school age group in high school rose steadily from 58 per cent to 94 per cent, with a 93.8 per cent high school graduation rate compared to 75 per cent in the United States. In 1985 the percentage of high school graduates entering college was 38.2 per cent, below the 45.6–52.5 per cent figure for the United States, but well ahead of France's 26.5 per cent, West Germany's 26.5 per cent, and Britain's 21.4 per cent. About 75 000 engineers annually graduate from Japanese colleges compared to 72 000 in the United States with twice the population.[34]

Even more important than instilling the basic elements of reading, writing and arithmetic, has been the system's outstanding job of socializing Japanese youth into the traditional values of groupism, hierarchy, and conformity, and making them productive members of Japan's economy. This socialization function is achieved by a variety of means. Education in Japan is centralized under the Ministry of Education's powerful control, which among other things sets the national curriculum and textbooks for all schools and universities. One simple but effective means of socialization is to keep students in school as much as possible. The Japanese school year is 240 days long, including Saturdays, compared to about 180 for the United States. By the time they graduate from high school, Japanese students will have been in school about three years more than their American counterparts. Japanese students generally start school much earlier than Americans – 40 per cent of three-year-olds and 92 per cent of four-year-olds are either in preschools or daycare centers.[35]

Another effective means of socialization has been the 'examination hell' (jijoku juken) for both high school and college. As in all other aspect of Japanese society, the schools are ranked in a strict hierarchy – high schools on their ability to send their students on to the best universities, universities on their ability to send their graduates to the most prestigious corporations or ministries. The 'college entrance war' (juken senso) is particularly fierce as only a percentage will succeed in entering the school of their choice. Exams are scheduled so that students cannot sit for more than two national university exams, and the competition has got worse as test scores improve. With the motto 'four hours pass, five hours fail' referring to the amount they should sleep at night, students begin studying years before. A vast $5 billion industry of cram schools (Juku) has emerged to service the needs of students struggling to get into the best high schools or universities, entrance to which will in turn guarantee them the best career choices. In 1982 47.3 per cent of high school students were enrolled in over 35 000 juku which range in size from small rooms to chains with a million students. About 2 per cent of the average family income goes to juku.[36]

Because the exams test knowledge rather than thinking, students spend years cramming thousands of facts into their heads without understanding their significance. Most students confess they soon forget most of what they learned soon after the exam is over. The value of the exam, however, is not its content but the effort that goes into preparing for it. The very fact that Japan's best and brightest students spend several years of their lives single-mindedly preparing for the exams deeply socializes within them such values as total dedication to a goal, conformity, and competition – the very attributes that corporations in particular are looking for in their recruits. Juku in turn devote as much time instilling a 'mind over matter mentality' (seishinshugi) as information in students. It is thought that anyone can succeed as long as they try hard enough – an attitude that failed to win World War II for Japan, but has certainly been more effective in contemporary battles. Accompanied by constant harangues from their teachers to try harder, students endure continual memorization and repetition drills, usually as groups.

Aside from the examination system, there are many other important ways Japan's school system socializes young people into traditional values. School uniforms, weekly morals classes, and minute attention to one's behavior including how to sit, talk, arrange one's desk, and bow all play a role. In a system similar to that of the corporations, Japanese classes are treated as one large group in which there is no tracking into ability or remedial groups, and students are never dropped or skipped ahead. Instead, they are divided into small groups (han) of four to six students, which serve as the primary unit for discipline, chores, and study. The han compete fiercely with each other for class honors. The school carefully monitors the students' outside behavior as well, prescribing strict curfews, activities, study time, and even when to go to bed and get up. Discipline is rarely direct; instead teachers use the group's peer pressure to keep mavericks in line.

Even school clubs, which one might think would be an outlet for individual preference and relaxation, help socialize students into Japanese etiquette and values. Everyone is required to join a club and is prevented from joining more than one. What is important about each club is not its formal purpose, but how it shapes each student's behavior. Lower ranking members of any club could relate the experience of a high school basketball player: 'when you meet a sempai (senior) you have to bow three times. Returning home after practice you weren't allowed to go home before your sempai. Even though I lived close to school I didn't get home until eight every night because I had to walk the sempai home'.[37]

Although Japan's school system has been an immense success at socializing Japanese into traditional values, those values are the very antithesis of internationalism. In his book 'The Education Factory' Satoshi Kamata compares Japan's education system with its factories, arguing that 'both are dedicated to turning out defect-free products. Japanese schools are structured like conveyor belts that leave no room for individuality . . . (Schools) decide everything for you, from your hair style to telling you what type of human being you should be'.[38] A US Department of Education report on the system pointed out that a 'basic characteristic of Japanese secondary education and university entrance examinations is adherence to the view that there is only one right answer'.[39] Student questions are considered rude and 'unJapanese'. As a result, Japanese may be good at memorization but often have extremely weak analytical and reasoning abilities.

Although the government proudly proclaims Japan to be a '100 per cent literate society', in fact there is a great deal of illiteracy that simply is not reported. The elevator system of advancement without tracking or remedial education leads to a severe problem of students 'falling to the bottom of the system' (ochikobore). By fifth grade 25 per cent of the students had fallen two or more years behind in reading, and 10 per cent read at only a first or second grade level.[40] Stevenson writes that 'there are Japanese children with serious difficulties in learning how to read, and the severity of their problems is at least as great as that of American children'.[41] One of the reasons for the juku is the need for slow-learning ochikobore to simply attempt to keep up with their fellow-students. As the statistics show, many never catch up and become the school equivalent of the 'by the window gang' (mado niwa zoku) of the incompetent corporate worker awaiting retirement.

There are many other problems with Japan's secondary school system that would make foreigners hesitate to use it as a model. An increasing problem is 'bullying' (ijime); in 1984 11.5 per cent of high schools experienced some sort of violence.[42] Another increasing problem is students who refuse to go to school (Tokokyohi) because of all the associated stress and repression. Like bullying 'school refusal' is more prevalent in junior than senior high school. The number of students absent for more than 50 days rose from 23 584 in 1975 to 52 080 in 1986, and the percentage of those who stayed home because they hated school rose from 11.4 per cent to 21.2 per cent.[43]

Japan's hierarchial school system provides inherently unequal opportunities for students. Rohlen writes that 'reputation is a self-fulfilling prophecy. The school drawing the best applicants has no trouble retaining its high reputation, and the schools at or near the bottom can do little to change their destiny'.[44] The limited number of public schools forces many families to send their children to private schools. These factors along with the high cost of juku means that poorer students have far less opportunity to advance than wealthier students. Children from the lowest 20 per cent of income families have only a one-in-three chance of attending a university compared to a nine-in-ten chance for those from the top 20 per cent; four out of five Tokyo University students are from professional or executive homes.[45]

All industrial nations face these same problems to varying extents. One distinct characteristic of Japan's school system, however, is its treatment of Japanese students who have lived abroad. In 1986 over 41 155 elementary and junior high school students returned from living with their families overseas, of which only 40 per cent had attended one of the 82 Japanese schools overseas while 20 per cent had no access to Japanese education.[46] These 'returnees' (kikoku shijo) are neglected by Japan's school system, and teased, bullied, or ostracized (murahachibu) by students. Why does Japan's xenophobia extend even to Japanese students who have lived overseas? Because the returnees do such 'unJapanese' things as ask questions and do not conform to the values and behavior the system tries so hard to socialize students into.

There are some signs of change. For example, before 1984 Mitsui did not hire Japanese who had been educated abroad, but since then, recognizing that returnees can be a tremendous resource, now sends recruiters overseas looking for them. However, the vast majority of corporations still discriminate against returnees. The government has been even slower to respond to the returnee's plight. Although the problem has been around for decades, it was not until October 1988 that the Ministry of Education first asked the schools to try to accommodate the returnees.

A similar trade off exists for Japan's higher education system. Like its lower schools, Japan's higher education system is the antithesis of internationalism. The schools do a great job of socialization but fall far short of turning out thinking, creative individuals. The 'old boy' networks developed at the better universities feed directly into Japan's governing triad while university clubs provide a similar socialization experience as their high school counterparts. Yet, even the author of 'Japan as Number One' admits that 'analytical rigor in the classroom is lacking, and attendance is poor . . . the Japanese student in his essays is more likely to follow guidelines than develop his originality'.[47] Edwin Reischauer's condemnation goes even further: 'the squandering of four years at the college level on poor teaching and very little study seems an incredible waste of time for a nation so passionately devoted to efficiency'.[48]

Perhaps the major reason why university students receive such an unchallenging education is the faculty seniority system. Although the corporate seniority system has been a vital aspect of big business dynamism, the faculty seniority system has had exactly the opposite effect, turning out not only poorly educated students, but research generally considered well below international standards of scholarship. For example, while most of its social scientists are churning out mountains of Nihonjinron tracts, Japan has produced only seven nobel prize winners.

Universities are hierarchically structured, both between and within departments. Each department is composed of several chairs (koza) consisting of a full professor, an associate professor, several assistant professors, and lecturers. Those below the professor dedicate themselves to carrying out the full professor's research, and rarely have time to enjoy any independent research. Professors (sensei) pick their disciples (deshi) from their undergraduates. About 95 per cent of the teachers at Tokyo University and 90 per cent at Kyoto University were students at the school they eventually taught at.[49] Tenure is automatic to everyone even if their teaching or research skills are not as vigorous as their loyalty to the professor. New disciples receive tenure in a couple of years, are promoted by strict seniority rather than merit, and spend about ten years at each level, reaching a professorship about their mid–40s.

The koza system obviously leads to a notoriously inbred, parochial, and unoriginal academic environment in which the 'scholars' tend to rework the same tired themes with no challenge from or interest in outside views. Just as students would never challenge their teacher's views, no disciple would ever challenge the views of his sensei. Despite its poor teaching and scholarly output, the Education Ministry defends koza because they give academics 'stability and security'.[50]

Another obstacle to any insignificant internationalization is the extremely low percentage of foreign teachers and students. In 1985 only 900 out of 110 000 teachers were foreign; until November 1986 none was allowed tenure at the national universities. An even lower percentage of students are foreign – in 1985 foreign students numbered only 15 000 (0.4 per cent) out of 2.2 million students. About 85 per cent of the foreign students were from Asia; of the total number of foreign students 29 per cent were from Taiwan, 20 per cent South Korea, 18 per cent China, 12 per cent Southeast Asia. Only 5 per cent of the foreign students were American in contrast to the over 13 000 Japanese students in the United States, almost more than the total number of foreign students in Japan. In comparison there were over 350 000 foreign students (3.1 per cent of the total) in the United States, 100 000 (10.8 per cent) in France, 57 000 (6.2 per cent) in West Germany, and 52 000 (10.8 per cent) in Britain. Although in 1985 Prime Minister Nakasone announced a plan to have 100 000 foreign students by the year 2000, only 6800 entered under the new system of relaxation in 1986.[51]

Both the Nakasone administration and Maekawa Report targeted education as a prime target for internationalization. This goal is in the hands of the National Council of Education Reform (formed in 1983) which directly reports to the Prime Minister rather than the Ministry of Education. Yet Japan's school system is unlikely ever to achieve an genuine internationalization despite stated government policy. Perhaps the major reason is that education reform policy aims at deeply contradictory goals. Nakasone stated that 'educational reform should aim to preserve and further develop the traditional Japanese culture . . . well balanced personalities and creative power . . . so that these future Japanese citizens may be able to contribute to the international community with a Japanese consciousness'.[52] A Council report proclaims that an 'emphasis on individuality is considered the fundamental guiding principal' and it criticizes the 'excessive emphasis on memorization [that] has produced many conformist people who are unable to think independently and creatively'.[53] The report goes on to recommend decentralizing and loosening control over the system, and identifies the 'national challenge of finding a balance between group harmony and individuality in Japanese culture' and ends by asking: 'How can we foster individuality and creativity while at the same time maintaining respect for harmony as part of our culture?'[54]

The answer is, of course, that it cannot – Japanese groupism and Western individualism are complete opposites. Although Western individualism exists within a group context, Japanese groupism has no place for the individual and is unlikely to create one. Genuine individuality revolves around choice: the ability to choose one's lifestyle, career, and workplace. Yet, while individuals are free to choose, they must take responsibility for their choice. One important constraint on choice its impact on one's group. Although the individual is free to choose an option that runs counter to his group – whether it be his family, school, religion, workplace, or society as a whole – he must be prepared to accept responsibility for the costs as well as the benefits. The best American corporations combine a dynamic blend of both individualism and groupism, with an emphasis on the former. At firms like Hewlett-Packard or IBM, individuals devote themselves to their company out of free choice. In contrast, Japanese society provides few opportunities for individuals to live freely and choose. Groups – whether they be families, schools, or firms – choose on behalf of their individual members. Genuine individuality cannot exist within Japanese society.

Creativity, however, is a separate problem, and can be achieved within a Japanese context. Japanese corporations have proven to be very creative at innovation. If the corporation's problem-solving methods were used in the classrooms, they might make for a much more dynamic interchange of ideas than the present assumption that there is only one right answer to every problem and emphasis on rote memorization rather than thinking. But the biggest culprit behind the lack of creativity is the college examination system which tests the ability to memorize facts rather than to creatively reason. Using an American style aptitude college entrance test would free students from literally years of dreary memorization for more creative, individual pursuits.

MINORITIES AND WOMEN

How a society treats its minority groups indicates its relative ability to genuinely internationalize. Although Japanese like to think of themselves as belonging to a 'pure race', and the Japanese government's 1980 Human Rights Report to the UN publically claimed that there were no minorities in Japan, in fact about 4 per cent of the population belongs to a range of distinct minority groups. Ethnic minorities include Koreans (650 000), Chinese (50 000), Ainu (60 000). Okinawans (1 million), foreigner workers (770 000), and refugees (5000), while cultural minorities include the untouchable class (burakumin, 3 million), atomic bomb victims (hibakusha, 20 000), racially mixed (konketsuji – 50 000), and returnees (kikoku shijo). Although women make up more than 50 per cent of the population, they can be considered a type of minority too because of their inferior status.

Like every industrial society, Japan faces problems of overcoming discrimination against minority groups and assimilating them into society's mainstream. Although progress has been made, all of Japan's minority groups face varying degrees of discrimination in terms of employment, school, housing, and marriage. In some cases legislation has been passed to deal with these problems, but has often been criticized as merely expressing principles (tatemae) while discrimination persists (honne).

The problem of discrimination is directly addressed in Article 14 of the Constitution: 'All of the people are equal under the law and there shall be no discrimination in political or economic or social relations because of race, creed, sex, social status, or family origin'. After considerable pressure from the affected minority, and at times foreign governments, Tokyo has passed a number of laws attempting to deal with minority groups that continue to suffer discrimination in such things as work, school, housing, and marriage. For example, the 1969 Special Measures Law for Assimilation closed all pre-twentieth century family registers (koseki) to prevent potential employers, schools, or marriage partners from determining whether or not the candidate was from the burakumin class, although burakumin claim it has not significantly affected their status. In 1978 the Supreme Court ruled in the McLean Decision that foreigners have the same freedom of expression as Japanese – although it hinted that visa extensions could be revoked if the foreigner exercised his right in a way that disturbed Japan's harmony. The 1986 Equal Employment Bill was passed in order for Japan to live up to the 1980 UN resolution on the status of women, but Japanese women groups claim it is merely a statement of principles. Until 1987 the children of a foreign male married to a Japanese could not be citizens unless the child was illegitimate, but the law was changed after concerted foreign protest.

What specific problems do minorities still face in Japan? Burakumin are Japan's largest and, aside from the Ainu, oldest minority group. Their exact origins are unknown, but the burakumin class is based on families that were involved in impure professions like skinning or funerals, with their ranks augmented by criminals and other outcasts. Originally called eta (people of great filth) and hinin (non-human), their present name, burakumin literally means village people and refers to their ghetto within each town or city. During the Tokugawa era, laws were passed formalizing their inferior status and inability to move elsewhere.

The burakumin are the most politically active of all Japan's minority groups. A variety of groups emerged in the Meiji era to campaign for equal rights, and as a result the new government officially abolished the burakumin class. While these groups were originally relatively moderate, they became increasingly active during the early twentieth century led by the Leveler's Society (Suiheisha) formed in 1922. Like all other political groups, the Levelers were disbanded in 1941. Following the war, three burakumin groups emerged, affiliated with the JSP, JCP, and LDP, respectively. After resisting the pressure for civil rights throughout the 1940s and 1950s, the LDP finally passed a bill in 1960 aimed at investigating their conditions. The Commission took five years before it issued a report in 1965 acknowledging that widespread discrimination continued to exist. It took another four years for the Diet to pass the 1969 Special Measure Law outlawing discrimination. Despite all these measures and efforts, discrimination has continued through today as most Japanese consider burakumin inferior in intelligence and ability.

The Koreans first trickled into Japan during the early twentieth century after Japan conquered Korea, but their population expanded enormously during World War II as millions of Koreans were imported as slave labor for Japan's mines and factories. Although the number dropped dramatically from 1945 when there were 2.3 million Koreans in Japan to 500 000 two years later, their population has since expanded to its present level of nearly 700 000.

Considered an inferior 'race', Koreans have suffered enormous discrimination from their first arrival. An estimated 4000 were murdered following the Kanto earthquake of 1924 when a rumour spread that Koreans were poisoning the wells, and untold thousands died from being worked to death during the war. Since 1945, in addition to the standard discrimination in terms of housing, jobs and private schools that all minority groups face, Koreans suffer the additional indignity of being forced to give up their Korean names before they can become citizens, and fingerprinting as alien residents. Politically, the Koreans are divided between those favoring the North and others the South, and their internal divisions have prevented the emergence of any powerful group to champion Korean rights.

The Ainu (Utari, friend') are the original people of the Japanese islands, and they suffered a fate of declining population, expropriation of land, and continued discrimination similar to the American Indians. Although the remaining Ainu live on reservations served by the 1974 Utari Policy Program, the government does not officially recognize them as a minority. Socio-economically, the Ainu are the worst off of Japan's minority groups. Seven per cent of Ainu are on welfare, a figure six times the national average, while only 78 per cent of those eligible attend high school and only 8 per cent college.[55]

Japan's largest minority group after the burakumin are the Okinawans. After an independent existence of thousands of years, the Ryukyu Islands were annexed by Japan in 1872. Although the Ryukyus were made a province, the Okinawans have suffered continuing discrimination up to the present. The worst came during the invasion of the Islands in 1945 when one-third of the population, or 150 000 were killed either in crossfires, bombardments, or even directly by the Japanese soldiers who drove them out of their shelters. The Ryukyu Islands were administered by the United States until being returned to Japan in 1972, and one sign of their inferior status was the government's compliance with the handover of the Okinawans to the United States. At the time Emperor Hirohito said to MacArthur that he hoped 'that the United States will continue the military occupation of Okinawa and other islands of the Ryukyus . . . to provide protection for Japan'.[56]

Surveys indicate that the Okinawan's anti-Japanese feelings remain high. A 1982 survey revealed that only 4 per cent had formed friendly relations with other Japanese, while 40.3 per cent felt awkward with Japanese, only 15.3 per cent thought marriage with Japanese desirable while more – 20.2 per cent – said it was undesirable.[57] In a September 1987 poll, only 57 per cent welcomed the Emperor's proposed visit in 1987 while 11 per cent opposed it; 47 per cent felt no special closeness and only 37 per cent did. The rate of high school compliance for displaying the Japanese flag (Hinomaru) or singing the anthem (Kimigayo) is zero.[58] Despite these hard feelings there are no Okinawan civil rights groups.

The status of women improved enormously during the Occupation. Before 1945 women not only lacked civil rights, but human rights as well; voting rights have been the least important change for women. Traditionally, women had little choice over marriage or divorce. Marriages were arranged and the woman had little choice over her spouse. A woman could be easily divorced for a variety of reasons, including not bearing a male heir. During hard times, daughters were regularly sold into prostitution. In contrast, the 1947 Constitution grants women equal political, economic, and social rights with men. Subsequent laws require both marriage and divorce to be based on mutual consent, while the 1985 Equal Employment Bill theoretically grants women equal economic rights.

Yet discrimination persists. Statistically, women have made rapid strides in the workplace: for example, in 1965 only 45 per cent of working women were married, while now about 70 per cent are. There are two large surges of women workers, the first of women aged 18 to 28 followed by a ten-year dip as women marry and then a gradual rise after age 35 as the children enter school. The quality of work, however, leaves much to be desired. A 1987 survey of 1000 firms found that only 150 had women at the kacho (section-chief) level, and fewer than 20 have women in positions above that level. Altogether only 7.3 per cent of working women have a subordinate. Sumitomo bank claims the largest number of high administrators (sogo shoku): 50 women out of 12 000 total. Women, on average, earn only half as much as men. There are, however, 80 000 women presidents of small, often one or two person, firms.[59]

Women are not covered by the company lifetime employment system and in 1984 90 per cent of all part-time workers were women. In the firms a woman's job is essentially ornamental, consisting mostly of 'smiling, bowing, and pouring tea'. One firm's employment requirements explicitly warned against hiring women who 'wear glasses, are very short, speak in loud voices, have been divorced, or are daughters of college professors'.[60] Women are discriminated against in higher education as well. In 1980 men accounted for 82 per cent of all four-year college students and women 90 per cent of all junior-college students. In terms of studies, 70 per cent of men enrolled in law, economics or applied sciences, but only 20 per cent of women.[61]

In politics there have been only five female Cabinet ministers and eight parliamentary vice-ministers since 1948. After the 1986 elections the House of Representatives was 98.6 per cent male; only 1.4 per cent of prefectural level councillors, 3.2 per cent of municipal councillors and 7.7 per cent of ward councillors were women. There were no women governors. Before the election, when asked whether his faction would field any women candidates, Prime Minister Takeshita said no because campaigning 'is too physically tough for women'.[62] The bureaucracy is no better. It did try to be progressive though when in 1986 it allowed women to take two Saturdays off a month and dropped the requirement that women wear uniforms. Of the 1987 entering class, women numbered 128 of 1669. That same year, out of 6500 middle-ranking administrators in the bureaucracy, 36 were women. Not to be outdone, the Self Defense Force recently announced that it will accept women to the Defense Academy after 1990.[63]

Women face social discrimination as well. For example, about half of women receive no alimony at all during a divorce and the rest a lump payment of two to three million yen ($15–20 000). Most divorce is by mutual consent; few go to court because of the immense time and money involved. The husband generally keeps the children. Twice as many women as men refuse to inherit their parent's estate, implying they are pressured to renounce it. About 40 per cent of all marriages result from an arranged meeting in which the couple must decide after three or four dates whether they want to marry or not. After the wedding the marriage settles down into a traditional routine where the women pours her energies into her children and the home.

Why does this discrimination persist? Boys and girls are socialized from birth to follow the traditional roles of men as bread-winners and women as bread-bakers. According to Confucian tradition, women are considered morally, intellectually, and emotionally inferior to men. It is said a woman must serve three masters in her life: first her father, then her husband, and finally her son. These attitudes are manifested in the Japanese language, which has different speech for males and females; while male language to females is direct and blunt, women must speak indirectly and subserviently to men.

Discrimination against women in the workplace becomes a self-fulfilling prophecy which is used to justify continued discrimination. It is assumed that women will work only to find a husband, and even if a woman should want to continue working after marriage, her first commitment is to her home. Since women will only work three or four years after graduation, it is considered a waste of time to train, pay, and provide them with responsible jobs. Of course, since there are no opportunities, women do drop out to get married since that is the only viable option society gives them. More than two-thirds, or 71 per cent of Japanese men think a woman's place is in the home, compared to 34 per cent of American men, and only 13 per cent of Swedish men.[64]

The 1986 Equal Employment Bill provides an excellent example of the relative power of women in Japan. In July 1980 Japan reluctantly signed the UN-sponsored Convention on Elimination of all forms of Discrimination against Women, which required all signatories to pass legislation to fulfill the goals of equal opportunity. Originally the Japanese delegation was not going to sign but decided to so so that the LDP could pick up some additional female votes in the upcoming election. At first women groups enthusiastically supported the original bill while Keidanren and Nikkeiren lobbied first to table the bill, and then had it rewritten so that no significant reforms would go through. Feminist groups then opposed the bill because it provides no guarantee of protection against discrimination but does away with current protective provisions such as menstrual leave, restrictions on overtime, holiday, and night work. Employers are only requested to strive for equality in hiring and promotion, while women are still prevented from working more than 24 hours overtime a month.

Will the status of women change in the future as Japan's population ages and more women are needed to fill the labor shortage? Or even then will they simply take the more menial jobs while men continue to dominate the important positions? As in the case of other minorities, any institutional convergence towards more international standards of equal opportunity and non-discrimination are undercut by the persistence of traditional attitudes and informal institutions.

The status of and opportunities for women and other minorities will change little in the forseeable future.

CONCLUSION

In all three interrelated areas examined – the Japanese perception of themselves and the world, the school system's role in socializing Japanese into those perceptions, and the impact of those perceptions on minorities – Japan clearly is not only unlikely to achieve any significant degree of internationalization, but may actually become increasingly nationalistic. How will Japan's new nationalism affect its international relations? Ivan Morris argues that Japan's 'sense of isolation and the resultant paranoia, persecution mania, and belief in uniqueness all combine to lead nationalism into dangerous channels'.[65]

Into what 'dangerous channels' could Japan's new nationalism lead? Morris and many other analysts have pointed out a cyclical pattern in Japan's relations with the outside world. Each cycle has four phases. The first phase comes after a period of isolation when foreign influences begin to filter into Japan. During this time there is deep debate among Japan's élite between the traditionalists who oppose those foreign influences and the accommodationists who favor them. During the second phase the accommodationists win out and enthusiastically open the flood gates to the foreign institutions, ideas, and values, and use them to solve domestic development problems and political conflicts. The third phase comes when Japan's system has saturated its needs for foreign influences, and a slow xenophobic reaction starts to gather force. The final phase results in a total rejection of foreign relations and isolation from the world. Japan has undergone four complete turns of this cycle (Chinese/Korean cultural sphere during the fifth-tenth century and thirteenth century, Western cultural sphere during the sixteenth century, and mid-nineteenth century to 1945 and some argue it may be in the third phase of the fifth.

Is Morris right? Will Japan's current saturation with foreign influences and growing nationalism lead to another rejection of the outside world and isolationism. The answer is a resounding no! Japan's prosperity is too interdependent with the outside world for Tokyo ever to abandon it in some mad Tokugawa-style isolation or World War II style national banzai charge into self-destruction.

Yet Japan's economic and political conflicts with its partners will deepen with its own interrelated growing confidence and power. Japan's new nationalism will increasingly clash with the mainstream Japanese definition of internationalization as the 'smooth promotion of Japan's national interests; the achievement of Japan's economic goals overseas without rocking the boat in international waters'.[66]

Will the new nationalists or old neo-mercantilists win out? The worst case scenario sees demands on Japan to trade fairly, extend genuine aid, and assist world environmental problems continuing to build as Japan becomes increasingly wealthy and powerful. This foreign pressure in turn reinforces the Japanese self-perception that they are a 'martyr' nation besieged, scape-goated, and bashed by jealous rivals. In response, Tokyo will take increasingly aggressive, openly self-serving stands on world trade and environmental issues. Japanese paranoia becomes a self-fulfilling prophecy as its continued neo-mercantilism provokes foreign protectionism and an eventual world trade war which impoverish everyone.

This scenario is unlikely to happen; cooler heads on all sides will prevail to manage growing conflicts. Yet clearly Japan's new nationalism will continue to grow. No other country is experiencing a similar degree of nationalistic introspection and historical revisionism. Even the Soviet Union has recently started openly to come to honest terms with its own barbarous past. In contrast, rather than promote their own 'glasnost' policy, Japanese at every level of society, from academics to politicians to the proverbial man in the street, are actually systematically distorting their history to depict Japan in the best possible light and widen the Japanese perception gap between themselves and the rest of humanity.

Despite these disturbing trends, Japan and the rest of the world will survive Nihonjinron. The nationalist chorus will stiffen the government's already immobilist stand on most international issues. But the chorus will never take over policy as it did in the 1930s. While Japan will never achieve any significant degree of genuine internationalization, its government will equally never do anything irresponsible enough to jeopardize the country's hard won wealth and power.

NOTES

1.   Peter Dale, *The Myth of Japanese Uniqueness*.
2.   Ibid., p. 15.
3.   Ibid., p. 3.
4.   Ibid., p. 16.
5.   Ibid., p. 17.
6.   Ibid., p. 17.
7.   Ross Mouer and Yoshio Sugimoto, *Images of Japanese Society*, p. 388.
8.   *Japan Economic Journal*, 23 April 1988.
9.   Kenneth Pyle 'The Future of Japanese Nationality', *Journal of Japanese Studies*, vol. 8, no. 2, Summer 1982, p. 239.
10. *Far Eastern Economic Review*, 19 February 1987.
11. Mouer and Sugimoto, op. cit., p. 397.
12. Chikara Higashi, *Japan's Internationalization*, p. 116.
13. Ibid., p. 57.
14. Hong N. Kim, 'Japanese-Korean Relations in the 1980s'. *Asian Survey*, vol. 27, no. 5, May 1987, p. 504.
15. *Independent*, 13 January, 1989.
16. *International Herald Tribune*, 26 April, 1988.
17. *Independent*, 13 January 1989.
18. *International Herald Tribune*, 17 December 1988.
19. *Far Eastern Economic Review*, 18 February 1988.
20. *The Listener*, 8 December 1988.
21. Ibid.
22. Pyle, op. cit., pp. 297–300.
23. Shupei Kumon, 'Some Principles Governing the Thought and Behavior of Japanists', *Journal of Japanese Studies*, vol. 8, no. 1, Winter 1982, p. 6.
24. *Far Eastern Economic, Review*, 18 February, 1988.
25. Ibid.
26. Ibid.
27. Ibid.
28. Ibid.
29. Mouer and Sugimoto, op. cit., p. 382.
30. Ibid., p. 388.
31. Dale, op. cit., p. 19.
32. Mouer and Sugimoto, op. cit., p. 390.
33. *Japanese Education Today*, United States Department of Education, 1987, p. 63.
34. Ibid., p. 23.
35. Ibid., p. 22.
36. Ibid., pp. 11–14.
37. *Japan Times Weekly*, 30 April 1988.
38. Ibid.
39. *Japanese Education Today*, p. 34.
40. Ibid., p. 45.

41. Harold Stevenson, *et al.*, *Child Development and Education in Japan*, p. 225.
42. *Japanese Education Today*, p. 37.
43. *Japan Times Weekly*, 30 April 1988.
44. Thomas Rohlen *Japan's High Schools*, p. 122.
45. *Japanese Education Today*, p. 54.
46. *International Herald Tribune*, 12 October 1988.
47. Ezra Vogel, *Japan as Number One*, p. 162.
48. Edwin Reischauer in Benjamin Duke, *The Japanese School*, p. xviii.
49. *Japanese Education Today*, p. 52.
50. *Economist*, 23 April 1988.
51. *Japanese Education Today*, p. 55.
52. Ibid., p. 64.
53. Ibid., p. 65.
54. Ibid., p. 66.
55. Takaki Mizuto, 'Ainu, the Invisible Minority', *Japan Quarterly*, vol. 34, no. 2, April 1987, p. 145.
56. Masato Yamazaki, 'History Textbooks that Provoke an Asian Outcry', *Japan Quarterly*, vol. 34, no. 1, January 1988, p. 10.
57. Ibid.
58. Hidetoshi Nishimura, 'Flag and Anthem,' *Japan Quarterly*. vol. April 1988, p. 155.
59. *Economist*, 14 May 1988.
60. Ibid.
61. Ibid.
62. Ibid.
63. Ibid.
64. Ibid.
65. Ivan Morris, *Nationalism and the Right Wing in Japan*, p. 424.

14 Economic Internationalization or Nationalism?

Although Japan will clearly never achieve any significant psychological or social internationalization, there is a possibility that it may eventually realize a relatively significant political and economic internationalization. But to do so, Tokyo must abandon the neo-mercantilist policies that have brought the country such tremendous wealth and power, and instead convert Japan into a liberal superpower with extensive responsibility for maintaining the world economy, much as Britain and the United States did during their respective heydays as hegemons.

This conversion from neo-mercantilism to liberalism involves a massive change in two interrelated policy areas. First, Japan must bring up the quality of life of its people to the level of other industrial countries. Measured by the old standard of living indices of per capita income, Japan's population is the world's second richest, with an average $19 500 each; measured by a quality of living index like the parity purchasing equation, Japan's real per capita income drops to a mere $13 000, on a par with most industrial countries.[1] If measured by other quality of life indices like per capita park acreage, sewage hook-ups, or leisure time, Japan is by far the poorest of the OECD countries. The culprit behind the huge gap between Japan's standards of living and poor quality of life is the government whose policies continue to promote industry at the expense of people.

Thus, genuine economic internationalization means in part stimulating the domestic economy by dismantling Japan's still bewildering array of import and investment barriers that have helped Japanese industries become the world's most dynamic at the expense of Japanese consumers and foreign producers; the Kafkaesque distribution system, hundreds of industrial cartels, and bureaucratic obstacles must all go. But it also means shifting the emphasis from crude standard of living measurements of 'economic development' such as per capita income and GNP growth rates to quality of life measurements like more and better leisure time, public parks, and good housing.

358

This policy shift will contribute to Japan's international responsibilities as a world economic superpower. But liberalism involves much more than simply shifting from export-led to domestic-led economic growth. As an economic superpower, Japan must significantly increase its contributions to defense and aid to the level of its allies, serve as an engine of world economic growth – a responsibility which includes running trade deficits with developing countries and resolving the debt crisis, allow a dramatic increase in foreign refugees and workers, and stop contributing to and start resolving such global environmental problems as the green-house effect, depletion of the ozone layer, and destruction of the rain forests.

Twenty-five years of persistent foreign pressure and internal change have resulted in some slow, uneven progress in Japan's contributions to the world political economy: the more obvious barriers to foreign imports of goods, services, and capital have been grudgingly dismantled, in volume terms Japan now dispenses more foreign aid than any other country and has the world's third largest defense budget after the United States and Soviet Union. As Japan's economy has become increasingly complex and sophisticated, it has split between those economic interests who favor significant internationalization of some areas and those who remain opposed. Examples abound. Keidanren favors the dismantlement of Japan's agricultural trade barriers while the farmers remain adamantly opposed to any concessions. MITI favors greater foreign procurements by the giant corporation NTT, while MPT fights to continue the traditional 'buy Japan' policies. MFA wants significantly to untie and increase aid while the other ministries argue for its continued use as an export subsidy for Japanese goods and services. The Maekawa Report calls for greater leisure time, while virtually all the other ministries and business federations remain opposed.

Despite these changes, there are many interrelated obstacles to any genuine shift from neo-mercantilism to liberalism. Entrenched economic interests clamouring for continued protection are reinforced by the prevailing Japanese perceptions that, in the words of Chikara Higashi, 'still see Japan as somewhat vulnerable and unique, and believe it should be treated as a special case among the world's nations. Others believe that Japan alone is asked to endure painful economic changes to please other nations which suffer from symptoms of 'advanced nation disease'.[2] A related problem is a misunderstanding of what internationalization actually means. Although a February 1989 Tokyo Broadcasting survey indicated that

62 per cent of Japanese agreed that their country is now a world economic power with international responsibilities while only 31 per cent disagreed, few seem to grasp what genuine internationalization entails.[3] Former minister of MOF and MITI Michio Watanabe, summed up the common perception of internationalization as merely 'the shift from an export-led to a domestic demand-led growth'.[4] For most bureaucrats and businessmen, internationalization simply means a more sophisticated version of nationalism – more 'tatemae' concessions on trade, aid, and defense issues while Japan's policies remain essentially neo-mercantilist. For most Japanese people, internationalization means occasionally going to a foreign film or restaurant, and possibly studying a foreign language or even travelling abroad, but it rarely includes the desire for foreign news, friends, students, workers, refugees or even goods.

This élite and mass confusion over the meaning of internationalization prevails despite a 'consensus building' series of government reports throughout the 1980s, such as MITI's 1980 'Policy Visions for the 1980s', EPA's 1983 'Japan in the Year 2000', MITI's 1986 'Japan in the Global Community: Its Role and Contribution on the Eve of the Twenty-first Century', and the 1986 Maekawa Report, which all shared the same theme that Japanese had genuinely to open up their hearts, minds, and markets to the rest of the world. Like its predecessors, the Maekawa Commission Report published on 7 April 1986, just before Prime Minister Nakasone's summit with President Reagan in Washington and four weeks before the Big Seven summit meeting in Tokyo, provides a simple list of 'goals' involving more open markets, deregulation, leisure time, and consumption. Although it was clearly a 'tatemae' public relations gesture to allay continued foreign criticism, Nakasone was widely condemned across the political economic spectrum at home when he promised Reagan that he would implement the Report.

This chapter will analyze the internationalization of Japan's political economy in two broad, interrelated areas. The first section focuses on quality of life issues such as leisure time, welfare, and personnel consumption. The second section will examine how far Japan has assumed its other international obligations in such areas as stimulating domestic demand, opening its trade and investment markets, and contributing more to foreign aid, defense, and the environment.

INTERNATIONALIZING JAPAN'S QUALITY OF LIFE

Every survey on the subject indicates that 90 per cent of Japanese believe they are middle class. This perception is reinforced by some statistical methods that show Japan's society is the OECD's most egalitarian after Australia.[5] In contrast, many Japanese privately admit that they do not feel as rich as the surveys and some statistical methods indicate. The economist Kimihiro Masamura writes that 'Japan's middle class is not really middle class by anyone else's standard . . . Japan's middle class is lower class', and he then goes on to talk of a growing 'have and have not' gap between homeowners and the 'new poor' or 'given up becoming rich' (akiramerichi) rentier class.[6]

Which image is correct? Is Japan the immensely rich, predominantly middle-class country that some statistics argue, or is the infamous 1979 Economic Community Report closer to the mark when it asserted that 'Japanese are workaholics living in rabbit hutches'? In terms of a raw per capita income of $19 500 in 1987, Japan was the OECD's second richest country, behind Switzerland's phenomenal $27 000 per capita income, but well ahead of America and Germany's $18 400, and nearly twice Britain's $11 800. Yet this figure does not accurately reflect economic reality for several reasons. When measured by purchasing power parity, Japan's per capita income sinks to a mere $13 000, the same as France's and slightly more than Britain's $12 000 but behind America's $18 200 and West Germany's $13 300.[7] Continuing trade barriers and an inefficient distribution system push up prices for goods to a point where not only imports are more expensive, but Japanese often pay twice the price for Japanese-made consumer goods like cameras, automobiles, or televisions as foreign consumers.

Not only is Japan's real per capita income about 60 per cent of the standard measurement, but some wealth distribution measurements that include property ownership and after-tax income reveal that Japan actually ranks twelfth among the 18 OECD countries in wealth distribution and seventh in household income distribution.[8] With the spiralling boom in land prices, the gap between those who own and those who do not continues to widen. Another source of inequality is the tax system, which discriminates against salaried workers, who are taxed at source, in favor of farmers, small businessmen, and shopowners who pay few taxes and usually own their own land. In 1987 the official real income growth for salaried workers was only 1 per cent compared to 4.3 per cent for independent business owners. In reality, because of the unequal tax burden, the gap was much greater.[9]

Even if Japan's purchasing power was greater and distribution of income more egalitarian, most Japanese would have little chance to enjoy it. Japanese workers annually spend as much as 250 to 300 more hours on the job than their American or British counterparts, and as much as 400 to 450 hours more than French or German workers; which means they annually work five to nine weeks more than their OECD rivals. But this dismal figure may actually be much worse, since many overtime hours never enter the official statistics. Clearly, the EC Report was right to label Japanese 'workaholics': whether they are by choice is another matter.

But even if the government could solve these lack of purchasing power and leisure-time problems, Japan's quality of life would still rank at the bottom of the OECD on most indices. The EC Report's description of Japanese living in rabbit hutches is an exaggeration, but Japanese do have the worst living conditions in the OECD. The average number of OECD housing units per 1000 inhabitants is 400 compared to Japan's 320, while its average floor area per person is 35 square meter's compared to Japan's 26 meters. Japan has the largest average number of persons per household (3.3), the second lowest number of houses per 1000 inhabitants, and the highest average mortgage rates – $308 000 paying $2200 a month, or 57 per cent of income. Between 1985 and 1986 speculation boosted commercial land prices 34.4 per cent and residential prices 18.8 per cent. Only 2.4 per cent of Japan's total surface area is used for housing, compared to industry's 0.4 per cent and agriculture's 14.6 per cent. About 34 per cent of farm land lies within urban areas.[10]

Japan's poor quality of life is revealed in a range of other indices. Its 53.8 persons per telephone compares to Sweden's 85.6, Switzerland's 77.6 and America's 71.0; its percentage of paved roads at 55 per cent compares to America's 75 per cent, Britain's 95 per cent, France's 96 per cent, and Germany's 99 per cent; Japan's traffic deaths per 100 million vehicle kilometers of 3.5 are far above the American 2.0; its 33 per cent sewage hook-up rate less than half the American rate of 72 per cent, and one-third Britain's 97 per cent rate.[11] Tokyo's 2.1 square meters of park space is miniscule compared to Paris's 12.2, London's 30.4, Bonn's 37.4, or Washington's 45.7 square meters per person.[12] Japanese use 30 per cent of their income on food, twice the American average of 15 per cent. Although the world's favorite travel spots seem overrun by Japanese tou: groups, in 1986 only 5.6 per cent of the population travelled abroad compared to 16.3 per cent of Americans, 18.2 per cent of French, 34.7 per cent of Germans, and 44.6 per cent of British.[13] Although a 1985 survey by the Prime Minister's Office indicated that 71.2 per cent were satisfied with their lives and only 28 per cent disatisfied,[14] Japan has the OECD's second highest per capita consumption of tranquilizers, one in three Japanese have been treated for stress-related illness, and 'death from overwork' (Karoshi) is becoming an increasingly important issue.[15] The only indicators in which Japan scored better than other OECD countries were its high life-expectancy of 75 years and low crime rate.

Given this overwhelmingly poor quality of life, why do 90 per cent of Japanese consider themselves middle class? Poor survey methodology accounts for much of the discrepancy. The words for upper- (joryu) and middle- (churyu) class have a very positive image while there is no good term for lower class – 'karyu' refers to the lower part of a stream but not a social class, while the prefix 'ge' in 'geryu' (lower-class) has negative connotations of inferiority, and the word is considered taboo. Thus, most people did not consider themselves joryu and without an acceptable term for lower-class simply marked themselves as 'churyu'.[16] But other methodological shortcomings include the failure to account for property income and social security benefits, which would have increased the number of those considered rich, and using after-tax income, which would have converted many middle class into lower class. Welfare recipients were excluded from the polls altogether. Cultural factors accounted for the strong middle-class identity as well. Japanese are socialized not to stand out in either a positive or negative sense. Thus, hardly anyone wanted to admit to being either poorer or richer than they actually were, and described themselves as middle class whether they were or not.[17]

Important political implications flow from the identification of 95 per cent of the population as either upper or middle class. Japan is experiencing a growing conservatism similar to that of the other industrial countries. Although LDP and JSP voter support fell steadily throughout the 1960s and 1970s, LDP strength has grown throughout the 1980s, while the JSP continues to lose Diet members. This shift paralleled Japan's development from an advanced industrial nation with its class divisions into the early stages of a post-industrial or 'new middle-mass' (chukan-taishu) society where class and ideological identities weaken and political pragmatism becomes the order of the age.[18]

What is fuelling the new conservatism (hoshu fukkatsu)? One major reason has been the LDP's pragmatic policies of coopting and taking credit for any popular ideas of the left, such as the environmental and welfare issues of the 1970s. Another is the LDP's ability to maintain a skewed electoral system that if corrected, would probably force them to form a coalition government with the center parties. Continued economic growth allows the LDP to receive tremendous amounts of cash from the business world, which it in turn distributes among the voting blocks around election time. Meanwhile, as the cheerleader of Japan's 'new nationalism', the LDP sways many patriotic floating voters into the conservative camp. The left and center parties remain fragmented and ineffectual. Finally, memories of the 1970s oil shocks reinforce the conservative idea that the less government, the better; the costly welfare policies of the 1970s have given way to the belt-tightening 'administrative reforms' of the 1980s.

These new neo-conservative, new middle-mass, or post-industrial values are revealed by a host of surveys and new expressions. Between 1973 and 1978 alone there was a marked drop in those polled who favored a policy emphasis on welfare (from 48 per cent to 31 per cent) and people's rights (from 11 per cent to 8 per cent), and a corresponding rise in those who favored economic development (10 per cent to 21 per cent) and law and order (from 12 per cent to 17 per cent).[19] Although this would appear to be a return to traditional growth at all costs, in fact the emphasis is on quality rather than quantity growth. There is a clear split in public opinion between those with industrial, instrumental (majime-shiko) and traditional (dento-shiko) values, an those with post-industrial, anti-traditional (dento-ridatsu), and consumer (asobi-shiko) values. Increasing numbers of Japanese are beginning to ask uncharacteristically introspective and anti-materialist questions about the proper lifestyle (kurashimuki), purpose of life (ikigai), satisfaction with life (seikatsu manzoku do), or what to do with all one's money (kanemari gensho). Japanese commentators describe such questioners as the 'new humanity' (shinjinrui).

Although there is clearly a growing minority of Japanese who are concerned with post-industrial values, and numerous government reports throughout the 1980s have promised policies to convert Japan into a post-industrial country, how far will any changes go? Although the government could theoretically reduce the current 48-hour work week to a 40-hour work week, it is extremely unlikely that any serious effort will be made to achieve an average OECD style work week anytime soon. Although the work year peaked in 1960 with 2432 hours and then declined steadily to 2064 in 1973, it gradually rose to a height of 2168 hours in 1985, then declined to 2138 in 1986, still an average 250–500 more hours than in any other OECD country. In 1986 only 22.1 per cent of all firms with 30 or more workers had a full six-day work week, while 77.1 per cent officially had five-day work weeks. The catch is that only 27 per cent offered a real two-day weekend on a continuous basis: 16.7 per cent had two-day weekends twice a month, 14.7 per cent once a month, and only 7.7 per cent three times a month, compared to almost all Western workers enjoying five-day work weeks. Altogether, only 28 per cent of industrial workers, composing 6.2 per cent of Japanese firms had five-day weeks in 1986.[20]

Why do Japanese work so much? Japan's 48-hour work week is a major reason. If Japan's work week were between 35 and 40 hours, as in the other OECD countries, firms might be less inclined to push for overtime. Because the work-week is so long, Japanese actually do not work much official overtime; in 1988 the monthly average was 21.8 hours. Another reason is that there are fewer paid holidays in Japan than in other industrial countries; Japanese workers enjoy only 12 a year compared to 19 in the United States, 23 in Britain, and 26 in France. Unlike the other OECD countries where national holidays are mandatory and workers can volunteer to work at double-time pay, Japan's are voluntary; firms, not the government, determine whether or not their employees work that day. Although this seems harsh, a 1986 Prime Minister's Office survey revealed that only 41 per cent wanted more free time, while 56 per cent were satisfied; half who wanted more free time were under the age of 30.[21]

Continual foreign pressure on Tokyo to reduce the official work week to remove an 'unfair' advantage of Japanese business along with bureaucratic rivalry caused the government to start the leisure bandwagon in the early 1970s, and then accelerate it throughout the 1980s, as both government and big business have issued a series of reports and actions calling for a gradual reduction in the work week. MITI fuelled a nascent leisure debate in 1972 when it created the semi-official Office for the Development of Leisure. Not to be outdone, MOE followed up MITI's initiative in 1973 with its own

Japanese Society for the Promotion of Leisure Culture. The two oil shocks temporarily submerged the debate, but it surfaced again in August 1983 when financial institutions agreed to take off one Saturday a month. Two years later MITI announced the creation of a Leisure Development Center to guide the development of a market that was worth $300 billion that year. The following year, the Maekawa Report called for a 40-hour work week and a reduction of total work hours to 1800 by March 1983. Every summer since the Department of Labor has echoed the call for a five-day week, and in June 1986 declared leisure a national task. Starting on 1 December 1987, the government actually began to practice what it preached when it closed its offices two Saturdays a month. In March 1988 the Post Office Savings Bank announced it would close on Saturdays in 1989, an action which allowed the commercial banks to follow suit. In February 1989 all government offices began closing two Saturdays a month, and in March all financial institutions, post offices, and stock exchanges followed suit, directly affecting 2 million workers but indirectly millions of others. Although both the business federations, Keidanren and Nikkeiren, and the labor federation Rengo, were long opposed to any work week reduction, in early 1989 they too agreed to support the policy.

But even if Japan's official work week and national holidays were comparable to those of other industrial countries, there would be little effect on the actual work week. For example, most older workers at the major firms are allowed two weeks holiday a year, yet the average vacation taken is a mere 5.1 days while most overtime is never recorded.

Why? As in all other aspects of Japan's political economy, there is a vast difference between the official (tatemae) situation and the actual (honne) situation. Just as a web of invisible but very real barriers impedes competitive imports, a web of invisible but very real barriers prevents Japanese workers from enjoying their vacation rights. Peer pressure and knowledge that to take 'too much' vacation would kill any advancement prospects and instead propel the worker into the 'by the window gang' (mado niwa zoku), which spend their careers drinking tea and reading newspapers, is a much more effective means of keeping Japanese 'workaholics' than any official policies. This 'invisible coercion' will remain the norm in all Japanese businesses despite the growing desire among young people for more leisure time. Japanese workers will become increasingly dissatisfied with their lives, but there is nothing they can do about it.

In fact, the government can officially reduce the work week and proudly point to such policies as proof that it is 'internationalizing' while the work week remains the same, much as it reduces visible trade barriers, then claims Japan has the world's most open economy and foreigners do not sell more because they do not try hard enough. The effect of both policies is the same – Japan officially appears to be 'internationalizing' and can then accuse foreign critics of 'Japan bashing' while it retains its comparative advantage and neo-mercantilist policies.

How significant is the steady shift in Japanese values from the traditional 'suppress personal interest and serve public goals' (messhi hoko) to the 'new humankind' (shinjinrui) quality of life adherents that the mass media play up? As always, the increasing number of people identifying with quality of life concerns may be more apparent than real. Japan has already gone through several 'quality of life' booms, but the emphasis was mostly materialistic, and led by clever marketing strategies rather than any deep social movement. The mass media and business cooperated to induce the 'three sacred treasure' (sanshu no jingi) boom of the late 1950s in which Japanese families scrambled to buy a washing machine, refrigerator, and vacuum cleaner, and in the mid-1960s, a buying surge around the '3Cs' – color television, 'cooler' (air conditioner), and car. The mass media claimed to identify a 'home before work' preference (mai-homu shugi) in the 1960s and resurrected the trend as the 'new family' orientation of the 1970s. Pundits have already labelled the new Heisei era as one of 'me-ism' (watashi-shugi).[22]

But as overtime hours and attitudes reveal, the slogans failed to ignite any genuine shift towards quality of life issues. Public and private employment continued to socialize workers into the traditional (suppress personal interest and serve public goals' values); anyone espousing 'my home' and 'new family' values continues to be considered unmanly. Leisure spending as a percentage of family income actually dropped slightly from 1970 to 1984, from 9.0 per cent to 8.9 per cent. Although only 45 per cent of people now use leisure time as simply a means to recharge their energy compared to 72 per cent before, while people who saw leisure as valuable in itself doubled from 15 per cent to 36 per cent, most Japanese still use leisure time to prepare for work (hataraku tame ni asobu) rather than work as a means to enjoy one's leisure (asobu tame ni hataraku).[23]

The rapid 'greying of Japanese society' will at once stimulate a growing leisure industry for retirees while forcing Japanese employees to work just as hard and long to pay for it. Because of an increased life expectancy (from 50 for men and 54 for women in 1947 to 75.2 for men and 80.9 for women in 1988) and declining birth rate (from 3.7 in 1950 to 1.8 in 1988), Japan's population is rapidly aging. In 1985 the percentage of Japan's population over 65 was only 10.3, slightly less than America's 11.8 per cent and well below Germany's 15.0 per cent. It is estimated that by the year 2020, however, the percentage of Japanese over 65 will reach 25 per cent, with pension costs rising from 4.2 per cent of GNP at present to 13.4 per cent then.[24]

Who is going to pay for all these retirees? During the 1980s the government has cut back the generous pension and health programs it originally created in the early 1970s because of popular demand. The 1982 Old People's Health Bill cut back medical care for the elderly, while the 1985 Pension Reform Act reduced the percentage of pensions to wages from a possible 83 per cent to 68 per cent. Robotization and computerization will increase productivity and cut back the number of blue- and white-collar workers demanded by industry, while foreign workers and women will increasingly fill important jobs. Yet government belt tightening and increased productivity will fill only part of the gap, the increased demands for and on workers will increase in the twenty-first century. Wages will rise steadily as both foreign and domestic firms scramble to acquire a dwindling supply of workers, labor mobility will increase, the savings rate will drop steadily, and Japan's comparative advantage in many industries will weaken.

INTERNATIONAL RESPONSIBILITIES

'New humanity' attitudes towards increased leisure time will not alone change Japan's quality of life, and the requirements of a rapidly aging society may actually increase demands on the workforce in the long run. As usual in Japan, the most powerful force for change will come from the outside. There is a very strong link between improving Japan's quality of life and fulfilling international responsibilities. The continual foreign pressure on Tokyo to abandon its neo-mercantilist policies for liberalism means dismantling a range of non-tariff barriers that have prevented Japanese consumers from completely enjoying the fruits of their role as producers. The benefits for

Japanese of more genuine transfers of foreign aid, defense, and technology to the needy, or leadership in global environment problems by Tokyo, may be far less apparent, but, in many ways, no less important. Everyone – Japanese and foreigners alike – benefits from an increasingly stable, prosperous world that is confronting a range of worsening environmental catastrophies. After over two decades of consistent foreign pressure, Tokyo has significantly increased its international contributions in many areas.

Throughout the late 1980s Tokyo not only agreed to shift from export-led to domestic-led growth, but has actually followed up its promises with several policies that have resulted in significant changes. One significant step has been to reverse its national tax policy that rewarded saving and often penalized consumption. In December 1988, after three years of political struggle, the Diet finally approved a sweeping tax reform bill that eliminates a range of savings rewards, simplifies the tax code, imposes a 3 per cent valued added tax on almost all goods, and hands over a huge tax cut. Although the value added tax will boost the prices of many basic items, it will vastly cut prices on foreign luxury goods such as automobiles, refrigerators, and large televisions, whose excise taxes often reached 30 per cent. Thus, even the value added tax should stimulate consumption.

Although the tax code was an important reason for Japan's high savings rate, it was not the only one. Japanese families set aside huge chunks of their monthly income in order to save for such major expenditures as their children's education or marriage, the purchase of a home, and eventual retirement. Unbridled land speculation throughout the 1980s severely boosted the price of a home, thus forcing families to save more and longer. Tokyo commercial property prices rose 160 per cent between 1983 and 1987, and 260 per cent in the three central Tokyo wards. Although politicians with inside information and considerable funds were benefiting from and stimulating the boom as much as anyone, the government finally overode vested interests in August 1987, and required that all prices of property larger than 500 square meters in Tokyo has to be government approved, while purchasers who resold their land within two years would be heavily taxed. In November the requirement was extended to all property over 100 square meters. At the same time the government proved its still vast powers of 'administrative guidance' by 'advising' financial institutions to curb their property loans. By late Fall, property loans had dropped from 38 per cent to 6 per cent of all loans. These policies burst the 'bubble'. By September 1987 office prices throughout Japan had tumbled 20–30 per cent, while Tokyo prices dropped by 4.4 per cent. These actions were followed up in March 1988, when the tax break was abolished which had allowed capital gains from property to go untaxed if the money was immediately ploughed back into property. By early 1989 property sales were half the level of a year and a half earlier.[25]

Tokyo has used supplementary budgets geared to infrastructure development projects as another means of stimulating domestic growth. In 1982 public works spending was only 1.4 trillion yen. In 1986, however, as part of its promise to stimulate the domestic economy, the government passed a 28.7 trillion yen supplementary public works budget, a figure which jumped to 48.7 trillion yen in 1987, 56 trillion yen in 1988, and 58 trillion for 1989.[26] The MOF contributed to domestic growth by cutting the discount rate five times since 1986.

These government policies to reform taxes, cut property prices, and increase infrastructure development, along with the strong yen after September 1986, powerfully stimulated the domestic economy. In both 1986 and 1987 domestic growth boomed by 4.1 per cent and 4.5 per cent respectively, while exports actually declined by about 0.5 per cent each year. Domestic demand grew 6.6 per cent in 1988 and a further 4.7 per cent in 1989. Up through 1988 over 600 000 new jobs were created which brought the unemployment rate of 2.4 per cent to the lowest level since 1973. Profit margins from cost-cutting and strong domestic demand rose a dazzling 65.2 per cent from March to September 1988, to peak at 3.48 per cent, the highest level since 1969.[27]

These policies affected only a fraction of the web of restrictions on domestic consumption. Consumer credit remains extremely cramped by laws limiting credit cards which allow payments over time. Instead, credit cards must be repaid in full by the month's end. Thus, credit card transactions remain unpopular; they were only $12 billion, or less than 2 per cent of personal consumption in 1983, a percentage that is estimated will rise to only 2.9 per cent by 1990.[28] Credit cards are valued for their prestige rather than practical value.

Another disappointment has been the limited effects of the strong yen on domestic prices. Although the yen has doubled in value since the Group of Five agreement in September 1985, importers kept most of the profits to themselves and passed on only a fraction of the revaluation to consumers. A 1988 survey indicated that only 7.9

per cent felt they were benefiting from the high yen, and in fact only 11 trillion yen of 29 trillion yen ($230 billion) in lower prices since 1985 have been passed on to consumers.[29] Aside from importers, producers greatly benefited from the strong yen, as raw materials and energy prices dropped by almost half. For example, Japan paid $40 billion less in 1986 for oil, which dropped as a percentage of imports from 43.1 per cent in 1985 to 29.8 per cent in 1986.[30]

A reduction of Japan's huge trade and current account surpluses would improve the quality of life of Japanese and foreigners alike. Japan has immense trade surpluses with almost all its non-oil producing trade partners. Of Japan's $93 billion trade surplus in 1988, about $50 billion was with the United States and $20 billion with Europe. Needless to say, foreign pressures on Japan to open its markets have increased with the deficit.

Japan's superficial trade barriers are lower than elsewhere: its average tariff rate of 2.9 per cent is the OECD's lowest, while its quotas are average. Yet Tokyo did little to dismantle the bewildering web of non-tariff barriers that continue to discriminate against competitive foreign imports. Like the hydra that Hercules confronted, two new barriers seem to pop up for every one that the government claims to have removed.

These trade barriers not only give Japanese firms a range of profits, economies of scale, and technology transfers that give them a comparative advantage over their foreign rivals, but they also export unemployment. A recent US Department of Commerce study found that between 1979 and 1985 the United States suffered a net loss of more than 1.5 million manufacturing jobs, most from unfair trade. For example, in 1984 export-related employment was 6.5 per cent while imports resulted in a 7.8 per cent job loss, which translated into 1.1 million jobs lost that year alone. Since Japan's trade surplus accounted for over one-third of America's total trade deficit, over 350 000 jobs were lost because of Japan's predatory trade practices. Economists estimate that about 21 000 jobs are lost for every $1 billion of trade deficit. Japan's trade surplus of $60 billion in 1986 put 1 260 000 Americans on the streets.[31]

What are these non-tariff barriers that continue to strain Japan's relations with its rivals, as well as give Japanese firms such powerful advantages in the world economy? In Japan relationships between firms rather than comparative advantage of products are the primary basis for the exchange of goods and services. A foreign firm with a comparative advantage must not only provide a product that is not produced within the keiretsu, but often not produced by industry-wide cartels as well. Because of the keiretsu and cartels it is rare for a foreign producer to capture more than a miniscule market share. The government could remove these trade barriers simply by enforcing its anti-trust laws. Instead, Tokyo not only tolerates but encourages these unfair trade practices by administering a range of production, price, import, export, and market cartels which numbered 422 in 1986, and wink at hundreds of other cartels which collaborate against Japanese consumers and foreign producers alike. The Keiretsu also prevent the foreign take-over of Japanese firms. While Japanese bought $12 billion worth of American firms alone in 1988, only 17 Japanese companies were bought by foreign firms in 1988, a drop from 22 in 1987.[32]

The construction industry provides an excellent example of how Japan's 'markets' work. Japan has the world's largest annual public works budget, whose benefits are enjoyed only by Japanese construction firms. Bids are prearranged and rotated (dango) so that all Japanese firms benefit. Washington first protested the construction cartel in 1984, and after three years of tough negotiations Tokyo agree to allow American firms a tiny fraction of the work on the $8 billion Osaka airport and five other projects. This pattern is characteristic of Japan's response to trade conflicts. After first being accused of presiding over a closed market Tokyo initially denies that it is closed and simply repeats the mantra that foreign firms do not sell more because they do not try hard enough. After the foreign government provides ample evidence that it is trade barriers and not lack of foreign effort that is the cause, Tokyo digs in its heels and fiercely stonewalls any concessions. Negotiations drag on for years and are 'resolved' only after the foreign government threatens to retaliate. Exhausted by the struggle, the foreign government then accepts a 'symbolic' miniscule market share as a sign of Tokyo's 'sincerity'.

Another important action Tokyo could take if it were really serious about fulfilling its market opening promises would be to abolish the Large-scale Retail Store Law which gives small stores a veto power over proposed new stores larger than 27 000 square feet, about the size of a large convenience store. Because of the law the expansion of large retail stores declined from a 12 per cent to 2 per cent annual rate over the last eight years.[33] Japan's distribution system is more than twice as intricate as those of other OECD countries. Over 20 per cent of Japan's workforce is in the distribution system compared to 10 per cent in the United States and 9 per cent in Germany. Although it has only half the population, Japan's 1.6 million retailers are more numerous than America's 1.5 million. Most of these retailers act as the exclusive outlet for one of the keiretsu. The keiretsu tie in the small retailers by a variety of means including extensions of 90-day credit, sale or return policies, sole agent agreements whereby the manufacturer entangles thousands of wholesalers and retailers into large groups under their control, secret rebates, and controlled prices. For example, Matsushita and Toshiba control 27 000 and 14 000 distributors, respectively. Thus, Japanese consumers must pay retail prices an average 48 per cent higher than in the United States.[34] Again, Japan's government could remove this formidable non-tariff barrier by abolishing the Large Scale Retailing law and enforcing existing anti-trust laws.

Although Tokyo claims to have removed a range of bureaucratic practices that were used to impede imports, an investigation by Bergsten and Cline revealed that discriminatory Japanese administrative practices alone may cost American manufacturers $6–8 billion a year in lost sales.[35] Japan's weak patent laws allow Japanese firms a free rein to copy and improve on foreign patents. In addition, the government has not altered its 'buy Japan' policies. Even more irritating than private monopolies are the more than a hundred public corporations that restrict imports to a fraction of sales. Although the government has recently attempted to privatize several of these public companies, such as NTT, the Tobacco monopoly, and JNR, these firms have maintained their 'buy Japan' policies. NTT procures its components from its 'family' of over 1000 Japanese firms. Again, if Tokyo was sincere about trade liberalization it could simply enforce its anti-trust agreements and pass a law saying that any procurements must go to the lowest bidder.

Since the early 1960s, the OECD has been pressuring Tokyo to liberalize its financial markets. Between 1967 and 1980 Tokyo made a series of small reforms that gradually shifted financial policy from 'basically restrictive to basically free in principle'. In the November 1983 Yen-Dollar Accord between Japan and the United States, Tokyo agreed to liberalize capital flows, internationalize the yen, expand foreign participation, and deregulate domestic capital markets. Tokyo has followed up the agreement by easing restrictions on foreign financial institutions in several areas including deposit interest rates, money market instruments, certificates of deposit bond issues, securities and trust markets, and offshore banking.

Despite these changes, the essence of Tokyo's financial policy remains based on trying to maintain as cheap a yen as possible, protecting financial markets and institutions, and funnelling cheap loans to key industrial sectors. MOF's power over financial markets and institutions remains immense despite this shift in principle. For example, although Japan is supposedly dedicated to internationalizing the yen, the yen's share in foreign reserves rose from 2 per cent in 1976 to 5.2 per cent in 1984, compared to 65.1 per cent for the American dollar and 12 per cent for the Deutschmark, while only about 3 per cent of Japanese trade was denominated in yen compared to deutschmarks comprising 40 per cent of Germany's trade and dollars almost 100 per cent of America's trade.[36]

Thus, since 1986 Japan's huge current account and trade surpluses declined only slowly despite the yen's doubling in value and Tokyo's 'market opening' steps. The current account surplus peaked in 1986 at $94.1 billion, then declined to $84.5 billion in 1987, and $78.0 billion in 1988, while the trade surplus dropped from an astronomical $101.6 billion to $94.0 billion and $93.0 billion over the same years.[37] Japan's overall trade continued to rapidly expand. In 1987 exports grew by $237.9 billion or 10.6 per cent while imports increased $161.9 billion or 39.2 per cent. Japan's trade partners, however, did not equally benefit from these imports. As if by design, despite or perhaps because of Washington's weak dollar and powerful negotiation efforts, Japanese imports from the United States during this time grew only 0.2 per cent, while imports from the EC and East Asia grew 26.7 per cent and 57.3 per cent, respectively.

The most impressive result of Japan's liberalization policies was the share of manufactured goods in total imports which rose steadily from 31.5 per cent in 1985, to 44.1 per cent in 1986, 45.6 per cent in 1987, and almost 50 per cent in 1988. Altogether the ratio doubled between 1981 and 1988. During this time, although from a very low base, steel imports increased 68 per cent to five million tons, with half coming from South Korea and Taiwan, while industrial machinery surged 60 per cent to $2.2 billion. Japan's imports of consumer goods was even more impressive: between 1986 and 1987 imports of televisions increased from 25 000 to 370 000 and VCRs from 18 000 to and 138 000, respectively.[38] When measured by market share, however, the increased imports are not quite as impressive: foreign machinery's market share rose from 5.9 per cent 1985 to 6.8 per cent in 1986, chemical products from 5.7 per cent to 6.8 per cent, and metals remained the same at 4.9 per cent. Yet, despite this, Japan's trade deficit with the NICs actually rose 10 per cent in 1988 to $22 billion. A large percentage of these products actually flowed from Japanese foreign investments. In addition, Japanese imports have slowed down while exports are surging again as firms adjusted to the strong yen by increasing productivity. Many economists agree that Japan's huge current account and trade surpluses have reached a plateau and will actually either remain at the same level indefinitely or actually start an upward climb past $100 billion again.[39]

Tokyo claims that the direct foreign investments of Japanese firms will eventually aleviate much of the trade problem. Between 1985 and 1988 Japanese foreign investments in Europe increased 125 per cent to $25.1 billion, and in the United States 140 per cent to $61.6 billion.[40] But in reality, foreign investments actually stimulate exports; it is estimated that every $1 billion of Japanese foreign investments raises Japanese machinery exports by $436 million. Japanese manufacturing firms eventually carry over Japanese sub-contractors and financial firms to the foreign country, supplanting domestic producers.[41]

Tokyo's unwillingness sincerely to resolve its trade problems is only one aspect of internationalization. In 1988 Japan surpassed the United States to become the world's largest aid donor, by dispensing almost $10 billion in aid compared to $8.9 billion from the United States.[42] Yet even this seemingly generous contribution to the developing world was controversial after close inspection. As a percentage of World ODA, Japan's share has risen little over the past 15 years, from 8.5 per cent in 1970, dropping to 6.8 per cent in 1975, rising to 10.4 per cent in 1980, and on up to 13.3 per cent in 1986–87. As a percentage of GNP, Japanese aid has risen steadily from 0.21 per cent in 1976 to 0.32 in 1980, then actually falling to 0.31 in 1987. During these years Japan's percentage of ODA to GNP was well behind the OECD average of 0.34 per cent, 0.36 per cent, and 0.35 per cent, respectively. In 1987 Japan ranked 13th of the 18 OECD countries in terms of its aid as a percentage of GNP. Its grant element of total ODA continues to lag at the bottom of the OECD countries, and has actually dropped recently. In 1981 Japan's grant element to total ODA was 75.0 per cent compared to an OECD average of 90.2 per cent; in 1987 Japan's had dropped to 62.4 per cent compared to the OECD's 87.0 per cent. In 1987 Japan's grant element to the poorest countries was 86.2 per cent compared to the OECD average of 95.6 per cent, while statistically Japan and Italy shared the ignominy of having their private grants as a percentage of GNP recorded as zero compared to an OECD 0.03 per cent.

But the chief criticism of Japanese aid is that it remains largely tied to the purchase of Japanese goods and services, and thus acts chiefly as an export subsidy for Japanese corporations. Shoji Ochi, deputy president of the Japan Center for International Finance, a private banks' research institution established to analyze country risks, admitted that Tokyo's aid policy was still basically neo-mercantilist, saying 'Japan's ODA has so far been export-oriented, aimed at increasing Japan's exports to developing nations'. He then added that Tokyo's aid policy should shift more to 'influence the domestic policies of recipients'.[43] The Asahi Shimbun reports that even if loans are officially designated as untied, in reality 'the bidding is open only to companies from Japan and firms of the recipient nations'. Since Japanese companies are more competitive than the domestic firms they land such contracts 'almost 100 percent of the time'.[44] The actual quality of Japanese aid remains dismally low. In 1988 only 47 per cent of Japan's ODA was estimated to be genuinely untied compared to 78 per cent for France, 90 per cent for the United States, and 99 per cent for Britain.[45]

At the June 1988 Big Seven Toronto Summit, Takeshita promised 'greater Japanese contribution to the world' including $50 billion in aid over the next five years, a rise in foreign aid as a percentage of GNP to 0.4 per cent by 1992, and proposals to ease the world debt crisis. Takeshita also agreed to join Washington's $10 billion Marshall aid program for the Philippines.

Will Japan's aid become increasingly untied or will it remain mostly an effective export subsidy for Japanese firms? Two recent events illustrate the possibilities. In 1987 Tokyo announced it was granting $500 million to sub-Saharan Africa to be dispensed through Britain's semi-official Crown Agents to ensure that it was untied. Those familiar with Japan's neo-mercantilist aid policies looked in vain for the catch. The African aid contrasted completely with the much more typical tied aid exemplified by a 1985 grant to Bangkok's Thamassat University to establish a center for Japanese studies. The grant was conditional not only on using Japanese firms to build a new center, but in addition on every one of the 200 000 library books coming from Japan. The Thais protested that English books rather than Japanese books were urgently needed since so few Thais could speak Japanese. After long negotiations, the Japanese agreed to the purchase of English books, but stipulated that they be bought through Japanese distributors who would ship them first through Japan.[46]

Whether aid will even be predominantly genuine or remain a carefully formulated set of export subsidies for Japanese industry remains to be seen. But it is extremely unlikely that Japan will reverse a tied aid policy that has been so beneficial to Japanese firms and given them an advantage over their foreign rivals.

Japan has also been criticized for its miniscule contributions to two related areas, accepting refugees and foreign workers. Although Japan's official quota for resettling Indochinese refugees is 10 000, in fact only about 5000 have been admitted to date. Japan's no more than token and grudging effort to aid a global problem compares badly with the extensive efforts of other OECD countries like the United States and France which accepted a million each, and Canada, Australia, Britain, and West Germany over 100 000 each. The United States alone spent over $1 billion in resettling the refugees. It is unlikely that Japan will ever reach its quota; in 1987 it accepted only 69 Vietnamese, five Lao, and 126 Khmers, less than 200 people altogether.[47] In response to criticisms of its unwillingness to aid the refugees, Japan claims that the refugees would not fit into Japanese society and the country is too crowded to take them anyway. Yet, certainly, the cultures of the Western countries that have opened their doors and hearts to the refugees are far more alien, while countries like The Netherlands and Belgium are even more crowded than Japan, but they have not hesitated to receive tens of thousands of refugees. The refugee issue is an excellent example of Japan's essentially 'beggar thy neighbor' neo-mercantilist policies.

Japan uses the same 'racial purity' arguments to limit its number of foreign workers. Only about 60 000 foreigners received work visas in 1988, a drop in the bucket for an overall working population of 60 million. But it is estimated that between 70 000 and 300 000 foreigners are currently working illegally in Japan, and the number is growing as Japan's labor market tightens. Some analysts estimate that by 1992 there could be as many as 600 000 illegal foreign workers, comprising 1 per cent of Japan's working population.[48]

Before 1985 most foreign workers were prostitutes who worked the thousands of nightclubs that salarymen enjoy visiting after hours. But since then as the yen has grown increasingly powerful their ranks have been joined by tens of thousands of people from Pakistan, Bangledesh, Thailand, China, and the Philippines who enter on 90-

day tourist visas and find jobs for pay which is 60 per cent lower than Japanese workers obtain. The foreign workers are difficult to catch; only 1343 were expelled in 1987.[49] Surveys indicate that as many as one-fourth of all firms want to hire foreigners. Demand is particularly high in the construction industry, where it is estimated that 13.5 foreign workers are needed for every 100 skilled Japanese construction workers. One government report estimates that by the year 2000 Japan will suffer a shortfall of 2.7 million workers, while others counter that automation and women can overcome any gap.[50] Clearly, the more affluent Japan becomes, the fewer Japanese will want to work in dirty, tough jobs.

The Government and business are severely divided on whether or not to allow more foreign workers. Six ministries are currently negotiating over both policy and responsibilities for enforcing the policy. On one side are the ministries of Labor, Justice, Agriculture, Forestry and Fisheries, Transport, the Industrial Bank of Japan, and Foreign Affairs, joined by Nikkeiren and small and medium-sized firms, which, for varying reasons want more foreign workers as well as the responsibility for administering them. They are opposed by MITI, the Construction Ministry, Keidanren, and most large firms. The essential argument is between those economic sectors and their ministries who need cheap, unskilled labor in order to remain competitive, and those economic sectors and their ministry representatives who do not. The Ministry of Foreign Affairs is the only actor that argues for more workers to help fulfill Japan's responsibilities.

So far, those opposed to more foreign workers have been on top. In January 1989 Japan suspended its 90-day tourist visas for Pakistan and Bangledesh; now the only Asian countries that enjoy tourist visas are Malaysia, Singapore, and Iran. This exclusivist policy will endure for the short run, but eventually some highly controlled increase in foreign workers will occur as Japan's labor market continues to tighten. Again, Japan's restrictive policy compares starkly with those of other OECD countries that have accepted millions of foreign workers.

Another international responsibility that Japan has been pressured on for several decades is defense. Many have noted the irony that the world's biggest debtor nation continues to pay for the defense of the world's greatest creditor nation. Japan's energy and raw materials would be extremely vulnerable in the unlikely advent of a world war. About 70 per cent of Japan's crude oil imports and 20 per cent of its iron-ore imports pass through the Straits of Malacca, and another 4 per cent and 19 per cent respectively through the Lombok Strait, while about half of Japan's oil still flows through the Straits of Hormuz compared to about 5 per cent of America's oil.[51] During his January 1989 Washington visit, Prime Minister Takeshita merely repeated the words of three and a half decades of predecessors when he said: 'The foundation of friendly relations between our two countries is the steadfast framework based on the Japan-U.S. security treaty'.[52]

Yet, since the Korean War broke out in 1950, citing such things as Article 9 of the Constitution, pacifist sentiments among the populace, and East Asian opposition, Tokyo has successfully staved off repeated requests by Washington for Japan to assume any genuine responsibility for self-defense. Although in the 1980s it agreed to defend sealanes radiating 1000 miles from Tokyo Bay, exceeded the 1976 policy limiting defense spending to 1 per cent of GNP, and signed a military technology exchange agreement with the United States, these were largely 'tatemae' gestures without real substance. Morse points out that a fifth of the world's commercial ships are devoted to Japanese trade; yet despite its dependence on international sealanes, Tokyo 'has not indicated any intention of contributing to the safety of international waterways'.[53]

The issue of Japan's free ride on defense resurfaced in May 1987 after the USS Stark was hit by an Iraqi missile. The gut reaction was why Americans were dying to protect Japanese oil. Later that year, the House of Representatives adopted a resolution demanding that Japan spend 3 per cent of its GNP on defense. Assistant Secretary of State Richard Armitage in response said Japan could acquire necessary self-defense and sea-lane protection at 2 per cent of GNP.[54] Zbigniew Brezinski then followed suit, arguing that Japan should contribute 4 per cent of its GNP to aid and military spending, a burden comparable to that of the NATO countries. Tokyo responded to the renewed pressure in characteristically symbolic style; it contributed to a navigation system for the Gulf, promised new economic aid to strategically important Oman and Jordan, and further funding for American troops in Japan.

Tokyo's neo-mercantilist policies remain based on keeping the defense burden on the shoulders of the United States while Japan concentrates on developing its economy and capturing foreign markets. For example, the 1987 defense budget was 1.004 per cent of GNP, hardly a sacrifice compared to the 7 per cent and average 3 per cent of GNP that the Americans and West European, respectively, annually spend on defense. Japan now ranks tenth in the world in terms of absolute spending, down from eighth in the early 1980s.[55] Japan's alliance with the United remains one-sided; Tokyo is not required to aid the United States if it were attacked, while it remains completely dependent on the United States to counter any invasion. George points out that Japan's army 'would be incapable of repulsing even a limited and small scale invasion . . . (while) at worst Japan would be able to hold up an invader for only two days. Even by 1990 Japan will be unable to fulfill the strategic goals it has set up; it would not be able to defend the sea-lanes or even to provide air defense of its own territory'.[56]

The most powerful argument Japan uses to limit fulfilling its alliance responsibilities is Article 9. Literally interpreted, Article 9 renounces Japan's sovereign right of self-defense and any military force. But Supreme Court rulings in 1958 and the 1970s found that the article does not deny the right of self-defense, but simply limits Japan's offensive capability. This gives Japan's policy-makers considerable leeway to adjust defense policy to their political and Japan's economic needs. Although the government agreed to defend sea-lanes 1000 miles out from Tokyo Bay, it refused to send non-offensive mine-sweepers to the Persian Gulf; although it officially forbids any nuclear weapons on Japanese soil, it allows American ships carrying nuclear weapons to dock at Japanese ports.[57]

The maleability of Article 9 for Japanese policy-makers, however, was stretched to new lengths during Defense-Secretary-designate John Tower's confirmation hearings before the Senate in February 1989. In response to a question about Japan's defense, Tower correctly stated that Article 9 does not restrict Japan's defense spending to only a certain percentage of GNP. His Japanese counterpart, Defense Agency Chief Kichiro Tazawa, immediately and harshly criticized Tower's 'presumption to speak about Japan's constitution in such a manner' while Foreign Ministry officials criticized Tower's 'lack of understanding of the Japanese way of thinking'.[58] Unable rationally to argue against the truth of Tower's statement, Japanese officials typically resorted to 'Japan is unique' arguments while accusing Tower of 'Japan bashing'. These emotional tactics will remain highly effective as long as foreigners continue to allow Japan to get away with them. The dilemma is, of course, that anyone who even points out inconsistencies in Japanese positions, let alone criticizes those policies, is by definition a 'Japan basher'.

One of the most valuable benefits for Japan of America's security blanket has been the flow of high technology from the United States to Japanese corporations, ostensibly to build military equipment, but more often than not utilized for consumer products which were in turn used to capture markets from their American corporate rivals. For example, the United States allowed Japan to build its own version of the F–4 fighter bomber. Japan in turn has spun off the technology into hundreds of consumer products which included adapting the braking system to its 'bullet train' (Shinkansen). Finally awakening to Japan's achievement of technology superpower status, in 1981 Washington began negotiating with Tokyo for the licensing of Japanese technology. After two years of tough negotiations an agreement was finally signed in January 1983 in which Japan promised to transfer technology to the United States as long as it was confined to military applications. Japan did not want the United States to do what it had been doing for 30 years.

To date, however, while only three very minor technology transfers from Japan have occurred, in 1988 Washington agreed to give Tokyo key technology with which to build its next generation of fighter planes, the FSX. In doing so, Washington typically played into Tokyo's hands. Japan could have bought F–16s, the world's most advanced fighter, at half the cost, an action which would have helped alleviate some of Japan's $50 billion trade surplus with the United States. Instead, Tokyo will use America's technology to accelerate the achievements of its aerospace industrial policy. Within a generation, Japan's aerospace industry will rival that of the United States.

Clearly, Japan falls far short of assuming international responsibilities in aid or defense; its combined aid and defense budget is only 1.5 per cent of GNP compared to America's combined burden of 7.5 per cent of GNP. In international environmental issues, however, Japan is not merely a 'free rider', but is actually the major contributor to several worsening global catastrophes, the most serious of which is the destruction of the world's tropical forests. Japan consumes 40 per cent of the world's hardwood for a range of products which include disposable chopsticks. Japanese timber companies have already denuded much of Southeast Asia and Nigeria's tropical forests, and one-third of Brazil's. Last year, in Brazil alone, an area of tropical forest the size of Belgium was destroyed. Japan's banks are financing and construction firms building a highway from Peru's west coast into the heart of the Brazilian rainforest to gain access for its timber companies. Analysts fear Japan's highway will result in the rainforest's eventual destruction. The World Bank and Inter-American Development Bank had both refused to fund the project because of its consequences.[59]

The survival of humanity may well depend on the survival of the tropical forests. Although less than 1 per cent of the tropical plants have been tested for their medical value, over one-third of the pharmaceutical products sold in the United States are derivatives of the tropical forests. Potential cures for cancer, AIDS, or hundreds of other diseases may be found in the world's rapidly dwindling forests. But the major contribution of the tropical forest is to act as a giant air filter which takes the world's worsening air pollution and converts it into carbon dioxide. Without the tropical forests, the world's air pollution and consequent green-house effect will accelerate, heating the earth and unleashing a chain reaction of environmental catastrophies.

Japan has either reluctantly gone alone with other international agreements on the environment or openly defied them. In the early 1980s Tokyo finally agreed to shelve its plan to dump low-level nuclear materials in the Pacific Ocean after sustained protests of other Pacific nations. Although it reluctantly signed the 1981 Washington Convention on Endangered Species, Tokyo retained 12 exemptions, the most of any country. Meanwhile Japanese firms have cornered the market in the illegal ivory trade.

But while Tokyo at least made tatemae gestures of compliance on these pressing global environmental issues, it openly defied the 1985 ban of the International Whaling Commission (IWC) on whaling. Tokyo allows its whaling ships to hunt minke whales while claiming the whaling agreement signed by 38 states is simply racist 'Japan bashing', despite the fact that Norway and Iceland have also been censured. The attitude of Japanese on the whaling issue today is very similar to their attitude over 50 years ago during the Manchuria crisis. At that time Japanese rejected the international community's condemnation of its invasion of Manchuria by claiming the world was scapegoating Japan.

At first it may seem strange that Japan would be so exploitive of the global environment, given that its traditional culture revered nature while its own industrial pollution had become so horrific by the 1960s that Japan was designated the 'canary in the coalmine' as a testcase of the human tolerance for pollution.[60] In May 1976, Tokyo officially recognized 1548 victims of mercury poisoning with 186 dead and over 3500 additional victims awaiting certification, 350 victims of cadmium poisoning and 120 dead, 232 cases of hexavalent chromium poisoning and 41 dead, and over 30 000 victims of air pollution throughout Japan. Surveys indicated that 71 per cent of the inhabitants of Japan's seven largest cities, 48 per cent in other urban areas, and even 32 per cent in the countryside, suffered from pollution.[61] Although starting in 1958, the Ministry of Health and Welfare submitted a series of anti-pollution proposals, they were repeatedly struck down by MITI and the corporate world. However, in the mid-1960s, a grass-roots anti-pollution movement slowly gathered steam fuelled by mass media exposure of pollution victims, lawsuits, foreign criticism of Japanese pollution, and the opposition parties, which one by one joined the political bandwagon. In 1970 the LDP finally gave in and passed 14 laws that dealt with virtually all aspects of Japan's pollution. Since then this pollution has been greatly reduced and, characteristically, pollution control equipment has become a significant industry and export product.

But despite this experience, Japanese remain unconcerned about environmental problems. The citizens groups that emerged across Japan in the mid–1960s in response to local problems dissolved as soon as the problem was solved. There is no national environmental movement in Japan comparable to America's Common Cause, Friends of the Earth, Wilderness Association, or hundreds of smaller groups, or th∗ European 'green' parties. Surveys reveal that in contrast to their self-perception as nature-lovers, Japanese are actually highly materialistic and see nature as something to be exploited for their own needs. Even members of Japanese environmental groups are essentially materialistic.[62] A comparison of the attitudes of American and Japanese members of environmental groups revealed that: 62 per cent of Americans and only 12 per cent of Japanese strongly agreed that 'the balance of nature is very delicate and easily upset by human activities'; 70 per cent of Americans and only 7 per cent of Japanese agreed that 'the earth is like a spaceship with only limited resources and room'; 70 per cent of Americans and 11 per cent of Japanese thought that 'plants and animals do not exist primarily to be used for humans'; 60 per cent of Americans and 27 per cent of Japanese felt that 'people would be better off if they lived a more simple life without so much technology'; 86 per cent of Americans and 70 per cent of Japanese strongly disagreed that 'modifying the environment for human use seldom causes serious problems'; and 85 per cent of Americans and 69 of Japanese strongly disagreed that 'mankind was created to rule over the rest of nature'. Overall, 45 per cent of American environmentalists and only 17 per cent of Japanese environmentalists took an 'earth-first' view that humans should live in harmony with nature, while 47 per cent of Japanese and only 18 per cent of Americans had an exploitive materialistic view of nature.

If Japanese environmentalists hold such anti-nature views, Japan's actions on the rainforest, nuclear dumping, or whaling issues are much more understandable. Still, most foreign residents of Japan are surprised to find that Japanese are just as wasteful and exploitive at home as they are abroad. Although Japanese describe themselves as members of 'a small, poor, crowded country, devoid of natural resources', in order to justify continued neo-mercantilist policies, their use of resources is actually very wasteful. Japanese not only annually dispose of billions of wooden chopsticks, but also discard virtually anything else that breaks down. A stroll in any Japanese neighborhood, particularly the more affluent ones, on trash collection day reveals all kinds of electrical appliances, including televisions, stereos, and VCRs set out for disposal. In the interests of 'purity', second-hand shops are extremely rare and no one would conceive of holding a garage sale. Although Japan complains about its dependence on imported energy, the government refuses to adopt 'daylight saving time' that could annually save huge amounts of energy. It justifies its inaction with polls saying that most Japanese are opposed to daylight saving time because it is 'unnatural'.

Japan's highly materialistic values, traditional 'we-them' view of the world, and tendency to see any criticism as 'Japan bashing' will prevent Tokyo from taking any more initiative on environmental issues than they have on trade, defense, or aid. When Japan does agree to sign an international agreement it will only be after long, tough negotiations and lots of exemptions. Even then it will be merely a tatemae gesture while in reality Japanese firms continue to operate as they wish.

CONCLUSION

Japan has clearly fallen far short of fulfilling its international responsibilities in virtually all areas including trade, defense, aid, or the environment. But will this always be the case? Will Japan ever begin to give more to the world than it takes? Will Japan abandon the neo-mercantilist policies that have brought the country such tremendous wealth and po wer?

Lucian Pyle identifies four schools of thought on Japan's future role in the world, two of which – the realist and mercantilist – are closely related and have formed the basis for Japan's post–1945 foreign policy, while the other two – the progressive and new nationalists – are diametrically opposed and color Japanese foreign policy with rhetoric rather than substance.[63]

The realist and mercantilist schools are both essentially neo-mercantilist, yet differ in their tactics for maximizing Japanese wealth and power. The realists assert that Japanese foreign policy should be anchored securely in its relationship with the United States, which provides Japan with a nuclear and conventional military umbrella, continual technology transfers, and a vast, largely open market. As America's junior partner, Japan must coordinate its diplomacy with that of Washington, and increase its defense and particularly aid parallel to its growing economic power. In contrast, the mercantilists take America's nuclear umbrella and markets for granted, correctly reasoning that in its obsession with containing communism Washington would never do anything to jeopardize its relations with Tokyo. Instead, the mercantilists advocate an 'omnidirectional foreign policy' in which Tokyo deals with anyone on virtually any terms as long as it is profitable. Whereas the realists advocate some significant increases in opening Japan's markets, and defense and aid, the neo-mercantilists want only to make only symbolic gestures to allay criticism. Both would agree that the world political economy is changing from the old 'Westphalian' system based on a balance of military power to a 'Kantian' system in which a state's comprehensive security is preserved by interdependence.[64]

In contrast to the hard-nosed realism of the two mainstream schools, the progressives are essentially idealist, believing that 'Japan's unique mission in the postwar world is to demonstrate that a modern industrial nation could exist without arming itself, that Japan could show the world to a new world in which . . . nation-states, which were artificial creations, would disappear'. This view was popular among the opposition parties and many academics up through the early 1980s but has lost considerable influence among them since. It never influenced Japanese foreign policy, although its rhetoric was often used in presenting Japan's 'face . . . to the outside world'.[65] In contrast to the realists, mercantilists, and progressives who advocate the increased integration of Japan within the world political economy, the 'new nationalists' argue that Japan should distance itself from the rest of the world, particularly the West; it should trade with all nations but rely on none. Japan's independence will be guaranteed by creating a powerful nuclear and conventional military.

The new nationalists are increasingly vocal, but Japan's foreign policy will continue to be determined by the realists and mercantilists for the forseeable future, with the realists eventually becoming the dominant players. Although the progressives and new nationalists will remain outside the mainstream with minimal input into Japanese foreign policy, Pyle reminds us that Tokyo 'borrows freely of the rhetoric and ideas of all four approaches as suits their convenience'.[66] Progressive rhetoric, if not sentiments, will continue to filter into the international speeches of Japan's government and business diplomats while new nationalist sentiments, and occasionally rhetoric, will become increasingly ingrained in the minds of most Japanese. But Japanese foreign policy-makers will remain essentially realists. They know that Japan needs the world economy much more than the world economy needs Japan, and thus would never advocate anything that would jeopardize Japan's increasingly privileged position. Having taken over America's role as world banker and running neck-and-neck with the United States in the high technology race, it is inconceivable that Tokyo would ever risk a trade or military war that would could sever Japan from the world economy.

Most analysts agree with Pyle that a shift from neo-mercantilism to liberalism is unlikely. Kent Calder describes Japan as a 'reactive state' which fails to undertake major independent foreign economic policy initiatives when it has the power and national incentives to do so and responds to outside pressures '(gaiatsu) . . . erratically, unsystematically, and often incompletely'.[67] According to Calder, Japanese foreign policy-making is characterized as a 'complex mixture of strategy, hesitancy, and pragmatism'.[68] Iron triangles among the different ministries, industrial associations, and LDP 'policy tribes' will guarantee the continuation of neo-mercantilism. This fragmentation of decision-making authority has become a gordian knot regarding trade barriers which persistent foreign pressure and Japanese promises have failed to solve.

But changes are clearly occurring. Tokyo's traditional low profile strategy from 1945 through the 1980s during which it behaved 'in international society in the same way that merchants did in the samurai dominated society of pre-modern Japan',[69] is being challenged by more assertive neo-mercantilist strategies. Increasing numbers of Japanese want an international profile more appropriate to Japan's status as an economic superpower acting as the world's banker and technological leader.

Ronald Morse sees a danger in this. He points out that 'Japan's quest for foreign policy autonomy – the tension of acting or appearing to act in coordination with U.S. interests while charting an independent course – is critical in understanding the political and psychological difficulties Japanese officials feel as they move away from three decades of depending on U.S. leadership'.[70] Morse is critical of Japan's growing independence, saying that Tokyo 'has not been willing to act quickly and decisively in concert with the U.S. as an alliance partner, even where the costs to Japan are small and the benefits to the U.S., largely in symbolic terms, would be great'.[71] He goes on to site the Soviet gas pipeline, Middle East oil, and Iranian hostage issues as examples. These conflicts will increase as Japan becomes more powerful.

Only one thing is certain – Japan's power over the world economy will continue to grow. Japan's role as world banker seems secure into the indefinite future. Meanwhile the country is in the midst of leapfrogging the United States as the world's technological leader as well. At their current respective growth rates, Japan's GNP will surpass that of the United States within 12 years. Its domination of world manufacturing and financial markets will deepen. Whether Japan uses its wealth to help the world overcome a myriad of development problems or continues simply to use its wealth to create more wealth remains to be seen.

NOTES

1. *Economist*, 24 December 1989.
2. Chikara Higashi, *Internationalization in Japan*, p. 4.
3. *International Herald Tribune*, 24 February 1989.
4. Higashi, op. cit., p. xi.
5. Tadoa Ishizaki, 'Is Japan's Income Distribution Equal?', *Japanese Economic Studies*, vol. 14, no. 2, Winter 1985/86, p. 33.
6. *Businessweek*, 12 September 1988.
7. *Economist*, 24 December 1988.
8. Ishizaki, op. cit., pp. 33–40.

9.   *Businessweek*, 12 September 1988.
10. *Businessweek*, 12 September 1988; Shinji Fukukawa, 'A New Industrial Structure', *Speaking of Japan*, vol. 7, no. 73, January 1987, p. 8.
11. *Economist*, 24 December 1988.
12. Higashi, op. cit., p. 170.
13. *International Herald Tribune*.
14. Higashi, op. cit., p. 177.
15. *Economist*, 11 June 1988.
16. Nada Inada, 'The Hundred Million Middle-Class', *Japan Quarterly*, vol. 28, no. 1, January-March 1981, p. 85.
17. Ibid., pp. 85–6.
18. Yasusuke Murakami, 'Age of New Middle Mass Politics', *Journal of Japanese Studies*, vol. 8, no. 1, Winter 1982.
19. Sepp Linhart, 'From Industrial to Postindustrial Society', *Journal of Japanese Studies*, vol. 14, no. 2, Summer 1988.
20. *Japan Economic Journal*, 14 January 1989.
21. Ibid.
22. *Japan Economic Journal*, 21 January 1987.
23. Linhart, op. cit., p. 299.
24. Higashi, op. cit., p. 155.
25. *Economist*, 16 July 1988.
26. *Economist*, 29 October 1988.
27. *Far Eastern Economic Review*, 15 December 1988.
28. Higashi, op. cit., p. 149.
29. *Economist*, 28 January 1989.
30. Ibid.
31. Quoted in Fred Bergsten and William Cline, *The United States-Japan Problem*.
32. *Far Eastern Economic Review*, 26 January 1989.
33. *Economist*, 28 January 1989.
34. Ibid.
35. Bergsten, op. cit., p. 124.
36. Higashi, op. cit., p. 157.
37. Unless otherwise noted all trade statistics come from the annual *IMF Direction of Trade*.
38. *Japan Economic Journal*, 10 September 1988; *Economist*, 13 August 1988.
39. *Far Eastern Economic Review*, 2 February 1989.
40. *International Herald Tribune*, 13 December 1988.
41. *Economist*, 7 January 1989.
42. Unless otherwise noted all foreign aid statistics come from the annual *OECD Development Cooperation Reports*.
43. *Japan Economic Journal*, 28 May 1988.
44. *International Herald Tribune*, 27 June 1988.
45. Ibid.
46. Ibid.
47. *Far Eastern Economic Review*, 28 April 1988.
48. Ibid., 26 January 1989.
49. *Economist*, 13 August 1988, 3 December 1988.

50. *Far Eastern Economic Review*, 26 January 1989.
51. Muthiah Alagappa, 'Japan's Political and Security Role in the Asia-Pacific Region', *Contemporary Southeast Asia*, vol. 10, no. 1, June 1988, p. 40.
52. *Japan Economic Journal*, 18 February 1989.
53. Ronald Morse, 'Japan's Search for an Independent Foreign Policy', *Journal of Northeast Asian Studies*, vol. 3, no. 2, Summer 1984, p. 40.
54. Alagappa, op. cit., pp. 25, 37, 38.
55. Aurelia George, 'Japan and the United States', in J.A.A. Stockwin, *Dynamics and Immobolist Politics in Japan*, p. 281.
56. Ibid., p. 281.
57. See Morse, op. cit.
58. *Japan Economic Journal*, 18 February 1989.
59. *Economist*, 11 February 1989.
60. Quoted in Steven Reed, 'Environmental Politics', *Comparative Politics*, vol. 13, no. 3, April 1981.
61. Margaret Kean, 'Pollution and Policymaking in Japan', in T.J. Pempel (ed.), *Policymaking in Japan*, pp. 203–4.
62. John Pierce, *et. al.*, 'The New Environmental Paradigm in Japan and the United States', *Journal of Politics*, vol. 49, no. 1, February 1987, pp. 54–60.
63. Lucian Pyle, 'The Future of Japanese Nationality', *Journal of Japanese Studies*, vol. 8, no. 2, Summer 1982, pp. 242–61.
64. Ibid., p. 255.
65. Ibid.
66. Ibid., p. 242.
67. Kent Calder, 'Japanese Foreign Economic Policy Formation', *World Politics*, vol. 40, no. 4, July 1988, p. 519.
68. Ibid., p. 518.
69. Pyle, op. cit., p. 228.
70. Morse, op. cit., p. 28.
71. Ibid., p. 28.

Bibliography

Abegglen, James C. and Hout, Thomas M., 'Facing up to the Trade Gap with Japan', *Foreign Affairs*, pp. 146–68, Fall 1978.

Abegglen, James, *The Strategy of Japanese Business* (Cambridge, Mass. Ballinger, 1984).

Abegglen, James, Kaisha, *The Japanese Corporation: The New Competitors In World Business* (New York: Basic Books, 1985).

Adams, F. Gerald, and Kleinl (eds) *Industrial Policy for Growth and Consequences* (Lexington, Mass.: Lexington Books, 1983).

Adler, Vernon R., 'Who Says You Can't Crack Japanese Markets', *Harvard Business Review*, January-February, 1987, no. 1, pp. 52–6.

Akao, Nobutoshi, *Japan's Economic Security* (New York: St. Martin's Press, 1983).

Aichi, Kiichi, 'Japan's Legacy and Destiny of Change', *Foreign Affairs*, pp. 21–38, October 1969

Akita, George, *Foundations of Constitutional Government in Modern Japan, 1868–1900* (Cambridge, Mass: Harvard University Press 1967).

Alagappa, Muthiah, 'Japan's Political and Security Role in the Asia Pacific Region', *Contemporary Southeast Asia*, vol. 10, no. 1, June 1988.

Alexander, Arthur, *Barriers To United States Service Trade In Japan*, Hong W. Tan (Santa Monica, California: Rand Corporation, 1984).

Alexander, Robert J., 'Is the U.S. Substituting a Speculative Economy for a Productive One?', *Journal of Economic Issues*, vol. xx, no. 2, June 1986.

Allen, George C., *Japan's Place in Trade Strategy: Larger Role in Pacific Region* (London: Atlantic Trade Study, 1968).

Allinson, Gary, 'Japan's Keidanren and its New Leadership', *Pacific Affairs*, vol. 60, no. 3, Fall 1987.

Allinson, Gary D., 'Politics in Contemporary Japan: Pluralist Scholarship in the Conservation Era', *Journal of Asian Studies*, vol. 48, no. 2, May 1989.

Altschiller Donald, (ed.), *Free Trade Versus Protectionism* (New York: H.W. Wilson Press, 1988).

Ames, Walter L., 'Buying a Piece of Japan Inc.: Foreign Acquisitions in Japan', *Harvard International Law Journal*, vol. 27, Special Issue, 1986.

Anchordoguy, Marie, 'Mastering the Market: Japanese Government Targeting of the Computer Industry', *International Organization*, vol. 42, no. 3, Summer 1988.

Andrews, Kenneth R., and Salter, M.S. 'The Automobile Crisis and Public Policy', *Harvard Business Review*, vol. 59, no. 1, January/February 1981.

Armour, Andrew (ed.) *Asia and Japan: The Search for Modernization and Identity* (London: Athlone Press, 1985).

Arnold, James, 'Japanese Economic Nationalism: Protectionism versus Internationalism', *Canadian Review of Studies in Nationalism*, vol. 10, no. 2, Fall 1983.

Arnold, James, 'Study of Japanese Economic Nationalism: A Bibliographical Essay', *Canadian Review of Studies in Nationalism,* vol. 10, no. 2, Fall 1983.

Asada, Sado (ed.) *Japan and the World 1853–1952: A Bibliographical Guide to Japanese Scholarship in Foreign Relations* (New York: Columbia University Press, 1989).

Ashley, Richard K., 'The Poverty of Neorealism', *International Organization,* pp. 225–86, vol. 38, no. 2, Spring 1984.

Atarashii, Kinju, 'Japan's Economic Cooperation Policy Towards the ASEAN Countries', *International Affairs* (Great Britain), vol. 61, no. 1, Winter, 1984–85.

Avery, William: Rapkin, David (eds), *America in a Changing World Political Economy* (New York: Longman 1982).

Axline, W. Andrew, 'Underdevelopment, Dependence, and Integration: the Politics of Regionalism in the Third World', *International Organization.* pp. 83–106, vol. 31, no. 1, Winter 1977.

Baerwald, Hans, *Party Politics in Japan* (Boston: Allen & Unwin, 1986).

Bailey, Martin Neil and Chakrabarti, Alok K. 'Innovation and U.S. Competitiveness', *The Brookings Review,* Fall 1985, vol. 4, no. 1, pp. 14–21.

Balassa, Bela, *The Newly Industrializing Countries in the World Economy* (New York: Pergamon, 1981).

Balassa, Bela, *et al., Developing Strategies in Semi-Industrializing Countries,* World Bank Research Publication (Baltimore: Johns Hopkins University Press, 1982).

Balassa, Bela, 'Dependency and Trade Orientation', *The World Economy,* vol. 9, no. 3, September 1986, pp. 239–58.

Balassa, Bela, *Japan in the World Economy* (Washington, DC: Institute for International Economics, 1988).

Baldwin, David A., 'International Political Economy and the International Monetary System', *International Organization,* pp. 487–512, vol. 32, no. 2, Spring 1978.

Ballon, Robert J., *Foreign Investment and Japan* (Tokyo: Kodansha International, 1972).

Baranson, Jack, *The Japanese Challenge to US Industry* (Lexington, Mass.: Lexington Books, 1981).

Baranson, Jack, *Robots in Manufacturing: Key to International Competitiveness* (Mt. Airy, Md.: Lomond, 1983).

Barfield, Claude E. and Schambra William (eds), *The Politics of Industrial Policy* (Washington DC.: American Enterprise Institute for Public Policy Research, 1986).

Barnds, William (ed.) *Japan and the United States: Challenges and Opportunities* (New York: New York University Press, 1979).

Barnhardt, Michael, *Japan Prepares for Total War: The Search for Economic Security, 1919–1941* (Ithaca: Cornell University Press, 1987).

Bartel, Richard D., 'Industrial Policy as an International Issue', *Challenge,* vol. 23, no. 6, January/February 1981.

Bedeski, Michael, 'Japanese Foreign Policy Under Nakasone: The

Dilemma of an Economic Superpower', *Etudes Internationale*, vol. 15, no. 2, June 1984.

Behrman, Jack, *Industrial Policy: International Structuring and Transnationalism* (Lexington, Mass.: Lexington Books, 1984).

Benjamin, Roger and Kudrle, Robert T. (eds), *The Industrial Future of the Pacific Basin* (Boulder, Colorado: Westview Press, 1984).

Bergsten, C. Fred, 'The New Economics and U.S. Foreign Policy', *Foreign Policy*, pp. 199–221, January 1972.

Bergsten, C. Fred, 'What to Do About the U.S.–Japan Economic Conflict', *Foreign Affairs*, pp. 1059–76, Summer 1982.

Bergsten, C. Fred, *The United States-Japan Economic Problem* (Washington, DC: Institute for International Economics, 1985).

Bhattacharya, Anindya, *The Asia Dollar Market: International Offshore Financing* (New York: Praeger, 1977).

Blake, David and Walter, Robert, *The Politics of Global Economic Relations* (Englewood Cliffs, New Jersey: Prentice-Hall, 1983).

Blaker, Michael, *Japanese International Negotiating Style* (New York: Columbia University Press, 1977).

Blaker, Michael, *The Politics of Trade: U.S. and Japanese Policymaking for the Gatt Negotiations* (New York: East Asian Institute, 1978).

Blauvelt, Jennifer Durlasher, *Sources of Asian/Pacific Economic Information* (Westmead, England: Gower Press, 1981).

Block, Fred, *The Origins of International Economic Disorder: A Study of U.S. International Monetary Policy from World War II to The Present* (Berkeley: University of California Press, 1977)

Bloom, Justin, 'A New Era for U.S.–Japan Technical Relations? Problems and Prospects', *Journal of Northeast Asian Studies*, Summer 1987.

Blumenthal, Tuvia, and Lee, Chung H., 'Development Strategies of Japan and the Republic of Korea', *The Developing Economies*, vol. 23, no. 2, September 1985.

Bobrow, David and Knudrle, Robert T., 'How Middle Powers Can Manage Resource Weakness', *World Politics*, vol. 39, no. 4, July 1987.

Boger, Karl, *Postwar Industrial Policy in Japan: An Annotated Bibliography* (New Jersey: Scarecrow Press, 1988).

Boltho, Andrea, 'Was Japan's Industrial Policy Successful?', *Cambridge Journal of Economics*, vol. 9, no. 2, June 1985.

Borden, William, *The Pacific Alliance: United States Foreign Economic Policy and the Japanese Trade Recovery, 1947–55* (Madison: University of Wisconsin Press, 1984).

Borrus, Michael *et al.*, *U.S.–Japanese Competition in the Semi-Conductor Industry*, Policy Papers in International Affairs 17 (Berkeley, California: Institute of International Studies, University of California, 1982).

Boyd, Gavin (ed.), *Region Building in the Pacific* (New York: Pergamon Press, 1982).

Boyd, Gavin (ed.), *Regionalism and Global Security* (Lexington, Mass: Lexington Books, 1984).

Brainard, Lawrence J., 'Current Illusions about the International Debt Crisis', *The World Economy*, Vol. 8, No. 1, March 1985, pp. 1–10.

Braddon, Russell, *The Other Hundred Years War: Japan's Bid for Supremacy* (London: Collins Press, 1983).

Bronte, Stephen, *Japanese Finance: Markets and Institutions* (London: Euromoney Publications, 1982).

Bressand, Albert, 'Mastering the "World Economy" ', *Foreign Affairs,* pp. 745–72.

Bronfenbrenner, Martin and Yasuba, Yasukichi, 'Economic Welfare, in Kozo Yamamura and Yasukichi Yasuba (eds), *The Political Economy of Japan: Volume 1, The Domestic Transformation* (Stanford: Stanford University Press, 1987).

Brooks, John and Orr, William, 'Japan's Foreign Assistance', vol. 25, no. 3, March 1985.

Brown, William S., 'Industrial Policy and Corporate Power', *Journal of Economic Issues,* vol. 19, no. 2, June 1985.

Bryant, William E., *Japanese Private Economic Diplomacy: An Analysis of Business–Government Linkages* (New York: Praeger, 1975).

Brzezinski, Zbigniew, 'Japan's Global Engagement', *Foreign Affairs,* pp. 270–82, January 1972.

Burkman, Thomas W., *The Occupation of Japan: The International Context* (Norfolk, Virginia: Liskey Lithograph, 1984).

Burks, Ardath W., *Japan: A Postindustrial Power* (Boulder, Colorado: Westview Press, 1984).

Burnett, Robert W., *Beyond War: Japan's Concept of Comprehensive National Security* (McLean, Virginia: Pergamon–Brassey's International Defense Publishers, 1984).

Burstein, Dan, *Yen! Japan's New Financial Empire and Its Threat to America* (New York: Simon & Schuster, 1989).

Buss, Claude A. (ed.) *National Security Interests in the Pacific Basin* (Stanford: Hoover Institute Press, 1985).

Buzan, Barry, 'Economic Structure and International Security', *International Organization,* Vol. 38, No. 4, Autumn 1984, pp. 597–624.

Calder, Kent E. and Hofheinz, Roy Jr., *The Eastasia Edge* (New York: Basic Books, 1982).

Calder, Kent E., 'Opening Japan', *Foreign Policy,* No. 47, Summer 1982, pp. 82–98

Calder, Kent, 'Japanese Foreign Economic Policy Formation', *World Politics,* vol. 40, no. 4, July 1988.

Calder, Kent E., 'The Rise of Japan's Military-Industrial Complex', *Asia Pacific Community,* no. 17, Summer 1982.

Calista, Samuel, 'Japanese Values and Perceptions of U.S. Values', vol. 16, no. 4, January 1984.

Calton, Jerry M., 'Industrial Policy, International Competitiveness, and the World Auto Industry', *Journal of Contemporary Business,* vol. 11, no. 1, June 1982.

Campbell, John Creighton, *Contemporary Japanese Budget Politics,* (Berkeley: University of California Press, 1977.)

Caporaso, James A., 'Introduction: Dependence, and Dependency in the Global System', *International Organization,* pp. 1–12, vol. 32, no. 1, Winter 1978.

Caporaso, James A., 'Dependence, and Power in the Global System: A Structural and Behavioral Analysis', *International Organization,* pp. 13–44, vol. 32, no. 1, Winter 1978.

Caporaso, James A., 'Theory and Method in the Study of International Integration', pp. 228–53, vol. 25, no. 2, Spring 1972.

Castle, Emery and Kenzo, Hemmi (eds), *U.S.–Japanese Agricultural Trade Relations,* (Washington, D.C: Resources for the Future, 1982).

Chang, C.S., *The Japanese Auto Industry and the U.S. Market* (New York: Praeger, 1981).

Chapman, J.W.M., Drifte, R. and Row, I.T.M., *Japan's Quest for Comprehensive Security: Defense-Diplomacy-Dependence* (New York: St. Martin's Press, 1983).

Chen, Edward, *Hypergrowth in the Asian Economies* (New York: Holmes & Meier, 1979).

Cheng, Hang-seng *(Financial Policies and Reform in Pacific Basin Countries* (Lexington, Mass.: Lexington Books, 1986).

Christopher, Robert C., *The Japanese Mind: The Goliath Explained* (New York: Linden Press, 1983).

Clark, Gregory, 'Japan in Asia: A Cultural Comparison', *Asia Pacific Community,* No. 17, Summer 1982, pp. 60–3.

Cleaver, Charles Grinnell, *Japanese and Americans: Cultural Parallels and Paradoxes* (Minneapolis: University of Minnesota Press, 1976).

Cohen, Jerome B. (ed.) *Pacific Partnership: United States–Japan Trade Prospects and Recommendations for the Seventies* (Lexington, Mass: Lexington Books, 1972)

Cohen, Stephen, *The Making of United States International Economic Policy* (New York: Praeger, 1977).

Cohen, Stephen S. and Zysman, John, 'Can America Compete', *Challenge,* vol. 29, no. 2, May/June 1986.

Cohen, Warren (ed.), *New Frontiers in American–East Asian Relations,* (New York: Columbia University Press, 1983).

Cole, Robert E. (ed.) *The Japanese Automobile Industry: Model and Challenge for the Future?* Michigan Papers in Japanese Studies 3. Ann Arbor: Center for Japanese Studies, University of Michigan, 1981).

Cole, Robert E. and Yakushiji, Taizo (eds), *The American and Japanese Auto Industries in Transition* (Tokyo: Technova, 1984).

Copper, John, 'U.S.–Japanese Relations', *Asia Affairs: An American Review,* vol. 10, no. 4, 1984.

Cummings, Bruce, 'The Origins and Development of the Northeast Asian Political Economy: Industrial Sectors, Product Cycles, and Political Consequences', *International Organization,* pp. 1–40, vol. 38, no. 1, Winter 1984.

Curtis, Gerald, *The Japanese Way of Politics* (New York: Columbia University Press, 1988).

Cusumano, Michael A., *The Japanese Automobile Industry* (Cambridge, Mass: Harvard University Press, 1985).

Cypher, James M., 'Military Spending, Technical Change, and Economic Growth: A Disguised Form of Industrial Policy', *Journal of Economic Issues,* vol. xxi, no. 1, March 1987, pp. 33–59.

Czinkota, Michael and Tesar, George (eds), *Export Policy: A Global Assessment* (New York: Praeger, 1982).

Czinkota, Michael and Woronoff, Jon, *Japan's Market: The Distribution System* (New York: Praeger, 1986).

Dale, Peter, *The Myth of Japanese Uniqueness* (New York: St. Martin's Press, 1986).

Davidson, William H., *The Amazing Race: Winning the Technorivalry with Japan* (New York: John Wiley, 1984).

Davis, John, 'The Institutional Foundations of Japanese Industrial Policy', *California Management Review*, vol. 27, no. 4, Summer 1985.

De Mente, Boye, *Japanese Business Etiquette* (Englewood Cliffs, N.J.: Prentice-Hall, 1981).

Dell, Edmund, 'Off Free Trade and Reciprocity', *The World Economy*, vol. 9, no. 2, June 1986, pp. 125–40.

Destler, I.M. and Sato, Hideo (eds), *Coping with the U.S.–Japanese Economic Conflicts* (Lexington, Mass.: Lexington Books, 1982).

Diebold, William, *Industrial Policy as an International Issue* (New York: McGraw-Hill, 1980).

Doi, Takeo, *The Anatomy of Japanese Dependence* (Tokyo: Kodansha, 1981).

Doi, Teruo, 'The Role of Intellectual Property Law in Bilateral Licensing Transactions between Japan and the United States', in *Law and Trade Issues of the Japanese Economy*.

Donnely, Michael, 'Setting the Price of Rice: A Study in Political Decision making', in T.J. Pempel, *Policy Making in Japan*.

Dore, Ronald, *Flexible Rigidities: Industrial Policy and Structural Adjustments in the Japanese Economy* (London: Athalone Press, 1986).

Dow, Tsung-I, 'The Meaning of the Confucian Work Ethic as the Source of Japan's Economic Power', *Asian Profile*, vol. 11, no. 3, June 1983.

Dower, J.W., *Empire and Aftermath: Yoshida Shigeru and the Japanese Experience, 1878–1954* (Cambridge, Mass.: Harvard University Press, 1979).

Downen, Robert and Dickson Bruce (eds), *The Emerging Pacific Community: A Regional Perspective* (Boulder: Westview Press, 1984).

Dreslter, J.M. and Sato, Hideo (eds), *Coping with United States-Japan Economic Conflicts* (Lexington, Mass: Lexington Books, 1982).

Drucker, Peter F., 'Japan: the Problems of Success', *Foreign Affairs*, pp. 564–78, April 1978.

Drysdale, Peter (ed.), *Direct Foreign Investment in Asia and the Pacific* (Toronto: Univertsity of Toronto Press, 1972).

Dubhashi, F.R., 'Economic Planning in Japan', *Indian Journal of Public Administration*, vol. 30, no. 3, August 1984.

Duncan, William, *United States–Japan Auto Diplomacy* (Cambridge, Mass.: Ballinger, 1973).

Dunn, James A., 'Automobiles in International Trade: Regime Change or Persistence', *International Organization*, vol. 41, no. 2, Spring 1987.

Duvall, Raymond D., 'Dependence and Dependenica Theory: Notes Toward Precision of Concept and Argument', *International Organization*, pp. 51–78, vol. 32, no. 1, Winter 1978.

Eguchi, Yujiro, 'Japanese Energy Policy', *International Affairs*, vol. 56, no. 2, April 1980.

El-Agraa, A.M., *Japan's Trade Frictions: Realities or Misconceptions* (New York, St. Martin's Press, 1988).

Emerson, John K., *Arms, Yen, and Power: The Japanese Dilemma* (New York, Dunellen, 1971).

Emery, Robert F., *The Japanese Money Market* (Lexington, Mass: Lexington Books, 1984).

Entwistle, Basil, *Japan's Decisive Decade: How a Determined Minority Changed the Nation's Course in the 1950s* (London: Grosvenor Books, 1985).

Fagen, Richard, 'A Funny Thing Happened on the Way to the Market: Thoughts on Extending Dependency Ideas', *International Organization*, pp. 287–300, vol. 32, no. 1, Winter 1978.

Feigenbaum, Edward and McCorduck, Pamela (eds), *The Fifth Generation Computer: Artificial Intelligence and Japan's Computer Challenge to the World* (Reading, Mass: Addison-Wesley, 1983).

Feld, Werner J., Jordan, Robert S. and Hurwitz Leon (eds), *International Organizations: A Comparative Approach* (New York: Praeger, 1983).

Feldman, Robert A., *Japanese Financial Markets: Deficits, Dilemmas, and Deregulation* (Boston: MIT Press, 1986).

Fletcher, Miles, 'Intellectuals and Fascism in Early Showa Japan', *Journal of Asian Studies*, vol. 39, no. 1, November 1979.

Fletcher, William M., *The Search for a New Order: Intellectuals and Facism in Prewar Japan* (Chapel Hill: University of North Carolina Press, 1982).

Frank, Isaiah (ed.), *The Japanese Economy in International Perspective* (Baltimore: Johns Hopkins University Press, 1975).

Frankel, Jeffrey A., *The Yen/Dollar Agreement: Liberalizing Japanese Capital Markets* (Washington, DC: Institute for International Economics, 1984).

Franko, Lawrence, *The Threat of Japanese Multinationals: How the West Can Respond* (New York: John Wiley, 1983).

Freedman, David, *The Misunderstood Miracle: Industrial Development and Policy Change in Japan* (Ithaca: Cornell University Press, 1988).

Freeman, Christopher, *Technology Policy and Economic Performance: Lessons from Japan* (New York: Pinter, 1987).

Frenkel, Orit, 'Flying High: A Case Study of Japanese Industrial Policy', *Journal of Policy Analysis and Management*, vol. 3, no. 3, Spring 1984.

Fried, Edward, Treise, Philip and Yoshida, Shigenobu, *The Future Course of U.S.–Japan Economic Relations* (Washington, DC: Brookings Institute, 1983).

Fukai, Shigeko, 'Japan's Energy Policy', *Current History*, April 1988.

Fukui, Haruhiro, *Party in Power: The Japanese Liberal-Democrats and Policy-Making* (Berkeley: University of California Press, 1970).

Fukushima, Haruhiro, 'Japan's Real Trade Policy', *Foreign Policy*, no. 59, Summer 1985.

Fukuzawa, Shiji, 'A New Industrial Structure', *Speaking of Japan*, vol. 7, no. 73, January 1987.

Fullerton, Stuart, 'International Trade: Reforming Japan's Trade Policy', *Harvard International Law Journal,* vol. 8, no. 4, December 1985.

Furuya, Kenichi, 'Labor-Management Relations in Postwar Japan', *Japan Quarterly,* vol. 27, no. 1, 1980.

George, Aurelia, 'The Japanese Farm Lobby and Agricultural Policymaking', *Pacific Affairs,* vol. 54, no. 3, Fall 1981.

Gibney, Frank, 'The View from Japan', *Foreign Affairs,* pp. 97–111, October 1971.

Gibney, Frank, *The Fragile Superpower* (Tokyo: Charles E. Tuttle, 1979).

Gibney, Frank (ed.), *The Whole Pacific Catalog* (Los Angeles: Access Press, 1981).

Gilpin, Robert G., *U.S. Power and the Multinational Corporation* (New York: Basic Books, 1975).

Gilpin, Robert, *War and Change in World Politics* (Cambridge: Cambridge University Press, 1981).

Gilpin, Robert G., 'The Richness of the Tradition of Political Realism', *International Organization.* pp. 287–304, vol. 38, no. 2, Spring 1984.

Gilpin, Robert G., *The Political Economy of International Relations* (Princeton, N.J.: Princeton University Press, 1987).

Girling, John, 'Agents of Influence', *Australian Outlook,* vol. 38, no. 2, August 1984.

Gold, Bela, 'Some International Differences in Approaches to Industrial Policy', *Contemporary Policy Issues,* vol. 4, no. 1, January 1986.

Grady, Robert C., 'Reindustrialization, Liberal Democracy, and Corporate Representation', *Political Science Quarterly,* no. 3, 1986, pp. 415–32.

Green, Robert and Lutz, James, *The United States and World Trade: Changing Patterns and Dimensions* (New York: Praeger, 1978).

Gregory, Gene, 'Japan's Telecom Industry Rushes into the Information Age', *Telephony,* vol. 206, no. 20, May 1984.

Goodman, Herbert, 'Japan and the World Energy Crisis' in Dan Okimoto, *Japan's Economy.*

Gordon, Bernard K. and Kenneth J. Rothwell (eds) *The New Political Economy of the Pacific* (Cambridge, Mass: Ballinger, 1975).

Government Decisionmaking in Japan: Implications for the United States, prepared for the Woodrow Wilson Centre, Washington, D.C., 1982.

Gowa, Joanne, 'Hegemons, IOs, and Markets: the Case of the Substitution Account', *International Organization,* pp. 661–84, vol. 38, no. 4, Autumn 1984.

Gowa, Joanne, 'Cooperation and International Relations', *International Organization,* Winter 1986, vol. 40, no. 1, pp. 167–86.

Grady, Robert C., 'Reindustrialization, Liberal Democracy, and Corporate Representation', *Political Science Quarterly,* no. 3, 1986, pp. 415–32.

Gressner, Julian, *Partners in Prosperity: Strategic Industries for the United States and Japan* (New York: McGraw-Hill, 1984).

Guerrieri, Paolo and Padovan, Pier Carlo, 'Neomercantilism and International Economic Stability', *International Organization,* 1986, vol. 40, no. 1, pp. 167–86.

Guttman, William, 'Japanese Capital Markets and Financial Liberalization', *Asian Survey,* vol. 27, no. 12, December 1987.

Guttman, David S., 'Protecting Intellectual Property: An American Viewpoint', *Speaking of Japan,* vol. 5, no. 41, May 1984.

Hadley, Eleanor M., *Antitrust in Japan* (Princeton, N.J.: Princeton University Press, 1970).

Hadley, Eleanor M., 'The Secret of Japan's Success', *Challenge,* vol. 26, no. 2, May/June 1983.

Haliday, Jon and McCorduck, Gavin, *Japanese Imperialism Today* (New York: Monthly Review Press, 1973).

Hall, John and Jansen, Marius (eds), *Studies in the Institutional History of Japan* (Princeton, New Jersey: Princeton University Press, 1968).

Hall, John, *Japan: From Prehistory to Modern Times* (New York: Delacorte Press, 1970).

Hamada, Tetsuo, 'Corporate Culture and Environment in Japan', *Asian Survey,* vol. 25, no. 12, December 1985, pp. 1214–28.

Hamilton, Pamela, 'Protection for Software Under U.S. and Japanese Law', *Boston College International and Comparative Law Review,* vol. 7, no. 2, Summer 1984.

Hasegawa, Sukehiro, *Japanese Foreign Aid: Policy and Practice* (New York: Praeger, 1975).

Hayashi, Risuke, 'Japanese Views', *Asia Pacific Community,* Summer 1979, no. 5, pp. 15–26.

Hayden, Eric W., 'Internationalizing Japan's Financial System', *Japan's Economy: Coping with Change in the International Environment* (Boulder, Colorado: Westview Press, 1982).

Hayden, Lesbril, 'The Political Economy of Substitution Policy: Japan's Response to Lower Oil Prices', *Pacific Affairs,* vol. 61, no. 2, Summer 1988.

Henderson, John, *Foreign Enterprise in Japan: Laws and Policies* (Chapel Hill: University of North Carolina Press, 1973).

Higashi, Chikara, *Japanese Trade Policy Formulation* (New York: Praeger, 1983).

Higashi, Chikara, *The Internationalization of the Japanese Economy* (Boston: Kluwer Academic Publications, 1987).

Hillman, Jimmy S. and Rothenberg, R.A., 'Wider Implications of Defending Japan's Rice Farmers', *The World Economy,* Vol. 8, No. 1, March 1985, pp. 43–62.

Hiraoka, L.S., 'U.S.–Japanese Competition in High Technology Fields', *Technological Forcasting and Social Change,* vol. 26, no. 1, August 1984.

Hiraoka, Tatsuo, 'Japan's Increasing Investments Abroad', *Futures,* vol. 17, no. 5, October 1985.

Hiraoka, Leslie S., 'A History of Assimilation: Japan's Technology Trade', *Speaking of Japan,* vol. 7, no. 71, November 1986.

Hirasawa, Kazushige, 'Japan's Emerging Foreign Policy', *Foreign Policy,* pp. 155–72, October 1975.

Holland, Harrison, *Managing Diplomacy Between the United States and Japan* (Stanford: Hoover Institute, 1984).

Hollerman, Leon (ed.), *Japan and the United States: Economic and Political Adversaries* (Boulder: Westview Press, 1980).

Hollerman, Leon, 'Disintegrative Versus Integrative Aspects of Interdependence: The Japanese Case', *Asian Survey*, Vol. XX, No. 3, March 1980, pp. 324–48.

Hoffman, Arthur (ed.), *Japan and the Pacific Basin* (Paris: Atlantic Institute for International Affairs, 1980).

Holsti, K.J., 'A New International Politics? Diplomacy in Complex Interdependence', *International Organization*, Vol. 32, No. 2, Spring 1978, pp. 513–30.

Holsti, Ole, Silverson, Randolph, George, Alexander (eds), *Change in the International System* (Boulder, Colorado: Westview Press, 1980).

Holsti, Kal J., 'Politics in Command: Foreign Trade as National Security Policy', *International Organization*, Summer 1986, vol. 40, no. 3, pp. 643–71.

Hopkins, Terrence and Wallerstein, Immanuel, *World Systems Analysis; Theory and Methodology* (Beverly Hills: Sage, 1982).

Horne, James, *Japan's Financial Markets: Conflict and Consensus in Policymaking* (London: Allen & Unwin, 1985).

Horvath, Dezso and McMillan, Charles, 'Industrial Planning in Japan', *California Management Review*, vol. 23, no. 1, Fall 1980.

Hrebrenaur, Ronald J., *The Japanese Party System: From One Party Rule to Coalition Government* (Boulder, Colorado: Westview Press, 1986).

Hunsberger, Warren S., *Japan and the United States in World Trade* (New York: Harper & Row 1964).

Ike, Nobutaka, *Japanese Politics* (New York: Alfred Knopf, 1973).

Imai, K., 'Iron and Steel: Industrial Organization', *Japanese Economic Studies*, vol. 3, no. 2, Winter 1974/75.

Inada, Nada, 'One-hundred Million Japanese', *Japan Quarterly*, vol. 28, no. 1, January–March 1981.

Inagaki, Takeshi, 'Rocket Readiness', *Japan Quarterly,* April–June 1988.

Inoguchi, Takashi and Tomoaki Iwai, *'Zoku Giin' No Kenkyu* (Tokyo: Nihon Keizai Shinbunsha, 1987).

Inoguchi Takashi Inoguchi and Okimoto, Daniel (eds), *The Political Economy of Japan: Volume 2, The Changing International Context,* (Stanford: Stanford University Press, 1988).

Ishii, Ryosuke, *A History of Political Institutions in Japan* (Tokyo: University of Tokyo Press, 1980).

Ishida, Takeshi, *Japan's Political Culture: Change and Continuity* (New Brunswick and London: Transaction Books, 1983).

Ishida, Hideto, 'Anticompetitive Practices in the Distribution of Goods and Services in Japan: the Problem of Distribution Keiretsu', *Journal of Japanese Studies*, vol. 9, no. 2, Summer 1983.

Ishizaki, Tadoa, 'Is Japan's Income Distribution Equal?', *Japanese Economic Studies,* vol. 14, no. 2, Winter 1985/86.

Ito, Keiichi, 'Japan's Defense Policy and Limited Budget', *Asia Pacific Community*, Summer 1985, no. 29, pp. 13–24.

Itoh, Hiroshi (ed.), *Japan's Foreign Policy Making* (Buffalo: State University of New York, 1982).

Jain, Hem C. 'The Japanese System of Human Resource Management', *Asian Survey,* vol. 27, no. 9, September 1987.

'Japan Special Report', *Middle East Economic Development* (MEED), December 1988.

Japanese Industrial and Trade Collusion, prepared for the Subcommittee on Economic Goals and Intergovernmental Policy of the Joint Economic Committee, Washington, DC, 1986.

Japanese Overseas Investment: A Complete Listing (Tokyo: Oriental Economist, 1981).

Johnson, Chalmers, *Japan's Public Policy Companies* (Washington, DC: AEI-Hoover Policy Studies, 1978).

Johnson, Chalmers, *MITI and the Japanese Miracle: The Growth of Industrial Policy, 1925–1975* (Stanford: Stanford University Press, 1982).

Johnson, Chalmers (ed.), *The Industrial Policy Debate* (San Francisco: ICS Press, 1984).

Johnson, Chalmers, 'The Institutional Foundations of Japanese Industrial Policy', *California Management Review,* vol. 27, no. 4, Summer 1985.

Johnson, Chalmers, 'Reflections on the Dilemma of Japanese Defense', *Asian Survey,* vol. xxvi, no. 5, May 1986, pp. 557–72.

Jones, T.M. *et al.,* 'Industrial Policy: Influencing the International Marketplace', *Journal of Contemporary Business,* vol. 11, no. 1, 1982.

Kabashima, 'Supportive Economic Growth in Japan', *World Politics,* vol. 36, no. 3, April 1983.

Kabashima, Ikui and Broadbent, Jeffrey, 'Referent Pluralism: Mass Media and Politics in Japan', *Journal of Japanese Studies,* Summer 1986.

Kajima, Morinosuke, *Modern Japan's Foreign Policy* (Tokyo: Tuttle, Charles E. 1969).

Kaplan, Eugene, *Japan: The Government–Business Relationship* (Washington, DC: Government Printing Office, 1972).

Kashiwagi, Yusuke, 'Going Global: The Internationalization of the Yen and the Tokyo Financial Market', *Speaking of Japan,* vol. 8, no. 79, July 1987.

Katsuo, Satoh, 'Japan's Economic Success: Industrial Policy or Free Market', *Cato Journal,* vol. 4, no. 2, Fall 1984.

Katz, Joshua and Friedman, Tilly (eds), *Japan's New World Role* (Boulder, Colorado: Westview Press, 1985).

Katzenstein, Peter J., 'International Interdependence: Some Long Term Trends Changes', *International Organization,* pp. 1021–34, vol. 29, no. 4, Autumn 1975.

Kawaii, Kazuo, *Japan's American Interlude* (Chicago: University of Chicago Press, 1960).

Kawahito, Kiyoshi, *The Japanese Steel Industry: With an analysis of the U.S. Steel Import Problem'* (New York: Praeger, 1972).

Kegley, Charles W. and Howell, Llewellyn D. Jr., *International Organization,* pp. 997–1020, vol. 29, no. 4, Autumn 1975.

Kegley, Charles and McGowan, Pat (eds), *The Political Economy of Foreign Policy Behavior* (Beverly Hills: Sage, 1981).

Keohane, Robert and Nye, Joseph (eds), *Power and Interdependence: World Politics in Transition* (Boston: Little, Brown, 1977).

Keohane, Robert, *After Hegemony: Cooperation and Discord in the World Political Economy* (Princeton, N.J.: Princeton University Press, 1984).

Keohane, Robert, 'Reciprocity in International Relations', *International Organization,* Winter 1986, vol. 40, no. 1, pp. 1–28.

Kershner, Thomas, *Japanese Foreign Trade* (Lexington, Mass.: Lexington Books, 1975).

Kim, Young, *Japanese Journalists and Their World* (Charlottesville: University of Virginia, 1981).

Kindleberger, Charles P., *The World in Depression* (London: Allen Press, 1973).

Kindleberger, Charles P., 'Hierarchy Versus Inertial Cooperation', *International Organization,* Autumn 1986, vol. 40, no. 4, pp. 841–8.

Kinmouth, Earl H., 'Japanese Patents: Olympic Gold or Public Relations Brass', *Pacific Affairs,* vol. 61, no. 1, Spring 1988.

Kiyuna, Kenneth, 'Japanese and American Companies', *Asian Affairs,* vol. 10, no. 2, Summer 1983.

Koh, B.C. and Jae-ln Kim, 'Paths to Advancement in Japanese Bureaucracy', *Comparative Politics Studies,* Vol. 15, No. 3, October 1983, pp. 289–313.

Kojima, Kiyoshi, *Direct Foreign Investment: A Japanese Model of Multinational Business Operations* (London: Croom Helm, 1978).

Kojima, Kiyoshi, *Japan and a New World Economic Order* (Boulder, Colorado: Westview Press. 1977).

Kolde, Endel Jakob, *The Pacific Quest: The Concept and Scope of an Oceanic Community* (Lexington, Mass: Lexington Books, 1976).

Konosuke, Odaka, Kunosuke, Ono and Adachi, Fumihiko, *The Automobile Industry in Japan* (Tokyo, Kinokuniya, 1988).

Kosobric, Richard (ed.), *Northeast Asia and the U.S.: Defense Partnership and Trade Rivalries* (Chicago, Chicago Council on Foreign Relations, 1983).

Krasner, Stephen, *Defending the National Interests: Raw Materials Investments and U.S. Foreign Policy* (Princeton, N.J.: Princeton University Press, 1978).

Krasner, Stephen (ed.), *International Regimes* (Ithaca: Cornell University Press, 1982).

Krasner, Stephen (ed.), *Structural Conflict: The Third World Against Global Liberalism* (Berkely: University of California Press, 1985).

Krause, Lawrence and Sekiguchi, Sueo, (eds), *Economic Interaction in the Pacific Basin* (Washington, DC: Brookings Institute, 1980).

Krause, Lawrence, *U.S. Economic Policy Toward the Association of Southeast Asian Nations: Meeting the Japanese Challenge* (Washington, DC: Brookings Institute, 1982).

Krause, Lawrence and Muramatsu, Harumi, 'Bureaucrats and Politicians in Japanese Policymaking', *American Political Science Review,* vol. 78, no. 1, March 1984.

Kubota, Akira, 'Japan: Social Structure and Work Ethic', *Asia Pacific Community,* no. 20, Spring 1983.

Kubota, Akira, 'Japan's External Economic Relations: Trade Barriers Versus Perception Barriers', *Asia Pacific Community*, no. 30, Fall 1986, pp. 119–34.

Kuroda, Yasumasa, *et al.*, 'The End of Westernization and the Beginning of New Modernization in Japan', *Arab Journal of the Social Sciences*, vol. 2, no. 1, April 1987.

Langdon, F.C., *Japan's Foreign Policy* (Vancouver: University of British Columbia Press, 1973).

Langdon, Frank, 'The Security Debate in Japan', *Pacific Affairs*, September 1985, vol. 58, no. 3, pp. 397–410.

Langdon, Frank, 'Japan–U.S. Trade Friction: The Reciprocity Issue', *Asian Survey*, vol. 23, no. 5, May 1983.

Lavoie, Don, 'Two Varieties of Industrial Policy: A Critique', *Cato Journal*, vol. 4, no. 2, Fall 1984.

Laxer, James, *Decline of the Superpowers: Winners and Losers in Today's Global Economy* (New York: Praeger, 1989).

Lawrence, Robert Z. and Litan, Robert E. 'Living with the Trade Deficit: Adjustment Strategies to Preserve Free Trade', *The Brookings Review*, Fall 1985, vol. 4, no. 1, pp. 3–13.

Lebra, Takie Sugiyama and Lebra, William, *Japanese Culture and Behavior* (Honolulu: East–West Book, University of Hawaii Press, 1974).

Lebra, Takie Sugiyama, *Japanese Patterns of Behavior* (Honolulu: University Press of Hawaii, 1976).

Lee, Chae-Jin and Sato, Hideo, *U.S. Policy Towards Japan and Korea: A Changing Influence Relationship* (New York: Praeger, 1982).

Lee, Ching, 'Japanese Foreign Investment Theories', *Economic Development and Cultural Change*, vol. 32, no. 4, July 1984.

Lee, Chong-Sik, *Japan and Korea: The Political Dimension* (Stanford, California: Hoover Institute Press, 1985).

Lee, Jung Bock, *The Political Character of the Japanese Press* (Seoul: Seoul National University Press, 1985).

Lincoln, Edward J., 'Disentangling the Mess in U.S.–Japan Economic Relations', *The Brookings Review*, Fall 1985, vol. 4, no. 1., pp. 22–7.

Lincoln, Edward J., *Japan: Facing Economic Maturity* (Washington, DC: Brookings Institute, 1988).

Linhart, Sepp, 'From Industrial to Postindustrial Society', *Journal of Japanese Studies*, vol. 14, no. 2, Summer 1988.

Linder, Staffan, *The Pacific Century; Economic and Political Consequences of Asian-Pacific Dynamism* (Stanford: Stanford University Press, 1986).

Lochmann, Michael, W., 'The Japanese Voluntary Restraint on Automobile Exports', *Harvard International Law Journal*, vol. 27, no. 1, Winter 1986.

Loutfi, Martha F., *The Net Cost of Japanese Foreign Aid* (New York: Praeger, 1973).

Lynn, Loreta, 'Japanese Robotics', *Annuls of the American Academy of Political and Sociological Sciences*, vol. 470, November 1983.

Machizuki, Mike, 'Japan's Search for Strategy', *International Security*, Vol. 8, No. 3, Winter 1983/84, pp. 152–79.

MacIntosh, Malcolm, *Japan Rearmed* (New York: St. Martin's Press, 1986).

Magaziner, Ira C. and Hout, Thomas M, *Japanese Industrial Policy*, Policy Papers in International Affairs 15 (Berkeley: Institute of International Studies, University of California, 1980).

Malik, Rex, 'Japan's Fifth Generation Computer', *Futures*, Vol. 15, No. 3, June 1983, pp. 205–11.

Mannari, Hiroshi and Harumi Befu (eds), *The Challenge of Japan's Internationalization, Organization, and Culture* (Nishinomiya, Japan: Kwansei Gkuin University, Kodansha, 1983).

Maruyama, Masao, *Thought and Behavior in Japanese Politics* (New York: Oxford University Press, 1969).

Mason, Ha, *International Business in the Pacific Basin* (Lexington, Mass: Lexington Books, 1978).

Matsuzaka, Hideo, 'The Future of Japanese–ASEAN Relations', *Asia Paficic Community*, No. 3, Summer 1983, pp. 11–21.

McCormick, Gavan and Sugimoto, Yoshio, *Democracy in Contemporary Japan* (Amronk, New York: M.E. Sharpe, 1986).

McCraw, Thomas K. (ed.), *America Versus Japan* (Boston: Harvard Business School Press, 1986).

McCulloch, Rachel, 'Points of view: Trade Deficits, International Competiveness, and the Japanese', *California Management Review*, vol. 27, no. 2, 1984.

McKenna, Regis, *et al.*, 'Industrial Policy and International Competition in High Technology', *California Management Review*, vol. 26, no. 2, Winter 1984.

McKeown, Timothy J., 'Hegemonic Stability Theory and 19th Century Tariff Levels in Europe', *International Organization*, pp. 73–92, vol. 37, no. 1, Winter 1983.

McLean, Mick (ed.), *The Japanese Electronics Challenge* (New York: St. Martin's Press, 1982).

McLean, Mick (ed.), *Mechatronics: Developments in Japan and Europe*, (Westport, Ct.: Technova, Quorum Books, 1983).

McMillan, Charles, *The Japanese Industrial System* (Berlin: De Gruyter, 1985).

McRae, Hamish, *Japan's Role in the Emerging Securities Market*, Occasional Paper No. 17 (New York: Group of Thirty, 1985).

Milner, Helen V. and David B. Yoffie, 'Between Free Trade and Protectionism: Strategic Trade Policy and a Theory of Corporate Trade Demands', *International Organization*, vol. 43, no. 2, Spring 1989.

Minor, John, 'Decision-makers and Japanese Foreign Policy', *Asian Survey*, vol. 25, no. 13, December 1985.

Mochizuki, 'Japanese Search for Strategy', *International Security*, vol. 8, no. 3, Winter 1983–84.

Mowery, David C. and Rosenberg, Nathan, 'Commercial Aircraft: Cooperation and Competition Between the U.S. and Japan', *California Management Review*, vol. 27, no. 4, Summer 1985.

Mowery, David C. and Rosenberg, Nathan, *The Japanese Commercial Aircraft Industry Since 1945: Government Policy, Technical*

Development and Industrial Structure (Stanford: Stanford University Press, 1985).

Moran, Theodore H., 'Multinational Corporations and Dependency: A Dialog for Dependentistas and Non-dependentistas', *International Organization*, pp. 79–100, vol. 32, no. 1, Winter 1978.

Moritaka, Hayashi, 'Japan and Deep Seabed Mining', *Ocean Development and International Law*, vol. 17, no. 4, 1986.

Morrison, Charles E., *Threats to Security in East Asia Pacific: National and Regional Perspectives* (Lexington, Mass.: Lexington Books, 1981).

Morse, Ronald (ed.) *The Politics of Japan's Energy Strategy* (Berkeley, California: Institute of East Asian Studies, 1981).

Morse, Ronald, 'Japan's Search for an Independent Foreign Policy', *Journal of Northeast Asian Studies*, vol. 3, no. 2, Summer 1984.

Muldoon, Robert D., 'Rethinking the Ground Rules for an Open World Economy', *Foreign Affairs*, pp. 1078–99, Summer 1983.

Murakami, Yasusuke, 'The Age of New Middle-Mass Politics', *Journal of Japanese Studies*, vol. 8, no. 1, Winter 1982.

Murakami, Yasusuke and Kosai, Yutake, *Japan in The Global Community: Its Role and Contribution on the Eve of the Twenty-First Century* (Tokyo: University of Tokyo Press, 1987).

Najita, Tetsuo and J. Victor Koschmann (eds), *Conflict in Modern Japanese History* (Princeton, N.J.: Princeton University Press, 1982).

Nakamura, Takafusa, *The Postwar Japanese Economy: Its Development and Structure* (Tokyo: University of Tokyo Press, 1981).

Nakamura, Takafusa, 'Japanese Perspectives on U.S.–Japan Trade Relations', *Asia Affairs: An American Review*, vol. 12, no. 4, Winter 1985–86.

Nakane, Chie, *Japanese Society* (Berkeley: University of California Press, 1970).

Nakasone, Soridaijin, 'Japan's Choice: A Strategy for World Peace', *Atlantic Community Quarterly*, vol. 22, no. 3, Fall 1984.

Najima, Tetsuo, *Japan: The Intellectual Foundations of Modern Japanese Politics* (Chicago: University of Chicago Press, 1980).

Nathan, Leah, 'A Matter of Control', *Business Month*, September 1988.

Nester, William, *Japan's Growing Power over East Asia and the World Economy: Ends and Means* (London: Macmillan, 1990).

Nishihara, 'Expanding Japan's Credible Defense Role', *International Security*, vol. 8, no. 3, Winter 1983–84.

Nivola, Pietro S., 'The New Protectionism: U.S. Trade Policy in Historical Perspective', *Political Science Quarterly*, no. 4, 1986, pp. 577–600.

Noguchi, Yukio, 'Public Finance', in Kozo Yamamura and Yasukichi Yasuba (eds), *The Political Economy of Japan: Volume 1, The Domestic Transformation* (Stanford: Stanford University Press, 1987).

Nukazama, 'Yen for Dollars', *World Economy*, vol. 6, no. 3, September 1983.

Ohkawa, Kazushi and Ranis, Gustav (eds), *Japan and the Developing Countries: A Comparative Analysis* (New York: Basil Blackwell, 1985).

Ohrnae, Kenichi, *Japan Business Obstacles and Opportunities* (New York: McKinsey, 1983).

Ohmae, Kenichi, *Beyond National Borders: Reflections on Japan and the World* (Homewood, Ill., Dow Jones-Irwin, 1987).

Okazaki, Hisahiko, *A Grand Strategy for Japanese Defense* (New York: University Press of America, 1986).

Okimoto, Daniel, *Japan's Economy: Coping with Change in the International Environment* (Boulder, Colorado: Westview Press, 1982).

Okimoto, Daniel, Sugano, Takuo and Weinstein, Franklin B. (eds), *Competitive Edge: The Semiconductor Industry in the U.S. and Japan* (Stanford: Stanford University Press, 1984).

Okimoto, Daniel and Rohlen, Thomas (eds), *Inside the Japanese System: Readings on Contemporary Society and Political Economy* (Stanford: Stanford University Press, 1988).

Okimoto, Daniel, *Between MITI and the Marketplace: Japanese Industrial Policy for High Technology* (Stanford: Stanford University Press, 1989).

Okita, Saburo, 'Japanese–American Economic Troubles: Lowering the Temperature', *International Security,* Vol. 7, No. 2, Fall 1982, pp. 198–203.

Okita, Saburo, 'The Role of the Trade Ombudsman in Liberalizing Japan's Markets', *The World Economy,* Vol. 7, No. 3, September 1984, pp. 241–56.

Olsen, Lawrence, *Japan in Postwar Asia* (New York: Prayer 1970).

Olsen, Robert, *U.S. Foreign Policy and the New International Order* (Boulder, Colorado: Westview Press, 1981).

O'Neil, Robert (ed.), *Security in East Asia* (Hant, GU.: Gower, 1984).

Organization for Economic Cooperation and Development, *The Industrial Policy of Japan* (Paris: OECD, 1972).

Oshima, Harry T., 'Reinterpreting Japan's Postwar Growth', *Economic Development and Social Change,* Vol. 31, No. 10, October 1982.

Ozaki, Robert, *The Control of Imports and Foreign Capital in Japan* (New York: Praeger 1972).

Ozaki, Robert, *The Japanese: A Cultural Portrait* (Tokyo: Charles E. Tuttle, 1978).

Ozaki, Hisahiko, 'Japanese Security Policy: A Time for Strategy', *International Security,* vol. 7, No. 2, Fall 1982, pp. 188–97.

Ozaki, Robert and Arnold, Walter (eds), *Japan's Foreign Relations: A Global Search for Economic Security* (Boulder, Colorado: Westview Press, 1985).

Ozaki, Robert, 'The Humanistic Enterprise System in Japan', *Asian Survey,* vol. 28, no. 12, December 1985.

Ozawa, Terutomo, *Japan's Technological Challenge to the West, 1950–74* (Cambridge, Mass.: MIT Press, 1974).

Ozawa, Terutomo, *Multinationalism, Japanese Style* (Princeton, N.J.: Princeton University Press, 1978).

Ozawa, Terutomo, 'Japan's New Resource Diplomacy: Government Backed Group Investment', *Journal of World Trade Law,* vol. 14, no. 1, January–February 1980.

Passin, Herbert and Iriye, Akira (eds), *Encounter At Shimoda: Search For a New Pacific Partnership* (Boulder, Colorado: Westview Press, 1979).

Patrick, Hugh, and Rosovsky Henry (eds), *Asia's New Giant: How the Japanese Economy Works* (Washington, DC: Brookings Institute, 1976).

Patrick, Hugh, 'The Future of the Japanese Economy', *Journal of Japanese Studies,* Summer 1977.

Patrick, Hugh, and Meissner, Larry (eds), *Japan's High Technology Industries: Lessons and Limitations of Industrial Policy* (Seattle: University of Washington Press, 1986).

Patrick, Hugh and Tachi, Ryuichiro (eds), *Japan and the United States Today: Exchange Rates, Macroeconomic Policies, and Financial Market Innovations* (New York: Columbia University Press, 1986).

Peck, Merton J., Levin, Richard and Goto, Akira, 'Picking Losers: Public Policy Toward Declining Industries in Japan', *Journal of Japanese Studies,* vol. 13, no. 1, Winter 1987.

Pempel, T.J. (ed.), *Policymaking in Contemporary Japan* (Ithaca: Cornell University Press, 1977).

Pempel, T.J. 'Japanese Foreign Economic Policy: the Domestic Bases for International Behavior', *International Organization,* pp. 722–74, vol. 31, no. 4, Autumn 1977.

Pempel, T.J., *Policymaking in Contemporary Japan* (Boulder, Colorado: Westview Press, 1978).

Pempel, T.J., *Policy and Politics in Japan: Creative Conservatism* (Philidephia: Temple University Press, 1982).

Pempel, T.J., *Japan: The Dilemma of Success* (New York: Foreign Policy Association, 1986).

Pepper, Thomas, Janow, Merrit E. and Wheeler, Jimmy W., *The Competition: Dealing with Japan* (New York: Praeger, 1985).

Pepper, Thomas, *The Japanese Challenge* (New York: Cromwell, 1979).

Peritz, Rene, 'Japan's Foreign Policy at Mid-Decade: A Critique', *Asian Profile,* vol. 13, no. 1, February 1985.

Petri, Peter A., *Modeling Japanese–American Trade: A Study of Symmetrical Interdependence* (Cambridge, Mass.: Harvard University Press, 1988).

Pierce, John, *et al.,* 'The New Environmental Paradigm in Japan and the United States, *Journal of Politics,* vol. 49, no. 1, February 1987.

Pinder, John (ed.), *National Industrial Strategies and World Economy* (London: Croom Helm, 1982).

Ping, Lee Poh, 'Malaysian Perceptions of Japan Before and During the "Look East" Period', *Asia Pacific Community,* Summer 1985, no. 29, pp. 25–34.

Prestowitz, Cylde, *Trading Places: How We Allowed Japan to Take the Lead* (New York: Basic Books, 1988).

Pugel, Thomas, 'Japan's Industrial Policy: Instruments, Trends, Effects', *Journal of Comparative Economics,* vol. 8, no. 4, December 1984.

Pugel, Thomas (ed.), *Fragile Interdependence: Economic Issues in United States–Japan Trade and Investments* (Lexington, Mass.: Lexington Books, 1986).

Pyle, Lucian, 'The Future of Japanese Nationality', *Journal of Japanese Studies,* vol. 8, no. 2, Summer 1982.

Pyle, Kenneth, *The Making of Modern Japan* (Lexington, Mass.: D.C. Heath, 1978).

Quo, F. Quei (ed.) *Politics of the Pacific Rim: Perspectives on the 1980s* (Burnaby, B.C.: Simon Fraser University, San Francisco University Publishers, 1982).

Quo, F. Quei, 'Japan's Role in Asia', *International Journal,* vol. 38, no. 2, Spring 1983.

Ramsted, Yugue, 'Free Trade Versus Fair Trade: Import Barriers as a Problem of Reasonable Values', *Journal of Economic Issues,* Vol. xxi, No. 1, March 1987, pp. 5–22.

Reading, Brian, *Investing in Japan* (Cambridge: Woodhead-Faulkner, 1978).

Redford, Lawrence (ed.), *The Occupation of Japan: Economic Policy and Reform* (Norfolk, Va.: The Memorial, 1980).

Reed, Steven, 'Environmental Politics in Japan', *Comparative Politics,* vol. 13, no. 3, April 1981.

Reich, Robert B., 'Making Industrial Policy', *Foreign Affairs,* pp. 852–81, Spring 1982.

Reich, Robert B., 'The Threat of the Global Corporation', *Canadian Business,* vol. 56, no. 8, August 1983.

Reich, Robert B., 'What Kind of Industrial Policy', *Journal of Business Strategy,* vol. 5, no. 1, Summer 1984.

Reich, Robert B., 'Beyond Free Trade', *Foreign Affairs,* pp. 773–804, Spring 1983.

Reichauer, Edwin, *The Japanese* (Toyko: Charles E. Tuttle, 1977).

Reynolds, Peter, 'Foreign Investment in Japan: The Legal and Social Climate', *Texas International Law Journal,* vol. 18, no. 1, Winter 1983.

Rice, Richard, 'Economic Mobilization in Wartime Japan', *Journal of Asian Studies,* vol. 38, no. 4, August 1979.

Richardson, Bradley and Taizo Ueda (eds), *Business and Society in Japan: Fundamentals for Businessmen* (New York: Praeger, 1981).

Rix, Alan, *Japan's Economic Aid: Policy-Making and Politics,* (New York: St. Martins Press, 1980).

Robertson, John, 'Japanese Offshore Banking', *Fletcher Forum,* vol. 8, no. 2, Spring 1983.

Rodrik, Dani, 'Managing Resource Dependency: The United States and Japan in the Markets for Copper, Iron Ore, and Bauxite', *World Development,* vol. 10, no. 7, 1982.

Rohrlich, Paul Egan, 'Economic Culture and Foreign Policy: The Cognitive Analysis of Economic Policymaking', *International Organization,* Winter 1987, vol. 41, no. 1, pp. 61–92.

Roemer, John E., *U.S.–Japanese Competition in International Markets: A Study of the Trade-Investment Cycle in Modern Capitalism* (Berkeley: University of California Press, 1975).

Rohrlich, Paul Egan, 'Economic Culture and Foreign Policy: The Cognitive Analysis of Economic Policymaking', *International Organization,* Winter 1987, vol. 41, no. 1, pop. 61–92.

Rosecrance, R. *et al.*, 'Whither Interdependence?', International Organization, pp. 425–72, vol. 31, no. 3, Summer 1977.

Rosecrance, Richard, *The Rise of the Trading State: Commerce and Conquest in the Modern World* (New York: Basic Books, 1986).

Rosecrance, Richard and Gutowitz, William, 'Measuring Interdependence: A Rejoinder', *International Organization*, pp. 553–56, vol. 35, no. 3, Summer 1981.

Rosenau, James N., 'Hegemons, Regimes, and Habit Driven Actors in World Politics', *International Organization*, Autumn 1986, vol. 40, no. 4, pp. 849–94.

Russett, Bruce, 'Dimension of Resource Dependence: Some Elements of Rigor in Concept and Policy Analysis', *International Organization*, pp. 481–500, vol. 38, no. 3, Summer 1984.

Samuels, Richard, *The Business of the Japanese State* (Ithaca: Cornell University Press, 1987).

Sakoh, Katsuro and Trezise, Philip H., 'Japanese Economic Success: Industrial Policy or Free Market?', *Cato Journal*, vol. 4, no. 2, Fall 1984.

Sato, Ryuzo and Wachtel, Paul (eds), *Trade Friction and Economic Policy* (New York: Cambridge University Press, 1985).

Sato, Kazuo and Hochino, Yasuo, *The Anatomy of Japanese Business*, Armonk, New York: M.E. Sharpe, 1984).

Sato, Kazuo, 'Saving and Investment', in Yamamura, Kozo and Yasuba, Yasukichi (eds), *The Political Economy of Japan: Volume 1, The Domestic Transformation* (Stanford: Stanford University Press, 1987).

Sato, Seizaburo and Tetsuhisa, Matsuzaki, *Jiminto Seiken* (Tokyo: Chuo Koronsha, 1986).

Saxonhouse, Gary, 'What is all this about Industrial Targeting in Japan', *World Economy*, vol. 6, no. 3, September 1983.

Saxonhouse, Gary, 'Japan's Intractable Trade Surplus in a New Era', *The World Economy*, vol. 9, no. 3, September 1986, pp. 239–58.

Saxonhouse, Gary and Yamamura, Kozo, *Law and Trade Issues of the Japanese Economy* (Seattle: University of Washington Press, 1986).

Scalipino, Robert (ed.), *The Foreign Policy of Modern Japan* (Berkeley: University of California Press, 1977).

Schaller, Michael, *The American Occupation of Japan: The Origins of the Cold War in Asia* (Oxford: Oxford University Press, 1985).

Schlosssentein, Steven, *Trade War: Greed, Power, and Industrial Policy on Opposite Sides of the Pacific* (New York: Gongdon Weed, 1984).

Schmiegelow, Michele (ed.), *Japan's Response to Crisis and Change in the World Economy* (Armonk, New York: M.E. Sharpe, 1987).

Schmitter, Philippe and Lehmbruch, Gerhard, *Trends Toward Corporate Intervention* (London: Sage, 1979).

Scott, B.R., 'National Strategy for Stronger U.S. Competitiveness', *Harvard Business Review*, vol. 62, no. 2, March/April 1984.

Sekiguchi, Sueo, *Japanese Direct Foreign Investment* (Montclair, N.J.: Allanehld, Osmun, 1979).

Sekiguchi, Haruichi, 'Myth and Reality of Japan's Industrial Policy', *World Economy*, vol. 8, no. 4, December 1985.

Selim, Hassam M., *Development Assistance Policies and the Performance of Aid Agencies* (London: Macmillan, 1983).

Shapiro, Michael, *Japan: In the Land of the Brokenhearted* (New York: H. Holt, 1989).

Shibata, Tokue, *Public Finance in Japan* (Tokyo: University of Tokyo Press, 1986).

Shibusawa, Masahide, 'Japan and its Region', *Asia Pacific Community*, Summer 1985, no. 29, pp. 25–34.

Shinkai, Yoichi, 'The Internationalization of Finance in Japan', in Inoguchi, Takashi and Okimoto, Daniel (eds), *The Political Economy of Japan: Volume 2, The Changing International Context* (Stanford, California: Stanford University Press, 1988).

Sigur, Gaston and Young, Kim, *Japanese and U.S. Policy in Asia* (New York: Praeger, 1982).

Silk, Leonard, 'The United States and the World Economy', *Foreign Affairs*, Vol. 65, No. 3, Fall 1986, pp. 458–76.

Sills, David L. (ed.), *International Encyclopedia of the Social Science* (Macmillan and the Free Press, U.S.A.)

Slaughter, Jane and Parker, Mike, *Choosing Sides*.

Slover, John (ed.), *Government Policy Towards Industry in the United States and Japan* (New York: Cambridge University Press, 1988).

Smith, Robert, *Japanese Society: Tradition, Self and the Social Order* (London: Cambridge University Press, 1984).

Snidal, Duncan 'The Limits of Hegemonic Stability Theory', *International Organization*, Autumn 1985, vol. 39, no. 4, pp. 579–614.

Sobel, Robert, *Car Wars: The Untold Story* (New York: E.P. Dutton, 1984).

Sobel, Robert, *IBM V. Japan: The Struggle for the Future* (New York: Stein & Day, 1986).

Spanier, John, *Games Nations Play: Analyzing International Politics* (New York: Holt, Rinehart & Winston, 1984).

Spencer, John, 'Japan: Stimulus or Scapegoat', *Foreign Affairs*, vol. 62, no. 1, Fall 1983.

Spindler, J. Andrew, *The Politics of International Credit: Private Finance and Foreign Relations in Germany and Japan* (Washington, DC: Brookings Institute, 1984).

Staniland, Martin, *What Is Political Economy?: A Study of Social Theory and Underdevelopment* (New Haven: Yale University Press, 1985).

Stein, Arthur A., 'The hegemon's Dilemma: Great Britain, the United States, and the International Economic Order', *International Organization*, pp. 355–86, vol. 38, no. 2, Spring 1984.

Statistical Yearbook for Asia and the Pacific (Bangkok: UN, 1984).

Stockwin, J.A.A., *Japan: Divided Politics in a Growth Economy* (New York: W.W. Norton, 1982).

Stockwin, John, 'Understanding Japanese Foreign Policy', *Review of International Studies*, vol. 11, no. 2, April 1985.

Stockwin, J.A.A., *Dynamics and Immobilist Politics in Japan* (London: Macmillan, 1988).

Strange, Susan (ed.), *Paths to International Political Economy* (London: Allen & Unwin, 1984).

Striner, Herbert E., *Regaining the Lead: Policies for Economic Growth* (New York: Prayer, 1984).

Suzuki, Yoshio, *Money, Finance and Macroeconomic Performance in Japan* (New Haven: Yale University Press, 1986).

Tai, Chong-Soo, 'The Relationship Between Economic Development and Social Equality in Japan, Korea, and Taiwan: A Comparative Analysis Using Regression Models', *Asian Profile,* vol. 14, no. 1, February 1986.

Taira, Koji, 'Colonialism in Foreign Subsidiaries: Lessons from Japanese Investment in Thailand', *Asian Survey,* April 1980.

Taira, Koji, 'Labor Federation in Japan', *Current History,* April 1988.

Tanaka, Yuki, 'Nuclear Power Plant Gypsies in High Tech Society', Bulletin of Concerned Asia Scholars, vol. 18, no. 1, 1986, p. 3.

Tasca, Diane (ed.) *U.S.–Japanese Economic Relations: Cooperation, Competition, Confrontation* (New York: Pergamon Press, 1980).

Tasker, Peter, *The Japanese: A Major Exploration of Modern Japan* (New York: Dutton Press, 1989).

Tatsuno, Sheridan, *The Technopolis Strategy: Japan, High Technology, and The Control of the Twenty-First Century* (New York: Prentice Hall, 1986).

Taylor, R. *The Sino–Japanese Axis: A New Force in Asia* (New York: St. Martins Press, 1985).

Tenderten, Gianni Fodella (ed.), *Japan's Economy in a Comparative Perspective* (Kent: Paul Norbury, 1983).

Tetreault, Mary Ann, 'Measuring Interdependence', *International Organization,* pp. 429–43, vol. 34, no. 3, Summer 1980.

Tetreault, Mary Ann, 'Measuring Interdependence: A Response', *International Organization,* pp. 557–60, vol. 35, no. 3, Summer 1981.

Thurow, Lester, *The Japanese Management Challenge* (Cambridge, Mass.: MIT Press, 1985).

Toffler, Alvin, *The Third Wave* (New York: Morrow, 1980).

Trezise, Philip H., 'Industrial Policy is Not the Major Reason for Japan's Success', *Brookings Review,* vol. 1, no. 3, Spring 1983.

Trezise, Phil, 'Japan's Miracles Revisited', *Society,* vol. 22, no. 1, November–December 1984.

Tsuji, Kiyoaki (ed.) *Public Administration in Japan* (Tokyo: University of Tokyo Press, 1980).

Tsurumi, Yoshi, *The Japanese Are Coming: A Multinational Interaction of Firms and Politics* (Cambridge: Ballinger, 1976).

Tsurumi, Yoshi, *Technology Transfer and Foreign Trade: The Case of Japan, 1950–66* (New York: Arno Press, 1980).

Tsurutani, Taketsugu, 'Old Habits, New Times: Challenges to Japanese–American Security Relations', *International Security,* Vol. 7, No. 2, Fall 1982, pp. 175–87.

Tsurutani, Taketsugu, 'The LDP in Transition: Mass Membership Participation in Party Leadership Selection', *Asian Survey,* vol. 20, no. 8, August 1980.

Tung, Rosalie, *Business Negotiations with the Japanese* (Lexington, Mass.: Lexington Books, 1984).

Uchino, Tasuo, *Japan's Postwar Economy* (Tokyo: Kodansha, 1983).

Ueno, Hiroya and Muto, Hiromichi 'The Automobile Industry of Japan', *Japanese Economic Studies,* vol. 3, no. 1, Fall 1974.

Vernon, Raymond, *Two Hungry Giants: The United States and Japan in the Quest for Oil and Ores* (Cambridge, Mass.: Harvard University Press, 1983).

Viner, Aron, *The Emerging Power of Japanese Money* (Homewood, Ill.: Dow Jones-Irwin, 1988).

Viner, Aron, *Inside Japan's Financial Markets* (Homewood, Ill.: Dow Jones-Irwin, 1988).

Vogel, Erza, *Comeback – Case by Case: Building the Resurgence of American Business* (New York: Simon & Schuster, 1985).

Vogel, Erza, 'Pax Nipponica', *Foreign Affairs,* vol. 64, no. 4, Spring 1986.

Wakaizumi, Kei, 'Japan's Role in a New World Order', *Foreign Affairs,* pp. 310–26, January 1973.

Ward, Robert, 'The Future of Area Studies', *Society,* vol. 22, no. 4, May–June 1985.

Watanabe, Koji, 'Japan and Southeast Asia: 1980', *Asia Pacific Community,* No. 10, Fall 1980, pp. 83–97.

Whalen, Charles J., 'A Reason to Look Beyond Neoclassical Economics: Some Major Shortcomings of Orthodox Theory', *Journal of Economic Issues,* vol. xxi, no. 1, March 1987, pp. 259–80.

Ward, Robert E. (ed.), *Political Development in Modern Japan* (Princeton, N.J.: Princeton University Press, 1968).

Ward, Robert E. and Yoshikazu, Sakamoto (eds), *Democratizing Japan: The Allied Occupation* (Honolulu; University of Hawaii Press, 1987).

Welfield, John, *An Empire in Eclipse: Japan in the Postwar American Alliance System: A Study in the Interaction of Domestic Politics and Foreign Policy* (London: Athalone Press, 1988).

Weil, F.A., 'U.S. Industrial Policy: A Process in Need of a Federal Industrial Coordination Board', *Law and Policy in International Business,* vol. 14, no. 4, 1983.

Weinstein, Franklin (ed.) *U.S.–Japan Relations and the Security of East Asia: The Next Decade* (Boulder, Colorado: Westview Press, 1978).

Weinstein, Martin E., *Northeast Asian Security After Vietnam* (Urbana, Chicago: University of Illinois Press, London, 1982).

Wheeler, Jimmy W., *Japanese Industrial Development Policies in the 1980s: Implications for U.S. Trade and Investment: Final Report* (Croton-on-Hudson, New York: Hudson Institute, 1982).

White, John, *The Politics of Foreign Aid* (New York: St. Martin's Press, 1974).

Williams, Justin, *Japan's Political Revolution Under MacArthur: A Participants Account* (Athens: University of Georgia Press, 1979).

Wilson, Robert, Ashton, Peter and Egan, Thomas, *Innovation, Competition, and Government Policy in the Semi-Conductor Industry* (Lexington, Mass.: Lexington Books, 1980).

Wineberg, Arthur, 'The Japanese Patent System: A Non-Tariff Barrier to Foreign Businesses?', *Journal of World Trade,* vol. 22, no. 1, Fall 1988.

Wright, Richard and Pauli Gunter, *The Second Wave: Japan's Global Assault on Financial Services* (New York: St. Martin's Press, 1987).

Wolf, Marvin J., *The Japanese Conspiracy: The Plot to Dominate Industry Worldwide* (New York: Empire Books, 1983).

Wolferen, Karel B. Van, 'The Japan Problem', *Foreign Affairs*, Vol. 65, No. 2, Winter 1986/87, pp. 288–303.

Wolferen, Karel B. Van, 'Agreeing on Reality: Political Reporting by the Japanese Press, *Speaking of Japan*, vol. 5, no. 44, August 1984.

Wolferen, Karel B. Van, *The Enigma of Japanese Power* (London: Macmillan, 1989).

Wonnacott, Ronald, *Aggressive United States Reciprocity Evaluated with a New Analytical Approach to Trade Conflicts* (Montreal: Institute for Research on Public Policy, 1984).

Woodall, Brian, 'Response to the Japanese Challenge', *Asia Pacific Community*, Winter 1985, no. 2, pp. 63–80.

World Trade Competition: Western Countries and Third World Markets, Center for Strategic and International Studies (ed.) (New York: Praeger, 1981).

Woronoff, Jon, *World Trade War* (New York: Praeger, 1984).

Woronoff, Jon, *Japan's Commercial Empire* (Armonk, New York: M.E. Sharpe 1984)

Woronoff, Jon, *The Japan Syndrome: Symptoms, Ailments, and Remedies* (New Brunswick: Transaction, 1986).

Woronoff, Jon, *Politics and Japanese Way* (London: Macmillan, 1988).

Wu, Yuan-li, *Japan's Search for Oil: A Case Study on Economic Nationalism and International Security* (Stanford: Hoover Institute, 1977).

Yamamura, Kozo, *Economic Policy in Postwar Japan* (Berkeley: University of California Press, 1967).

Yamamura, Kozo (ed.), *Policy and Trade Issues of the Japanese Economy: American and Japanese Perspectives* (Seattle: University of Washington Press, 1982)

Yamamura, Kozo and Yasuba, Yasukichi (eds), *The Political Economy of Japan: Volume 1, The Domestic Transformation* (Stanford: Stanford University Press, 1987).

Yamauchi, 'Long Range Strategic Planning in Japanese R & D', *Futures*, vol. 15, no. 5, October 1983.

Yasutomo, Dennis, *Japan and the Asian Development Bank* (New York: Praeger, 1983).

Yoshida, Shigeru, *The Yoshida Memoirs: The Story of Japan in Crisis* (Westport, Connecticut: Greenwood Press, 1962).

Yoshino, Michael, *Japan's Multinational Enterprises* (Cambridge, Mass.: Harvard University Press, 1976).

Yoshino, Michael, and Lifson, Thomas B., *The Invisible Link: Japan's Sogo Shosha and the Organization of Trade* (Cambridge, Mass.: MIT Press, 1986).

Yoshihara, Kunio, *Sogo Sosha: The Vanguard of the Japanese Economy* (New York: Oxford University Press, 1982).

Yoshitani, Masaru, 'An Appraisal of Japan's Financial Policy', *The World Economy*, Vol. 6, No. 3, March 1983, pp. 27–38.

Yoshitomi, Masaru, 'An Appraisal of Japanese Financial Policies', *World Economy,* vol. 6, no. 1, March 1983.

Yoshitsu, Michael, *Japan and the San Francisco Peace Settlement* (New York: Columbia University Press, 1983).

Young, Alexander, *The Sogo Shosha: Japan's Multinational Trading Companies* (Boulder, Colorado: Westview Press, 1979).

Yutaka, Matsumura, *Japan's Economic Growth, 1945–60* (Tokyo: Tokyo News Sevice, 1961).

Zimmerman, William, 'Hierarchical Regional Systems and the Politics of System Boundaries', *International Organization,* pp. 18–36, vol. 26, no. 1, Winter 1972.

Zimmerman, William, *How To Do Business with the Japanese* (New York: Randon House, 1984).

Zysman, John and Tyson, Laura (eds), *American Industry in International Competitiveness: Government Policies and Corporate Strategies* (Ithaca, N.Y.: Cornell University Press, 1983).

Zysman, John, *Governments, Markets, and Growth: Financial Systems and the Politics of Industrial Change* (Ithaca, New York: Cornell University Press, 1983).

Index

414